Structured Credit Products

Structured Credit Products

Credit Derivatives and Synthetic Securitisation

Moorad Choudhry

John Wiley & Sons (Asia) Pte Ltd

Other Wiley Editorial Offices

John Wiley & Sons, Inc., 111 River Street, Hoboken, NJ, 07030, USA
John Wiley & Sons Ltd, The Atrium, Southern Gate, Chichester PO19 8SQ, England
John Wiley & Sons (Canada) Ltd, 22 Worcester Road, Rexdale, Ontario M9W 1L1,Canada
John Wiley & Sons Australia Ltd, 33 Park Road (PO Box 1226), Milton, Queensland 4064, Australia
Wiley — VCH, Pappelallee 3, 69469 Weinheim, Germany

Library of Congress Cataloging-in-Publication Data
978-0-470-82119-0

Typeset in 10.5/13 points, Times by Linographic Services Pte Ltd
Printed in Singapore by Saik Wah Press Pte Ltd
10 9 8 7 6 5 4 3

Contents

For *All Things Must Pass, Déjà Vu, Crumbling the Antiseptic Beauty, Songs for Beginners, The Smiths, Keep on Keepin' On!, The Price, Rattlesnakes, Easy Pieces, Brewing Up With Billy Bragg, Snap!, To Whom It May Concern, Hope and Despair, Played, The Rockingbirds, Years of Backwater*, and countless other LPs not heard for a long time …

" … but don't forget the songs that made you cry
And the songs that saved your life,
Yes you're older now, and you're a clever swine —
But they were the only ones that ever stood by you … "

Foreword

Since the early 1990s, the market for credit derivatives has grown, slowly at first, then explosively, into one of the most important markets for financial products. According to statistics available from the British Bankers Association, the total of outstanding notional positions in this market has roughly doubled each year for the past few years, and will likely reach over 4 trillion US dollars in 2004. In the early years of the credit-derivatives market, my own recollection is that the potential for this exceptional growth and success was discussed inside investment banks, but that few traders were truly confident that the market would soon support itself, in terms of liquidity and profitability for dealers. Standards had not been well established, and deals were few and far between. Indeed, it was not even clear that default swaps would become the plain-vanilla version of a credit derivative. For example, I had incorrectly (and, unfortunately, publicly) predicted in the early 1990s that default swaps would not become the predominant form of credit derivative because of settlement risk. It had seemed to me that there would remain significant uncertainty for the buyer of protection in establishing to a sufficient legal standard that default, of the contractually stipulated form, had actually occurred. It had also seemed to me that there would be thorny questions of deliverability of different forms of obligations of the underlying entity, under conditions that might or might not cause cross-acceleration of various forms of obligations. At that time, I had believed that put options, struck either at a price or at a yield spread, would become more popular than default swaps. Indeed, despite these settlement issues, not only have default swaps become the standard method of buying protection against default, they have also become the elemental building blocks for many other important financial products, such as synthetic collateralised debt obligations (CDOs) and default-swap index products, such as the TRAC-X (for "tradable credit index") family of products of J.P. Morgan and Morgan Stanley. The threat that cheapest-to-deliver optionality on default swaps could in some cases be large, expensive to cover, and difficult to hedge and price, did not disappear, but has been sufficiently mitigated under the recently modified ISDA standards for restructuring as a covered credit event, that the default-swap market appears set to become even more established and liquid as means of transferring credit risk.

Foreword

With his new book, Moorad Choudhry has filled a significant gap in the literature on credit derivatives. By bringing together helpful practical knowledge as well as quantitative modelling approaches, Moorad has significantly lowered the cost of entry to newcomers. He covers a wide range of issues, including screen-based data, the main classes of credit derivatives, credit risk measurement, hedging, deal mechanics, as well as basic pricing models. I admire the book, and plan to use it with my students here at Stanford University.

Perhaps I should be cautious about making predictions about the development of the credit derivatives markets, given my past forecast errors. Here goes anyway: I think there will be a problem with the emerging standard for quoting basket credit derivative prices, based on the "implied Gaussian copula correlation." The benefit of the copula approach is clear. Given spread data by name (or term structures of risk-neutral default probabilities), one can easily apply copula correlation parameters to price products that have combined exposure to a selection of obligors in the form of first-loss, synthetic mezzanine CDO tranches, and so on. My experiments, however, show that the implied copula correlation is often a very unstable pricing tool. For example, fixing the actual default correlation structure in the underlying collateral pool, a change in spreads alone can have dramatic effects on the implied copula correlation, especially for mezzanine loss protection. Even worse, perhaps, it remains to be shown that one can consistently apply a copula model to the task of mark-to-market risk analysis for a collateral pool. Consider, for example, the pricing of an option to become the buyer of protection in one year, at a stated exercise CDS rate, on the TRAC-X. A standard option pricing approach would call for simulating the market values of each of the underlying 100 names' default swaps as of the exercise date, scenario by scenario, with correlation, reflecting in each scenario and for each underlying name the effects of any defaults and changes in spreads before the exercise date. Certain models that are not based on a copula can be used for this purpose, but then one is placed in the position of reconciling the pricing of default-based basket products, such as default-loss tranches, by copula methods (the current market standard) and the pricing of option-based products by some other method. So far, this does not look easy!

Darrell Duffie
James Irvin Miller Professor of Finance
Graduate School of Business, Stanford University

Preface

A key risk assumed by investors in bonds or loans is *credit risk*, the risk that the bond or loan issuer will default on the debt. To meet the need of investors to hedge this risk, the market uses *credit derivatives*. These are financial instruments originally introduced to protect banks and other institutions against losses arising from default. As such, they are instruments designed to off load or take on credit risk. Since their inception, they have been used by banks, portfolio managers and corporate treasurers to enhance returns, to trade credit, for speculative purposes and as hedging instruments.

Credit derivatives are financial contracts designed to reduce or eliminate credit risk exposure by providing insurance against credit-linked losses. The principle behind credit derivatives is straightforward, and the flexibility of credit derivatives, arising from their status as over-the-counter (OTC) products, provides users with a number of advantages as they can be tailored to meet specific user requirements. The use of credit derivatives assists banks and other financial institutions with restructuring their businesses, because they allow banks to repackage and parcel out credit risk, while retaining assets on balance sheet (when required) and thus maintain client relationships. As the instruments isolate certain aspects of credit risk from the underlying loan or bond, it is possible to separate the ownership of credit risk from the other features of ownership associated with the credit-risky assets in question. In other words, credit can be considered an asset in its own right. It is this flexibility that has given rise to the market in structured credit products such as synthetic CDOs, which exist in many varieties. Both these products, in their plain vanilla credit derivative form and their more structured CDO form, are a positive development for market participants and an advancement for the capital markets, as they have effectively encouraged the process of disintermediation that began originally with the establishment of capital markets, bringing lenders and borrowers of capital closer together.

This book has been written with both market practitioners and post-graduate students in mind. It aims to provide a comprehensive description and analysis of credit derivatives instruments, and the structured finance products that use credit derivatives in their construction. The credit derivatives market has grown spectacularly, in a relatively short time, to become a key component of the capital markets and one that embraces a wide range of participants. At the same time, so-called synthetic securitisation structures have grown in size such that they match, in nominal terms, the size of the cash-based securitisation market. As such this book has a dual focus. First, we review all the credit derivative instruments, including credit default swaps, total return swaps and credit-linked notes. We consider the instruments themselves, their application and pricing. Then we look at the market in synthetic structured finance products, typified by the synthetic collateralised debt obligation (CDO), but also including synthetic mortgage-backed securities and repacks. We consider these instruments from the point of view of both the originator and investor.

Comments on the text are welcome and should be sent to the author care of John Wiley & Sons Pte (Asia).

Layout of the Book

This book is organised into 15 chapters. They are divided into two parts:

- Part I: credit derivative instruments
- Part II: structured credit products and synthetic securitisation

In Part I we discuss credit derivative instruments, their structure, application and pricing. In terms of organisation, we look first at unfunded credit derivatives in Chapter 2 and then at funded credit derivatives in Chapter 3. Following our discussion of pricing, we look in detail at the interplay between the cash (bond) and synthetic (credit derivative) markets in corporate credit, exemplified by the basis, in Chapters 7 and 8.

In Part II we discuss in detail the synthetic CDO, synthetic conduits and repack structures, and the synthetic MBS. We illustrate each stage in product development with case studies of real-world deals. We also provide an analysis of CDO returns and pricing, and an introduction to cashflow waterfall models.

Where appropriate throughout the text, we reference the most important literature on specific issues. A more technical background is supplied in the appendices and relevant readings referenced at the end of certain chapters.

Website

Further research on credit derivatives and synthetic structured finance products is available on the dedicated fixed income website at:

www.YieldCurve.com

This site also lists details of other books and articles written by Moorad Choudhry and other YieldCurve.com associates.

Acknowledgements

Special thanks to Professor Duffie for the excellent foreword, an honour for me who has been reading and learning from his books and articles for some time now.

Thanks to Malar at Wiley for all her great help with this book. Top stuff!

Many thanks to Peter Jones and Abukar Ali at Bloomberg for help with Bloomberg screens. Peter, it was a real pleasure working with you at the various Bloomberg seminars and TV shows! Thanks also to Victoria Moore at Bloomberg for help with permissions to reproduce their screens.

Thanks to Richard Pereira, Rod Pienaar, Suleman Baig, Aaron Nematnejad, Dr Chee Hau and Abukar Ali who co-authored some of the material here — these guys are market experts and it's great to have this input.

Thanks to Niall Considine at KBC Financial Products for enlightening me further on credit derivatives.

Thanks to Ketul Tanna for reviewing the proofs and for many expert insights.

Thanks to fab ladies Margaret Lee and Sheila Thorogood at Forest Road post office for making me feel so welcome ever since I moved to the area!

Hello and thanks to Mr Luciano Tavolotti at JP Morgan Chase Bank in Milan, a gentleman, a friend and great to work with.

Thanks to Ruth Kentish, the team administrator when I was at JP Morgan, for all her help! Thanks to Bruno Giombini in JP Morgan Milan, for closing deals at the drop of a hat.

Thank you to Isidro Jimenez Ovelar at Banco Bilbao Vizcaya for his help with their credit default swap price screens, your quick response really appreciated!

Finally, thanks to Anne Carter at KBC Financial Products for help during the production phase of this book — you're an absolute darling!

Moorad Choudhry
Surrey, England
March 2004

About the Author

Moorad Choudhry is Head of Treasury at KBC Financial Products in London. He previously worked at JP Morgan Chase Bank, Hambros Bank Limited, ABN Amro Hoare Govett Limited and the London Stock Exchange.

Dr Choudhry was educated at Claremont Fan Court school in Esher, Surrey, the University of Westminster, the University of Reading, Henley Management College and Birkbeck, University of London. He is a Visiting Professor at the Department of Economics, London Metropolitan University, a Senior Fellow at the Centre for Mathematical Trading and Finance, CASS Business School, and a Fellow of the Securities Institute. He is a member of the Education Advisory Board, ISMA Centre, University of Reading.

I

Credit Risk and
Credit Derivative Instruments

Credit risk is the risk of loss arising from the inability of a borrower to make interest and/or principal repayments on a loan. Anyone who has lent funds to a borrower that is not considered as default risk-free is exposed to a certain level of credit risk. While credit risk has been a factor for investor concern ever since the development of capital markets, it has received considerable attention among market participants since the 1990s. This attention has taken the form of ever-more sophisticated methods of measuring credit risk and managing credit risk. It is the latter that is the backdrop to this book. An understanding of the former is necessary, though, so we will begin with a look at credit risk and credit risk measurement.

Credit derivatives are important tools that are used in the managing and hedging of credit risk, and also for trading and speculating in credit, as we shall see. All credit derivatives are instruments, financial contracts in fact, that enable credit risk on a particular named asset or borrowing entity, the *reference entity*, to be transferred from one party to the contract to another. In essence, one party is buying protection on the reference entity from the counterparty, who is selling credit protection. The buyer pays a premium to the seller during the life of the credit derivative contract in return for receiving credit protection. The seller agrees to pay the buyer a pre-specified amount under certain conditions of default, or upon a restructuring event.

We begin with a look at credit risk and risk measurement. After our introduction to the concept of credit risk, we look in detail at all the important credit derivative instruments, their description, application and pricing. The main instruments are *credit default swaps* (also known as credit swaps or default swaps), *total return swaps* (also called total rate of return swaps) and credit-linked notes. Although all these instruments achieve the same end-goal of transferring credit risk exposure from a protection buyer to a protection seller, there are subtle differences between them. Credit-linked notes are fundamentally different to the other two types, as they are *funded* credit derivatives as opposed to *unfunded* ones. We explain this shortly. An instrument developed much earlier, the asset swap, is usually considered to be a credit derivative as well, so we also look at this product.

The passing of time, and all of its crimes,
Is making me sad again.

But don't forget the songs that made you cry
And the songs that saved your life,
Yes you're older now, and you're a clever swine —
But they were the only ones who ever stood by you ... .

— The Smiths, *Rubber Ring*
(Rough Trade Records) 1985

1

Credit Risk

Credit risk emerged as a significant risk management issue during the 1990s. In increasingly competitive markets, banks and securities houses began taking on greater credit risk from this period onwards. While the concept of "credit risk" is as old as banking itself, it is only recently that the nature and extent of it has increased dramatically. For example, consider the following developments:

- credit spreads tightened during the late 1990s onwards, to the point where blue chip companies such as General Electric, British Telecom and Shell were being offered syndicated loans for as little as 10–12 basis points over LIBOR. To maintain margin, or the increased return on capital, banks increased lending to lower-rated corporates, thereby increasing their credit risk both overall and as a share of overall risk;
- investors were finding fewer opportunities in interest rate and currency markets, and therefore moved towards yield enhancement through extending and trading credit across lower-rated and emerging market assets;
- the rapid expansion of high yield and emerging market sectors, again lower-rated assets, increased the magnitude of credit risk for investors and the banks that held and traded such assets.

The growth in credit risk exposure would naturally be expected to lead to more sophisticated risk management techniques than those employed hitherto. It was accompanied, however, by a rise in the level of corporate defaults and consequently higher losses due to credit deterioration, which led to a rigorous test of banks' risk management systems and procedures. It also led to a demand for the type of product that resulted in the credit derivative market.

The development of the credit derivatives market, and hence the subsequent introduction of structured credit products, was a response to the rising importance attached to credit risk management. For this reason, it is worthwhile beginning this book with a look at credit risk, credit ratings, default and credit risk measurement. So in this chapter we will look at the concept of credit risk, before considering the main way that it is measured in banks and financial institutions, using the technique known as credit *value-at-risk*. We also introduce two credit risk measurement methodologies. First, though, we look at the incidence of corporate defaults during the 1990s.

Corporate Default

During the second half of the 1990s and into the new century, credit risk and credit risk management have been topical issues in the financial markets industry. Viewed statistically, 1999 onwards appear to be years of excessive corporate default, when compared with the market experience in the previous two decades. This is vividly illustrated in Figure 1.1, which shows the monetary value of corporate defaults for the period 1980–2002. The average size of corporate bond defaults also rose significantly, as we show in Figure 1.2. Adjusted for inflation, the average size of default in 2002 was over five times that for the entire period 1980–2002.

Figure 1.1 Global corporate defaults, 1980–2002.

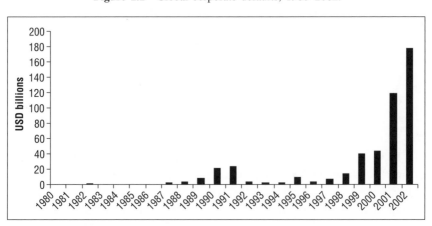

Source: S&P, CSFB. Used with permission.

Figure 1.2   Average size of corporate bond defaults.

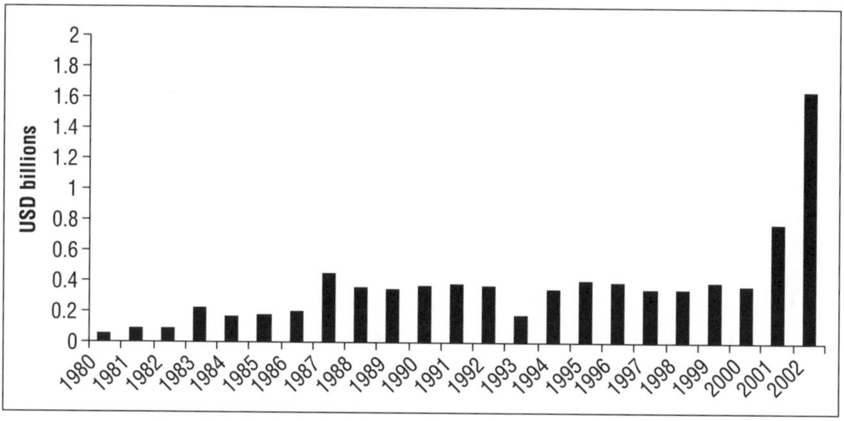

Source: Moodys, CSFB. Used with permission.

The excessive levels of corporate defaults provided confirmation that banks and bond investors needed to focus closely on credit risk management. They did this using a two-pronged approach, by concentrating on risk measurement and risk hedging. The former used so-called value-at-risk techniques, introduced earlier in the 1990s for market risk measurement, while the latter was accomplished with credit derivatives.

Credit Risk

There are two main types of credit risk that a portfolio of assets, or a position in a single asset, is exposed to. These are credit default risk and credit spread risk.

Credit default risk

This is the risk that an issuer of debt (obligor) is unable to meet its financial obligations. This is known as *default*. There is also the case of technical default, which is used to describe a company that has not honoured its interest payments on a loan for (typically) three months or more, but has not reached a stage of bankruptcy or administration. Where an obligor defaults, a lender generally incurs a loss equal to the amount owed by the obligor less any recovery amount that the firm recovers as a result of foreclosure, liquidation or restructuring of the defaulted obligor. This recovery amount is usually expressed as a percentage of the total amount and is known as the *recovery rate*. All portfolios with credit exposure exhibit credit default risk.

The measure of a firm's credit default risk is given by its *credit rating*. The three largest credit rating agencies are Moody's, Standard & Poor's and Fitch Ratings. These institutions undertake qualitative and quantitative analysis of borrowers and formally rate the borrower after their analysis. The issues considered in the analysis include:

- the financial position of the firm itself, for example, its balance sheet position and anticipated cash flows and revenues;
- other firm-specific issues such as the quality of management and succession planning;
- an assessment of the firm's ability to meet scheduled interest and principal payments, both in its domestic and in foreign currencies;
- the outlook for the industry as a whole, and competition within it, together with general assessments of the domestic economy.

The range of credit ratings awarded by the three largest rating agencies is shown at Figure 1.4. Ratings can also be seen on Bloomberg page RATD, shown at Figure 1.3. We discuss credit ratings again shortly.

Figure 1.3   Bloomberg screen RATD, long-term credit ratings.

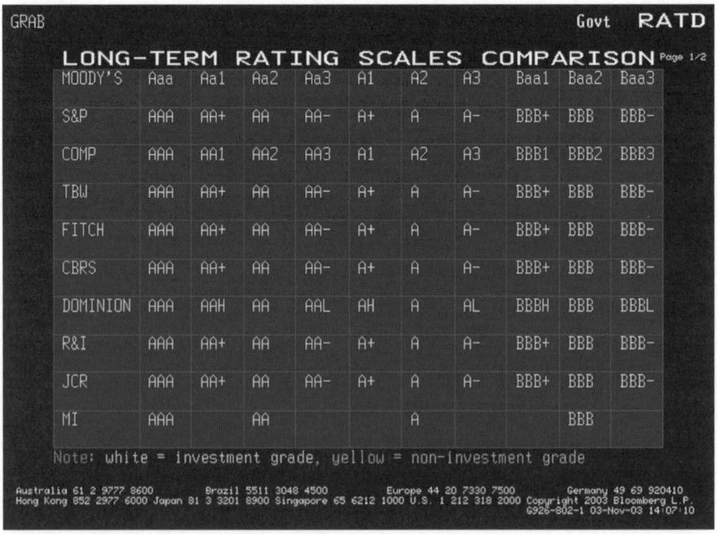

© Bloomberg L.P. Used with permission.

Figure 1.4   Long-term bond credit ratings.

Fitch	Moody's	S&P	Summary description
Investment grade — High creditworthiness			
AAA	Aaa	AAA	Gilt edged, prime, maximum safety, lowest risk
AA+	Aa1	AA+	High-grade, high credit quality
AA	Aa2	AA	
AA−	Aa3	AA2	
A+	A1	A+	Upper-medium grade
A	A2	A	
A−	A3	A−	
BBB+	Baa1	BBB+	Lower-medium grade
BBB	Baa2	BBB	
BBB−	Baa3	BBB−	
Speculative — Lower creditworthiness			
BB+	Ba1	BB+	Lower grade; speculative
BB	Ba2	BB	
BB−	Ba3	BB−	
B+	B1		
B	B	B	
B−	B3		
Predominantly speculative, substantial risk or in default			
CCC+		CCC+	Substantial risk, in poor standing
CCC	Caa	CCC	
CC	Ca	CC	May be in default, very speculative
C	C	C	Extremely speculative
		CI	Income bonds — no interest being paid
DDD			Default
DD			
D		D	

Credit spread risk

Credit spread is the excess premium, over and above government or risk-free risk, required by the market for taking on a certain assumed credit exposure. For example, Figure 1.5 shows the credit spreads in January 2003 for US dollar corporate bonds with different credit ratings (AAA, A and BBB). The benchmark is the on-the-run or *active* US Treasury issue for the given maturity. Note that the higher the credit rating, the smaller the credit spread. Credit spread risk is the risk of financial loss resulting from changes in the

Figure 1.5 US dollar bond yield curves, January 2003.

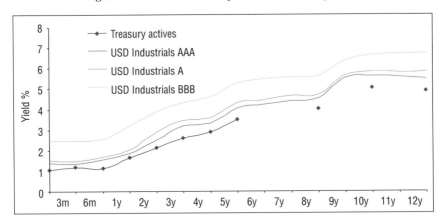

level of credit spreads used in the marking-to-market of a product. It is exhibited by a portfolio for which the credit spread is traded and marked-to-market. Changes in observed credit spreads affect the value of the portfolio and can lead to losses for investors.

The value-at-risk measurement methodology was first applied for credit risk by JPMorgan, which introduced the *CreditMetrics* tool in 1995. The measurement of credit risk requires a slightly different approach to that used for market risk, because the distribution of credit losses follows a different pattern to market risk. In the following sections we describe the approach used to measuring such risk.

Credit Ratings

The risks associated with holding a fixed interest debt instrument are closely connected with the ability of the issuer to maintain the regular coupon payments as well as redeem the debt on maturity. Essentially, the *credit risk* is the main risk of holding a bond. Only the highest quality government debt, and a small amount of supra-national and corporate debt are considered to be entirely free of credit risk. Therefore at any time the yield on a bond reflects investors' views on the ability of the issuer to meet its liabilities as set out in the bond's terms and conditions. A delay in paying a cash liability as it becomes due is known as technical default and is a cause for extreme concern for investors — failure to pay will result in the matter going to court as investors seek to recover their funds. In order to determine the ability of an issuer to meet its obligations for a particular debt issue, for the entire life of the issue, judgmental analysis of the issuer's financial strength and business prospects is required. There are a number of factors that must be considered, and larger banks, fund managers and corporates carry out their own *credit analysis* of individual borrowers' bond issues. The market also makes considerable use of formal *credit ratings* that are assigned to individual bond issues by a formal credit rating agency. In the international markets, arguably the two most influential ratings agencies are Standard & Poor's Corporation (S&Ps) and Moody's Investors Service, Inc (Moody's), based in the US. In the US domestic market, Fitch Investors Service, Inc (Fitch) also has a high profile, as does Dun & Bradstreet in the UK.

The specific factors that are considered by a ratings agency, and the methodology used in conducting the analysis, differ slightly amongst the individual ratings agencies. Although in many cases the ratings assigned to a particular issue by different agencies are the same, they occasionally differ and in these instances investors usually seek to determine what aspect of an issuer is given more weight in an analysis by which individual agency. Note that a credit rating is not a recommendation to buy (or equally, sell) a particular bond, nor is it a comment on market expectations. Credit analysis does take into account general market and economic conditions, but the overall point of credit analysis is to consider the financial health of the issuer and its ability to meet the obligations of the specific issue being rated. Credit ratings play a large part in the decision-making of investors, and also have a significant impact on the interest rates payable by borrowers.

A credit rating is a formal opinion given by a rating agency, of the *credit risk* for investors holding a particular issue of debt securities. Ratings are given to public issues of debt securities by any type of entity, including governments, banks and corporates. They are also given to short-term debt such as commercial paper as well as medium-term notes and long-term debt such as bonds.

Purpose of credit ratings

Investors in securities accept the risk that the issuer may default on coupon payments or fail to repay the principal in full on the maturity date. Generally credit risk is greater for securities with a long maturity, as there is a longer period for the issuer potentially to default. For example, if company issues ten-year bonds, investors cannot be certain that the company will still exist in ten years' time. It may have failed and gone into liquidation some time before that. That said, there is also risk attached to short-dated debt securities, indeed there have been instances of default by issuers of commercial paper, which is a very short-term instrument.

The prospectus or offer document for an issue provides investors with some information about the issuer so that some credit analysis can be performed on the issuer before the bonds are placed on the market. The information in the offer document enables investors to perform their own credit analysis by studying this information before deciding whether or not to invest in the bonds. Credit assessments take up time, however, and also require the specialist skills of credit analysts. Large institutional investors employ specialists to carry out credit analysis, however often it is too costly and time-consuming to assess every issuer in every debt market. Therefore investors commonly employ two other methods when making a decision on the credit risk of debt securities:

- name recognition;
- formal credit ratings.

Name recognition is when the investor relies on the good name and reputation of the issuer and accepts that the issuer is of such good financial standing, or sufficient financial standing, that a default on interest and principal payments is unlikely. An investor may feel this way about companies such as Microsoft or British Petroleum. However, the collapse of Barings Bank in 1995 suggested to many investors that it may not be wise to rely on name recognition alone in today's marketplace. The tradition and reputation behind the Barings name allowed the bank to borrow at LIBOR or occasionally at sub-LIBOR interest rates in the money markets, which put it on a par with highest-quality clearing banks in terms of credit rating. The Barings case illustrated that name recognition needs to be augmented by other methods to reduce the risk of loss due to unforeseen events. Credit ratings are increasingly used to make investment decisions about corporate or lesser-developed government debt.

Formal Credit Ratings

Credit ratings are provided by the specialist agencies. The major credit rating agencies are Standard & Poor's, Fitch and Moody's based in the United States. There are other agencies both in the US and other countries. On receipt of a formal request, the credit rating agencies carry out a rating exercise on a specific issue of debt capital. The request for a rating comes from the organisation planning the issue of bonds. Although ratings are provided for the benefit of investors, the issuer must bear the cost. However it is in the issuer's interest to request a rating as it raises the profile of the bonds, and investors may refuse to buy paper that is not accompanied with a recognised rating. Although the rating exercise involves a credit analysis of the issuer, the rating is applied to a specific debt issue. This means that, in theory, the credit rating is applied not to an organisation itself, but to specific debt securities that the organisation has issued or is planning to issue. In practice, it is common for the market to refer to the creditworthiness of organisations in terms of the rating of their debt. A highly-rated company such as Rabobank or Wells Fargo is therefore referred to as a "triple-A rated" company, although it is the banks' debt issues that are rated as triple-A.

The rating for an issue is kept constantly under review and if the credit quality of the issuer declines or improves, the rating will be changed accordingly. An agency may announce in advance that it is reviewing a particular credit rating, and may go further and state that the review is a precursor to a possible downgrade or upgrade. This announcement is referred to as putting the issue under *credit watch*. The outcome of a credit watch is, in most cases, likely to be a rating downgrade, however the review may re-affirm the current rating or possibly upgrade it. During the credit watch phase the agency will advise investors to use the current rating with caution. When an agency announces that an issue is under credit watch, the price of the bonds will fall in the market as investors look to sell out of their holdings. This upward movement in yield will be more pronounced if an actual downgrade results. For example, in October 1992 the government of Canada was placed under credit watch and subsequently lost its AAA credit rating; as a result there was an immediate and sharp sell-off in Canadian government eurobonds, before the rating agencies had announced the actual results of their credit review.

Ratings Changes Over Time

Ratings transition matrix

We have noted that the rating agencies constantly review the credit quality of firms they have rated. As may be expected, the credit rating of many companies will fluctuate over time as they experience changes in their corporate well-being. As a guide to the change in credit rating that might be expected over a one-year period, Moody's and S&P publish historical transition matrices, which provide average rating transition probabilities for each class of rating. An example is shown at Figure 1.6, which is Moody's one-year ratings transition matrix for 2002. These results are obtained from a sample of a large number of firms over many years. In Figure 1.6, the first column shows the initial rating and the first row the final rating. For instance, the probability of an A-rated company being downgraded to Baa in one year is 4.63%. The probability of the A-rated company defaulting in this year is 0.00%.

There are some inconsistencies in the ratings transition table and this is explained by Moody's as resulting from scarcity of data for some ratings categories. For instance, an Aa-rated company has a 0.02% probability of being in default at year-end, which is higher than the supposedly lower-rated A-rated company. Such results must be treated with caution. The conclusion from Figure 1.6 is that the most likely outcome at year-end is that the company rating remains the same. It may be that a one-year time horizon provides little real value, hence the rating agencies also publish transition matrices for longer periods, such as five and ten years.

Figure 1.6   Moody's one-year rating transition matrix.

	Aaa	Aa	A	Baa	Ba	B	Caa	Default
Aaa	93.40%	5.94%	0.64%	0.00%	0.02%	0.00%	0.00%	0.00%
Aa	1.61%	90.55%	7.46%	0.26%	0.09%	0.01%	0.00%	0.02%
A	0.07%	2.28%	92.44%	4.63%	0.45%	0.12%	0.01%	0.00%
Baa	0.05%	0.26%	5.51%	88.48%	4.76%	0.71%	0.08%	0.15%
Ba	0.02%	0.05%	0.42%	5.16%	86.91%	5.91%	0.24%	1.29%
B	0.00%	0.04%	0.13%	0.54%	6.35%	84.22%	1.91%	6.81%
Caa	0.00%	0.00%	0.00%	0.62%	2.05%	4.08%	69.20%	24.06%

We might expect an increased level of default as we move lower down the credit ratings scale. This is borne out in Figure 1.7, which is a reproduction of data published by Moody's. It shows one-year default rates by credit rating category, for the period 1985–200. We see that the average one-year default rate rises from zero for the highest-rated Aaa, to 15.7% for the B3 rating category. However, investors generally attach little value to one-year results. Figure 1.8 shows average cumulative default rates for five- and 10-year time horizons, for the same period covered in Figure 1.7. This repeats the results shown in Figure 1.7, with higher default rates associated with lower credit ratings.

Figure 1.7 One-year default rates 1985–2000.

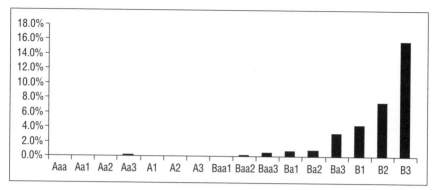

Source: Moody's. Reproduced with permission.

Figure 1.8 Five- and 10-year average cumulative default rates, 1985–2000.

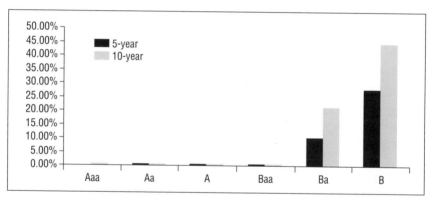

Source: Moody's. Reproduced with permission.

Corporate recovery rates

When a corporate obligor experiences bankruptcy or enters into liquidation or administration, it defaults on its loans. However this does not mean that all the firm's creditors will lose everything. At the end of the administration process, the firm's creditors will typically receive a portion of their outstanding loans, a *recovery* amount.[1] The percentage of the original loan that is received back is known as the *recovery rate*, which is defined as the percentage of par value that is returned to the creditor.

---

[1] This recovery may be received in the form of other assets, such as securities or physical plant, instead of cash.

The seniority of a loan strongly influences the level of the recovery rate. Figure 1.9 shows recovery rates for varying levels of loan seniority in 2002 as published by Moody's. The standard deviation for each recovery rate reported is high, which illustrates the dispersion around the mean and reflects widely varying recovery rates even within the same level of seniority. It is clear that the more senior a loan or a bond is, the higher the recovery rate it will have in the event of default.

Figure 1.9   Moody's recovery rates for varying levels of loan seniority, 2002.

Seniority	Mean	Standard deviation
Senior secured bank loans	60.70%	26.31%
Senior secured	55.83%	25.41%
Senior unsecured	52.13%	25.12%
Senior subordinated	39.45%	24.79%
Subordinated	33.81%	21.25%
Junior subordinated	18.51%	11.26%
Preference shares	8.26%	10.45%

Credit risk is measured using the value-at-risk (VaR) technique. This was first introduced as a market risk measurement tool, and subsequently applied to credit risk. Therefore in the next section we introduce the basics of the VaR methodology, which we required for an understanding of Credit VaR.

Value-at-Risk

The introduction of Value-at-Risk (VaR) as an accepted methodology for quantifying market risk is part of the evolution of risk management. The application of VaR has been extended from its initial use in securities houses to commercial banks and corporates, following its introduction in October 1994 when JPMorgan launched *RiskMetrics*™ free over the Internet.

Value-at-Risk is a measure of the worst expected loss that a firm may suffer over a period of time that has been specified by the user, under normal market conditions and a specified level of confidence. This measure may be obtained in a number of ways, using a statistical model or by computer simulation.

VaR is a measure of market risk. It is the maximum loss which can occur with X% confidence over a holding period of n days.

VaR is the expected loss of a portfolio over a specified time period for a set level of probability. For example, if a daily VaR is stated as £100,000 to a 95% level of confidence, this means that during the day there is a only a 5% chance that the loss the next day will be *greater* than £100,000. VaR measures the potential loss in market value of a portfolio using estimated volatility and correlation. The "correlation" referred to is the correlation that exists between the market prices of different instruments in a bank's portfolio. VaR is calculated within a given confidence interval, typically 95% or 99%. It seeks to measure the possible losses from a position or portfolio under "normal" circumstances. The definition of normality is critical and is essentially a statistical concept that varies by firm and by risk management system. Put simply however, the most commonly used VaR models assume that the prices of assets in the financial markets follow a normal distribution. To implement VaR, all of a firm's positions data must be gathered into one centralized database. Once this is complete, the overall risk has to be calculated by aggregating the risks from individual instruments across the entire portfolio. The potential move in each instrument (that is, each risk factor) has to be inferred from past daily price movements over a given observation period. For regulatory purposes this period is at least one year. Hence the data on which VaR estimates are based should capture all relevant daily market moves over the previous year.

The main assumption underpinning VaR — and which in turn may be seen as its major weakness — is that the distribution of future price and rate changes will follow past variations. Therefore the potential portfolio loss calculations for VaR are worked out using distributions from historic price data in the observation period.

VaR is therefore a measure of a bank's risk exposure — it a tool for measuring market risk exposure. There is no one VaR number for a single portfolio, because different methodologies used for calculating VaR produce different results. The VaR number captures only those risks that can be measured in quantitative terms, it does not capture risk exposures such as operational risk, liquidity risk, regulatory risk or sovereign risk.

Assumption of normality

A distribution is described as *normal* if there is a high probability that any observation from the population sample will have a value that is close to the mean, and a low probability of having a value that is far from the mean. The normal distribution curve is used by many VaR models, which assume that asset returns follow a normal pattern. A VaR model uses the normal curve to estimate the losses that an institution may suffer over a given time period. Normal distribution tables show the probability of a particular observation moving a certain distance from the mean.

If we look along a normal distribution table, we see that at -1.645 standard deviations, the probability is 5%. This means that there is a 5% probability that an observation will be at least 1.645 standard deviations below the mean. This level is used in many VaR models.

Calculation methods

There are three different methods for calculating VaR. They are:

- the variance/covariance (or *correlation* or *parametric* method);
- historical simulation;
- Monte Carlo simulation.

Variance–covariance method

This method assumes the returns on risk factors are normally distributed, the correlations between risk factors are constant and the delta (or price sensitivity to changes in a risk factor) of each portfolio constituent is constant. Using the correlation method, the volatility of each risk factor is extracted from the historical observation period. Historical data on investment returns is therefore required. The potential effect of each component of the portfolio on the overall portfolio value is then worked out from the component's delta (with respect to a particular risk factor) and that risk factor's volatility.

There are different methods of calculating the relevant risk factor volatilities and correlations. Two alternatives are:

- simple *historic volatility*: this is the most straightforward method but the effects of a large one-off market move can significantly distort volatilities over the required forecasting period. For example, if using 30-day historic volatility, a market shock will stay in the volatility figure for 30 days until it drops out of the sample range and correspondingly causes a sharp drop in (historic) volatility 30 days *after* the event. This is because each past observation is equally weighted in the volatility calculation;
- to weight past observations unequally: this is done to give more weight to recent observations so that large jumps in volatility are not caused by events that occurred some time ago. One method is to use exponentially-weighted moving averages.

Historical simulation method

The historical simulation method for calculating VaR is the simplest method and avoids some of the pitfalls of the correlation method. Specifically, the three main assumptions behind correlation (normally distributed returns, constant correlations, constant deltas) are not needed in this case. For historical simulation, the model calculates potential losses using actual historical returns in the risk factors and so captures the non-normal distribution of risk factor returns. This means rare events and crashes can be included in the results. As the risk factor returns used for revaluing the portfolio are actual past movements, the correlations in the calculation are also actual past correlations. They capture the dynamic nature of correlation as well as scenarios when the usual correlation relationships break down.

Monte Carlo simulation method

The third method, Monte Carlo simulation is more flexible than the previous two. As with historical simulation, Monte Carlo simulation allows the risk manager to use actual historical distributions for risk factor returns rather than having to assume normal returns. A large number of randomly generated simulations are run forward in time using volatility and correlation estimates chosen by the risk manager. Each simulation will be different, but in total the simulations will aggregate to the chosen statistical parameters (that is, historical distributions and volatility and correlation estimates). This method is more realistic than the previous two models and therefore is more likely to estimate VaR more accurately. However, its implementation requires powerful computers and there is also a trade-off in that the time required to perform calculations is longer.

The level of confidence in the VaR estimation process is selected by the number of standard deviations of variance applied to the probability distribution. A standard deviation selection of 1.645 provides a 95% confidence level (in a one-tailed test) that the potential estimated price movement will not be more than a given amount based on the correlation of market factors to the position's price sensitivity.

Explaining Value-at-Risk

Correlation

Measures of correlation between variables are important to fund managers who are interested in reducing their risk exposure through diversifying their portfolio. Correlation is a measure of the degree to which a value of one variable is related to the value of another. The correlation coefficient is a single number that compares the strengths and directions of the movements in two instruments' values. The sign of the coefficient determines the relative directions that the instruments move in, while its value determines the strength of the relative movements. The value of the coefficient ranges from -1 to $+1$, depending on the nature of the relationship. So if, for example, the value of the correlation is 0.5, this means that one instrument moves in the same direction by half of the amount that the other instrument moves. A value of zero means that the instruments are uncorrelated, and their movements are independent of each other.

Correlation is a key element of many VaR models, including parametric models. It is particularly important in the measurement of the variance (hence volatility) of a portfolio. If we take the simplest example, a portfolio containing just two assets, (1.1) below gives the volatility of the portfolio based on the volatility of each instrument in the portfolio (x and y) and their correlation with one another.

$$V_{port} = \sqrt{x^2 + y^2 + 2xy \cdot \rho(xy)} \tag{1.1}$$

where

x is the volatility of asset x
y is the volatility of asset y
ρ is the correlation between assets x and y.

The correlation coefficient between two assets uses the covariance between the assets in its calculation. The standard formula for covariance is shown at (1.2):

$$\text{Cov} = \frac{\sum_{i=1}^{n}(x_i - \bar{x})(y_i - \bar{y})}{(n-1)} \tag{1.2}$$

where the sum of the distance of each value x and y from the mean is divided by the number of observations minus one. The covariance calculation enables us to calculate the correlation coefficient, shown as (1.3):

$$r = \text{Cov}\frac{(1,2)}{\sigma_1 \sigma_2} \tag{1.3}$$

where σ is the standard deviation of each asset.

Equation (1.1) may be modified to cover more than two instruments. In practice, correlations are usually estimated on the basis of past historical observations. This is an important consideration in the construction and analysis of a portfolio, as the associated risks depend to an extent on the correlation between its constituents.

From a portfolio perspective, a positive correlation increases risk. If the returns on two or more instruments in a portfolio are positively correlated, strong movements in either direction are likely to occur at the same time. The overall distribution of returns is wider and flatter, as there are higher joint probabilities associated with extreme values (both gains and losses). A negative correlation indicates that the assets are likely to move in opposite directions, thus reducing risk.

It has been argued that in extreme situations, such as market crashes or large-scale market corrections, correlations cease to have any relevance, because all assets are moving in the same direction. However, under most market scenarios using correlations to reduce the risk of a portfolio is considered satisfactory practice, and the VaR number for a diversified portfolio is lower than that for an undiversified portfolio.

Simple VaR calculation

To calculate the VaR for a single asset, we calculate the standard deviation of its returns, using either its historical volatility or *implied volatility*. If a 95% confidence level is required, meaning we wish to have 5% of the observations in the left-hand tail of the normal distribution, this means that the observations in that area are 1.645 standard deviations away from the mean. Let us consider the following statistical data for a government bond, calculated using one year's historical observations:

Nominal:	£10 million
Price:	£100
Average return:	7.35%
Standard deviation:	1.99%

The VaR at the 95% confidence level is 1.645×0.0199 or 0.032736. The portfolio has a market value of £10 million, so the VaR of the portfolio is $0.032736 \times 10,000,000$ or £327,360. Therefore this figure is the maximum loss that the portfolio may sustain over one year for 95% of the time.

We may extend this analysis to a two-asset portfolio. In a two-asset portfolio, we stated at (1.1) that there is a relationship that enables us to calculate the volatility of a two-asset portfolio. This expression is used to calculate the VaR, and is shown at (1.4):

$$Var_{port} = \sqrt{w_1^2 s_1^2 + w_2^2 s_2^2 + 2w_1 w_2 \sigma_1 \sigma_2 r_{1,2}} \qquad (1.4)$$

where

w_1 is the weighting of the first asset;
w_2 is the weighting of the second asset;
σ_1 is the standard deviation or *volatility* of the first asset;
σ_2 is the standard deviation or volatility of the second asset;
$r_{1,2}$ is the correlation coefficient between the two assets.

In a two-asset portfolio, the undiversified VaR is the weighted average of the individual standard deviations. The diversified VaR, which takes into account the correlation between the assets, is the square root of the variance of the portfolio. In practice, banks calculate both diversified and undiversified VaR. The diversified VaR measure is used to set trading limits, while the larger undiversified VaR measure is used to gauge an idea of the bank's risk exposure in the event of a significant correction or market crash. This is because in a crash situation, liquidity dries up as market participants all attempt to sell off their assets. This means that the correlation relationship between assets ceases to have any impact on a book, as all assets move in the same direction. Under this scenario, it is more effective to use an undiversified VaR measure.

Although the description given here is very simple, nevertheless it explains what is the essence of the VaR measure. VaR is essentially the calculation of the standard deviation of a portfolio, which is the used as an indicator of the volatility of that portfolio. A portfolio exhibiting high volatility has a high VaR number. An observer may then conclude that the portfolio has a high probability of making losses. Risk managers and traders may use the VaR measure to help them to allocate capital to more efficient sectors of the bank, as the return on capital can now be measured in terms of return on risk capital. Regulators may use the VaR number as a guide to the capital adequacy levels that they believe the bank requires.

Variance–covariance value–at–risk

Calculation of variance–covariance VaR

In the previous section, we illustrated how VaR can be calculated for a two-asset portfolio. Here we illustrate how this is done using matrices.

Let us consider the following hypothetical portfolio, invested in two assets, as shown in Table 1.1. The standard deviation of each asset has been calculated on historical observation of asset returns. Note that *returns* are returns of asset prices, rather than the prices themselves. They are calculated from the actual prices by taking the ratio of closing prices. The returns are then calculated as the logarithm of the price relativities. The mean and standard deviation of the returns are then calculated using standard statistical formulae. This then gives the standard deviation of daily price relativities, which is converted to an annual figure by multiplying it by the square root of the number of days in a year, usually taken to be 250.

Table 1.1   Two-asset portfolio VaR.

Assets	Bond 1	Bond 2	
Standard deviation	11.83%	17.65%	
Portfolio weighting	60%	40%	
Correlation coefficient			0.647
Portfolio value			£10,000,000
Variance			0.016506998
Standard deviation			12.85%
95% c.i. standard deviations			1.644853
Value-at-Risk			0.211349136
Value-at-Risk £			£2,113,491

The standard equation (shown as (1.4)) is used to calculate the variance of the portfolio, using the individual asset standard deviations and the asset weightings. The VaR of the book is the square root of the variance. Multiplying this figure by the current value of the portfolio gives us the portfolio VaR, which is £2,113,491.

The RiskMetrics VaR methodology uses matrices to obtain the same results that we have shown here. This is because once a portfolio starts to contain multiple assets, the method we described above becomes inappropriate. Matrices allow us to calculate VaR for a portfolio containing many hundreds of assets, which would require assessment of the volatility of each asset and correlations of each asset to all the others in the portfolio. We can demonstrate how the parametric methodology uses variance and correlation matrices to calculate the variance, and hence standard deviation, of a portfolio. The matrices are shown in Choudhry (1999).

The variance-covariance method captures the diversification benefits of a multi-product portfolio because of the correlation coefficient matrix used in the calculation. For example, if the two bonds in our hypothetical portfolio have a negative correlation, the VaR number produced would be lower. It was also the first methodology introduced, by JP Morgan in 1994. To apply it, a bank requires data on volatility and correlation for the assets in its portfolio. This data is available from a number of sources including the *RiskMetrics* website, so a bank does not necessarily need its own data. It may wish to use its own datasets however, should it have them, to tailor the application to its own use. The advantages of the variance-covariance methodology are that:

- it is simple to apply, and straightforward to explain;
- datasets for its use are immediately available.

The drawbacks of the variance-covariance are that it assumes stable correlations and measures only linear risk, it also places excessive reliance on the normal distribution, and returns in the market are widely believed to have "fatter tails" than a true to normal distribution. This phenomenon is known as *leptokurtosis*, that is, the non-normal distribution of outcomes. Another disadvantage is that the process requires *mapping*. To construct a weighting portfolio for the *RiskMetrics* tool, cash flows from financial instruments are mapped into precise maturity points, known as grid points. However in most cases assets do not fit into neat grid points, and complex instruments cannot be broken down accurately into cash flows. The mapping process makes assumptions that frequently do not hold in practice.

Nevertheless the variance-covariance method is still popular in the market, and is frequently the first VaR method installed at a bank.

Historical VaR methodology

The historical approach to value-at-risk is a relatively simple calculation, and it is also easy to implement and explain. To implement it, a bank requires a database record of its past profit/loss figures for the total portfolio. The required confidence interval is then applied to this record, to obtain a cut-off of the worst-case scenario. For example, to calculate the VaR at a 95% confidence level, the 5th percentile value for the historical data is taken, and this is the VaR number. For a 99% confidence level measure, the 1% percentile is taken. The advantage of the historical method is that it uses the actual market data that a bank has recorded (unlike *RiskMetrics*, for example, for which the volatility and correlations are not actual values, but estimated values calculated from average figures over a period of time, usually the last five years), and so produces a reasonably accurate figure. Its main weakness is that as it is reliant on actual historical data built up over a period of time — generally at least one year's data is required to make the calculation meaningful. Therefore it is not suitable for portfolios with asset weightings that frequently change, as another set of data is necessary before a VaR number can be calculated.

In order to overcome this drawback, banks use a method known as *historical simulation*. This calculates VaR for the current portfolio weighting, using the historical data for the securities in the current portfolio. To calculate historical simulation VaR for our hypothetical portfolio considered earlier, comprising 60% of bond 1 and 40% of bond 2, we require the closing prices for both assets over the specified previous period (usually three or five years); we then calculate the value of the portfolio for each day in the period assuming constant weightings.

Simulation methodology

The most complex calculations use computer simulations to estimate value-at-risk. The most common is the Monte Carlo method. To calculate VaR using a Monte Carlo approach, a computer simulation is run in order to generate a number of random scenarios, which are then used to estimate the portfolio VaR. The method is probably the most realistic, if we accept that market returns follow a similar "random walk" pattern. However, Monte Carlo simulation is best suited to trading books containing large option portfolios, where price behavior is not captured very well with the *RiskMetrics* methodology. The main disadvantage of the simulation methodology is that it is time-consuming and uses a substantial amount of computer resources.

A Monte Carlo simulation generates simulated future prices, and it may be used to value an option as well as for VaR applications. When used for valuation, a range of possible asset prices are generated and these are used to assess what intrinsic value the option will have at those asset prices. The present value of the option is then calculated from these possible intrinsic values. Generating simulated prices, although designed to mimic a "random walk", cannot be completely random because asset prices, although not a pure normal distribution, are not completely random either. The simulation model is usually set to generate very few extreme prices. Strictly speaking, it is asset price *returns* that follow a normal distribution, or rather a *lognormal* distribution. Monte Carlo simulation may also be used to simulate other scenarios, for example the effect on option "greeks" for a given change in volatility, or any other parameters. The scenario concept may be applied to calculating VaR as well. For example, if 50,000 simulations of an option price are generated, the 95th lowest value in the simulation will be the VaR at the 95% confidence level. The correlation between assets is accounted for by altering the random selection programme to reflect relationships.

Credit Value-At-Risk

Introduction

Credit risk VaR methodologies take a portfolio approach to credit risk analysis. This means that:

- credit risks of each obligor across the portfolio are re-stated on an equivalent basis and aggregated in order to be treated consistently, regardless of the underlying asset class;
- correlations of credit quality movements across obligors are taken into account.

This allows portfolio effects, that is the benefits of diversification and risks of concentration, to be quantified.

The portfolio risk of an exposure is determined by four factors:

- size of the exposure;
- maturity of the exposure;
- probability of default of the obligor;
- systematic or concentration risk of the obligor.

Credit VaR, like market risk VaR, considers (credit) risk in a mark-to-market framework. It arises from changes in value due to credit events, that is, changes in obligor credit quality including defaults, upgrades and downgrades.

Nevertheless, credit risk is different in nature to market risk. Typically market return distributions are assumed to be relatively symmetrical and approximated by normal distributions. In credit portfolios, value changes are relatively small as a result of minor up/downgrades, but can be substantial upon default. This remote probability of large losses produces skewed distributions with heavy downside tails that differ from the more normally distributed returns assumed for market VaR models. This is shown in Figure 1.10.

This difference in risk profiles does not prevent us from assessing risk on a comparable basis. Analytical method market VaR models consider a

Figure 1.10   Comparison of distribution of market returns and credit returns.

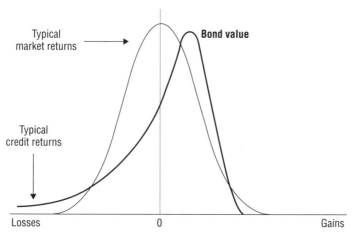

Typical market returns

Bond value

Typical credit returns

Losses   0   Gains

time horizon and estimate value-at-risk across a distribution of estimated market outcomes. Credit VaR models similarly look to a horizon and construct a distribution of value given different estimated credit outcomes.

When modeling credit risk the two main measures of risk are:

- distribution of loss: obtaining distributions of loss that may arise from the current portfolio. This considers the question of what the expected loss is for a given confidence level;
- identifying extreme or catastrophic outcomes: this is addressed through the use of scenario analysis and concentration limits.

To simplify modeling, no assumptions are made about the causes of default. Mathematical techniques used in the insurance industry are used to model the event of an obligor default.

Time horizon

The choice of time horizon will not be shorter than the time frame over which risk-mitigating actions can be taken. The investment bank CSFB (who introduced the *CreditRisk+* model shortly after the JP Morgan *CreditMetrics* model was introduced) suggested two alternatives:

- a constant time horizon such as one year;
- a hold-to-maturity time horizon.

The constant time horizon is similar to the *CreditMetrics* approach and also to that used for market risk measures. It is more suitable for trading desks. The hold-to-maturity approach is used by institutions such as insurance companies and similar fund managers.

Data inputs

Modeling credit risk requires certain data inputs, for example *CreditRisk+* uses the following:

- credit exposures;
- obligor default rates;
- obligor default rate volatilities;
- recovery rates.

These data requirements present some difficulties. There is a lack of comprehensive default and correlation data and assumptions need to be made at certain times. The most accessible data is compiled by the credit ratings agencies such as Moody's and Standard & Poor's.

We now consider two methodologies used for measuring credit value-at-risk, the *CreditMetrics* model and the *CreditRisk+* model.

CreditMetrics^{TM}

CreditMetrics is JPMorgan's portfolio model for analyzing credit risk, providing an estimate of value-at-risk due to credit events caused by upgrades, downgrades and default. A software package known as *CreditManager* is available that allows users to implement the *CreditMetrics* methodology.[2]

Methodology

There are two main frameworks in use for quantifying credit risk. One approach considers only two scenarios — default and no default. This model constructs a binomial tree of default versus no default outcomes until maturity. This approach is shown in Figure 1.11.

The other approach, sometimes called the RAROC (Risk Adjusted Return on Capital) approach holds that risk is the observed volatility of

---

[2]   The department in JPMorgan that developed *CreditMetrics* was transformed into a separate corporate entity, known as *RiskMetrics*, during 1998.

Figure 1.11   A binomial model of credit risk.

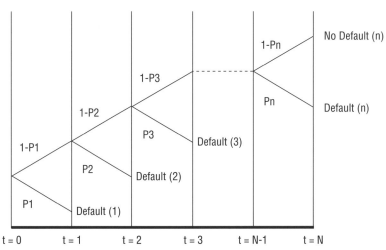

Source: JPMorgan, RiskMetrics technical document, 1997. Used with permission.

corporate bond values within each credit rating category, maturity band and industry grouping. The idea is to track a benchmark corporate bond (or index) that has observable pricing. The resulting estimate of volatility of value is then used as a proxy for the volatility of the exposure (or portfolio) under analysis.

The *CreditMetrics* methodology sits between these two approaches. The model estimates portfolio VaR at the risk horizon due to credit events that include upgrades and downgrades, rather than just defaults. Thus it adopts a mark-to-market framework. As shown in Figure 1.12, bonds within each credit rating category have volatility of value due to day-to-day credit spread fluctuations. The exhibit shows the loss distributions for bonds of varying credit quality. *CreditMetrics* assumes that all credit migrations have been realized, weighting each by a migration likelihood.

Time horizon

CreditMetrics adopts a one-year risk horizon. The justification given in its technical document[3] is that this is because much academic and credit agency data is stated on an annual basis. This is a convenient convention similar to the use of annualized interest rates in the money markets. The risk horizon

---

[3]   JPMorgan, *Introduction to CreditMetrics^{TM}*, JP Morgan & Co., 1997.

Figure 1.12 Distribution of credit returns by rating.

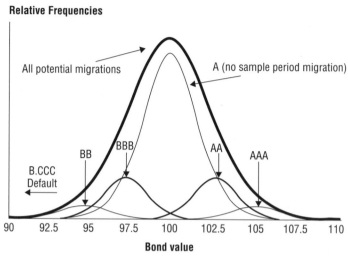

Relative Frequencies
All potential migrations
A (no sample period migration)
BB
BBB
AA
AAA
B.CCC
Default
90
92.5
95
97.5
100
102.5
105
107.5
110
Bond value

Source: JPMorgan, *RiskMetrics* technical document, 1997. Used with permission.

is adequate as long as it is not shorter than the time required to perform risk-mitigating actions. Users must therefore adopt their risk management and risk adjustments procedures with this in mind.

The steps involved in *CreditMetrics* measurement methodology are shown in Figure 1.13, described by JPMorgan as its analytical "roadmap".

Figure 1.13 Analytics road map for *CreditMetrics*.

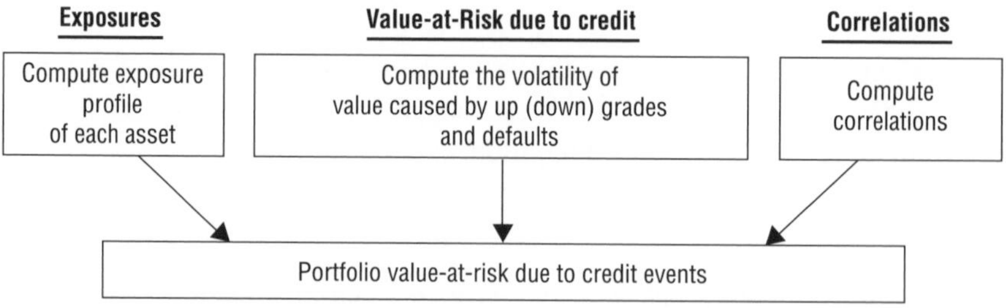

Exposures
Value-at-Risk due to credit
Correlations
Compute exposure profile of each asset
Compute the volatility of value caused by up (down) grades and defaults
Compute correlations
Portfolio value-at-risk due to credit events

Source: JPMorgan, RiskMetrics technical document, 1997. Used with permission.

The elements in each step are:

Exposures
User portfolio;
Market volatilities;
Exposure distributions.

VaR due to credit events
Credit rating;
Credit spreads;
Rating change likelihood;
Recovery rate in default;
Present value bond revaluation;
Standard deviation of value due to credit quality changes.

Correlations
Ratings series;
Models (eg., correlations);
Joint credit rating changes.

Calculating the Credit VaR

CreditMetrics methodology assesses individual and portfolio credit VaR in three steps:

Step 1:   it establishes the exposure profile of each obligor in a portfolio;
Step 2:   it computes the volatility in value of each instrument caused by possible upgrade, downgrade and default;
Step 3:   taking into account correlations between each of these events, it combines the volatility of the individual instruments to give an aggregate portfolio risk.

Step 1 — Exposure Profiles

CreditMetrics incorporates the exposure of instruments such as bonds (fixed or floating-rate) as well as other loan commitments and off-balance sheet instruments such as swaps. The exposure is stated on an equivalent basis for all products. Products covered include:

- receivables (or trade credit);
- bonds and loans;
- loan commitments;

- letters of credit;
- market-driven instruments.

Step 2 — Volatility of each exposure from up/downgrades and defaults

The levels of likelihood are attributed to each possible credit event of upgrade, downgrade and default. The probability that an obligor will change over a given time horizon to another credit rating is calculated. Each change (migration) results in an estimated change in value (derived from credit spread data and in default, recovery rates). Each value outcome is weighted by its likelihood to create a distribution of value across each credit state, from which each asset's expected value and volatility (standard deviation) of value are calculated.

There are three steps to calculating the volatility of value in a credit exposure:

- the senior unsecured credit rating of the issuer determines the chance of either defaulting or migrating to any other possible credit quality state in the risk horizon;
- revaluation at the risk time horizon can be by either (i) the seniority of the exposure, which determines its recovery rate in case of default or (ii) the forward zero-coupon curve (spot curve) for each credit rating category which determines the revaluation upon up/ downgrade;
- the probabilities from the two steps above are combined to calculate volatility of value due to credit quality changes.

Step 3 — Correlations

Individual value distributions for each exposure are combined to give a portfolio result. To calculate the portfolio value from the volatility of individual asset values requires estimates of correlation in credit quality changes. *CreditMetrics* allows for different approaches to estimating correlations including a simple constant correlation. This is because of frequent difficulty in obtaining directly observed credit quality correlations from historical data.

CreditManager^{TM}

CreditManager is the software implementation of *CreditMetrics* as developed by JPMorgan. It is a PC-based application that measures and analyses credit risk in a portfolio context. It measures the VaR exposure due to credit events across a portfolio, and also quantifies concentration risks and the benefits of diversification by incorporating correlations (following the methodology utilised by *CreditMetrics*). The *CreditManager* application provides a framework for portfolio credit risk management that can be implemented "off-the-shelf" by virtually any institution. It uses the following:

- obligor credit quality database: details of obligor credit ratings, transition and default probabilities, industries and countries;
- portfolio exposure database: containing exposure details for the following asset types: loans, bonds, letters of credit, total return swaps, credit default swaps, interest rate and currency swaps and other market instruments;
- frequently updated market data: including yield curves, spreads, transition and default probabilities;
- flexible risk analyses: with user-defined parameters supporting VaR analysis, marginal risk, risk concentrations, event risk and correlation analysis;
- stress testing scenarios: applying user-defined movements to correlations, spreads, recovery rates, transition and default probabilities;
- customized reports and charts.

CreditManager data sources include Dow Jones, Moody's, Reuters and Standard and Poor's. By using the software package, risk managers can analyze and manage credit portfolios based on virtually any variable, from the simplest end of the spectrum — single position or obligor — to more complex groupings containing a range of industry and country obligors and credit ratings.

Generally this quantitative measure is employed as part of an overall risk management framework that retains traditional, qualitative methods.

CreditMetrics can be a useful tool for risk managers seeking to apply VaR methodology to credit risk. The model enables risk managers to apply portfolio theory and VaR methodology to credit risk. It has several applications including prioritising and evaluating investment decisions and perhaps most important, setting risk-based exposure limits. Ultimately the model's sponsors claim its use can aid in maximizing shareholder value based on risk-based capital allocation. This should then result in increased liquidity in credit markets, the use of a marking-to-market approach to credit positions and closer interlinking of regulatory and economic capital.

CreditRisk+

CreditRisk+ was developed by Credit Suisse First Boston and can, in theory, handle all instruments that give rise to credit exposure including bonds, loans commitments, letters of credit and derivative instruments. We provide a brief description of its methodology here.

Modelling process

CreditRisk+ uses a two-stage modelling process as illustrated in Figure 1.14.

Figure 1.14 *CreditRisk+* modelling process.

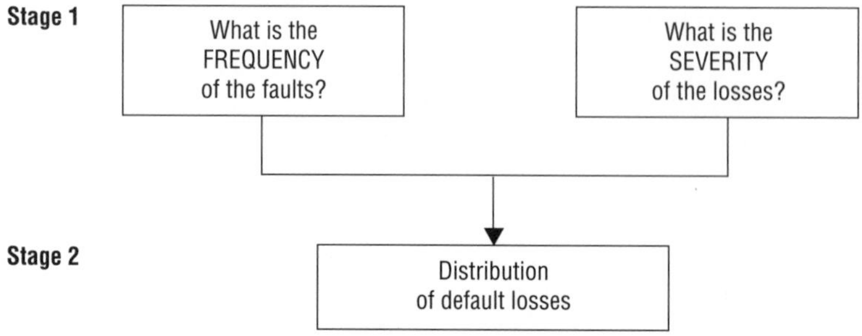

Stage 1	What is the FREQUENCY of the faults?	What is the SEVERITY of the losses?

Stage 2	Distribution of default losses

Source: CSFB, *CreditRisk+*, 1998. Reproduced with permission.

CreditRisk+ considers the distribution of the number of default events in a time period such as one year, within a portfolio of obligors having a range of different annual probabilities of default.

The annual probability of default of each obligor can be determined by its credit rating and then mapping between default rates and credit ratings. A default rate can then be assigned to each obligor (an example of what this would look like is shown in Figure 1.15). Default rate volatilities can be observed from historic volatilities.

Figure 1.15 One year default rates (%).

Credit rating	One year default rate (%)
Aaa	0.00
Aa	0.03
A	0.01
Baa	0.12
Ba	1.36
B	7.27

Correlation and background factors

Default correlation impacts the variability of default losses from a portfolio of credit exposures. *CreditRisk+* incorporates the effects of default correlations by using default rate volatilities and sector analysis.

Unsurprisingly enough, it is not possible to forecast the exact occurrence of any one default or the total number of defaults. Often there are background factors that may cause the incidence of default events to be correlated, even though there is no causal link between them. For example, an economy in recession may give rise to an unusually large number of defaults in one particular month, which would increase the default rates above their average level. *CreditRisk+* models the effect of background factors by using default rate volatilities rather than by using default correlations as a direct input. Both distributions give rise to loss distributions with fat tails.

Concentration

As noted previously, there are background factors that affect the level of default rates. For this reason, it is useful to capture the effect of concentration in particular countries or sectors. *CreditRisk+* uses sector analysis to allow for concentration. Exposures are broken down into an obligor-specific element independent of other exposures, as well as non-specific elements that are sensitive to particular factors such as countries or sectors.

Distribution of the number of default events

CreditRisk+ models the underlying default rates by specifying a default and a default rate volatility. This aims to take into account the variation in default rates. The effect of using volatility is illustrated in Figure 1.16, which shows the distribution of default rates generated by the model when rate volatility is varied. The distribution becomes skewed to the right when volatility is increased.

This is an important result and demonstrates the increased risk represented by an extreme number of default events. By varying the volatility in this way, *CreditRisk+* is attempting to model for real-world shock much in the same way that market risk VaR models aim to allow for the fact that market returns do not follow exact normal distributions, as shown by the incidence of market crashes.

Figure 1.16   *CreditRisk+* distribution of default events.

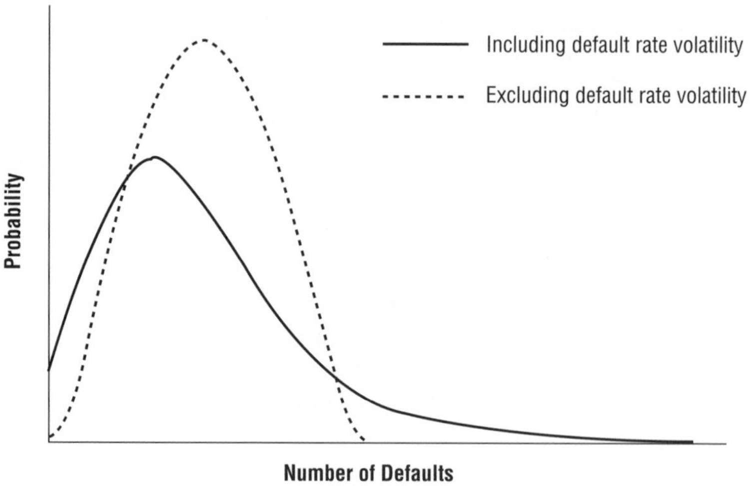

Application software

CSFB has released software that allows the *CreditRisk+* model to be run on Microsoft Excel® as a spreadsheet calculator. The user inputs the portfolio static data into a blank template and the model calculates the credit exposure. Obligor exposure can be analysed on the basis of all exposures being part of the same sector, alternatively up to eight different sectors (government, countries, industry, and so on) can be analysed. The spreadsheet template allows the user to include up to 4,000 obligors in the static data. An example portfolio of 25 obligors and default rates and default rate volatilities (assigned via a sample of credit ratings) is included with the spreadsheet.

The user's static data for the portfolio will therefore include details of each obligor, the size of the exposure, the sector for that obligor (if not all in a single sector) and default rates. An example of static data is given in Figures 1.17 and 1.18.

Figure 1.17   Example default rate data.

Credit rating	Mean default rate	Standard deviation
A+	1.50%	0.75%
A	1.60%	0.80%
A−	3.00%	1.50%
BBB+	5.00%	2.50%
BBB	7.50%	3.75%
BBB−	10.00%	5.00%
BB	15.00%	7.50%
B	30.00%	15.00%

Figure 1.18   Example obligor data.

Name	Exposure (£)	Rating	Mean default rate	Default rate standard deviation	Sector split general economy
Co name	358,475	B	30.00%	15.00%	100%
Co (2)	1,089,819	B	30.00%	15.00%	100%
Co (3)	1,799,710	BBB−	10.00%	5.00%	100%
Co (4)	1,933,116	BB	15.00%	7.50%	100%
Co (5)	2,317,327	BB	15.00%	7.50%	100%
Co (6)	2,410,929	BB	15.00%	7.50%	100%
Co (7)	2,652,184	B	30.00%	15.00%	100%
Co (8)	2,957,685	BB	15.00%	7.50%	100%
Co (9)	3,137,989	BBB+	5.00%	2.50%	100%
Co (10)	3,204,044	BBB+	5.00%	2.50%	100%

An example credit loss distribution calculated by the model is shown below. Figure 1.19 shows the distribution for the basic analysis for a portfolio at the simplest level of assumption — all obligors are assigned to a single sector. The full loss distribution over a one-year time horizon is calculated together with percentiles of the loss distribution (not shown here), which assess the relative risk for different levels of loss. The model can calculate distributions for a portfolio with obligors grouped across different sectors, as well as the distribution for a portfolio analysed over a "hold to maturity" time horizon.

Figure 1.19 Illustration of Credit Loss Distribution (single sector obligor portfolio).

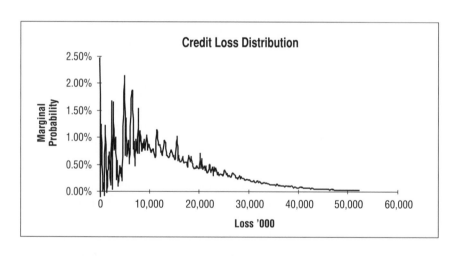

Summary of CreditRisk+ model

- *CreditRisk+* **captures the main characteristics of credit default events.** Credit default events are rare and occur in a random manner with observed default rates varying from year to year. The model's approach attempts to reflect this by making no assumptions about the timing or causes of these events and by incorporating a default rate volatility. It also takes a portfolio approach and uses sector analysis to allow for concentration risk.

- *CreditRisk+* **is capable of handling large exposure portfolios.** The low data requirements and minimum assumptions make the model comparatively easy to implement for firms.

However, the model is limited to two states of the world — default or non-default. This means that it is not as flexible as *CreditMetrics*, for example, and ultimately therefore not modeling the full exposure that a credit portfolio would be subject to.

Conclusion

Our discussion of credit risk, and the VaR methodology for measuring such risk, will be useful background for the following chapters. We are now in a position to consider the main instruments used to manage and trade credit risk.

References and Bibliography

Choudhry, M., *An Introduction to Value-at-Risk,* Securities Institute (Services) Publishing 1999.

I still remember those halcyon days,
When we leapt on stage though we couldn't play!
Furthermore, we had nothing to say ... .

— Orange Juice, "Satellite City",
from *You Can't Hide Your Love Forever* (Polydor Records) 1981

2

Credit Derivatives I: Unfunded Instruments[1]

Credit derivatives are financial instruments that enable credit risk on a specified entity or asset to be transferred from one party to another. Hence they are used to take on or lay off credit risk, with one party being the buyer of credit protection and the other party being the seller of credit protection. They have become a key tool in the management of credit risk for banks as well as other capital market participants. Credit derivatives allow investors to manage the credit risk exposure of their portfolios or asset holdings, essentially by providing insurance against a deterioration in credit quality of the borrowing entity.[2] If there is a technical default by the borrower[3] or an actual default on the loan itself, and the bond is marked down in price, the losses suffered by the investor can be recouped in part or in full through the payout made by the credit derivative. The introduction of credit derivatives has resulted in the isolation of credit as a distinct asset class. This has improved the efficiency of the capital market because market participants can separate the functions of credit origination and credit risk-bearing. Banks have been able to spread their credit risk exposure across the financial system, which arguably reduces *systemic* risk. Use of credit derivatives also

---

[1] The section on basket CDS was co-authored with Aaron Nematnejad when he was with Bloomberg L.P. He is now with Daiwa U.S.A. The authors are writing in their individual private capacity.

[2] The simplest credit derivative works exactly like an insurance policy, with regular premiums paid by the protection-buyer to the protection-seller, and a payout in the event of a specified credit event.

[3] A technical default is a delay in timely payment of debt interest or coupon, or non-payment of the coupon altogether.

improve market transparency by making it possible to better price specific types of credit risk.[4]

In this chapter we consider the various *unfunded* credit derivative instruments.[5] The following chapter looks at funded credit derivatives. We will go on later to look at various applications of the instruments and their pricing and valuation. We begin with some observations on market volumes and participants.

Market Volumes

Credit derivatives are a relatively recent innovation in the capital markets, but their use has seen rapid growth. They were first introduced in 1994. Figure 2.1 shows growth in credit derivatives volumes from 1997, with an estimate for 2004. This is data published by the British Bankers Association (BBA). The BBA estimate for 2004 is US$4 trillion. While this figure

Figure 2.1 Credit derivatives volume growth, 1997–2004 (forecast).

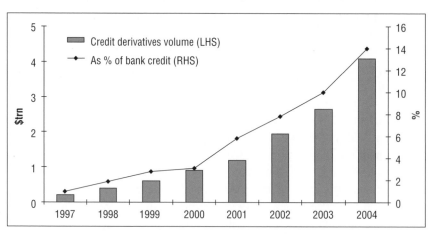

Source: BBA, Bank for International Settlements. Used with permission.

---

[4] Some commentators have suggested that credit derivatives have *reduced* market transparency because it may not be possible to track where credit risk has gone after it has been removed from bank balance sheets. It has also been suggested that use of credit derivatives increases systemic risk because they spread risk and hence increase risk of contagion. We will leave this sort of viewpoint to the media and regulatory authorities and concentrate on describing and analysing the instruments!

[5] This term is explained in this chapter. The next chapter looks at *funded* credit derivatives.

represents a small percentage of the total size of the over-the-counter (OTC) market (approximately US$100 trillion), it is still a significant number. This is because the underlying credit risk on most derivative contracts is no more than 5% of their notional value, whereas the corresponding risk for credit derivatives is essentially 100% of their notional value.

There are a number of different types of credit derivative instruments, which we will consider in detail later. The most commonly encountered contract is the *credit default swap*. As shown in Figure 2.2, credit default swaps made up approximately 45% of the market in 2003. There has also been significant growth in structured credit products such as *collateralised debt obligations* (CDOs), which are not strictly credit derivatives as such, and synthetic CDOs or *CSOs*, which make use of credit derivatives in their structure.

Although banks are the main users of credit derivatives, as both protection sellers and buyers, they are also used by a range of other participants. Figures 2.3 and 2.4 show the breakdown of each type of user. The figures suggest that banks are net buyers of protection while insurance companies (who are institutional investors) are net sellers of protection.

Figure 2.2   Credit derivative use by product, 2003.

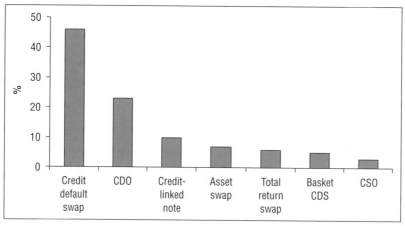

Source: BBA.

Figure 2.3 Protection sellers, 2003.

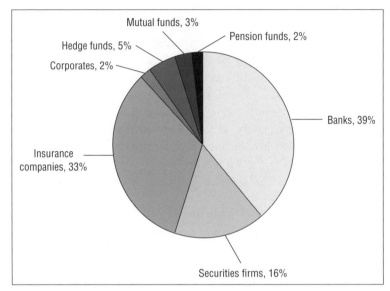

Source: BBA. Used with permission.

Figure 2.4 Protection buyers, 2003.

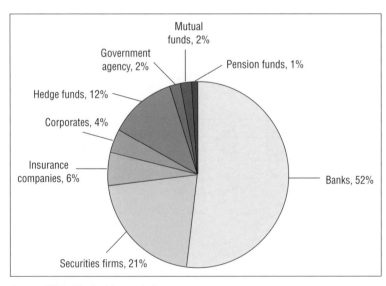

Source: BBA. Used with permission.

Credit Risk and Credit Derivatives

Credit derivatives are financial contracts designed to reduce or eliminate credit risk exposure by providing insurance against losses suffered due to *credit events*. A payout under a credit derivative is triggered by a credit event associated with the credit derivative's *reference asset* or *reference entity*. As banks define default in different ways, the terms under which a credit derivative is executed usually include a specification of what constitutes a credit event. The principle behind credit derivatives is straightforward. Investors desire exposure to debt that is not risk-free because of the higher returns this debt offers. However, such exposure brings with it concomitant credit risk. This can be managed with credit derivatives. At the same time, the exposure itself can be taken on synthetically if, for instance, there are compelling reasons why a cash market position cannot be established. The flexibility of credit derivatives provides users with a number of advantages and as they are over-the-counter (OTC) products they can be designed to meet specific user requirements. Some of the most common reasons for which they are used include:

- hedging credit risk: this includes credit default risk, dynamic credit risks and changes in credit quality;
- reducing credit risk with a specific client (*obligor*) so that lending lines to this client are freed up for other business;
- diversifying investment options.

We focus on credit derivatives as instruments that may be used to manage risk exposure inherent in a corporate or non-AAA sovereign bond portfolio, and to manage the credit risk of commercial bank loan books. The intense competition amongst commercial banks, combined with rapid disintermediation, has meant that banks have been forced to evaluate their lending policies, with a view to improving profitability and return on capital. The use of credit derivatives assists banks with restructuring their businesses, because they allow banks to repackage and transfer credit risk, while retaining assets on balance sheet (when required) and thus maintain client relationships. As the instruments isolate certain aspects of credit risk from the underlying loan or bond and transfer them to another entity, it becomes possible to separate the ownership and management of credit risk from the other features of ownership associated with the assets in question. This means that illiquid assets such as bank loans, and illiquid bonds, can have their credit risk exposures transferred — the bank owning the assets can protect against credit loss even if it cannot transfer the assets themselves.[6]

The same principles apply to the credit risk exposures of portfolio managers. For fixed-income portfolio managers, some of the advantages of using credit derivatives include the following:

- they can be tailor-made to meet the specific requirements of the entity buying the risk protection, as opposed to the liquidity or term of the underlying reference asset;
- they can be "sold short" without risk of a liquidity or delivery squeeze, as it is a specific credit risk that is being traded. In the cash market, it is not possible to "sell short" a bank loan for example, but a credit derivative can be used to establish synthetically the economic effect of such a position;
- as they theoretically isolate credit risk from other factors such as client relationships and interest rate risk, credit derivatives introduce a formal pricing mechanism to price credit issues only. This means a market is available in credit only, allowing more efficient pricing, and it becomes possible to model a term structure of credit rates;
- they are off-balance sheet instruments[7] and as such incorporate tremendous flexibility and leverage, exactly like other financial derivatives. For instance, bank loans are not particularly attractive investments for certain investors because of the administration required in managing and servicing a loan portfolio. However an exposure to bank loans and their associated return can be achieved using credit derivatives while simultaneously avoiding the administrative costs of actually owning the assets. Hence credit derivatives allow investors access to specific credits while allowing banks access to further distribution for bank loan credit risk.

Thus credit derivatives can be an important instrument for bond portfolio managers as well as commercial banks, who wish to increase the liquidity of their portfolios, gain from the relative value arising from credit pricing anomalies, and enhance portfolio returns.

---

[6] The bank may not wish to transfer the physical assets, in order to maintain client relationships. It can always transfer the assets in a securitisation transaction, which can also bring in funding (cash securitisation).

[7] When credit derivatives are embedded in certain fixed-income products, such as structured notes and credit-linked notes, they are then off-balance sheet but part of a structure that will have on-balance sheet elements. Funded credit derivatives are on-balance sheet.

Credit events

The occurrence of a specified credit event will trigger the termination of the credit derivative contract, and result in the transfer of the default protection payment from the protection seller to the protection buyer.

The following may be specified as "credit events" in the legal documentation between counterparties:

- downgrade in S&P and/or Moody's credit rating below a specified minimum level;
- financial or debt restructuring, for example occasioned under administration or as required under US bankruptcy protection;
- bankruptcy or insolvency of the reference asset obligor;
- default on payment obligations such as bond coupon and continued non-payment after a specified time period;
- technical default, for example the non-payment of interest or coupon when it falls due;
- a change in credit spread payable by the obligor above a specified maximum level.

The International Swap and Derivatives Association (ISDA) compiled standard documentation governing the legal treatment of credit derivative contracts. The standardisation of legal documentation promoted ease of execution and was a factor in the rapid growth of the market. The 1999 ISDA credit default swap documentation specified bankruptcy, failure to pay, obligation default, debt moratorium and restructuring to be credit events. Note that it does not specify a rating downgrade to be a credit event.[8]

A summary of the credit events as set forth in the ISDA definitions is given in Appendix 2.1.

The precise definition of "restructuring" is open to debate and has resulted in legal disputes between protection buyers and sellers. Prior to issuing its 1999 definitions, ISDA had specified restructuring as an event or events that resulted in making the terms of the reference obligation "materially less favorable" to the creditor (or protection seller) from an economic perspective. This definition was open to more than one interpretation and it caused controversy when determining if a credit event had occurred. The 2001 definitions specified more precise conditions,

---

[8]   The ISDA definitions from 1999, the restructuring supplement from 2001 and the 2003 definitions are available at www.ISDA.org.

including any action that resulted in a reduction in the amount of principal. In the European market, restructuring is generally retained as a credit event in contract documentation, but in the US market it is less common to see it included. Instead, US contract documentation tends to include as a credit event a form of *modified restructuring*, the impact of which is to limit the options available to the protection buyer as to the type of assets it could deliver in a physically-settled contract. Further clarification was provided in the 2003 ISDA definitions.[9]

Restructuring, modified restructuring and modified–modified restructuring

The original 1999 ISDA credit definitions defined restructuring among the standard credit events. The five specified definitions included events such as a reduction in the rate of interest payable, a reduction in the amount of principal outstanding and a postponement or deferral of payment. Following a number of high-profile cases where there was disagreement or dispute between protection buyers and sellers on what constituted precisely a restructuring, the Supplement to the 1999 ISDA limited the term to maturity of deliverable obligations. This was modified restructuring or Mod-R, which was intended to reduce the difference between the loss suffered by a holder of the actual restructured obligation and the writer of a CDS on that reference name. In practice this has placed a maturity limit on deliverable obligations of 30 months.

---

[9] The debate on restructuring as a credit event arose out of a number of events, notably the case involving a corporate entity, Conseco, in the US in 2000. It concerned the delivery option afforded the protection buyer in a physically-settled credit derivative, and the *cheapest-to-deliver* asset. Under physical settlement, the protection buyer may deliver any senior debt obligation of the reference entity. When the triggering credit event is default, all senior obligations of the reference entity generally trade at approximately equal levels, mainly because of the expected recovery rate in a bankruptcy proceeding. However, where the triggering event is restructuring short-dated bank debt, which has been restructured to give lending banks better pricing and collateral, the short-dated bonds will trade at a significant premium to longer-dated bonds. The pricing differential between the short-dated, restructured obligations and the longer-dated bonds results in the delivery option held by the protection buyer carrying significant value, as the protection buyer will deliver the cheapest-to-deliver obligation. Under the modified restructuring definition, where the triggering event is restructuring, the delivered obligation cannot have a maturity that is longer than the original maturity date of the credit derivative contract, or more than 30 months after the original maturity date.

The 2003 Definitions presented further clarification and stated that the restructuring event had to be binding on all holders of the restructured debt. The modified-modified restructuring definition or Mod-Mod-R described in the 2003 ISDA defines the modified restructuring term to maturity date as the later of:

- the scheduled termination date, and
- 60 months following the restructuring date

in the event that a restructured bond or loan is delivered to the protection seller. If another obligation is delivered, the limitation on maturity is the scheduled maturity date and 30 months following the restructuring date.

Credit Derivative Instruments

Before analysing the main types of credit derivatives, we now consider some generic features of all credit derivatives.

Background

Credit derivative instruments enable participants in the financial market to trade in credit as an asset, as they effectively isolate and transfer credit risk. They also enable the market to separate funding considerations from credit risk. A number of instruments come under the category of credit derivative. In this and the next chapter we consider the most commonly encountered credit derivative instruments. Irrespective of the particular instrument under consideration, all credit derivatives can be described as having the following characteristics:

- the *reference entity*: which is the asset or name on which credit protection is being bought and sold;[10]
- the credit event, or events: which indicate that the reference entity is experiencing or about to experience financial difficulty and which act as trigger events for termination of and payments under the credit derivative contract;

---

[10] Note that a contract may be written in relation to a *reference entity*, which is the corporate or sovereign name, or a *reference obligation*, which is a specific debt obligation of a specific reference entity. Another term for reference obligation is *reference asset* or *reference credit*. We will use these latter terms interchangeably in the book.

- the settlement mechanism for the contract: whether cash settled or physically settled;
- (under physical settlement), the deliverable obligation: that the protection buyer delivers to the protection seller on the occurrence of a trigger event.

Within this broad framework, it is common to see wide variations in detail among specific types of credit derivative instruments.

Funded and unfunded contracts

Credit derivatives are grouped into *funded* and *unfunded* instruments. In a funded credit derivative, typified by a credit-linked note (CLN), the investor in the note is the credit-protection seller and is making an upfront payment to the protection buyer when it buys the note. This upfront payment is the price of the CLN. Thus, the protection buyer is the issuer of the note. If no credit event occurs during the life of the note, the redemption value (par) of the note is paid to the investor on maturity. If a credit event does occur, then on termination (in effect, maturity of the bond), a value less than par will be paid to the investor. This value will be reduced by the nominal value of the reference asset that the CLN is linked to. The exact process will differ according to whether *cash settlement* or *physical settlement* has been specified for the note. We will consider this later.

In an unfunded credit derivative, typified by a credit default swap, the protection seller does not make an upfront payment to the protection buyer. Thus the main difference between funded and unfunded is that in a funded contract, the insurance protection payment is made to the protection buyer at the start of the transaction: if there is no credit event, the payment is returned to the protection seller. In an unfunded contract, the protection payment is made on termination of the contract on occurrence of a triggering credit event. Otherwise it is not made at all. Therefore, when entering into a funded contract transaction, the protection seller must find the funds at the start of the trade.

Credit derivatives such as credit default swaps have a number of applications and are used extensively for flow trading of single reference name credit risks or, in *portfolio swap* form, for trading a basket of reference obligations. Credit default swaps and credit-linked notes are used in structured products, in various combinations, and their flexibility has been behind the growth and wide application of the synthetic collateralised debt obligation and other credit hybrid products. We look at these later.

Compared to cash market bonds and loans, an unfunded credit derivative isolates and transfers credit risk. In other words, its value reflects (in theory) only the credit quality of the reference entity. Compare this to a fixed-coupon corporate bond, the value of which is a function of both interest rate risk and credit quality, where the return to the investor depends on the investor's funding costs.[11] The interest rate risk element of the bond can be removed by combining the bond with an interest rate swap, to create an *asset swap*. An asset swap removes the interest rate risk of the bond, leaving only the credit quality and the funding aspects of the bond. With an unfunded credit derivative, the funding aspect is removed as well, leaving only the credit element. This is because no up-front payment is required, resulting in no funding risk to the protection seller. The protection seller, who is the investor, receives a return that is linked only to the credit quality of the reference entity.

This separation of credit risk from other elements of the cash market is shown in Figure 2.5.

Figure 2.5   Credit derivatives isolate credit as an asset class and risk element.

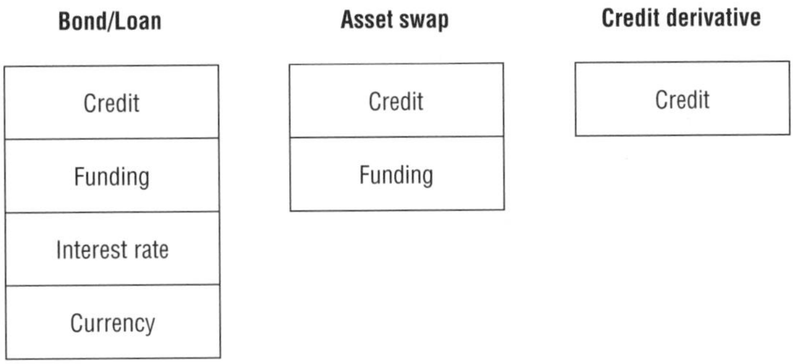

Bond/Loan	Asset swap	Credit derivative
Credit	Credit	Credit
Funding	Funding	
Interest rate		
Currency		

---

[11] Funding refers to the cost of funds of the investor. For a bank, funding is based on LIBID. For a traditional investor, such as a pension fund manager, funding is more problematic, as the funds are in theory invested directly with the pension fund and so acquired "free". However for economic purposes, such funds are valued at the rate that they can be invested in the money markets. For other investors, funding is based on LIBOR plus a spread, except for very highly-rated market participants such as the World Bank, who can fund at sub-LIBOR rates.

> **Example 2.1** Reference entity and reference obligation
>
> A reference obligation or reference asset is an obligation issued by a reference entity for which credit protection is required. The reference obligation usually has a pre-specified seniority, to facilitate ease of determination of the settlement payment. A higher seniority usually leads to a better recovery rate and hence a lower loss rate following a credit event.

Comparing credit derivatives to cash instruments

Both funded and unfunded credit derivatives act as alternatives to cash market products for investors. Funded credit derivatives are similar to cash bonds, but investors will need to assess their requirements more fully when assessing the relative merits of cash versus synthetic products.

In certain respects both products offer the same thing. The coupon cash flows of a corporate bond can be replicated using a credit default swap contract, and an investor can get synthetic access to a particular sovereign or corporate name in this way. In some cases the return can be higher for essentially the same commensurate risk. We can illustrate this with an hypothetical example. Assume a pension fund investor wishes to invest in the bonds of a hypothetical corporate credit, call it Jackfruit Music Limited, which is rated BBB−/Baa3. The investor can buy Jackfruit Music bonds or sell protection in Jackfruit Music instead. Either way, the investor is acquiring risk in Jackfruit Music.

Market makers quote the following for Jackfruit Music:

- Five-year bonds offered at 250 basis points over benchmark government bonds;
- Credit default swap bid-offer price is 225–230 bps;
- Bond asset swap price is Libor + 195 bps (five-year interbank swap spread is 55 bps).

Assume further that the investor is part of a Group entity and funds at Libor plus 10 basis points.

The alternatives are illustrated in Table 2.1.

Table 2.1   Jackfruit Music Ltd, buying bonds versus selling protection.

Buy Jackfruit 5-year bonds	Sell 5-yr protection on Jackfruit
Funded position	Unfunded position
Earn 195 basis points over Libor	Earn 225 basis points
Fund at Libor + 10.0	No funding cost
Net return 185 bps	Return 225 bps

By investing via the synthetic product, the investor earns a yield pick up of 40 basis points over the cash position. This sounds too good to be true and in some cases will be. However it illustrates the key issues. As we will see in Chapter 8, the CDS position in many cases exposes the investor to a greater risk exposure than the cash bond position, which is why the CDS price is in many cases higher. This difference between the CDS price and the cash bond price is known as the *basis*. The size of the basis is used as an indicator of deteriorating credit quality (or, as significant, potentially deteriorating credit quality) in a reference name.

Table 2.2 shows the key investor considerations for both markets.

Table 2.2   Cash versus synthetic market considerations.

Buy cash bonds	Sell credit protection
Funded position	Unfunded position
Investor holds a specific bond and its risk exposure is to that specific bond	Unless written into the contract specifically, investor is selling protection on all obligations of the reference issuer
Risk to specific bond which is marked-to-market and may be sold in market if buyer is available	In event of credit event, which may not be complete default or full administration, protection seller will settle at par, minus market price of cheapest eligible reference bond (or receive this bond, for which it pays par)
Return on bond is net amount of funding cost	Return is CDS offer price

We now consider the individual credit derivative instruments.

Credit Default Swaps

First, we describe the credit default swap (CDS), the most commonly traded credit derivative instrument.

Structure

The most common credit derivative is the *credit default swap, credit swap* or *default swap*.[12] This is a bilateral contract that provides protection on the par value of a specified reference asset, with a protection buyer that pays a periodic fixed fee or a one-off premium to a *protection seller*, in return for which the seller will make a payment on the occurrence of a specified credit event. The fee is usually quoted as a basis point multiplier of the nominal value. It is usually paid quarterly in arrears. The swap can refer to a specific single asset, known as the reference asset or underlying asset, a basket of assets, or a reference entity. The default payment can be paid in whatever way suits the protection buyer or both counterparties. For example, it may be linked to the change in price of the reference asset or another specified asset, it may be fixed at a pre-determined recovery rate, or it may be in the form of actual delivery of the reference asset at a specified price. The basic structure is shown in Figure 2.6.

Figure 2.6   Credit default swap.

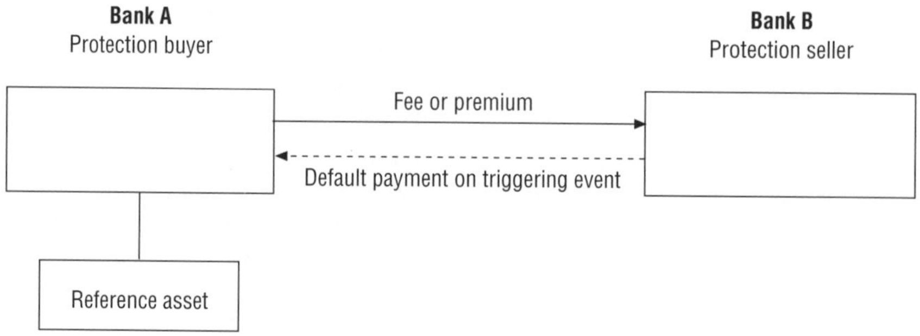

---

[12] The author prefers the first term, but the other two terms are common.

The credit default swap enables one party to transfer its credit risk exposure to another party. Banks may use default swaps to trade sovereign and corporate credit spreads without trading the actual assets themselves; for example, someone who has gone long a default swap (the protection buyer) will gain if the reference asset obligor suffers a rating downgrade or defaults, and can sell the default swap at a profit if they can find a buyer counterparty.[13] This is because the cost of protection on the reference asset will have increased as a result of the credit event. The original buyer of the default swap need never have owned a bond issued by the reference asset obligor.

The maturity of the credit default swap does not have to match the maturity of the reference asset and often does not. On occurrence of a credit event, the swap contract is terminated and a settlement payment is made by the protection seller, or *guarantor,* to the protection buyer. This termination value is calculated at the time of the credit event, and the exact procedure that is followed to calculate the termination value depends on the settlement terms specified in the contract. This will be either cash settlement or physical settlement. We look at these options later.

For illustrative purposes, Figure 2.7 shows investment-grade credit default swap levels during 2001 and 2002 for US dollar and euro reference entities (average levels taken), while Figure 2.7b shows sample CDS prices during September 2003.

Appendix 2.3 shows a sample term sheet for a CDS contract.

---

[13] Be careful with terminology here. To "go long" of an instrument generally is to purchase it. In the cash market, "going long the bond" means one is buying the bond and so receiving coupon — the buyer has therefore taken on credit risk exposure to the issuer. In a credit default swap, "going long" is to buy the swap, but the buyer is purchasing protection and therefore paying premium. The buyer has no credit exposure on the name and has in effect "gone short" on the reference name (the equivalent of "shorting a bond" in the cash market and paying coupon). So buying a credit default swap is frequently referred to in the market as "shorting" the reference entity.

Figure 2.7 Investment-grade credit default swap levels, 2001–2002.

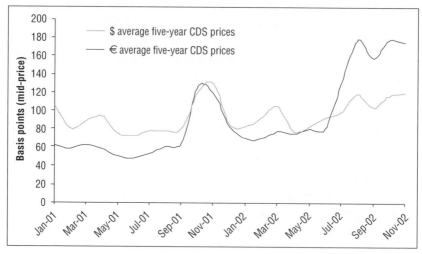

Source: Bloomberg.

Figure 2.7b Sample 5-year CDS swap premiums, September 2003.

Reference name	Mid-price bps	Moodys/S&P
Automobiles		
Ford Motor Co	318	Baa1/BBB−
General Motors	269	Baa1/BBB
GMAC	229	A3/BBB
Banks		
Bank of America	23	Aa2/A+
Wells Fargo	33	Aa2/ A+

Asia-Pacific region	Bid-Ask	Moodys/S&P
Hutchison Whampoa	96/106	A3/A−
PR China	22/26	A3/BBB
Rep of Korea	67/74	A3/A−
NEC	46/53	Baa2/BBB−
Qantas	74/84	Baa1/BBB+

Source: Morgan Stanley, Bloomberg, Risk.

Example 2.2 Credit default swap example

XYZ plc credit spreads are currently trading at 120 bps over five-year government bond maturities and 195 bps over 10-year government bond maturities. A portfolio manager hedges a US$10 million holding of 10-year paper by purchasing the following credit default swap, written on the five-year bond. This hedge protects for the first five years of the holding, and in the event of XYZ's credit spread widening, will increase in value and may be sold before expiry at profit. The 10-year bond holding also earns 75 bps over the shorter-term paper for the portfolio manager.

Term: 5 years
Reference credit: XYZ plc five-year bond
Credit event: The business day following occurrence of specified credit event
Default payment: Nominal value of bond × [100 − price of bond after credit event]
Swap premium: 3.35%

Assume that midway into the life of the swap there is a technical default on the XYZ plc five-year bond, such that its price now stands at US$28. Under the terms of the swap the protection buyer delivers the bond to the seller, who pays US$7.2 million to the buyer.

Bloomberg users can also access the price histories of CDS contracts on specific reference entities. This is done in the first instance by obtaining the tickers for each contract, which are listed by currency. So to obtain a ticker list for euro-denominated contracts, the user types

EUR CDS <Crncy> <go>

and this screen is shown at Figure 2.8. We have paged forward to obtain the ticker for British Telecom, and this is shown for various maturities at Figure 2.8. We then select the five-year CDS, detailed at Figure 2.9 which is the DES page for this contract. This gives the 52-week high and low for this contract as well as its current spread. From this page we can select the CDS spread curve by hitting 2 <go>, and for this example the curve is shown at Figure 2.10.

To view the historical range of this particular contract, we type the ticker and select GP, which is

CBTE5 <Crncy> GP <go>

and this screen is shown at Figure 2.11. To view this data in tabular form we hit "page forward", and this is reproduced at Figure 2.12.

Rolling maturity swaps and constant maturity swaps

A recent innovation in credit default swaps (during 2003) is that of rolling maturity swaps. This is where there is a set of rolling quarterly maturity dates, rather like the futures market. The dates are 20th March, 20th June, 20th September and 20th December. A CDS contract traded on any day with a (say) five-year maturity will mature on the relevant quarterly maturity date in five years. So for example the active three-year CDS contract on 20 April 2004 will mature on 20 June 2007. This will be the expiry date for all rolling maturity CDS contracts traded from that date until 21 June 2004, when the active-maturity CDS will expire on 20 September 2007, and so on.

A more recent innovation still (during 2004) is the constant maturity CDS. This is not a plain vanilla CDS. A constant maturity CDS has its maturity date reset periodically, say at three-month or six-month intervals. Its premium is also reset at each roll date, so a constant maturity swap has a varying premium. In theory a constant maturity CDS is of value to a loan portfolio manager who wishes to maintain the maturity of their hedges at a set period, without transacting new trades. For instance the portfolio manager may wish to maintain a constant five-year hedge for its portfolio because this is the most liquid part of the CDS curve. The premium of a constant maturity swap for a particular reference name will lie above that of a vanilla swap for the same name, say 10 or 15 basis points higher.

However a constant maturity swap carries price risk for the protection buyer (and conversely for the protection seller) because the portfolio manager does not know at what level the swap premium will be reset at each roll date. It may be simpler and less risky to simply roll actual contracts at quarterly or semi-annual intervals, with a new contract traded as each one matures.

Basket default swaps

The simplest CDS is the single-name credit default swap, which references one reference entity or the specific asset of an entity. A basket default swap is linked to a group of reference entities. There may be five, 10, 20 or more reference names in the basket. While it is possible to buy a CDS that covers all the named assets in the event of default, this is rare and the most common basket CDS provides protection on a selection of the names in the basket only. For instance, if there are q names in the basket, the basket CDS may be one of the following:

- first-to-default, which provides credit protection on the first default in the basket only;
- second to default, which provides credit protection on the second default in the basket (but not the first);
- n-th to default, which provides protection on the first n (out of q) defaults in the basket;
- last p-th to default, which provides protection on the last p (out of q) defaults.

Figure 2.8   Menu page, EUR CDS price histories.

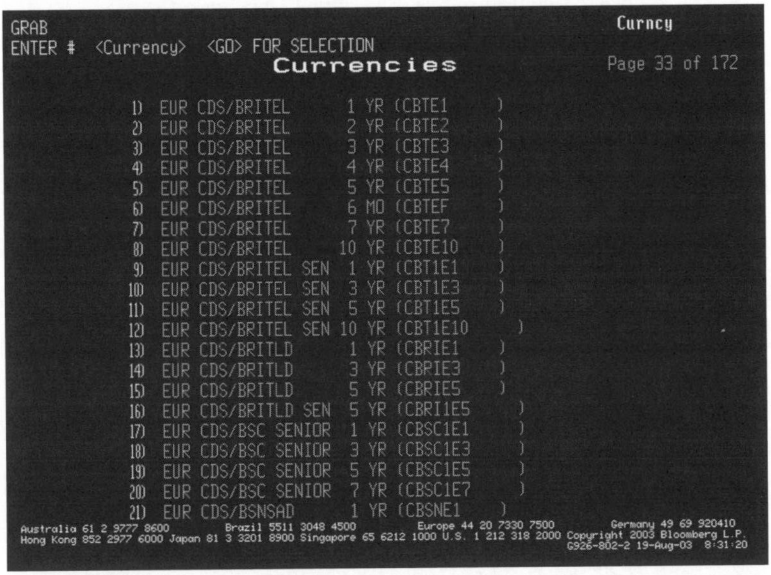

Figure 2.9   British Telecom 5-year CDS description.

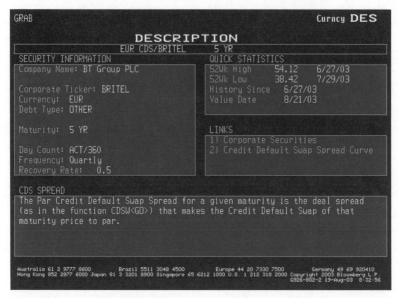

© Bloomberg L.P. Used with permission.

Figure 2.10   British Telecom, current CDS spread curve.

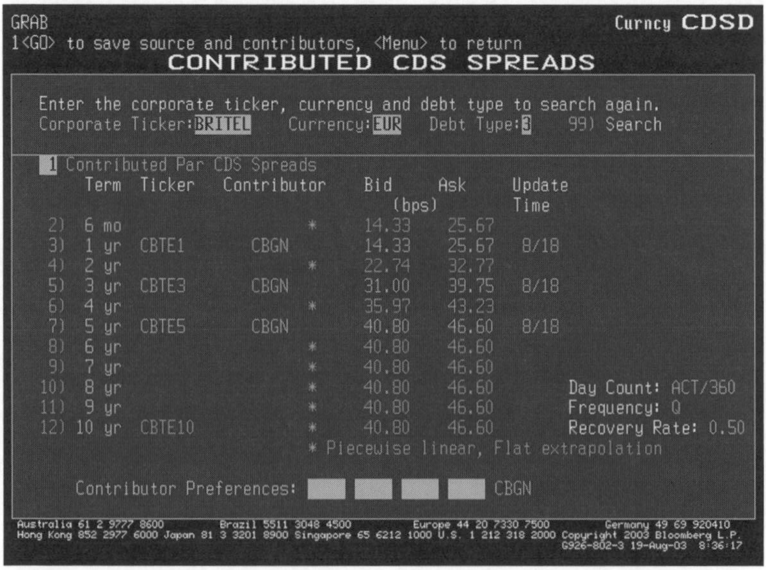

© Bloomberg L.P. Used with permission.

Figure 2.11 Selected BT CDS contract, price history.

© Bloomberg L.P. Used with permission.

Figure 2.12 Price history in table format.

© Bloomberg L.P. Used with permission.

Basket default swaps require special treatment in their pricing and valuation compared to single-name CDS contracts.

Basket default swaps are required for specific applications of credit exposure and hedging. First-to-default basket CDS are common in the market. They enable investors to spread out their credit risk but without increasing their downside credit risk exposure. The maximum loss for the investor in the basket is (as for a single-name CDS) par minus the recovery value of the first asset that experiences a credit event, which is the same risk exposure were they to be long the bond in the cash market. The advantage of the basket CDS though is that the protection premium paid to the investor will be a higher spread that that paid by any of the individual names in the basket. We illustrate this in the table below, with some hypothetical industry sectors. Each individual name does not pay more than 130 basis points, with an average premium of 107 basis points. However a first-to-default basket CDS on all these names will pay 285 basis points.

First-to-default basket CDS on hypothetical reference names

Reference name	Credit rating	Premium (bps)
Bank	AA/Aa	53
Non-bank financial	A/A2	120
Airline	BBB−/Baa2	130
Utility	BBB+/Baa1	110
Transport	BBB+/Baa2	120

CDS premium 285 basis points per annum — contingent payment of par minus recovery value of first default

The variations in basket CDS present different risk/return profiles. For example a second-to-default basket CDS will only pay protection after the second and subsequent reference asset has experienced a credit event. Thus it is a lower-risk investment with a lower level of credit risk exposure than the first-to-default basket, but paying a higher premium than a single-name CDS on any of the names in the basket.

Basket products also exist in funded form as credit-linked notes (see chapter 3), usually issued out of an SPV.

Illustration of a basket credit default swap

Figure 2.13 shows a basket credit default swap written on a portfolio of five reference names. The protection seller writes protection on the basket, for which it receives the CDS premium. A notional amount is specified for each reference entity in the basket. During the term of the CDS if one of the reference entities experiences a credit event, the protection seller will make a protection payment to the protection buyer, to the value of the pre-specified notional amount (minus the usual value in accordance with the type of settlement mechanism chosen.) On occurrence of a credit event, the affected reference entity is removed from the basket. However the CDS itself still runs to its original maturity date, covering the remaining entities in the basket.

Figure 2.13   Basket CDS.

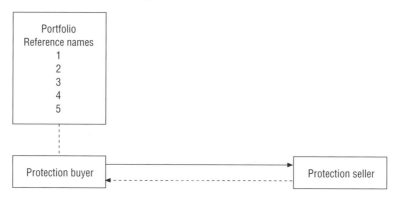

As an example consider a basket CDS as shown in Figure 2.13, written on a portfolio of five reference entities. A protection buyer enters into a basket CDS with a market maker with the following terms:

Trade date   17 February 2004
Value date   19 February 2004
Maturity date   19 Feb 2009
Notional amounts   USD 20 million for each entity
Portfolio notional value USD 100 million
Settlement   Cash
Premium   285 bps

Assume that one year into the transaction, one of the reference entities experiences a credit event. Its recovery value is determined to be 70%. The protection seller makes a payment of

$$USD\ 20\ million \times (1.00 - 0.70)$$

or USD 6 million at the time of the credit event. The affected reference name then drops out of the basket.

The CDS will then continue to maturity, and assuming the portfolio experienced no further credit evens, would expire on 19 February 2009 having not paid out any more cash flows (apart from the ongoing premium). The terms of the CDS would have changed to reflect a USF 80 million notional basket value, covering four reference entities.

If any of the remaining four entities experience a credit event, the same procedure will apply again. The main difference between a single name CDS and the basket is that the CDS would have terminated on occurrence of the credit event, whereas the basket will continue, albeit covering only for the remaining unaffected names, to its original maturity date. The key advantage of the basket CDS is that it typically offersd protection for multiple names at a lower cost than if the protection buyer had taken out a series of single-name CDS for each name in the portfolio.

The protection provided by the basket discussed above could also be traded in funded form, as a basket credit-linked note (CLN). In the example given above, the nominal value of the note would be USD 200 million, paid up front by the investor (protection seller). If we assume the same credit event as above, there will be a payout on occurrence of the credit event of USD 6 million, and on maturity of the note (assuming no further credit events) the redemption proceeds would be USD 180 million rather than USD 200 million. Investors receive a pro rata amount of the remaining total principal available in accordance with the amount of the note they are holding. If the CLN was issued as a series of notes with differing seniority, the senior notes would be paid off in full first before investors holding the more junior notes are paid their redemption proceeds.

The basket CLN is shown in Figure 2.14.

Figure 2.14   Basket CLN.

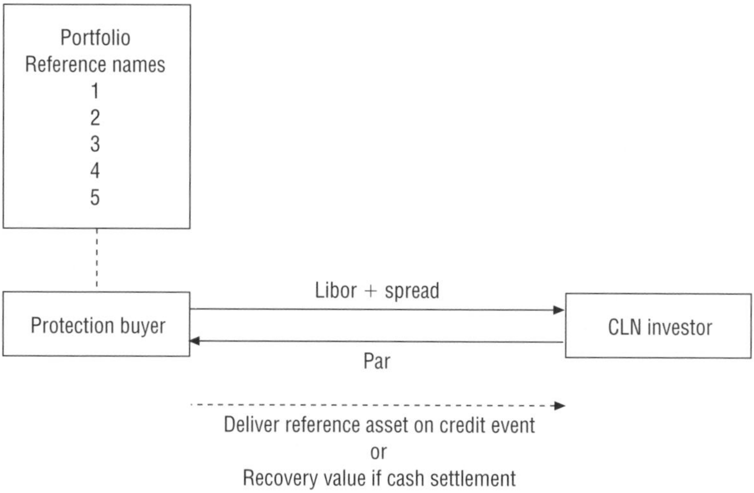

First to default portfolio CDS
==

A first-to-default CDS (FtD) is similar to the basket CDS described above, with one key difference: unlike with a standard basket CDS, on occurrence of a credit event the entire FtD CDS will terminate and settlement will be with regard to the entire notional amount following the first credit event affecting one of the reference entities.

If we assume the same circumstances as the earlier basket CDS, with the FtD CDS written on five reference entities for a notional total of USD 200 million, following the first credit event the swap will terminate with a settlement of USD 186 million.

As we see in the next section the key issue for those analysing FtD swaps is the correlation between the different reference entity names. Correlation is assessed with respect to each name's industrial sector, credit rating, geographical region and so on. In contrast to an investor in (say) a cash flow CDO, where diversifying among the names in the portfolio will reduce the risk exposure to the credit protection seller, with an FtD CDS greater diversity may infact increase the risk factor. This is because it may increase the probability of default or other credit event, since as soon as the first reference entity experiences a credit event, it triggers termination of the entire CDS. For this reason, a FtD CDS will be priced at a higher level than a basket CDS for the same reference name, to compensate investors for the higher resultant risk exposure.

Pricing considerations

For instance, consider that a fund manager is holding three bonds issued by three different issuers. If the fund manager is worried about one of the bonds defaulting it can buy a 1st-to-default swap contract. If instead it was to buy three different CDS's then in order for the contract to be used all three bonds would have to default. But if the fund manager does not believe that all three bonds would default then it would not be worth paying for three separate CDS contracts. Hence it is a cheaper hedge to buy a basket CDS that covers all three bonds in the portfolio and set the CDS as a nth-to-default swap contract.

The degree to which the nth-to-default basket would be cheaper than buying 3 separate CDS's depends on the default correlation between the reference entities in the basket. Consider two extreme examples; let us say that we have three bonds of different issuers and that all of them have a default correlation of 100%. This would mean that a fair price for the 1st to default is the same as the premium of the most expensive single name CDS. To explain the logic behind this let us take a look at this from a risk perspective. If we have CDS's on three reference entities A, B and C at a price of 50, 50 and 50 basis points respectively and all of them have the same time to default (by definition 100% default correlation) then the first to default premium should be the 50 basis points. If $t(i)$ is the time to default then all of them will default at time $t(i)$, and as only payments of the first to default will be made the seller of the 1st to default swap will charge the same premium as that of the single name CDS on say C.[14] Now let us assume that there is no default correlation between any of the above reference entities. Here the risk to the seller of the 1st to default is greater. We cannot take the perspective of selling one CDS, say C and assuming one payment will be made when C defaults and the seller of the CDS will not have to worry about the others defaulting, because their defaults are perfectly correlated and only a risk of 50 basis points can be attached. Here

---

[14] The above is a theoretical simplification for demonstration purposes. Using strict statistical definitions we imply the probability that one of the reference enteties has experienced a default on condition that none of the other refernce enteties have defaulted. Although the above is a simplification, in the limit of there being a 100% default correlation the above example is valid.

the 2 other reference entities can default at completely different times. Now from the perspective of the seller of the CDS if the three reference entities can default at different times the probability of a default occurring until the maturity of the basket contact is greater. This results in a higher premium than in the first case. By the above logic there is a simple formula for the 1st to default, 2nd to default and 1st two to default and this would be the sum of the premium between the 1st and second to default.

Essentially 1st to default baskets are an efficient way for portfolio managers to hedge their exposure when they believe that not all of the bonds in their portfolio can default within short periods of time. This makes it cheaper for them to hedge using basket CDS contracts.

Default correlation

A basket CDS is a *default correlation* instrument. The main determinant of the price of an nth-to-default basket is the correlation of default. So for instance assets issued within the same geographical or industrial sector will have a higher correlation of default than assets that are more diverse.

Let us say that we have a basket with 2 reference entities A and B. The default correlation is represented by:

$$\rho(ab) = \frac{\pi ab(T) - Qa(T)Qb(T)}{\sqrt{[Qa(1 - Qa)][Qb(1 - Qb)]}}$$

where $\pi(ab)$ is the probabilities of both reference entities a and b defaulting between time $t = 0$ and T, and $Qa(T)$ is the cumulative probability of a default at time T.

The above form is used when the default probabilities follow a normal distribution. A preferable method of structuring correlation relation when variables are not normally distributed is the *Gaussian Copula* approach. This subject is outside the scope of the book. Suppose that Ta and Tb are the times to default of reference entities a and b which are not normally distributed. Let Ta be the time to default of reference entity a and Tb be the time for B, we imply

$$\mu_a = N^{-1} [Qa(Ta)]$$
$$\mu_b = N^{-1} [Qb(Tb)]$$

here μ_a and μ_b are normally distributed which means that the correlation is $ab = \text{corr}[\mu_a(Ta), \mu_b(Tb)]$.

Quanto Default Swaps

A *quanto default swap* is a CDS in which the swap premium payments, and/or the cash proceeds in the event of termination, are in a different currency to that of the reference asset. Aan example is a CDS written on a euro-denominated bond, for which the premium is payable in US dollars. Quanto swaps are used to hedge holdings in bonds or bank loans that are in a different currency to the investor's "home" currency and may be illiquid or not traded.

Equity Default Swaps

Equity default swaps are the latest development in credit derivative products. They follow the same principles as credit default swaps, except that the reference asset is an equity asset rather than a bond or loan. This gives rise to two key differences between equity default swaps and credit default swaps:

- instead of a "credit event", the triggering event is the point when the reference stock hits a specified low barrier;
- the "recovery rate" is set at a pre-specified fixed level, for instance 50%.

All equity default swaps are cash settled instruments. Figure 2.15 illustrates the structure.

As with CDS, the terms of an equity default swap (EDS) are flexible and can be set to meet customer requirements. We illustrate the concept with an hypothetical example.

Figure 2.15 Equity default swap.

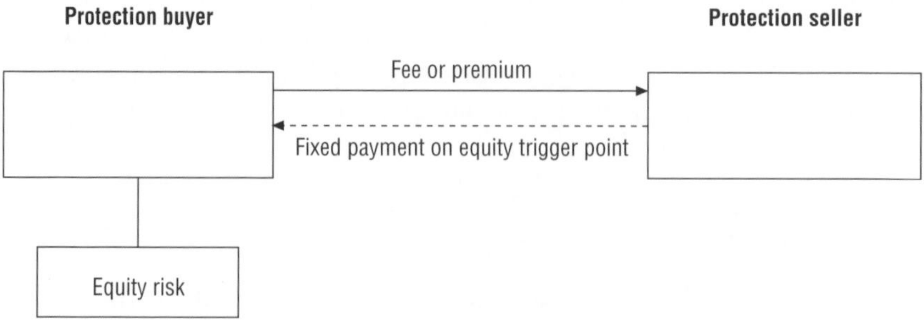

Example 2.3   Equity Default Swap

At trade date, the stock price of British Aerospace plc is £5.50. A protection buyer enters into a three-year EDS on this security, at a premium of 240 basis points. The trigger level is set at 50% and recovery rate 30%. The EDS will run for the three-year term, unless at any time the closing price of the stock on the London Stock Exchange is at or below £2.75, which is 50% of £5.50. If the stock closes at or below this price on any day during the next three years (the "equity event"), the EDS is immediately terminated and the contract is cash settled. The protection buyer will pay any remaining accrued premium, and the protection seller will pay 70% (that is, 100% − recovery rate) of the notional amount to the protection buyer.

In this example, the EDS protection seller receives the swap premium and pays 70% of the notional on an equity event. The EDS protection buyer pays the swap premium and receives 70% of the notional on occurrence of the equity event.

Typically, the premiums on an EDS are payable quarterly on the stock exchange expiry date, this is usually the third Friday of the month. In contrast to a CDS contract, there is only one "equity event", the fall of the stock price to the trigger level. On occurrence of the equity event, the contract is terminated and cash settlement takes place. The protection buyer will pay any remaining accrued premium, while the protection seller pays (100% — recovery value).

EDS prices

EDS premiums generally trade at higher levels than the CDS for the same reference name. This is because the probability of an equity falling by say, 50% (as in our example) or even 70%–80% can be expected to be higher than the probability of default. The protection seller is therefore taking on greater risk. The protection seller also has mark-to-market risk even if no equity event takes place, if a rise in volatility leads to higher premiums. Figure 2.16 shows indicative three-year EDS and CDS spreads for a sample of corporate entities. We see that the EDS spread is significantly higher compared to the CDS in all examples. The higher EDS prices reflects higher volatility and also (one assumes) different set recovery rates. The prices also indicate a positive correlation of higher CDS prices with higher EDS prices.

Figure 2.16   Three-year EDS and CDS spreads, May 2003.

Name	EDS (bps)	CDS (bps)
Aegon	575	75
Aviva	480	50
BBVA	310	25
British Aerospace	240	55
BT	465	85
Deutsche Telekom	431	125
Fortis	430	25
GlaxoSmithKline	222	20
Lloyds TSB	475	20
Prudential	480	45
RBoS	235	20
Shell	215	8
Telecom Italia	290	120
UBS	205	15
Unilever	210	25
Vodaphone	350	45

Source: JPMorgan Chase. Used with permission.

Given this positive correlation, market participants can use the EDS as a proxy for the CDS for any particular reference name, and use the EDS market as an alternative for taking on or laying off credit risk. In addition, there is scope for relative value trades between the two markets.

Applications

An investor may compare EDS and CDS spreads and select the market that offers the greatest value for taking on or hedging credit exposure. For example, assume that the EDS for a company is viewed as being expensive relative to its CDS price. Credit protection on the name can be funded by selling protection via an EDS and buying protection via a CDS. As the EDS will trade at higher premiums, the investor will have credit protection on the name while earning a net premium spread. For example, selling protection on British Aerospace at 240 bps and buying protection at 55 bps for say, twice the notional amount means that the investor is holding credit protection and earning 130 bps per annum (that is, $240 - (2 \times 55) = 130$). If there is a credit event, we assume that the equity event trigger is also breached, and the investor will pay out on the EDS but receive twice this amount through the CDS (we assume a 50% recovery here). The downside risk of this trade is of course that the equity event occurs without the credit event occurring.

We look at EDS valuation in Chapter 6.

Total Return Swaps

A *total return swap* (TRS), sometimes known as a *total rate of return swap* or *TR swap*, is an agreement between two parties that exchanges the total return from a financial asset between them. This is designed to transfer the credit risk from one party to the other. It is one of the principal instruments used by banks and other financial instruments to manage their credit risk exposure, and as such is a credit derivative. One definition of a TRS is given in Francis *et al* (1999), which states that a TRS is a swap agreement in which the *total return* of a bank loan or credit-sensitive security is exchanged for some other cash flow, usually linked to LIBOR or some other loan or credit-sensitive security.

The TRS trade itself can be to any maturity term, that is, it need not match the maturity of the underlying security. In a TRS, the total return from the underlying asset is paid to the counterparty in return for a fixed or floating cash flow. This makes it slightly different to other credit derivatives, as the payments between counterparties to a TRS are connected to changes in the market value of the underlying asset, as well as changes resulting from the occurrence of a credit event. So, in other words, TRS cash flows are not solely linked to the occurrence of a credit event — in a TRS the interest rate risk is also transferred. The transaction enables the complete cash flows of a bond to be received without the recipient actually buying the bond, which makes it a synthetic bond product and therefore a credit derivative. An investor may wish to receive such cash flows synthetically for tax, accounting, regulatory capital, external audit or legal reasons. On the other hand, it may be easier to source the reference asset synthetically — via the TRS — than in the cash market. This happens sometimes with illiquid bonds.

In some versions of a TRS, the actual underlying asset is actually sold to the counterparty, with a corresponding swap transaction agreed simultaneously. In other versions, there is no physical change of ownership of the underlying asset. This makes TRS akin to a synthetic repo transaction. This is discussed in Appendix 2.2.

Figure 2.17 illustrates a generic TR swap. The two counterparties are labelled as banks, but the party termed "Bank A" can be another financial institution, including cash-rich fixed-income portfolio managers such as insurance companies and hedge funds. In Figure 2.10, Bank A has contracted to pay the "total return" on a specified reference asset, while simultaneously receiving a LIBOR-based return from Bank B. The reference or underlying asset can be a bank loan such as a corporate loan or a sovereign or corporate bond. The total return payments from Bank A include the interest payments on the underlying loan as well as any appreciation in the market value of the asset. Bank B will pay the LIBOR-based return and it will also pay any difference if there is a depreciation in the price of the asset. The economic effect is as if Bank B owned the underlying asset, as such TR swaps are synthetic loans or securities. A significant feature is that Bank A will usually hold the underlying asset on its balance sheet, so that if this asset was originally on Bank B's balance sheet, this is a means by which the latter can have the asset removed from its balance sheet for the term of the TR swap.[15] If we assume Bank A has access to LIBOR funding, it will receive a spread on this from Bank B. Under the terms of the swap, Bank B will pay the difference between the initial market value and any depreciation, so it is sometimes termed the "guarantor" while Bank A is the "beneficiary".

Figure 2.17   Total return swap.

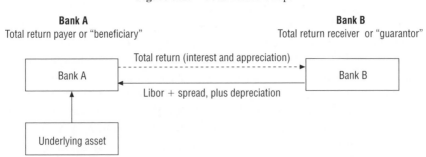

The total return on the underlying asset is the interest payments and any change in the market value if there is capital appreciation. The value of an appreciation may be cash settled, alternatively there may be physical

---

[15] Although it is common for the receiver of the LIBOR-based payments to have the reference asset on its balance sheet, this is not always the case.

delivery of the reference asset on maturity of the swap, in return for a payment of the initial asset value by the total return "receiver". The maturity of the TR swap need not be identical to that of the reference asset, and in fact it is rare for it to be so.

The swap element of the trade will usually pay on a monthly, quarterly or semi-annual basis, with the underlying asset being revalued or *marked-to-market* on the re-fixing dates. The asset price is usually obtained from an independent third party source such as Bloomberg or Reuters, or as the average of a range of market quotes. If the *obligor* of the reference asset defaults, the swap may be terminated immediately, with a net present value payment changing hands according to what this value is, or it may be continued with each party making appreciation or depreciation payments as appropriate. This second option is only available if there is a market for the asset, which is less likely in the case of a bank loan. If the swap is terminated, each counterparty is liable to the other for accrued interest plus any appreciation or depreciation of the asset. Commonly under the terms of the trade, the guarantor bank has the option to purchase the underlying asset from the beneficiary bank, and then deal directly with loan defaulter.

The TRS can also be traded as a funded credit derivative, and we look at this in the next chapter. The use of TRS for funding purposes is considered in Chapter 4.

Banks employ a number of methods to price credit derivatives and TR swaps. Essentially the pricing of credit derivatives is linked to that of other instruments, however the main difference between credit derivatives and other off-balance sheet products such as equity, currency or bond derivatives is that the latter can be priced and hedged with reference to the underlying asset, which can be problematic when applied to credit derivatives. Credit products pricing uses statistical data on likelihood of default, probability of payout, level of risk tolerance and a pricing model. With a TRS the basic concept is that one party "funds" an underlying asset and transfers the total return of the asset to another party, in return for a (usually) floating return that is a spread to LIBOR. This spread is a function of:

- the credit rating of the swap counterparty;
- the amount and value of the reference asset;
- the credit quality of the reference asset;
- the funding costs of the beneficiary bank;
- any required profit margin;
- the capital charge associated with the TRS.

The TR swap counterparties must consider a number of risk factors associated with the transaction, which include:

- the probability that the TR beneficiary may default while the reference asset has declined in value;
- the reference asset obligor defaults, followed by default of the TR swap receiver before payment of the depreciation has been made to the payer or "provider".

The first risk measure is a function of the probability of default by the TR swap receiver and the market volatility of the reference asset, while the second risk is related to the joint probability of default of both factors as well as the recovery probability of the asset.

A formal pricing formula for a TRS contract is given in Chapter 5.

Asset Swaps[16]

Description

Asset swaps pre-date the introduction of the other instruments we discuss in this chapter and strictly speaking are not credit derivatives: they are viewed as being part of the "cash market". However they are used for similar purposes and there is considerable interplay between the cash and synthetic markets using asset swaps, hence we include them here. An asset swap is a combination of an interest rate swap and a bond, and is used to alter the cash flow profile of a bond.[17] The asset swap market is an important segment of the credit derivatives market since it explicitly sets out the price of credit as a spread over LIBOR. Pricing a bond by reference to LIBOR is commonly used and the spread over LIBOR is a measure of credit risk in the cash flow of the underlying bond. This is because LIBOR — the rate at which banks lend cash to each other in the interbank market — is viewed as representing the credit risk of banks. As such it can be viewed as a AA or AA- credit rating. The spread over LIBOR therefore represents additional credit risk over and above that of bank risk.

Asset swaps are used to transform the cash flow characteristics of a bond, either fixed-rate into floating-rate or floating-rate into fixed-rate. This

---

[16] This section was co-written with Richard Pereira of Dresdner Kleinwort Wasserstein in London. The views represent those of the authors in their individual private capacity.

[17] For a background on interest rate swaps, you can look up any number of sources, for instance Das (1994), Kolb (1999), Decovny (1999), Choudhry (2001), and so on.

enables investors to hedge the currency, credit and interest rate risks to create investments with more suitable cash flow characteristics for themselves. An asset swap package involves transactions in which the investor acquires a bond position and then enters into an interest rate swap with the bank that sold them the bond. If it is a fixed-rate bond, the investor will pay fixed and receive floating on the interest rate swap. This transforms the fixed coupon of the bond into a LIBOR-based floating coupon.

For example, assume that a protection buyer holding a fixed-rate "risky" bond wishes to hedge the credit risk of this position via a credit default swap. By means of an asset swap, the protection seller (for example a bank) will agree to pay the protection buyer LIBOR +/− spread in return for the cash flows of the risky bond. In this way, the protection buyer (investor) may be able to explicitly finance the credit default swap premium from the asset swap spread income if there is a negative basis between them. If the asset swap is terminated, it is common for the buyer of the asset swap package to take the "unwind" cost of the interest rate swap.

Asset swaps have some similarities with TRS, but the key difference is that there is no concept of a "credit event" with an asset swap. Upon default of the underlying asset, a TRS will terminate, whereas with an asset swap the interest rate swap will continue until its scheduled maturity.

The generic structure for an asset swap is shown in Figure 2.18.

Figure 2.18   Asset swap structure.

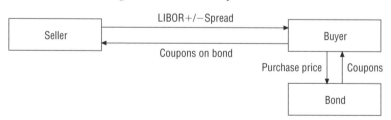

Illustration using Bloomberg

We can illustrate the asset swap spread for a credit-risky corporate bond using Bloomberg screens. In Figure 2.19 we show the 7% 2007 bond issued by British Telecom, a UK telecommunication company. The bond is denominated in US dollars. The screen is Bloomberg's YA page for yield analysis, which is obtained by typing:

BRITEL 7 07 <CORP> YA <GO>

Figure 2.19 Bloomberg screen YA for British Telecom 7% 2007 bond, as at 11 June 2003.

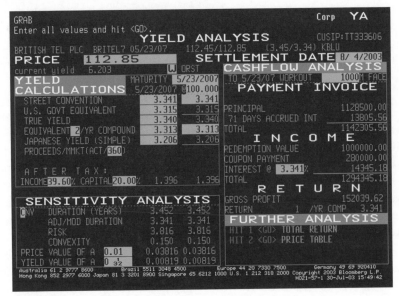

© Bloomberg L.P. Used with permission.

and shows the bond as at 4 August 2003, at an offered price of 112.85, which represents a yield of 3.340%. Combining this with an interest rate swap to create an asset swap will convert the bond's fixed-rate coupon to a floating-rate coupon for the bondholder, who pays fixed and receives floating in the associated interest rate swap.

To establish what the spread for this bond would be in an asset swap, we call up screen ASW. This is shown in Figure 2.20 and we see that the asset swap spread for the bond, which is rated Baa1 by Moody's and A- by S&P, is 30.7 basis points. The bond price on the screen is user-input at 112.85 as before. Another screen can be used to see the bond spread over other references and benchmarks, and this is shown at Figure 2.21. We see that the interpolated spread over US Treasuries is 69 basis points. This compares to a spread of just over 60 basis points over Treasuries at the time the bond was issued. In other words, the bond has cheapened in the market since issue in May 1997, when it was priced off the US 10-year active bond. This reflects market interest rate conditions generally as well as the fact that the issuer has been downgraded in that time.

Selecting the generic credit-risky industrials yield curve for USD bonds (numbered I52 on Bloomberg), we see that the asset swap spread is actually

Figure 2.20   Bloomberg screen ASW for British Telecom 7% 2007 bond, as at 4 August 2003 settlement.

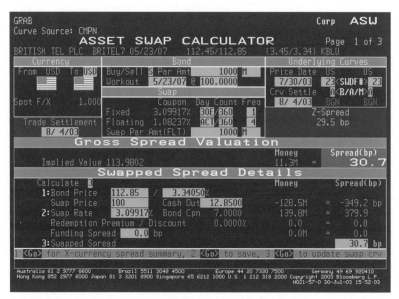

© Bloomberg L.P. Used with permission.

Figure 2.21   Determination of British Telecom 7% 2007 bond yield spreads, using Bloomberg screen YAS, as at 4 August 2003 settlement.

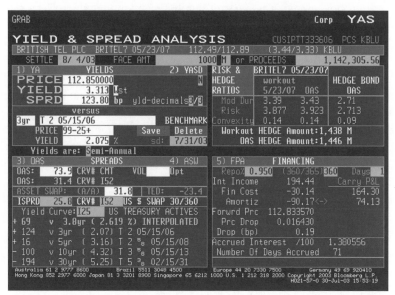

© Bloomberg L.P. Used with permission.

31.8 basis points for this bond also shown in Figure 2.21. This is because the screen has calculated the asset swap spread over a specific, and hence more appropriate yield curve, rather than the generic inter-bank LIBOR curve used by screen ASW.

Credit Options and Credit Spread Options

Credit options are also bilateral OTC financial contracts. A credit option is a contract designed to meet specific hedging or speculative requirements of an entity, which may purchase or sell the option to meet its objectives. A credit call option gives the buyer the right, but not the obligation, to purchase the underlying credit-sensitive asset, or a credit spread, at a specified price and specified time (or period of time). A credit put option gives the buyer the right, but not the obligation, to sell the underlying credit-sensitive asset or credit spread. By purchasing credit options, banks and other institutions can take a view on credit spread movements for the cost of the option premium only, without recourse to actual loans issued by an obligor. The writer of credit options seeks to earn premium income.

Credit option terms are similar to those used for conventional equity options. A *call* option written on a stock grants the purchaser the right, but not the obligation, to purchase a specified amount of the stock at a set price and time. A credit option can be used by bond investors to hedge against a decline in the price of specified bonds, in the event of a credit event such as a ratings downgrade. The investor purchases an option which has a payoff profile that is a function of the credit quality of the bond, so that a loss on the bond position is offset by the payout from the option.

As with conventional options, there are both vanilla credit options and exotic credit options. The vanilla credit option[18] grants the purchaser the right, but not the obligation, to buy (or sell if a *put* option) an asset or credit spread at a specified price (the *strike* price) for a specified period of time up to the maturity of the option. A credit option allows a market participant to take a view on credit only, and no other exposure such as interest rates. For example, consider an investor who believes that a particular credit spread, which can be that of a specific entity or the average for a sector (such as "all AA-rated sterling corporates"), will widen over the next six months. They can buy a six-month call option on the relevant credit spread, for which a one-off premium (the price of the option) is paid. If the credit spread does widen beyond the strike price during the six months, the option will be

---

[18] Sometimes referred to as the *standard* credit option.

in-the-money and the investor will gain. If not, the investor's loss is limited to the premium paid.[19]

Exotic credit options are options that have one or more of their parameters changed from the vanilla credit option, the same terms are used as in other option markets. Examples include the barrier credit option, which specifies a credit-event that *triggers* (activates) the option or inactivates it. A digital credit option has a payout profile that is fixed, irrespective of how much in-the-money it was on expiry, and a zero payout if out-of-the-money.

Credit spread options are options on specific credit spreads. The protection buyer pays an up-front premium to the protection seller. In return for this, on option exercise the protection buyer receives from the protection seller the difference between the yield on the underlying reference asset over a benchmark and the strike yield of the option. The benchmark might be a Treasury security or Euribor. With a *credit spread call*, the buyer has the right to buy the reference asset at a pre-specified strike yield. In a *credit spread put*, the buyer has the right to sell the reference asset at a pre-specified strike yield.

Under the call option, the payout on exercise increases as the credit spread decreases (the bond price is rising), and with the put option the payout increases as the credit spread widens. Credit spread options are used by banks and investors to protect against changes in credit spreads, or to trade credit spread volatility. Like other credit derivatives, they can be cash-settled or physically-settled. For a credit spread option under physical settlement, the protection buyer can sell the reference asset to the protection seller for the strike credit spread.

The reference asset on a credit option is usually a floating-rate note or a fixed coupon bond referenced via an asset swap. For a call credit spread option, which would be held if one had a negative view of the reference name, exercise will take place on occurrence of a credit event. The strike "price" for a credit spread option is quoted as a spread over Libor. For instance, an investor or hedger might buy an option that grants the right to enter into an asset swap with a strike price of Libor plus 50 basis points. As long as the asset swap spread remains below 50 basis points over Libor, the option will be in-the-money. The investor in this case has a positive view on the reference credit, which it has expressed by purchasing the call on the asset swap.

---

[19] Depending on whether the option is an American or European one will determine whether it can be exercised before its expiry date or on its expiry date only.

We illustrate this example at Figure 2.22.

Figure 2.22   A call option on an asset swap.

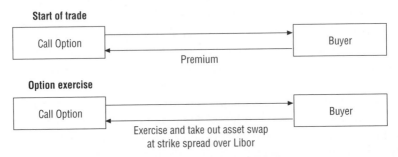

A credit spread option may be used instead of other unfunded credit derivatives to express a view on a particular reference credit. The value of the option is not linked to the general level of interest rates; being a pure credit view, it is linked to the fluctuation in the credit spread of the reference name relative to the spread specified in the strike price. For instance the value of a six-month call option that gives the buyer the right to enter into a three-year asset swap is a function of the three-year asset swap spread in six months time. So the option expresses a view on the forward credit spread. As with other types of options, a higher level of volatility (in this case volatility of credit spreads) will lead to a higher option value. Because a higher volatility increases the value of an option especially if there is a greater time-value, buying call credit spread option can also be undertaken as a view on credit spread volatility, providing the purchaser has hedged his position by purchasing the underlying reference credit.

Bloomberg Screens

The Bloomberg system provides a number of pages for CDS and asset swap analytics, as well as contributed pages for CDS prices.

Market prices are supplied by a number of investment banks. Most banks make their price screens available only to clients, or on request. Banco Bilbao Vizcaya Argentaria (BBVA) is a market-maker whose screen is available to all users. Their screen of CDS prices for the Utilities and Industrial sectors is shown in Figure 2.23, this shows three- and five-year indicative CDS quotes, both bid and offer, together with the change from the last quote. We show at Figure 2.23(a) and (b) two pages from the BBVA price menu, which is a comprehensive set of CDS prices across the sectors. Figures 2.24 and 2.25 show the main menu page and the Airline/Aerospace sector CDS page from BBVA.

Chapter 2   Credit Derivatives: Unfunded Instruments

Figure 2.23(a)   CDS prices page from BBVA, 19 April 2004.

N2N299 Govt   **BBCS**

```
7:58 Utilities / Energy                                      PAGE  1 / 2
                        3 Y - CDS Quotes           5 Y - CDS Quotes
Utilities / Energy  BID  /  ASK   CHG          BID  /  ASK   CHG  TIME
AGBAR              1)  10 /  20      7:25   16)  15 /  25      7:25
BIRKA              2)  25 /  35      7:25   17)  36 /  46      7:25
E.ON               3)  17 /  27      7:25   18)  23 /  33      7:25
ELEC. FRANCE       4)  15 /  25      7:25   19)  22 /  32      7:25
ELEC. PORTUGAL     5)  26 /  36      7:25   20)  35 /  45      7:25
ENBW               6)  26 /  36      7:25   21)  34 /  44      7:25
ENDESA             7)  31 /  41      7:25   22)  36 /  46      7:25
ENEL               8)  20 /  30      7:25   23)  25 /  35      7:25
ENECO HOLDING      9)     /          4/16   24)     /          4/16
ESSENT NV         10)  18 /  28      7:25   25)  25 /  35      7:25
GECC              11)  20 /  30      7:25   26)  22 /  32      7:25
IBERDROLA         12)  15 /  25      7:25   27)  26 /  36      7:25
NATIONAL GRID     13)  25 /  35      7:25   28)  38 /  48      7:25
RWE               14)  16 /  26      7:25   29)  26 /  36      7:25
SUEZ              15)  31 /  41      7:25   30)  41 /  51      7:25
Tel: +34 91 537 6087
INDICATIVE PRICES FOR CREDIT DEFAULT SWAPS ON STANDARD
ISDA 2003 DOCUMENTATION WITH 3 CREDIT EVENTS           BBVA
MATURITIES ARE ON QUARTERLY BASIS
Australia 61 2 9777 8600    Brazil 5511 3048 4500    Europe 44 20 7330 7500    Germany 49 69 920410
Hong Kong 852 2977 6000 Japan 81 3 3201 8900 Singapore 65 6212 1000 U.S. 1 212 318 2000 Copyright 2004 Bloomberg L.P.
                                                              G926-802-0 19-Apr-04  7:58:34
```

Figure 2.23(b)   CDS prices page from BBVA, 19 April 2004.

Page   N299 Govt   **BBCS**

```
7:58 INDUSTRIALS                                             PAGE  1 / 2
                     3 Y - CDS Quotes             5 Y - CDS Quotes
Industrials       BID  /  ASK   CHG          BID  /  ASK   CHG  TIME
BRISA             1)     /                16)  40 /  60      7:25
CIR INTL          2)     /                17) 270 / 280      7:25
DBFIN             3)     /                18)     /
DEUTSCHE POST     4)     /                19)  26 /  30      7:25
EKSPORTFINANS     5)     /                20)   5 /  12      7:25
FINMECANICA       6)  47 /  57      7:25  21)  56 /  66      7:25
FKI Plc           7)     /                22)  90 / 100      7:25
HAMMERSON Plc     8)     /                23)  40 /  50      7:25
HOLCIM            9)     /                24)  46 /  54      7:25
HUTCHISON WHAM   10)     /                25)     /
INVESTOR AB      11)     /                26)  50 /  60      7:25
ISS GLOBAL A/S   12)     /                27)     /
METSO            13) 125 / 150      7:25  28) 145 / 155      7:25
RENTOKIL         14)     /                29)  35 /  45      7:25
SCHNEIDER        15)  18 /  28      7:25  30)  48 /  58      7:25
Tel: +34 91 537 6087
INDICATIVE PRICES FOR CREDIT DEFAULT SWAPS ON STANDARD
ISDA 2003 DOCUMENTATION WITH 3 CREDIT EVENTS           BBVA
MATURITIES ARE ON QUARTERLY BASIS
Australia 61 2 9777 8600    Brazil 5511 3048 4500    Europe 44 20 7330 7500    Germany 49 69 920410
Hong Kong 852 2977 6000 Japan 81 3 3201 8900 Singapore 65 6212 1000 U.S. 1 212 318 2000 Copyright 2004 Bloomberg L.P.
                                                              G926-802-0 19-Apr-04  7:58:53
```

Figure 2.24   BBVA main credit default swap menu.

Menu   .N2199n Govt   **BBCS**

BBVA

CREDIT DEFAULT SWAPS

CREDIT DERIVATIVES INDICES
1) BBIB iBOXX Indices   11) Media
   CREDIT DEFAULT SWAPS   12) Oil/Gas
2) Spanish References   13) Retail
   CORPORATES   14) Telecoms
3) Airline/Aerospace/Defense   15) Tobacco
4) Autos   16) Utilities
5) Building Materials   FINANCIALS
6) Chemicals/Pharmaceuticals   17) Financials
7) Food   18) Insurance
8) Hotel/Leisure/Restaurants   LATAM & EM & SOVEREIGNS
9) Industrials   19) Latam & Emerging Markets
10) Iron/Steel   20) Sovereigns

Australia 61 2 9777 8600   Brazil 5511 3048 4500   Europe 44 20 7330 7500   Germany 49 69 920410
Hong Kong 852 2977 6000 Japan 81 3 3201 8900 Singapore 65 6212 1000 U.S. 1 212 318 2000 Copyright 2004 Bloomberg L.P.
                                                                    G926-802-0 19-Apr-04 7:59:01

Figure 2.25   BBVA Airline and Aerospace sector CDS prices,
19 April 2004.

3   N2N299 Govt   **BBCS**

7:59 **AIRLINE/AEROSPACE/DEFENSE**   PAGE 1 / 1

AIRLINE/AEROSPACE		3 Y – CDS Quotes				5 Y – CDS Quotes			
DEFENSE		BID	/	ASK	CHG		BID	/ ASK	CHG TIME
AIR FRANCE	1)	60	/	70	7:25	9)	75	/ 85	7:25
BRITISH AIRPOR	2)	32	/	42	7:25	10)	41	/ 51	7:25
BAE SYSTEMS	3)	45	/	55	7:25	11)	55	/ 65	7:25
BRITISH AIRWAY	4)	250	/	400	7:25	12)	250	/ 260	7:25
EADS	5)	22	/	32	7:25	13)	32	/ 42	7:25
LUFTHANSA	6)	55	/	65	7:25	14)	65	/ 75	7:25
ROLLS ROYCE	7)	35	/	45	7:25	15)	59	/ 69	7:25
THALES	8)	19	/	29	7:25	16)	28	/ 38	7:25

Tel: +34 91 537 6087
INDICATIVE PRICES FOR CREDIT DEFAULT SWAPS ON STANDARD
ISDA 2003 DOCUMENTATION WITH 3 CREDIT EVENTS   **BBVA**
MATURITIES ARE ON QUARTERLY BASIS

Australia 61 2 9777 8600   Brazil 5511 3048 4500   Europe 44 20 7330 7500   Germany 49 69 920410
Hong Kong 852 2977 6000 Japan 81 3 3201 8900 Singapore 65 6212 1000 U.S. 1 212 318 2000 Copyright 2004 Bloomberg L.P.
                                                                    G926-802-0 19-Apr-04 7:59:12

Other screens are supplied for analysis of CDS written on individual bonds. We illustrate these with selected bonds. Our first example is a bond issued by Toyota Motor Credit, the 5.5% 2008, which is a US dollar-denominated bond. Figure 2.26 shows the description of the bond, which is Bloomberg's DES page. We select this bond on the Bloomberg system by typing:

Toyota 5.5 08 <Corp> DES <GO>

which brings up the DES page. This is a highly-rated bond, with a AAA rating from S&P and a Aa1 rating from Moody's. To look at the bond's yield spread to various benchmarks, we select screen YAS, which is shown in Figure 2.27. We see that the bond has a 34 basis point interpolated yield spread to US Treasuries, but a negative spread to the swap curve. This is confirmed in Figure 2.28, which is Bloomberg page ASW and shows the bond's asset swap spread. A negative asset swap spread is common with AAA-rated bonds, indicating that these bonds fund at sub-LIBOR rates in the cash market. Page RVS graphs the spread of the bond's historical yield against the interest rate swap curve, and we see from Figure 2.29 that this bond had only recently started to trade at a negative spread to the swap curve.

Figure 2.26   Bloomberg page DES for Toyota $5\frac{1}{2}$% 2008 bond.

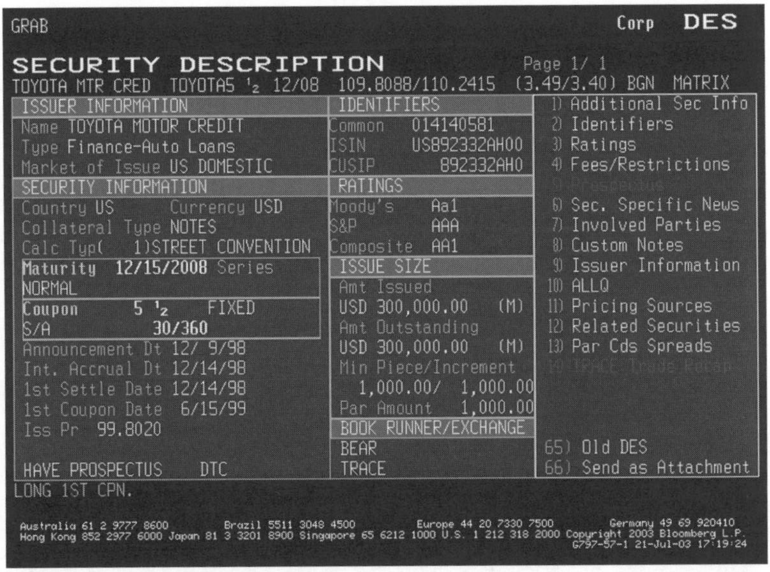

Figure 2.27   Bloomberg page YAS for Toyota $5\frac{1}{2}\%$ 2008 bond, 21 July 2003.

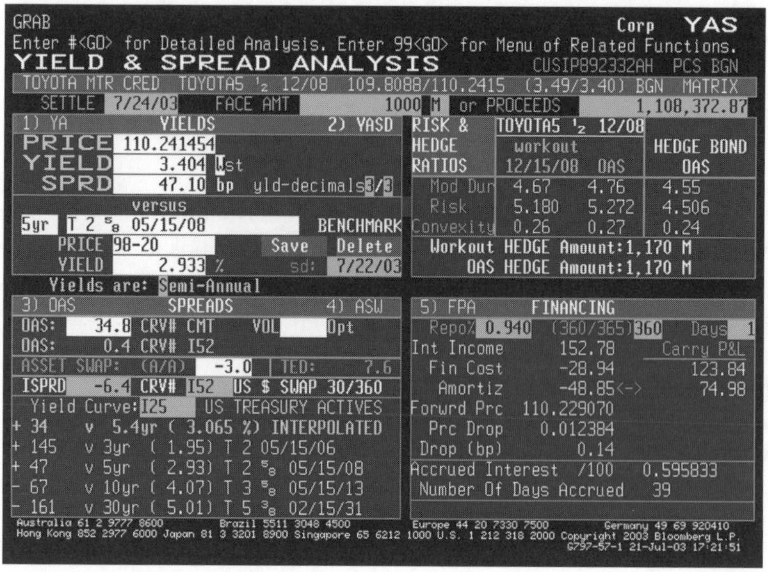

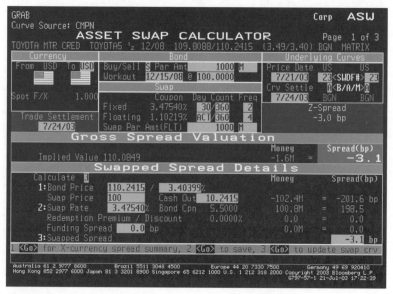

© Bloomberg L.P. Used with permission.

Figure 2.28   Bloomberg page ASW for Toyota $5\frac{1}{2}\%$ 2008 bond, 21 July 2003.

© Bloomberg L.P. Used with permission.

Figure 2.29   Bloomberg page RVS for Toyota $5\frac{1}{2}\%$ 2008 bond, 21 July 2003.

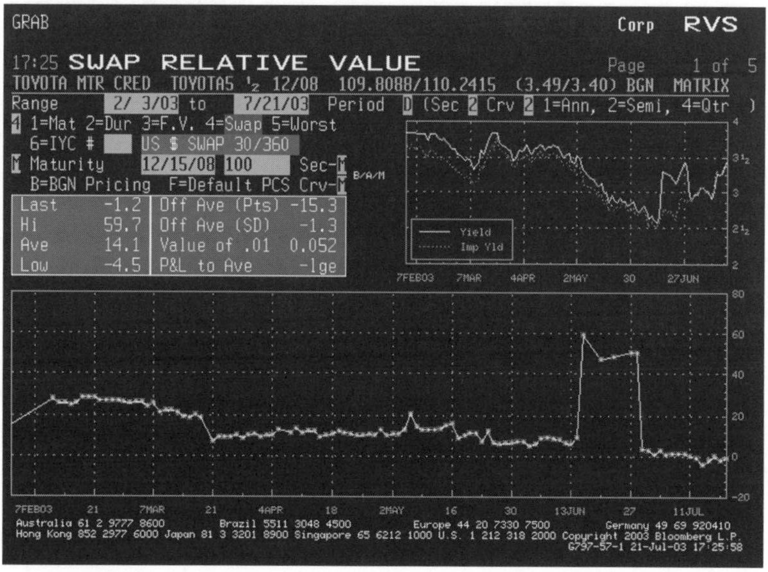

© Bloomberg L.P. Used with permission.

To undertake analysis of a CDS written on this bond, we select screen CDSW. This is shown at Figures 2.30 and 2.31. Screen CDSW calculates the price of a CDS on the selected bond using one of three pricing approaches, noted as:

- discounted spreads;
- the JPMorgan model;
- the modified Hull-White model.

Pricing models are discussed in Chapter 5. As well as selecting the pricing model, the user also selects the benchmark yield curve and the credit-risky yield curve, from which the CDS is priced off. The user also selects the recovery rate.

We can see from Figure 2.30 that the discounted spreads approach gives a five-year CDS price of 68.3 bps, whereas selecting the Hull-White model gives a price for the same CDS of 70.73 bps.

From screen CDSW it is possible to view the contributing yield curves that have been used in pricing the CDS. We will use a different bond to illustrate this. Figure 2.32 shows page DES again, this time for the Ford 6.75% 2008 bond. This bond is rated BBB by S&P and A3 by Moody's.

Figure 2.30 Bloomberg page CDSW for Toyota 5.5% 2008 bond, 21 July 2003.

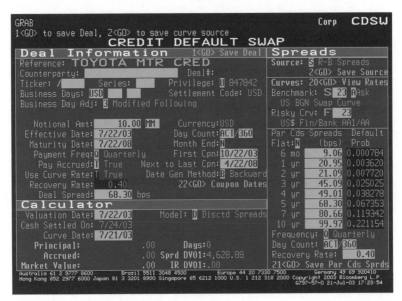

© Bloomberg L.P. Used with permission.

Figure 2.31 Bloomberg page CDSW for Toyota 5.5% 2008 bond, 21 July 2003, using Hull-White Pricing Model.

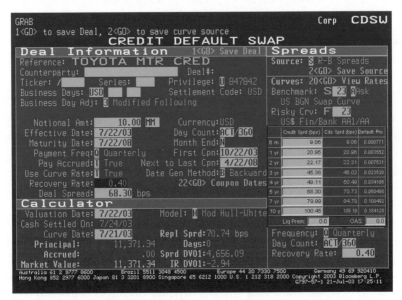

© Bloomberg L.P. Used with permission.

Figure 2.33 is page CDSW again, for the Ford Motor Credit bond, this time with the JPMorgan model selected. Selecting:

$$20 <GO>;$$

brings up the contributing yield curve used with this page, shown in Figure 2.34.

In addition to calculating the CDS price, screen CDSW also provides a risk measure for the CDS contract. This is shown in Figure 2.33 as 'Spread DV01'. This is a measure of how much the contract value changes for a 1 basis point change in the credit spread. From the screen, we can see this is $4,206. Changing the recovery rate will impact the spread, we see the impact of this in Figure 2.35, which is CDSW again for the same Ford bond but now showing different values after the change in recovery rate from 40% to 30%. We see that for a five-year CDS, a recovery rate of 30% has changed the DV01 value to $4,278. The CDS premiums are unchanged.

Finally, we show screen ASW for this bond in Figure 2.36. This indicates an asset swap spread of 216 bps, compared to the five-year CDS spread of 277 bps. This is an example of a positive basis, which we explore in Chapter 8.

Figure 2.32   Bloomberg DES screen showing Ford 6.75% 2008 bond.

```
5 Corp DES                                      N219 Corp   DES

SECURITY DESCRIPTION                Page 1/ 1
FORD MOTOR CRED  F 6 ¾ 08/15/08    105.0483/105.2983   (5.42/5.36) BGN  MATRIX
┌ISSUER INFORMATION────────┬IDENTIFIERS──────────┬ 1) Additional Sec Info
│Name FORD MOTOR CREDIT CO │CUSIP      345397GX5 │ 2) Identifiers
│Type Finance-Auto Loans   │ISIN    US345397GX54 │ 3) Ratings
│Market of Issue US DOMESTIC│BB number  DD5304223│ 4) Involved Parties
│SECURITY INFORMATION      │RATINGS              │ 5) Custom Notes
│Country US    Currency USD│Moody's    A3        │ 6) Issuer Information
│Collateral Type NOTES     │S&P        BBB-      │ 7) ALLQ
│Calc Typ(  1)STREET CONVENTION│Fitch   BBB+     │ 8) Pricing Sources
│Maturity   8/15/2008 Series│ISSUE SIZE          │ 9) Prospectus Request
│NORMAL                    │Aggr Amt Iss    *    │10) Related Securities
│Coupon    6 ¾    FIXED    │USD    300,000.00 (M)│11) Issuer Web Page
│S/A        30/360         │Aggr Amt Out    *    │12) Par Cds Spreads
│Announcement Dt  8/ 5/93  │USD    300,000.00 (M)│
│Int. Accrual Dt  8/18/93  │Min Piece/Increment  │
│1st Settle Date  8/18/93  │    1,000.00/ 1,000.00│
│1st Coupon Date  2/15/94  │Par Amount   1,000.00│
│Iss Pr   99.4150          │BOOK RUNNER/EXCHANGE │
│SPR @ ISS  100.0 vs T 5 ¾ 08/03│JPM             │65) Old DES
│HAVE PROSPECTUS    DTC    │TRACE                │66) Send as Attachment
└COMMIT BY MBIA TO INSURE $12.65MM W/CUSIP:345397RY1. $350M PURCH & INS'D BY MBIA
W/CUSIP:345397TQ6. SHORT 1ST CPN.
Australia 61 2 9777 8600      Brazil 5511 3048 4500    Europe 44 20 7330 7500    Germany 49 69 920410
Hong Kong 852 2977 6000 Japan 81 3 3201 8900 Singapore 65 6212 1000 U.S. 1 212 318 2000 Copyright 2004 Bloomberg L.P.
                                                          G926-802-3 14-Apr-04 13:58:34
```

© Bloomberg L.P. Used with permission.

Figure 2.33 Bloomberg page CDSW for Ford 6% 2008 bond, 24 July 2003.

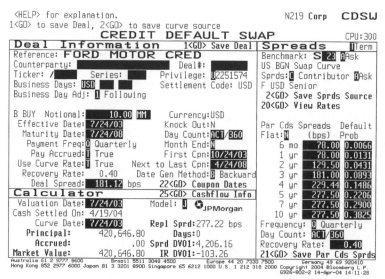

© Bloomberg L.P. Used with permission.

Figure 2.34 Contributing yield curve for Figure 2.33, 24 July 2003.

```
<HELP> for explanation.                              N219 Corp   CDSW
<Menu> to return
                    CREDIT  DEFAULT  SWAP                      CPU:300
  Deal  Information        1<GO> Save Deal  Spreads        Term
  Reference: FORD  MOTOR  CRED            Benchmark: S 23 Ask
                          Rates
    Benchmark: S23 (US BGN Curve:Ask)
  Risky Curve: Benchmark + Cntr Sprds
    Base Date:  7/28/03

                 Benchmark       Risky    Adjusted   Cds Sprds  Risky Curve
         Term Dts   Par     Spot   Term Dts Benchmark  (bps)
  6 mo   1/28/04  1.1200   1.1200  1/26/04  1.1201      78.00    1.9001
  1 yr   7/28/04  1.2000   1.2000  7/26/04  1.1989      78.00    1.9789
  2 yr   7/28/05  1.7500   1.7554  7/25/05  1.7155     129.50    3.0105
  3 yr   7/28/06  2.3950   2.4163  7/25/06  2.3476     181.00    4.1576
  4 yr   7/30/07  2.9399   2.9853  7/25/07  2.8797     229.44    5.1741
  5 yr   7/28/08  3.4000   3.4762  7/25/08  3.3316     277.50    6.1066
  7 yr   7/28/10  4.0300   4.1676  7/26/10  3.9490     277.50    6.7240
 10 yr   7/29/13  4.5900   4.8115  7/25/13  4.4946     277.50    7.2696
                  MMkt:ACT/360            ACT/360 Quartly
                  Swap: 30/360 Semi

                        MENU  to return
Australia 61 2 9777 8600      Brazil 5511 3048 4500      Europe 44 20 7330 7500      Germany 49 69 920410
Hong Kong 852 2977 6000 Japan 81 3 3201 8900 Singapore 65 6212 1000 U.S. 1 212 318 2000 Copyright 2004 Bloomberg L.P.
                                                                  G926-802-2 14-Apr-04 14:12:27
```

© Bloomberg L.P. Used with permission.

Figure 2.35   Bloomberg page CDSW for Ford 6% 2008 bond, impact of
change in recovery rate on DV01 value.

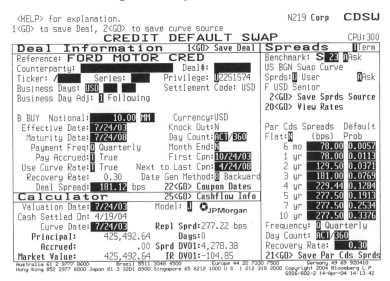

© Bloomberg L.P. Used with permission.

Figure 2.36   Bloomberg page ASW for Ford 6% 2008 bond,
24 July 2003.

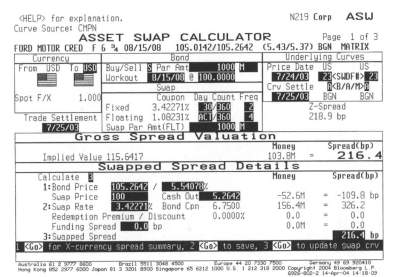

© Bloomberg L.P. Used with permission.

Using Bloomberg screen CDSW when breaking a CDS deal

In certain cases a dealer may cancel or "break" a CDS contract that it has entered into earlier, rather than netting it out by taking out a CDS contract on the other side. This may be done for its own reasons or at customer request. Screen CDSW may then be used to value the contract at the breaking date, which confirms the one-off payment that is due from the protection buyer.

Figure 2.37 shows screen DES for the 7% 2007 bond issued by British Telecom plc. Its asset swap spread, shown by Figure 2.38, is around 58 basis points on 12 August 2003. Assume that a dealer has entered into a £10 million notional five-year CDS contract referencing this bond as at May 2002 that matures on the same day as the bond itself. Assume further that the dealer wishes to cancel this contract; the start and end dates for the contract are entered on screen CDSW and a flat credit curve is used. The curve itself is set at 58 basis points. As at the break date, the value of the contract under these conditions, for a 35% recovery rate, is shown to be £280,160 at Figure 2.39.

Figure 2.37   Screen DES for British Telecom 7% 2007 bond.

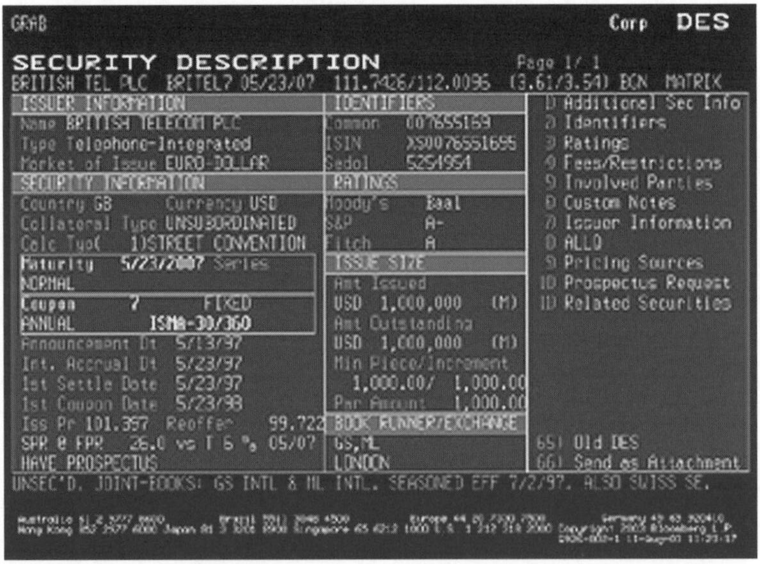

© Bloomberg L.P. Used with permission

Figure 2.38   Screen ASW for British Telecom 7% 2007 bond as at
12 August 2003.

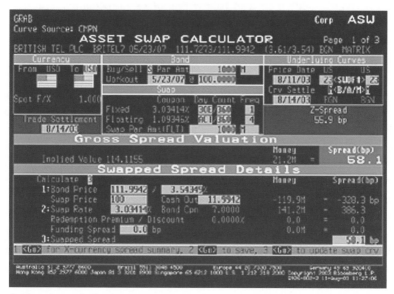

© Bloomberg L.P. Used with permission

Figure 2.39   Screen CDSW used to value CDS contract for British Telecom
traded in May 2002 as at 12 August 2003

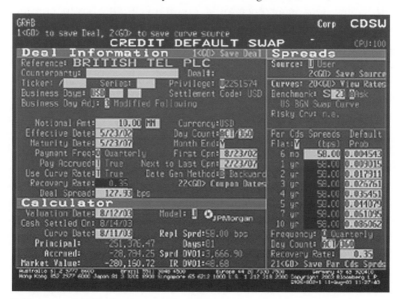

© Bloomberg L.P. Used with permission

Settlement

Credit derivative settlement can follow one of two procedures, specified at deal inception. We consider these here.

With all credit derivatives, upon occurrence of a credit event, a credit event notice must be submitted. Typically, the notice must be supported by information posted on public news systems such as Bloomberg or Reuters. When used as part of a structured product, the terms of the deal may state that a credit event must be verified by a third-party *verification agent*. Upon verification, the contract will be settled in one of two ways, cash settlement or physical settlement.

A report from the BBA suggests that between 75%–85% of credit derivatives written in 2002 were physically-settled, while about 10%–20% were cash-settled. About 5% of contracts were settled under the *fixed amount* approach, under which the protection seller delivers a pre-specified amount to the protection buyer ahead of the determination of the reference asset's recovery value. However as the fixed amount approach is essentially cash settlement, we will consider it as such and prefer the more technical term for it noted below.

Contract settlement options

Credit derivatives have a given maturity, but will terminate early if a credit event occurs. On occurrence of a credit event, the swap contract is terminated and a settlement payment is made by the protection seller or guarantor to the protection buyer. This termination value is calculated at the time of the credit event, and the procedure that is followed to calculate the termination value depends on the settlement terms specified in the contract. Credit derivatives specify either physical or cash settlement. In physical settlement, the protection buyer transfers the deliverable obligation (usually the reference asset or assets) to the protection seller, with the total principal outstanding equal to the nominal specified in the default swap contract. The protection seller simultaneously pays to the buyer 100% of the nominal. In cash settlement, the protection seller pays the buyer the difference between the nominal amount of the default swap and the final value for the same nominal amount of the reference asset. This final value is usually determined by means of a poll of dealer banks. This final value is, in theory, the recovery value of the asset, however as the recovery process can take some time, often the reference asset market value at time of default is taken and this amount is used in calculating the final settlement amount paid to the protection buyer.

The settlement mechanisms are shown in Figure 2.40 and follow the following process:

- *Cash settlement:* the contract may specify a pre-determined pay-out value on occurrence of a credit event. This may be the nominal value of the swap contract. Such a swap is known as a *fixed amount* contract or in some markets as a *digital credit derivative.* Alternatively, the termination payment is calculated as the difference between the nominal value of the reference asset and either its market value at the time of the credit event or its recovery value. This arrangement is more common with cash-settled contracts.[20]

- *Physical settlement:* on occurrence of a credit event, the buyer delivers the reference asset to the seller, in return for which the seller pays the face value of the delivered asset to the buyer. The contract may specify a number of alternative assets that the buyer can deliver — these are known as *deliverable obligations.* This may apply when a swap has been entered into on a reference name rather than a specific obligation (such as a particular bond) issued by that name. Where more than one deliverable obligation is specified, the protection buyer will invariably deliver the asset that is the cheapest on the list of eligible assets. This gives rise to the concept of the *cheapest-to-deliver,* as encountered with government bond futures contracts, and is in effect an embedded option afforded to the protection buyer.

Figure 2.40   Physical and cash settlement.

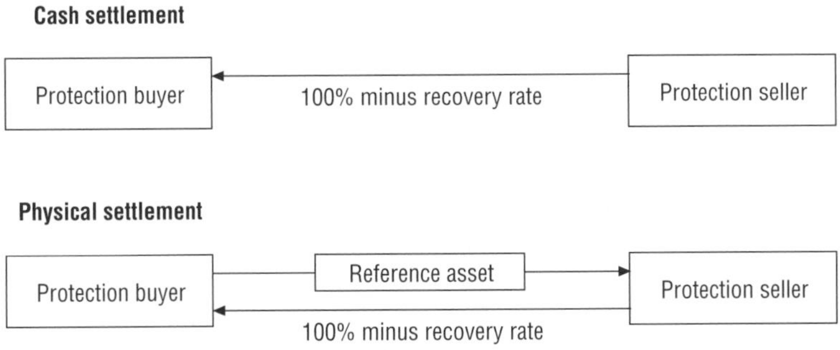

Cash settlement

Physical settlement

---

[20] Determining the market value of the reference asset at the time of the credit event may be a little problematic — the issuer of the asset may be in default or administration. An independent third-party *Calculation Agent* is usually employed to make the termination payment calculation.

In theory, the value of protection is identical irrespective of which settlement option is selected. However, under physical settlement the protection seller can gain if there is a recovery value that can be extracted from the defaulted asset, or its value may rise as the fortunes of the issuer improve.

Swap market-making banks often prefer cash settlement because there is less administration associated with it, since there is no delivery of a physical asset. For a CDS used as part of a structured product, cash settlement may be more suitable because such vehicles may not be set up to take delivery of physical assets. Another advantage of cash settlement is that it does not expose the protection buyer to any risks should there not be any deliverable assets in the market, for instance due to shortage of bond or asset liquidity. Should this occur, the buyer may find the value of their settlement payment reduced. Nevertheless, physical settlement is widely used because counterparties wish to avoid the difficulties associated with determining the market value of the reference asset under cash settlement.[21] Physical settlement also permits the protection seller to take part in the creditor negotiations with the reference entity's administrators, which may result in improved terms for them as holders of the asset.

Cash settlement is sometimes adopted even for contracts that are physically settled in situations when, for one reason or another, it is not possible to deliver a physical asset, for example, if none is available.

Market requirements

Different market participants have different requirements and so may have their own preferences with regard to the settlement mechanism. A protection seller may prefer physical settlement for particular reference assets if they believe that a higher recovery value for the asset can be gained by holding onto it and/or entering into the administration process. A protection buyer may have different interests. For example, unless the protection buyer already holds the deliverable asset (in which case the transaction they have

---

[21] Credit derivative market-makers may value two instruments written on the same reference entity, and with all other terms and conditions identical except that one is cash settled and the other physically settled, at the same price. This is because while the protection buyer has a delivery option and will deliver the cheapest bond available, an option that carries value, in a cash settled contract the protection buyer will nominate this same bond to be used in the calculation of the settlement of the contract. Therefore the value of the delivery option may not result in a higher price quote from a market-maker for a physically delivered contract.

entered into is a classic hedge for an asset already owned), they may prefer cash settlement, if they have a negative view of the reference obligation and have used the CDS or other credit derivative to create a synthetic short bond position. Alternatively, the protection buyer may prefer physical settlement because they view the delivery option as carrying some value.

Risks in Credit Default Swaps

To conclude this chapter, we consider some risk exposures that investors take on when trading in credit derivatives.

Unintended risks in credit default swaps

As credit derivatives can be tailored to meet specific requirements in terms of reference exposure, term to maturity, currency and cash flows, they have enabled market participants to establish exposure to specific entities without the need for them to hold the bond or loan of that entity. This has raised issues of the different risk exposure that this entails compared to the cash equivalent. A Moody's special report highlights the unintended risks of holding credit exposures in the form of default swaps and credit-linked notes.[22] Under certain circumstances, it is possible for credit default swaps to create unintended risk exposure for holders, by exposing them to greater frequency and magnitude of losses compared to that suffered by a holder of the underlying reference credit in cash form.

In a credit default swap, the payout to a buyer of protection is determined by the occurrence of credit events. The definition of a credit event sets the level of credit risk exposure of the protection seller. A wide definition of "credit event" results in a higher level of risk. To reduce the likelihood of disputes, counterparties can adopt the ISDA Credit Derivatives definitions to govern their dealings. The Moody's paper states that the ISDA definitions at the time did not unequivocally separate and isolate credit risk, and in certain circumstances credit derivatives can expose holders to additional risks. The paper suggested that differences in definitions can lead to unintended risks being taken on by protection sellers. Two examples from the paper are cited below as illustration.

---

[22] Jeffrey Tolk, "Understanding the Risks in Credit Default Swaps", *Moody's Investors Service Special Report*, March 16, 2001

Extending loan maturity

The bank debt of Conseco, a corporate entity, was restructured in August 2000. The restructuring provisions included deferment of the loan maturity by three months, higher coupon, corporate guarantee and additional covenants. Under the Moody's definition, as lenders received compensation in return for an extension of the debt, the restructuring was not considered to be a "diminished financial obligation", although Conseco's credit rating was downgraded one notch. However, under the ISDA definition, the extension of the loan maturity meant that the restructuring was considered to be a credit event, and thus triggered payments on default swaps written on Conseco's bank debt. Therefore this was an example of a loss event under ISDA definitions that was not considered by Moody's to be a default.

It was the Conseco case that led to the adoption of the modified restructuring ISDA definitions of 2003.

Risks of synthetic positions and cash positions compared

Consider two investors in XYZ, one of whom owns bonds issued by XYZ, while the other holds a credit-linked note (CLN) referenced to XYZ. Following a deterioration in its debt situation, XYZ violates a number of covenants on its bank loans, but its bonds are unaffected. XYZ's bank accelerates the bank loan, but the bonds continue to trade at 85 cents in the dollar, coupons are paid and the bond is redeemed in full at maturity. However, the default swap underlying the CLN cites "obligation acceleration" (of either bond or loan) as a credit event, so the holder of the CLN receives 85% of par in cash settlement and the CLN is terminated. However the cash investor receives all the coupons and the par value of the bonds on maturity.

These two examples illustrate how, as credit default swaps are defined to pay out in the event of a very broad range of definitions of a "credit event", portfolio managers may suffer losses as a result of occurrences that are not captured by one or more of the ratings agencies rating of the reference asset. This may result in a potentially greater risk for the portfolio manager, compared to the position were it to actually hold the underlying reference asset. Essentially, therefore, it is important for the range of definitions of a "credit event" to be fully understood by counterparties, so that holders of default swaps are not taking on greater risk than is intended.

Measuring risk for a CDS contract

Banks calculate a quantitative measure of the risk exposure of their CDS positions. The approach used follows the same value-at-risk principles used for earlier asset class products, namely it calculates the sensitivity of a contract to variations in market parameters. The main risk measure regards the sensitivity of the CDS to a change in the primary credit curve, and is known as Spread01 or usually "Credit01".

Credit01 is a measure of the change in the mark-to-market value of a CDS contract for a 1 basis point parallel shift upwards in the credit-risky curve. The precise definition differs depending on whether one is measuring the risk on a bought or sold protection position. The value of a short credit (buy protection) CDS position increases as credit spreads widen, while the value of a long credit (sell protection) position decreases as credit spreads widen. Generally, the market quotes the Credit01 value of a long credit (sold protection) contract as negative, which matches the sign for a short credit position. Essentially Credit01 is similar in concept to the "PVBP" or DV01 (Dollar01) interest-rate risk measure for a cash bond holding.

The change in the mark-to-market value is given by:

$$\text{Notional} \times \text{Credit01} \times \Delta\text{Spread}$$

with this value being negative or positive depending on whether the holder is buying or selling protection.

There is also an interest-rate sensitivity measure for CDS contracts, although this sensitivity is relatively insignificant unless one is experiencing high market volatility. The risk measure of sensitivity to changes in he interest rate yield curve (the Libor curve) is known as IR01 or Libor01, and measures the change in value of the contract for a 1 basis point upward parallel shift in the Libor curve.

Credit Default Swap Benchmark Indices[23]

The highly liquid nature of the CDS market has meant that a benchmark index can be constructed with relative ease. Credit default swap indices are now compiled by a number of banks and quoted for trading. Goldman and Deutsche are among the 11 banks that started a US high yield credit default

---

[23] This section was co-authored with Abukar Ali. The views and representations are those of the authors in their individual private capacity.

swap index which tracks the credit default swap of 100 companies (below investment grade issues). These indices for different sectors are now available and can be found for instance on the Bloomberg by inputting

CDX CDS <corp><go>.

Figure 2.42 shows the valuation or the mark to market value of the USD Finance sector iBoxx index . Figure 2.43 shows a list of all the reference entities that make up the index.

JPMorgan Chase & Co and Morgan Stanley formed a similar index called TRAC-X which also lists a US and Euro high-yield credit default index. The TRAC- X Europe comprises the 100 most actively traded names in the European credit default swap market. This is shown at Figure 2.44.

Figure 2.41   CDS spreads for ticker CDS.

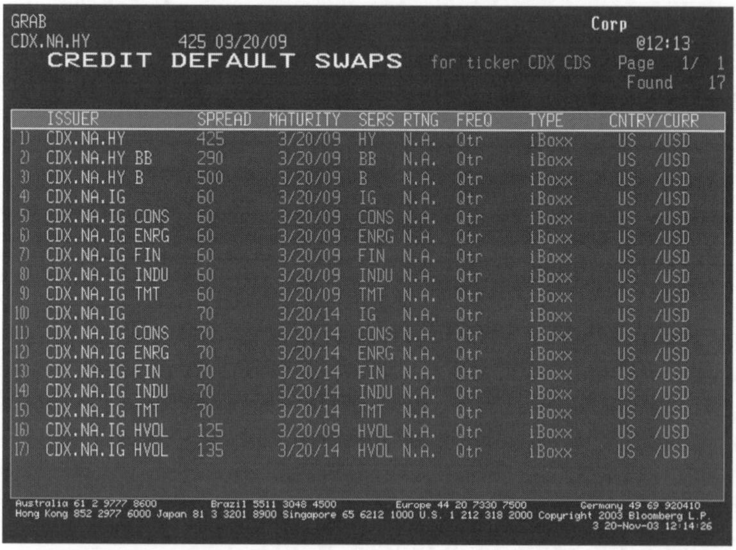

© Bloomberg L.P. Used with permission.

Figure 2.42   Value of iBoxx CDS.

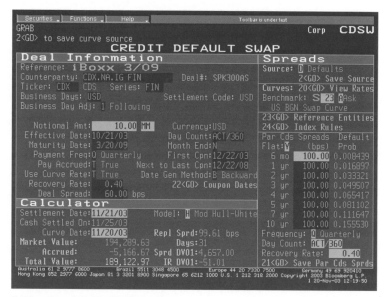

© Bloomberg L.P. Used with permission.

Figure 2.43   Reference entities for iBoxx index.

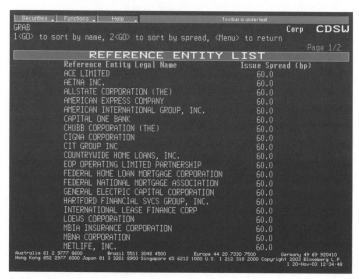

© Bloomberg L.P. Used with permission.

Figure 2.39   TRAC-X index.

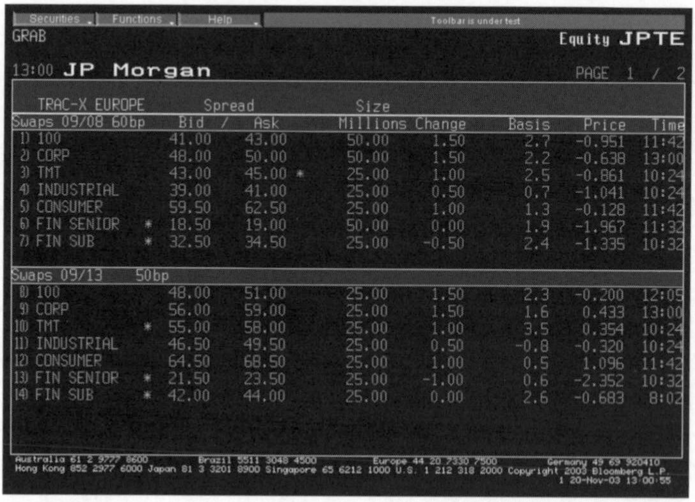

© Bloomberg L.P. Used with permission.

iBoxx® CDS index term sheet

Counterparty:	ABC Fund LLC
Trade Date:	February 24, 2004
Effective Date:	February 25, 2004
Schedule Termination Date:	March 20, 2009
Floating Rate Payer (Seller)	Counterparty
Fixed Rate Payer (Buyer)	XYZ Securities Ltd
Calculation Agent:	XYZ Securities Ltd
Index:	iBoxx CDX.NA.HVOL ®
Traded Rate	107.5 bps
Fixed Rate	125 bps
XYZ Receives (Pays)	$256,517
Amount Traded	$25,000,000

We list above an example of a term sheet for an iBoxx contract. This is a CDS index of 100 reference names that can be traded in unfunded and funded form. The details below are of a contract for a CDS written on the iBoxx index. The hypothetical bank is "XYZ Securities" and the counterparty is an hypothetical hedge fund called "ABC Fund".

The "fixed rate" refers to the coupon on the Index at its inception. There is a fixed coupon set at the start of trading in the index, this is set at "fair value" based on the aggregate value of all the single-name CDS prices for each reference entity in the index (100 names in all). Over the time the traded value of the Index fluctuates to reflect changes in the value of underlying names. The current price is calculated by taking the cashflows representing the underlying CDSs and discounting them at he risky rate.

To arbitrage between the Index and the underlying names, a trader will put on a position in the Index contract and the opposite position in single-name CDSs for each of the constituent names. This would be undertaken when the "traded value" of the Index CDS was felt to not reflect the fair value given the current price of each of the underlying names. Given that this would involve administration for 101 CDS contracts, as well as paying the bid-offer spread, the amount of divergence from fair value would need to be sufficiently high to make the trade worthwhile, say 10 bps or more.

Investors can also trade in the funded credit derivative for iBoxx, via the iBoxx note. This also has a fixed coupon set at inception, and its price fluctuates as the value of the reference names fluctuates.

The following figures are iBoxx price screens for CDS and CLNs as published by BBVA on Bloomberg, which we show here. Figure 2.45 shows prices for the funded and unfunded iBoxx credit index products, while figures 2.46 and 2.47 show the constituents of the index, also presented by BBVA.

Figure 2.45   BBVA iBoxx funded and unfunded price quotes, March 2004.

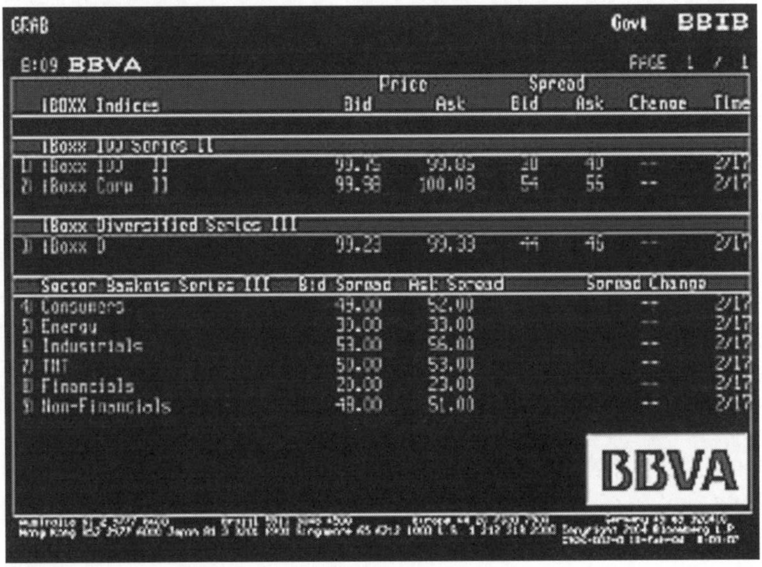

© Bloomberg L.P. © BBVA. Used with permission.

Figure 2.46 iBoxx constituent names, from BBVA.

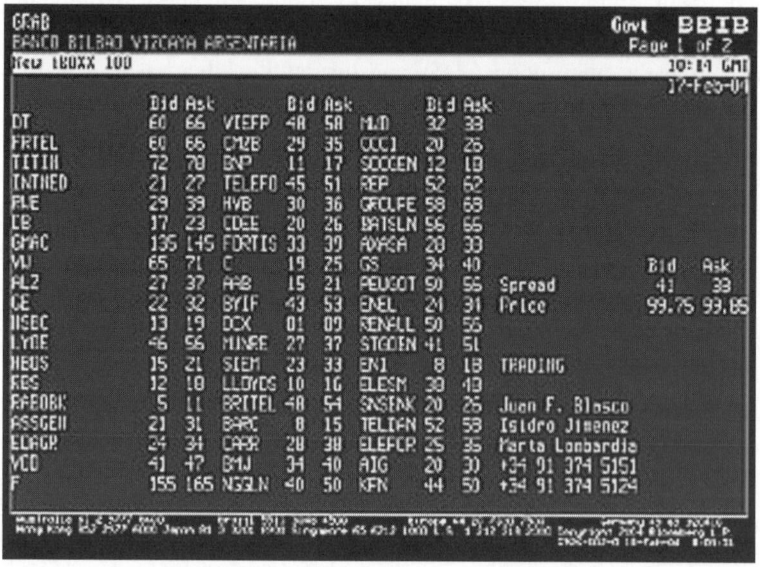

© Bloomberg L.P. © BBVA Used with permission.

Figure 2.47 iBoxx, constituent names.

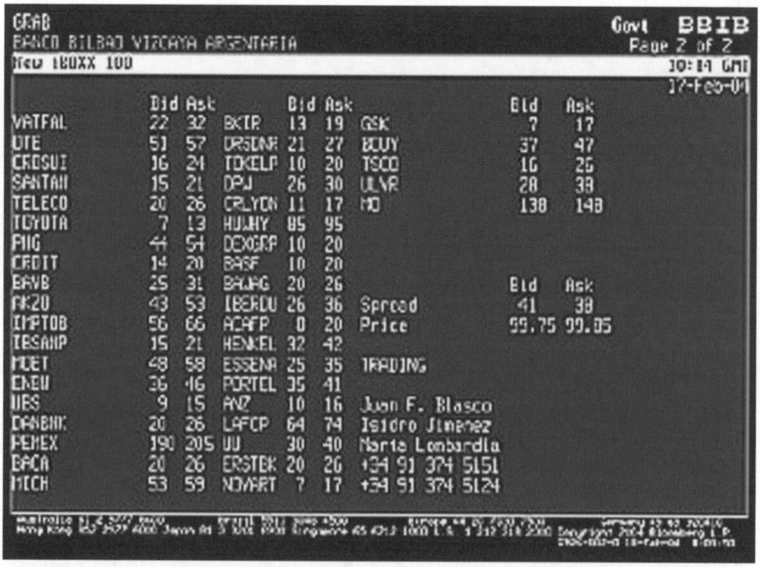

© Bloomberg L.P. © BBVA Used with permission.

Appendix 2.1   ISDA 2003 Credit Derivative Definitions

Bankruptcy

A reference entity voluntarily or involuntarily files for bankruptcy or insolvency protection, or is otherwise unable to pay its debts.

Failure to pay

Failure of a reference entity to make due payments greater than a specified payment requirement (commonly $1 million or more), taking into account a pre-specified grace period to prevent accidental triggering of the contract due to administrative errors.

Restructuring and modified restructuring

A reference entity agrees to a capital restructuring (such as a change in a loan obligation's seniority), deferral or reduction of loan, change in currency or composition of a material debt obligation such as interest or principal payments. "Material" is generally considered to be $10 million or more. Market participants may elect an alternative definition of restructuring known as *modified restructuring* to limit the maturity and type of obligations that may be delivered by the protection seller, to reduce the "cheapest-to-deliver" option.

Obligation acceleration

Obligations of the reference entity have become due and payable earlier than they would have been due to default, other than a Failure to Pay.

Obligation default

Obligations of the reference entity have become capable of being declared due and payable before they otherwise would have due to a default other than a Failure to Pay.

Repudiation/moratorium

A reference entity or government authority rejects or challenges the validity of the obligation.

Appendix 2.2   Total Return Swap and Repo

Repo is short for "sale and repurchase" agreement, and is a collateralised loan. The legal definition is a sale of a bond by one party (or other collateral) in return for cash, with a simultaneous agreement to buy back that bond at an agreed future date. On the buy-back date, the original sale proceeds are returned together with interest on the amount, this interest being charged at the repo rate.

There are economic similarities between a TRS and a repo transaction. A repo seller does not remove the collateral bond from its balance sheet, and there is no transfer of economic effects, including market and credit risk. In a TRS the total return payer or beneficiary lays off these risks to the swap counterparty. The counterparty desires this economic exposure, but the TRS enables it to achieve this without taking on the associated financing cost. However both trades are funding transactions, in effect financed purchases of an asset, and in that respect are similar.

Consider a situation where the potential total return receiver owns an asset such as a bond, and requires financing for it (or is about to purchase the asset and requires financing). It could sell the bond to a counterparty that is prepared to be a TRS payer and simultaneously enter into a TRS with this counterparty. This is illustrated in Figure A2.1. In Figure A2.1, if Bank A had entered into a classic repo with Bank B, with the repo rate set at Libor plus a spread, the repo trade would be economically identical to the bond sale and TRS.[24]

The main difference is that the transaction is governed by the International Swap and Derivatives Association (ISDA) Swap agreement as opposed to a repo agreement. This changes the way the trade is reflected on the bank's balance sheet, and takes it off-balance-sheet. This is one of the main motivations for entering into this type of trade. So the transaction works as follows:

(a) the institution sells the security at its market price;
(b) the institution then executes a swap transaction for a fixed term, exchanging the total return on the security for an agreed rate on the relevant cash amount;
(c) on maturity of the swap the institution repurchases the security at the market price.

---

[24] This trade is also common with equity or convertible bonds as underlying assets.

Figure A2.1 Repo and TRS.

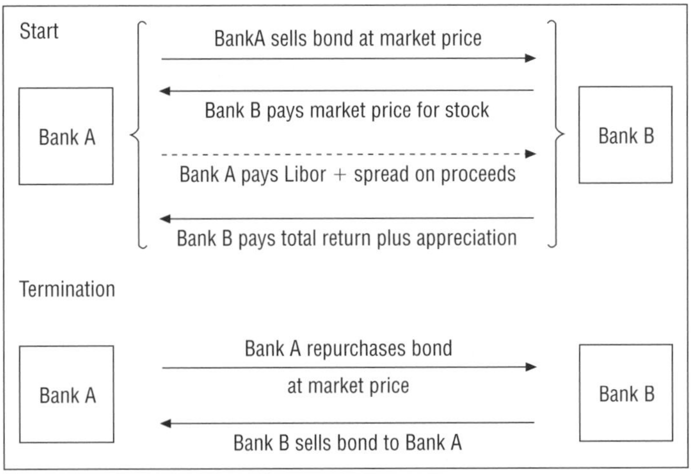

```
Start          ┌─  BankA sells bond at market price  ─┐
               │  ◄─────────────────────────────────  │
               │      Bank B pays market price for stock │
  ┌────────┐   │  ─────────────────────────────────►   │   ┌────────┐
  │ Bank A │ ◄─┤   Bank A pays Libor + spread on proceeds├─► │ Bank B │
  └────────┘   │  ◄─────────────────────────────────    │   └────────┘
               └─  Bank B pays total return plus appreciation ─┘

Termination
                         Bank A repurchases bond
  ┌────────┐             at market price              ┌────────┐
  │ Bank A │  ─────────────────────────────────►     │ Bank B │
  └────────┘  ◄─────────────────────────────────     └────────┘
                 Bank B sells bond to Bank A
```

In theory each leg of the transaction can be executed separately with different counterparties; in practice, the trade is bundled together and so is economically identical to a repo.

The similarities between repo and TRS has resulted in repo traders employing the latter to help manage their books. The swaps are used if they offer a cheaper funding rate and if there is a need to remove assets from the balance sheet for the term of the swap. Often TRS are used as financing instruments by equity market makers. It is unlikely that a repo trader would employ TRS for short-term funding, or longer-term funding in high-quality assets such as gilts. However, long-term funding and funding of high-yield or exotic assets may need to be funded via a TRS. In addition, repo desks are exposed to credit risk in the same way that other lending desks are so exposed; a TRS or other credit derivative may be used to reduce this credit exposure where the bank does not wish to physically sell the asset.

In another application, assume that a bond trader believes that a particular bond that is not currently on his book is about to decline in price. To reflect this view the trader may:

- sell the bond in the market and cover the resulting short position in repo. The cash flow out is the coupon on the bond, with capital gain if the bond falls in price. Assume that the repo rate is floating, say Libor plus a spread. The trader must be aware of the funding costs of the trade, so that unless the bond can be covered in repo at GC,[25] the funding will be at a loss. The yield on the bond must also be lower than the Libor plus spread received in the repo;
- as an alternative, enter into a TRS in which they pay the total return on the bond and receives Libor plus a spread. If the bond yield exceeds the Libor spread, the funding will be negative; however, the trade will gain if the trader's view is proved correct and the bond falls in price by a sufficient amount. If the breakeven funding cost (which the bond must exceed as it falls in value) is lower in the TRS, this method will be used rather than   the repo approach. This is more likely if the bond is special.

Total return swaps are increasingly used as synthetic repo instruments, most commonly by investors that wish to purchase the credit exposure of an asset without purchasing the asset itself. This is conceptually similar to what happened when interest-rate swaps were introduced, which enabled banks and other financial institutions to trade interest-rate risk without borrowing or lending cash funds.

Balance sheet impact

Under a TRS an asset such as a bond position may be removed from the balance sheet. As we noted earlier, in order to avoid adverse impact on regular internal and external capital and credit exposure reporting a bank may use TRS to reduce the amount of lower-quality assets on the balance sheet. This can be done by entering into a short-term TRS with, say, a two-week term that straddles the reporting date.

Bonds are removed from the balance sheet if they are part of a sale plus TRS transaction. This is because legally, the bank selling the asset is not required to repurchase bonds from the swap counterparty, nor is the total return payer obliged to sell the bonds back to the counterparty (or indeed sell the bonds at all on maturity of the TRS). This does not occur under a classic repo or sell/buy-back, which remain balance sheet transactions.

---

[25] That is, the bond cannot be special.

Appendix 2.3   CDS Term Sheet

For illustrative purposes, we show here an example of a typical term sheet for an hypothetical single-name CDS transaction. The entity XYZ Bank plc is the CDS market maker.

XYZ Bank plc
London branch

Draft Terms — Credit Default Swap

1. General Terms

Trade Date	Aug 5, 2003
Effective Date	Aug 6, 2003
Scheduled Termination Date	Jul 30, 2005
Floating Rate Payer ("Seller")	XYZ Bank plc, London branch.
Fixed Rate Payer ("Buyer")	ABC Investment Bank plc
Calculation Agent	Seller
Calculation Agent City	New York
Business Day	New York
Business Day Convention	Following
Reference Entity	Waterford International Inc
Reference Obligation	Primary Obligor: Waterford International Inc Maturity: Jun 30, 2020 Coupon: 0% CUSIP/ISIN: 947074AB6/US947074AB67 Original Issue Amount: 910,000,000
Reference Price	100%
All Guarantees	Not Applicable

2. Fixed Payments

Fixed Rate Payer	USD 7,000,000
Calculation Amount Fixed Rate	0.3% per annum
Fixed Rate Payer Payment Date(s)	Oct 30, Jan 30, Apr 30, Jul 30, starting Oct 30, 2003
Fixed Rate Day Count Fraction	Actual/360

3. Floating Payments

Floating Rate Payer Calculation Amount	USD 7,000,000
Conditions to Payment	Credit Event Notice (Notifying Parties: Buyer or Seller) Notice of Publicly Available Information: Applicable (Public Source: Standard Public Sources. Specified Number: Two)
Credit Events	Bankruptcy Failure to Pay (Grace Period Extension: Not Applicable. Payment Requirement: $1,000,000)
Obligation(s)	Borrowed Money

4. Settlement Terms

Settlement Method	Physical Settlement
Settlement Currency	The currency in which the Floating Rate Payer Calculation Amount is denominated.

Terms Relating to Physical
Settlement

Physical Settlement Period	The longest of the number of business days for settlement in accordance with the then-current market practice of any Deliverable Obligation being Delivered in the Portfolio, as determined by the Calculation Agent, after consultation with the parties, but in no event shall be more than 30 days.
Portfolio	Exclude Accrued Interest
Deliverable Obligations	Bond or Loan
Deliverable Obligation	Not Subordinated
Characteristics	Specified Currency — Standard Specified Currencies Maximum Maturity: 30 years Not Contingent Not Bearer Transferable Assignable Loan Consent Required Loan
Restructuring Maturity Limitation	Not Applicable
Partial Cash Settlement of Loans	Not Applicable
Partial Cash Settlement of Assignable Loans	Not Applicable
Escrow	Applicable

5.   Documentation

Confirmation to be prepared by the Seller and agreed to by the Buyer. The definitions and provisions contained in the 2003 ISDA Credit Derivatives Definitions, as published by the International Swaps and Derivatives Association, Inc., as supplemented by the May 2003 Supplement, to the 2003 ISDA Credit Derivatives Definitions (together, the "Credit Derivatives Definitions"), are incorporated into the Confirmation.

6.   Notice and Account Details

Telephone, Telex and/or   Buyer:

Facsimile Numbers and   Phone:

Contact Details for Notices   Fax:
Seller: A.N. Other
Phone: +1 212-xxx-xxxx
Fax: +1 212-xxx-xxxx

Account Details of Seller

Risks and characteristics

Credit Risk. An investor's ability to collect any will depend on the ability of XYZ Bank plc to pay.

Non-Marketability. Swaps are not registered instruments and they do not trade on any exchange. It may be impossible for the transactor in a swap to transfer the obligations under the swap to another holder. Swaps are customized instruments and there is no central source to obtain prices from other dealers.

Appendix 2.4   Regulatory Capital Treatment of Credit Derivatives

All banking activity is subject to regulatory capital treatment, as defined in the Bank for International Settlements (BIS) Basel capital accord of 1988. The Basel rules are described in Choudhry (2001).

The Basel rules define banking activity in terms of the Banking book and the Trading book. Banking book activity would include traditional bank lending such as loans to corporates, while the Trading book is where investment banking operations such as market making and derivatives trading is concentrated. All banks are required to put up regulatory capital against all their banking and trading book operations.

Briefly, for banking book operations, a bank must put up capital against all its assets in accordance with their "risk weight", and a minimum of 8% of the nominal value of the assets. Higher risk assets carry a higher risk-weight, as shown below.

Basel Risk Weights for banking book assets

Assets	Counterparty Risk Weight
Cash and Sovereign debt (mostly OECD, domestic currency)	0%
Loans to OECD banks	20%
Loans secured by residential mortgages	50%
Loans to corporates and non-OECD	100%

As lending to corporates carries the highest capital charge, this business is the most expensive and demands the highest return on capital.[1] As corporate loan books began to become more expensive to maintain, banks sought ways of reducing the capital impact of these loans.

---

1 For instance, a loan of $100 million to a corporate, being 100% risk-weighted, requires that the bank sets aside $8 million of capital. A similar size position in a US Treasury would require no capital, while a loan to another bank would require $1.6 million. Capital is defined as equity and long-term subordinated debt.

This led to the growth in use of credit derivatives and also structured products like CDOs and synthetic CDOs. If a bank buys credit protection on a corporate loan that is held on its book, its capital requirement against that loan is significantly reduced. In effect, if entering into a credit default swap and buying protection from an OECD banking counterparty, the risk weighting on the underlying reference loan reduces from 100% to 20%.[2]

Since the Basel Accord came into effect in 1992, various drawbacks in its construction have been highlighted and the BIS had been working to implement a replacement accord, known as Basel II. This seeks to define risk categories more accurately, and under Basel II there is a higher number of risk categories, defined by credit ratings. Basel II is scheduled to be published in final form at the end of 2004, with scheduled implementation at the end of 2006.

The table below shows the new risk categories for capital allocation.

Basel II counterparty risk weights.

Asset type	AAA to AA−	A+ to A−	BBB+ to BBB−	BB+ to BB−	B+ to B−	Below B− (including defaulted)	Unrated
Sovereigns	0	20	50	100	100	150	100
Banks, option 1[3]	20	50	100	100	100	150	100
Banks, option 2[4] > three months	20	50	50	100	100	150	50
Banks, option 2 < three months	20	20	20	50	50	150	20
Corporates	20	50	100	100	150	150	100

Impact on credit derivatives

Under Basel I, banks had a great incentive to enter into credit derivative contracts, due to the impact on their balance sheet and the reduced cost of capital that resulted. Under Basel II, some of this incentive may be reduced;

---

2 This is a deliberately simple example and assumes that the maturity of the credit derivatives contract matches the maturity of the underlying corporate loan. If the CDS is of a shorter maturity, then only a partial capital relief would apply.

3 Risk weighting based on the sovereign in which the bank is incorporated.

4 Risk weighting based on the rating of the individual bank.

for instance, banks would not necessarily need to buy credit protection on high credit-quality corporate loans. Considering the table above for example, the risk weight of a loan to a corporate rated at AA would be 20%. Buying credit protection on this loan from an AA-rated bank would not reduce this charge, while buying protection from an A-rated bank would actually increase the charge, to 50%.

The same impact may be observed in the structured product market, as the incentive to securitise certain assets is also reduced.

References and Bibliography

Das, S., *Swaps and Financial Derivatives*, IFR Publishing 1994.

Ducovney, S., *Swaps*, 2nd edition, FT Prentice Hall 1999.

Francis, J., J. Frost, J. Whittaker, *The Handbook of Credit Derivatives* (New York, NY: McGraw Hill, 1999).

Gregory, J., *Credit Derivatives: The Definitive Guide*, RISK Publishing 2003.

Kolb, R., *Futures, Options and Swaps*, Blackwell 2000.

I remember as a child looking up to older brothers and longing to experience all their great adventures. Years later I found most of those things to be a great disappointment. What had looked so good as a child, seemed dull when I came to experience it.

— Dexy's Midnight Runners, "Until I Believe in my Soul",
from *Searching for the Young Soul Rebels*
(Mercury Records) 1982

3

Credit Derivatives: Funded Instruments

We have noted that credit derivative instruments exist in funded and unfunded variants. The previous chapter looked at unfunded credit derivatives. In this chapter we consider funded credit derivatives, by which we mean principally the credit-linked note and also some total return swaps.

Credit-Linked Notes

Credit-linked notes (CLNs) are a form of credit derivative. They are also, in all their forms, bond instruments for which an investor pays cash, in order to receive a periodic coupon and, on maturity or termination, all or part of its initial purchase price back. That makes CLNs similar to bonds. The key difference is that the return on the CLN is explicitly linked to the credit performance of the reference security or reference entity. Like all credit derivatives, CLNs are associated with a reference entity, credit events and cash or physical settlement.

CLNs are funded credit derivatives. The *buyer* of the note is the investor, who is the *credit protection seller* and is making an upfront payment to the protection buyer when it buys the note. Thus, the *credit protection buyer* is the *issuer* of the note. If no credit event occurs during the life of the note, the par redemption value of the note is paid to the investor on maturity. If a credit event does occur, then on maturity, a value less than par will be paid to the investor. This value will be reduced by the nominal value of the reference asset that the CLN is linked to. The exact process will differ according to whether *cash settlement* or *physical settlement* has been specified for the note. We will consider this later.[1]

As with credit default swaps, CLNs are used in structured products, in various combinations, and their flexibility has been behind the growth and wide application of the synthetic collateralised debt obligation and other credit hybrid products.

Description of CLNs

Credit-linked notes exist in a number of forms, but all of them contain a link between the return they pay and the credit-related performance of the underlying asset. A standard credit-linked note is a security, issued directly by a financial or corporate entity or by a special purpose legal entity (SPV or SPE), which has an interest payment and fixed maturity structure similar to a vanilla bond. The performance of the note however, including the maturity value, is linked to the performance of a specified underlying asset or assets as well as that of the issuing entity. Notes are usually issued at par. The notes are often used by borrowers to hedge against credit risk, and by investors to enhance the yield received on their holdings. Hence, the issuer of the note is the credit protection buyer and the buyer of the note is the credit protection seller.[2]

Essentially credit-linked notes are hybrid instruments that combine a pure credit risk exposure with a vanilla bond. The credit-linked note pays regular coupons, however the credit derivative element is usually set to allow the issuer to decrease the principal amount, and/or the coupon interest, if a specified credit event occurs.

Figure 3.1 shows Bloomberg screen SND and their definition of the CLN. We also show an earlier page from the same screen, Figure 3.2, which indicates that a CLN is also viewed as a *structured note*.

---

[1]   In an era before fancy terminology, a bank would make a loan to (say) a corporate, in return for which the bank would receive interest payments on the loan up until the loan maturity date, upon which the original loan would be repaid in full ("par"). During the life of the loan, if the borrower ("obligor") experiences any financial difficulty or downturn in corporate performance, it may not be able to service the loan interest, or may default on the loan repayment. The bank lender has taken on an exposure to the credit performance of the obligor. The original funded credit derivative ...?!

[2]   Some market participants think of CLNs as being issued only by SPVs or as part of structured products. However, as we illustrate in the example in this chapter they are also issued by corporations.

Chapter 3 Credit Derivatives: Funded Instruments

Figure 3.1 Bloomberg screen SND: definition of credit-linked note.

Page 11/ 12

Credit Linked Notes (CLN): A hybrid debt security that offers investors a synthetic credit exposure to a specified Reference Entity or basket of Reference Entities. This credit exposure can be gained through a variety of methods including (but not limited to): a credit default swap, a credit spread swap, a total return swap, or as a repackaged note where the issuer passes through the risk of an underlying credit to the noteholder in exchange for an enhanced return. For example, a note might provide for its principal repayment to be reduced below par in the event that a reference obligation defaults.
20) Example: EC771465 <CORP> DES. A note that is linked to the credit of Sodexho Alliance SA. Following a credit event on the underlying reference obligation, this note will be redeemed early at less than par.

Repackaged Notes: A debt instrument secured by an underlying asset where the cashflows of that asset are reprofiled through a derivative contract while the credit risk is passed through to the investor of the Repackaged Note.
21) Example: EC785183 <CORP> DES. A note that is secured by Roche Holdings convertible notes and a swap agreement. Following an event of default on all or part of the underlying, this note will be redeemed early at an amount based on the underlying.

Page <FWD> for FFIEC 034 Structured Note Call Reporting Revision

Australia 61 2 9777 8600   Brazil 5511 3048 4500   Europe 44 20 7330 7500   Germany 49 69 920410
Hong Kong 852 2977 6000 Japan 81 3 3201 8900 Singapore 65 6212 1000 U.S. 1 212 318 2000 Copyright 2004 Bloomberg L.P.
G926-802-2 14-Apr-04 14:22:15

© Bloomberg L.P. Used with permission.

Figure 3.2 Bloomberg screen SND: definition of structured note.

Page 2/ 12

Structured Note — Definition

The use of the term **structured note** is imprecise among market participants. Bloomberg appreciates the sensitivity to the identification of any bond as such, since special treatment is mandated for **structured notes** by various U.S. banking regulations. It is for precisely this reason that Bloomberg has elected to use the Structured note definition as employed by U.S. banking regulations.

Structured notes are hybrid securities combining a fixed-income instrument with a series of derivative components. As a result, the bond's coupon, average life, and/or redemption value can become exposed to the forward movement in various indices, equity prices, foreign exchange rates, mortgage-backed security prepayment speeds, etc. When combined with the nature of the options typically embedded within these structures--including complex call features, caps, and/or floors--exotic payoff scenarios and random cashflows can be expected. Excluded from this category are fixed-income securities that are issued by sovereign governments, where the structure is considered to be standard domestic convention.

Page <FWRD> for Structured Note product types

Australia 61 2 9777 8600   Brazil 5511 3048 4500   Europe 44 20 7330 7500   Germany 49 69 920410
Hong Kong 852 2977 6000 Japan 81 3 3201 8900 Singapore 65 6212 1000 U.S. 1 212 318 2000 Copyright 2004 Bloomberg L.P.
G926-802-2 14-Apr-04 14:23:32

© Bloomberg L.P. Used with permission.

As with credit default swaps, credit-linked notes may be specified under cash settlement or physical settlement. Specifically:

- under cash settlement, if a credit event has occurred, on termination the protection seller receives the difference between the value of the initial purchase proceeds and the value of the reference asset at the time of the credit event;
- under physical settlement, on occurrence of a credit event, the note is terminated. At maturity, the protection buyer delivers the reference asset or an asset among a list of deliverable assets, and the protection seller receives the value of the original purchase proceeds minus the value of the asset that has been delivered.

Figure 3.3 illustrates a cash-settled credit-linked note.

CLNs may be issued directly by a financial or corporate entity or via a Special Purpose Vehicle (SPV). They have been issued with the form of credit-linking by taking on one or more of a number of different guises. For instance, a CLN may have its return performance linked to the issuer's, or a specified reference entity's, credit rating, risk exposure, financial performance or circumstance of default. The return of a CLN is linked to the performance of the reference asset. CLNs are described in some texts as being "collateralised" with the reference security, but this is incorrect. The reference security may not be owned by the issuer of the CLN, so it could not possibly be described as being "collateral" for the CLN.[3]

In some texts a CLN is described as being the equivalent of a risk-free bond and a short position in a credit default swap. While this description is not incorrect, one cannot see the point of stating it. A CLN is a bond with a return, that is principal and/or interest payments, that is/are linked to the credit performance of a linked reference asset or reference entity, which may be the issuer. The investor in the note is selling credit protection on the reference asset or entity.

---

[3] Beware of this sort of jargon being used by bankers or capital market lawyers, or even in some text-books. The proceeds of a CLN issue may be invested in collateral, as part of a CSO structured product (see Chapter 10), but, in its plain vanilla form it is not collateralised by anything. This is as silly as saying that a bond issued by a corporate cannot be a CLN (because it has not been issued by an SPV), even though the bond may, for example, have its coupon payment linked to the credit rating of the issuer or another reference entity.

Figure 3.3 Credit-linked note.

Credit-linked note on issue

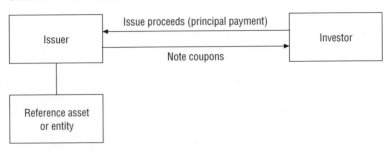

No credit event

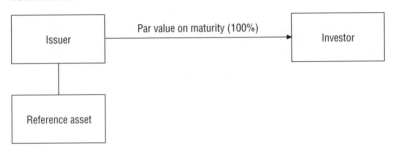

Credit event

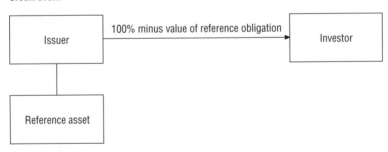

Figure 3.4 shows Bloomberg screen CLN and a list of the various types of CLN issue that have been made.

Figure 3.5 shows a page accessed from Bloomberg screen "CLN", which is a list of CLNs that have had their coupon affected by a change in the reference entity's credit rating, as at October 2002.

Figure 3.4 Bloomberg screen CLN.

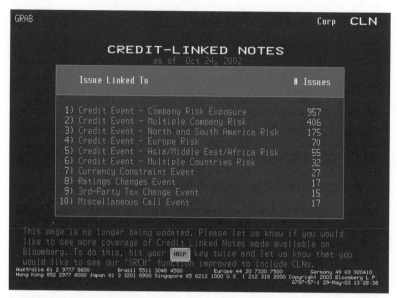

© Bloomberg L.P. Used with permission.

Figure 3.5 Bloomberg screen showing a sample of CLNs impacted by change in reference entity credit rating, October 2002.

Issuer	Settle Date	Cpn	Crncy	Maturity Date	Rating Changes Exposure
1) BHFBK	04/28/1998	6.25	DEM	04/28/2006	Govt of Ukraine
2) BSPIR	03/21/2000	7.00	EUR	02/20/2010	B-Spires
3) CATTLE	10/21/1999	8.63	GBP	12/07/2007	Cattle PLC
4) CNTCNZ	09/14/2000	FRN	AUD	09/14/2007	Contact Energy
5) CNTCNZ	09/14/2000	FRN	USD	09/14/2007	Contact Energy
6) HI	11/13/1997	FRN	USD	11/13/2013	Household Fin Co
7) IFCTF	08/04/1997	7.88	USD	08/04/2002	Indust Fin Corp
8) IFCTF	08/04/1997	7.75	USD	08/04/2007	Indust Fin Corp
9) KPN	06/13/2000	FRN	EUR	06/13/2002	KPN NV
10) KPN	06/13/2000	FRN	EUR	06/13/2002	KPN NV
11) KPN	06/13/2000	6.05	EUR	06/13/2003	KPN NV
12) METALF	07/25/2000	6.75	EUR	07/25/2005	MetallGesell Fin
13) METALF	07/25/2000	6.75	EUR	07/25/2005	MetallGesell Fin
14) OSTDRA	02/16/2000	Var	EUR	02/16/2007	Oester Draukraft
15) SIRSTR	06/25/1998	FRN	USD	10/06/2006	Bk Tokyo-Mitsub
16) SOULN	03/26/1998	6.89	GBP	03/26/2008	Southern Water
17) SPIRES	01/26/1998	FRN	DEM	10/24/2007	Greece

© Bloomberg L.P. Used with permission.

Example illustrations

CLNs come in a variety of forms. For example, consider a bank issuer of credit cards that wants to fund its credit card loan portfolio via an issue of debt. The bank is rated as AA-. In order to reduce the credit risk of the loans, it issues a two-year credit-linked note. The principal amount of the bond is 100 per cent (par) as usual, and it pays a coupon of 7.50%, which is 200 basis points above the two-year benchmark. The equivalent spread for a vanilla bond issued by a bank of this rating would be around 120 basis points. With the CLN though, if the incidence of bad debt amongst credit card holders exceeds 10% then the terms state that note holders will only receive $85 per $100 nominal. The credit card issuer has, in effect, purchased a credit option that lowers its liability in the event that it suffers from a specified credit event, which in this case is an above-expected incidence of bad debts. The credit card bank has issued the credit-linked note to reduce its credit exposure, in the form of this particular type of credit insurance. If the incidence of bad debts is low, the note is redeemed at par. However, if there is a high incidence of such debt, the bank will only have to repay a part of its loan liability. In this example, the reference assets linked to the CLN is the credit card loan portfolio.

Investors may wish to purchase the CLN because the coupon paid on it will be above what the credit card bank would pay on a vanilla bond it issued, and higher than other comparable investments in the market. In addition, such notes are usually priced below par on issue. Assuming that the notes are eventually redeemed at par, investors will also have realized a substantial capital gain.

The majority of CLNs are issued directly by banks and corporates, in the same way as conventional bonds.

An example of such a bond is shown in Figure 3.6. This shows Bloomberg screen DES for a CLN issued by British Telecom, the 8.125% note due in December 2010. The terms of this note state that the coupon will increase by 25 basis points for each one-notch rating downgrade below A-/A3 suffered by the issuer during the life of the note. The coupon will decrease by 25 basis points for each ratings upgrade, with a minimum coupon set at 8.125%. In other words, this note allows investors to take on a credit play on the fortunes of the issuer.

Figure 3.7 shows Bloomberg screen YA for this note, as at 12 May 2003. We can see that a rating downgrade meant that the coupon on the note changed to 8.375%.

Part I: Credit Risk and Credit Derivative Instruments

Figure 3.6   Bloomberg screen DES for British Telecom plc 8.125% 2010 credit-linked note issued on 5 December 2000.

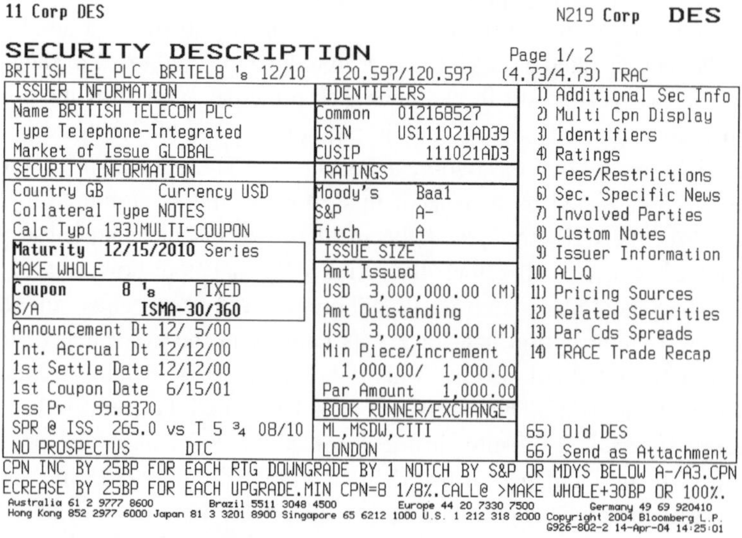

```
11 Corp DES                                              N219 Corp   DES
SECURITY DESCRIPTION                        Page 1/ 2
BRITISH TEL PLC  BRITEL8 '₈ 12/10    120.597/120.597   (4.73/4.73) TRAC
┌─ISSUER INFORMATION───┬─IDENTIFIERS───────────┐ 1) Additional Sec Info
│Name BRITISH TELECOM PLC│Common    012168527   │ 2) Multi Cpn Display
│Type Telephone-Integrated│ISIN    US111021AD39 │ 3) Identifiers
│Market of Issue GLOBAL │CUSIP      111021AD3   │ 4) Ratings
├─SECURITY INFORMATION─┤─RATINGS───────────────┤ 5) Fees/Restrictions
│Country GB    Currency USD│Moody's    Baa1     │ 6) Sec. Specific News
│Collateral Type NOTES  │S&P        A-          │ 7) Involved Parties
│Calc Typ( 133)MULTI-COUPON│Fitch     A         │ 8) Custom Notes
│Maturity  12/15/2010 Series│─ISSUE SIZE────────┤ 9) Issuer Information
│MAKE WHOLE             │Amt Issued            │ 10) ALLQ
│Coupon     8 '₈   FIXED│USD  3,000,000.00 (M) │ 11) Pricing Sources
│S/A        ISMA-30/360 │Amt Outstanding       │ 12) Related Securities
│Announcement Dt 12/ 5/00│USD  3,000,000.00 (M)│ 13) Par Cds Spreads
│Int. Accrual Dt 12/12/00│Min Piece/Increment  │ 14) TRACE Trade Recap
│1st Settle Date 12/12/00│    1,000.00/ 1,000.00│
│1st Coupon Date  6/15/01│Par Amount   1,000.00 │
│Iss Pr   99.8370       ├─BOOK RUNNER/EXCHANGE──┤
│SPR @ ISS  265.0 vs T 5 ³₄ 08/10│ML,MSDW,CITI │ 65) Old DES
│NO PROSPECTUS      DTC │LONDON                 │ 66) Send as Attachment
CPN INC BY 25BP FOR EACH RTG DOWNGRADE BY 1 NOTCH BY S&P OR MDYS BELOW A-/A3.CPN
ECREASE BY 25BP FOR EACH UPGRADE.MIN CPN=8 1/8%.CALL@ >MAKE WHOLE+30BP OR 100%.
Australia 61 2 9777 8600    Brazil 5511 3048 4500    Europe 44 20 7330 7500    Germany 49 69 920410
Hong Kong 852 2977 6000 Japan 81 3 3201 8900 Singapore 65 6212 1000 U.S. 1 212 318 2000 Copyright 2004 Bloomberg L.P.
                                                              G926-802-2 14-Apr-04 14:25:01
```

© Bloomberg L.P. Used with permission.

Figure 3.7   Bloomberg screen YA for British Telecom CLN, as at 12 May 2003.

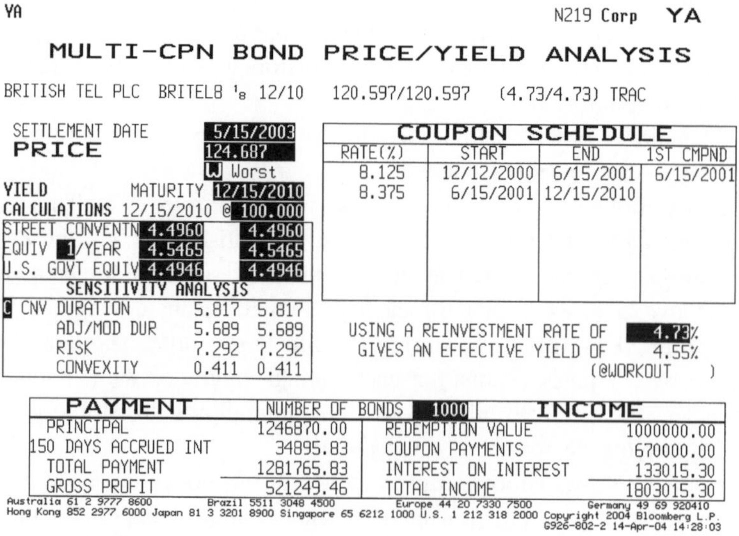

```
YA                                                       N219 Corp   YA
MULTI-CPN BOND PRICE/YIELD ANALYSIS
BRITISH TEL PLC  BRITEL8 '₈ 12/10    120.597/120.597   (4.73/4.73) TRAC

SETTLEMENT DATE    5/15/2003    ┌──────COUPON SCHEDULE──────┐
PRICE              124.687      │RATE(%)│ START  │  END   │1ST CMPND│
                   [W] Worst    │ 8.125 │12/12/2000│6/15/2001│6/15/2001│
YIELD      MATURITY 12/15/2010  │ 8.375 │6/15/2001│12/15/2010│        │
CALCULATIONS 12/15/2010 @ 100.000
STREET CONVENTN 4.4960   4.4960
EQUIV  1/YEAR   4.5465   4.5465
U.S. GOVT EQUIV 4.4946   4.4946
     SENSITIVITY ANALYSIS
C CNV DURATION  5.817    5.817
   ADJ/MOD DUR  5.689    5.689   USING A REINVESTMENT RATE OF   4.73%
   RISK         7.292    7.292   GIVES AN EFFECTIVE YIELD OF    4.55%
   CONVEXITY    0.411    0.411                      (@WORKOUT   )

┌─────PAYMENT──────┬─NUMBER OF BONDS 1000─┬──────INCOME──────┐
│PRINCIPAL         │  1246870.00 │REDEMPTION VALUE  │1000000.00│
│150 DAYS ACCRUED INT│  34895.83 │COUPON PAYMENTS   │ 670000.00│
│TOTAL PAYMENT     │  1281765.83 │INTEREST ON INTEREST│133015.30│
│GROSS PROFIT      │   521249.46 │TOTAL INCOME      │1803015.30│
Australia 61 2 9777 8600    Brazil 5511 3048 4500    Europe 44 20 7330 7500    Germany 49 69 920410
Hong Kong 852 2977 6000 Japan 81 3 3201 8900 Singapore 65 6212 1000 U.S. 1 212 318 2000 Copyright 2004 Bloomberg L.P.
                                                              G926-802-2 14-Apr-04 14:28:03
```

© Bloomberg L.P. Used with permission.

Figure 3.8 is the Bloomberg DES page for a USD-denominated CLN issued directly by Household Finance Corporation.[4] Like the British Telecom bond, this is a CLN with its return linked to the credit risk of the issuer, but in a different way. The coupon of the HFC bond was issued as floating USD-LIBOR, but in the event of the bond not being called from November 2001, the coupon would be changed to the issuer's two-year "credit spread" over a fixed rate of 5.9%. In fact, the issuer called the bond with effect from the coupon change date. Figure 3.9 shows the Bloomberg screen YA for the bond and how its coupon remained the same as at the first issue until the call date.

Another type of credit-linking is illustrated in Figure 3.10. This is a JPY-denominated bond issued by Alpha-Sires, which is a medium term note (MTN) program vehicle set up by Merrill Lynch. The note itself is linked to the credit quality of Ford Motor Credit. In the event of a default of the reference name, the note will be called immediately. Figure 3.11 shows the rate fixing for this note as at the last coupon date. The screen snapshot was taken on 6 June 2003.

Figure 3.8   Bloomberg screen DES for Household Finance Corporation CLN.

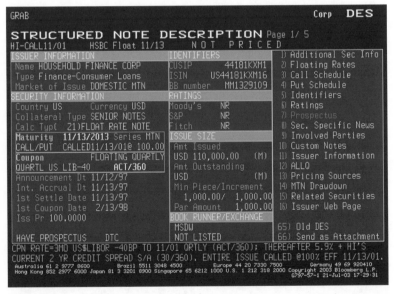

© Bloomberg L.P. Used with permission.

---

[4]   HFC was subsequently acquired by HSBC.

Part I: Credit Risk and Credit Derivative Instruments

Figure 3.9   Bloomberg screen YA for Household Finance Corporation CLN, showing bond called (screen as at 21 July 2003).

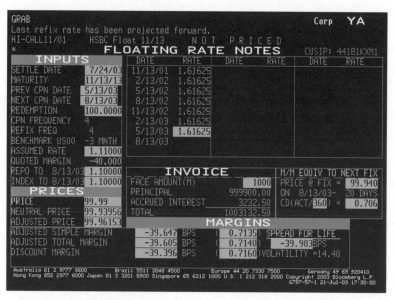

© Bloomberg L.P. Used with permission.

Figure 3.10   Bloomberg screen DES for Ford Motor Credit-reference linked CLN issued by Alpha-Sires MTN program.

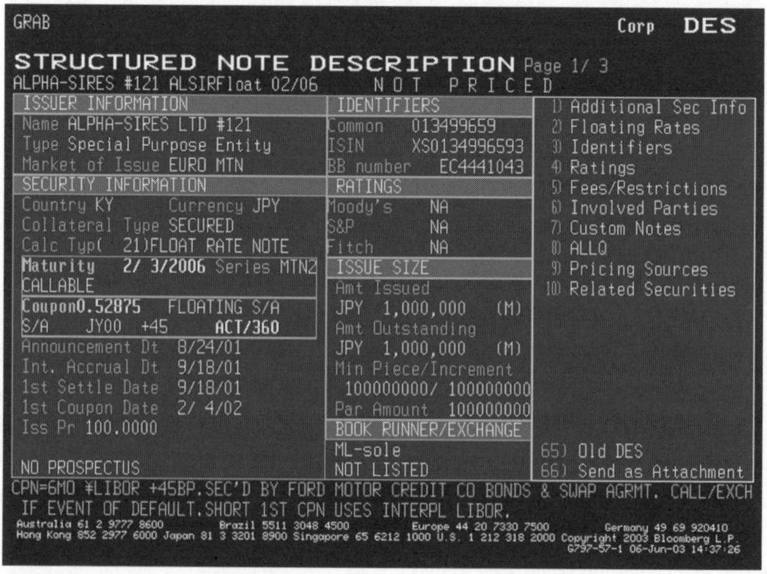

© Bloomberg L.P. Used with permission.

124

Figure 3.11   Bloomberg screen YA for Ford Motor Credit-linked CLN as at
6 June 2003.

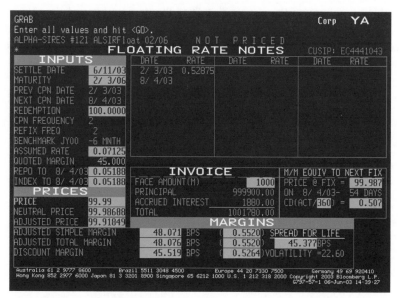

© Bloomberg L.P. Used with permission.

CLNs and Structured Products

As with other credit derivatives, CLNs are used as part of synthetic securitisation structures and structured products. We introduce this use here, while a detailed description of these products is given in Chapter 14.

Simple structure

Structured products such as synthetic collateralised debt obligations (CDOs) may combine both CLNs and credit default swaps, to meet issuer and investor requirements. For example, Figure 3.12 shows a credit structure designed to provide a higher return for an investor on comparable risk to the cash market. An issuing entity is set up in the form of a special purpose vehicle (SPV), which issues CLNs to the market. The structure is engineered so that the SPV has a neutral position on a reference asset. It has bought protection on a single reference name by issuing a funded credit derivative, the CLN, and simultaneously sold protection on this name by selling a credit default swap on this name. The proceeds of the CLN are invested in risk-free collateral such as T-bills or a Treasury bank account. The coupon on the CLN will be a spread over Libor. It is backed by the collateral account and the fee generated by the SPV in selling protection with the credit default swap. Investors in the CLN have exposure to the reference asset or entity, and the repayment of the note is linked to the performance of the reference entity. If a credit event occurs, the maturity date of the CLN is brought forward and the note is settled as par minus the value of the reference asset or entity.

Figure 3.12   CLN and credit default swap structure on single reference name.

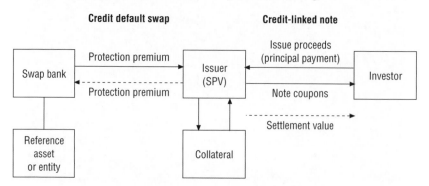

The first-to-default credit-linked note

A standard credit-linked note is issued in reference to one specific bond or loan. An investor purchasing such a note is writing credit protection on a specific reference credit. A CLN that is linked to more than one reference credit is known as a *basket credit-linked note*. A development of the CLN as a structured product is the First-to-Default CLN (FtD), which is a CLN that is linked to a basket of reference assets. The investor in the CLN is selling protection on the first credit to default.[5] Figure 3.13 shows this progression in the development of CLNs as structured products, with the *fully-funded synthetic* collateralised debt obligation (CDO) being the vehicle that uses CLNs tied to a large basket of reference assets.

An FtD CLN is a funded credit derivative in which the investor sells protection on one reference entity in a basket of assets, whichever is the first to default. The return on the CLN is a multiple of the average spread of the basket. The CLN will mature early on occurrence of a credit event relating

---

[5] "Default" here meaning a credit event as defined in the ISDA definitions.

to any of the reference assets. Note that settlement can be either of the following:

- physical settlement: with the defaulted asset(s) being delivered to the noteholder;
- cash settlement: in which the CLN issuer pays redemption proceeds to the noteholder calculated as (principal amount multiplied by the reference asset recovery value).[6]

Figure 3.13 Progression of CLN development.

Figure 3.14 shows a generic FtD credit-linked note.

To illustrate, let us consider an FtD CLN issued at par with a term to maturity of five years and linked to a basket of five reference assets with a face value (issued nominal amount) of $10 million. An investor purchasing this note will pay $10 million to the issuer. If no credit event occurs during the life of the note, the investor will receive the face value of the note on maturity. If a credit event occurs on any of the assets in the basket, the note will redeem early and the issuer will deliver a deliverable obligation of the reference entity, or a portfolio of such obligations, for a $10 million nominal amount. An FtD CLN carries a similar amount of risk exposure on default to a standard CLN, namely the recovery rate of the defaulted credit. However, its risk exposure prior to default is theoretically lower than a standard CLN, as it can reduce default probability through diversification. The investor can obtain exposure to a basket of reference entities that differ by industrial sector and by credit rating.

The matrix in Figure 3.15 illustrates how an investor can select a credit mix in the basket that diversifies risk exposure across a wide range — we show a hypothetical mix of reference assets to which an issued FtD could be linked. The precise selection of names will reflect investors' own risk/return profile requirements.

---

[6] In practice, it is not the "recovery value" that is used, but the market value of the reference asset at the time the credit event is verified. Recovery of a defaulted asset follows a legal process of administration and/or liquidation that can take years, the final recovery value may not be known with certainty for some time.

Figure 3.14   First-to-Default CLN structure.

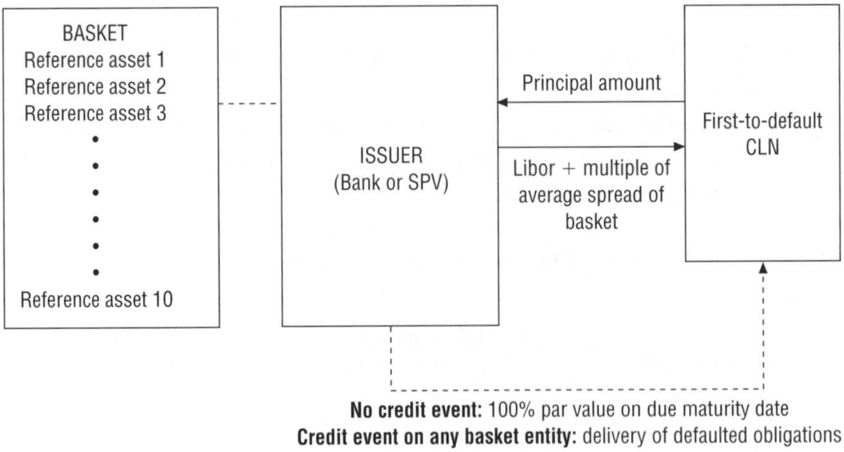

No credit event: 100% par value on due maturity date
Credit event on any basket entity: delivery of defaulted obligations

Figure 3.15   Diversified credit exposure to basket of reference assets: hypothetical reference asset mix.

	Auto-mobiles	Banks	Elec-tronics	Insurance	Media	Telecoms	Utilities
Aaa							
Aa1							
Aa2			Sun Alliance				
Aa3		RBoS					
A1							
A2							Powergen
A3	Ford					British Telecom	
Baa1			Philips		News Intl		
Baa2							
Baa3							

The FtD CLN creates a synthetic credit entity that features a note return with enhanced spread. Investors receive a spread over LIBOR that is the average return of all the reference assets in the basket. This structure serves

128

to diversify credit risk exposure while benefiting from a higher average return. If the pool of reference assets is sufficiently large, the structure becomes similar to a *single-tranche CDO*. This is considered in Chapter 8.

Principal Protected Structures

Principal protected structures are instruments that were designed to meet investor demand for products that offered an element of capital guarantee. Because they offer an exposure to credit risk, and can be used to transfer credit risk exposure, they may be designated as a form of credit derivative. As the cost of a principal protected structure is paid up-front on issue, we discuss them here as part of "funded" credit derivatives.

Certain investors desire to hold highly-rated or investment-grade rated assets but in a form that guarantees at least their initial investment on maturity. That is, the purchase price of par is not at risk during the term of the investment. This guarantee is structured into the investment instrument in the credit derivatives market, in the form of a principal protected credit-linked note. The note is issued usually by an SPV that has been set up by the structuring investment bank. In essence the principal protected note is a funded credit derivative and is a form of CLN. The typical structure is that of a 100% principal protected note with an embedded credit default swap. The swap is linked to a specified reference credit. On occurrence of a credit event, the note stops paying coupons, but is redeemed at par on the original stated maturity date. Any type of credit derivative, such as a basket CDS, can be embedded into a principal protected note. So another type of structure is one where the coupons of the principal protected note are linked to the risk on a CDO mezzanine or equity tranche. Any default results in a decrease or termination of the remaining coupons. On maturity the par value is paid back to the investor.

Funded Total Return Swap

As we saw in Chapter 2, the total return swap (TRS) is an unfunded credit derivative. However TRSs can also be traded in funded form, where an up-front payment is made in return for the "total return" of the reference asset. This makes the funded TRS similar to the synthetic repo discussed in Appendix 2.2.

A variation of the generic TRS that is a funded credit derivative has been used in structured credit products such as synthetic collateralised debt obligations (CDO).[7] An example of this is the Jazz I CDO B.V., which is a vehicle that can trade in cash bonds as well as credit default swaps and total return swaps. It has been called a hybrid CDO for this reason. In the *Jazz* structure, the TRS is a funded credit derivative because the market price of the reference asset is paid upfront by the *Jazz* vehicle to the swap counterparty. In return, the swap counterparty pays the principal and interest on the reference asset to Jazz CDO. The Jazz CDO has therefore purchased the reference asset synthetically, and paid up-front the purchase price. The TRS in this case is physically-settled. On occurrence of a pre-defined credit event, the swap counterparty delivers the asset to the CDO and the TRS is terminated. Because these are funded credit derivatives, a liquidity facility is needed by the vehicle, which it will draw on whenever it purchases a TRS. This facility is provided by the arranging bank to the structure, which in this case was Deutsche Bank AG.

The TRS arrangement in the *Jazz* structure is shown in Figure 3.16. The Jazz I CDO is discussed in detail in Chapter 10.

Figure 3.16   Total return swap as used in Jazz I CDO BV.

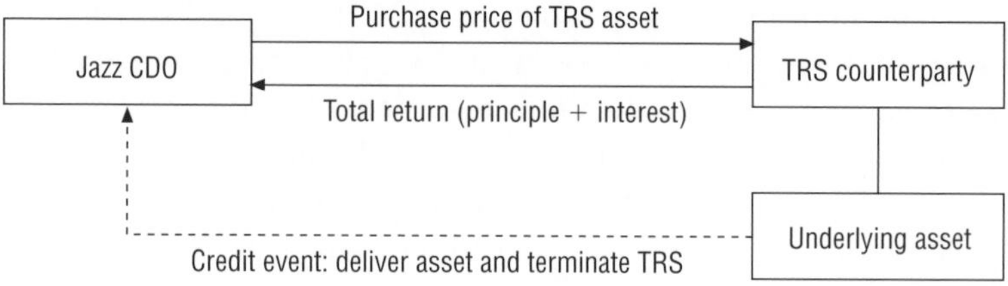

The Portfolio CLN

To conclude this chapter, we produce here for illustrative purposes the term sheet that relates to an hypothetical Portfolio CLN. This is a note issued by an SPV that references a basket of 50 different corporate bonds. Readers will; be able to get a flavour of the market's description of these products from this term sheet, and the list of the reference portfolio that is detailed within it. There is also a description of the return of the CLN and how it is linked to the performance of the bonds in the basket.

---

[7] These are covered in Chapter **10**.

Static Portfolio Credit-Linked Note

Indicative terms and conditions

For illustrative purposes we show here a sample term sheet for an hypothetical credit-linked note that has been issued by an hypothetical Jersey SPV ("Golden Claw Funding Limited"). The CLN is referenced to a static tranche of a seven-year portfolio of 50 (synthetic) assets and pays a quarterly coupon of Euribor plus 2.2% on an Act/360 basis.

Issuer	Golden Claw Funding Limited a special purpose vehicle incorporated in Jersey
Format	Bearer Medium Term Notes
Trade Date	11th December 2003
Issue Date	8th January 2004
Scheduled Maturity Date	20th March 2011
Scheduled Credit	3 Business Days prior to the Scheduled
Observation End Date	Maturity Date
Principal Amount	EUR 100,000,000
Issue Price	100 %
Reference Entity	Each of the Reference Entities specified in the Schedule, and any Successors of any of them
Loss Threshold	Implicit Portfolio Size multiplied by the Lower Boundary
Lower Boundary	5.95%
Upper Boundary	6.95%
Tranche Size	Upper Boundary minus Lower Boundary
Implicit Portfolio Size	Principal Amount divided by Tranche Size

Combined Collateral	1. EUR 100,000,000 of Erste Europaische Pfandbrief Und Kommunalkreditbank AG • % bonds due 20 March 2011, ISIN [to be confirmed] (the "Collateral Securities") 2. A swap agreement with the Swap Counterparty comprising an Asset Swap element and a Credit Swap element (the "Swap Agreement")
Interest Rate	3 month Euribor + 220 bps
Interest Payment Dates	Quarterly on March 20th, Jun 20th, September 20th and December 20th each year, starting with a long first coupon on 20th March 2004, Act/360, Following
Interest Amount and Accrual of Interest	**Interest Bearing Amount * Interest Rate * Day Count Fraction** 1. Interest Amount shall be determined by the Calculation Agent on the Payment Observation Date based on the Interest Bearing Amount as at that Payment Observation Date and shall be payable to the Noteholders on the relevant Interest Payment Date 2. For the avoidance of doubt, Interest Amounts shall not be calculated on a weighted average basis 3. No Interest shall accrue after the Scheduled Maturity Date
Interest Bearing Amount	Principal Amount less the Notional Reduction Amount
Notional Reduction Amount	On any date, an amount determined by the Calculation Agent equal to: (1) the aggregate of the Implicit Credit Positions of all Non-determined Reference Entities existing on such date **plus**

	(2) Accumulated Loss calculated as of such date **Minus** (3) Implicit Portfolio Size multiplied by Lower Boundary, Subject to a maximum of the Principal Amount and a minimum of zero.
Non-determined Reference Entity	On any date, any Reference Entity in respect of which: (a) a Credit Event has occurred on or prior to, or (b) if a Potential Failure to Pay is Applicable, a Potential Failure to Pay exists on, that date and no Price Determination Date has occurred in respect thereof.
Implicit Credit Position	With respect to any Reference Entity means the Implicit Portfolio Size multiplied by the Credit Position
Accumulated Loss	Aggregate of all Triggered Reference Entity Losses
Triggered Reference Entity	Each Reference Entity in respect of which a Credit Event has occurred and a Final Price has been determined
Triggered Reference Entity Loss	With respect to any Triggered Reference Entity means: the Implicit Portfolio Size multiplied by the Credit Position multiplied by the Credit Swap Loss
Credit Swap Loss	The difference between 100% and the Final Price of the Reference Obligation of the Triggered Reference Entity, as determined by the Calculation Agent
Additional Interest Payment Loss	If any Non-determined Reference Entities exist on the Payment Observation Date relating to an Interest Payment Date, the Deferral Number of Business Days

	following the Price Determination Date in respect of each such Reference Entity.
Price Determination Date	In respect of a Reference Entity the date on which either (i) the Final Price is determined in relation to a Credit Event or (ii) if Potential Failure to Pay is Applicable, a Potential Failure to Pay has been cured
Payment Observation Date	The Observation Day Number of Business Days prior to each Interest Payment Date (including the Scheduled Maturity Date)
Redemption Amount	Provided no Early Redemption Event ("Credit Event") has occurred, the Notes will redeem on the Scheduled Maturity Date at the Interest Bearing Amount calculated as of the Payment Observation Date preceding the Scheduled Maturity Date (including in the Notional Reduction Amount the Implicit Credit Positions of all the Non-determined Reference Entities).

If on such day any Non-determined Reference Entities exist, then on the Additional Instalment Date in respect of any such Reference Entity, a further instalment of principal shall be payable, which shall equal:

1. The Interest Bearing Amount calculated in respect of the final Interest Payment Date on the Price Determination Date in respect of the relevant Reference Entity

Minus

2. Either (a) the Interest Bearing Amount calculated in respect of the final Interest Payment Date on the last preceding Price Determination Date in respect of another Reference Entity

that was a Non-determined Reference Entity on the Payment Observation Date or (b), if no such Price Determination Date has occurred, the Interest Bearing Amount calculated in respect of such last Interest Payment Date prior to the Scheduled Maturity Date, subject to a minimum of zero. Subject to a minimum of zero. Notwithstanding the foregoing, where on any Payment Observation Date on which no Non-determined Reference entities exist, the Interest Bearing Amount is zero, the Notes will redeem on the related Interest Payment Date and both the Redemption Amount and Interest Amount due on such day shall be zero.

Redemption following Early Redemption Events	Notwithstanding any other provision, if an Early Redemption Event (including default by the issuer of the Collateral Securities and tax events) occurs the Collateral Securities will be liquidated and the Notes will redeem on the Early Redemption Date at the Early Redemption Amount
The Early Redemption Amount	The liquidation proceeds of the Collateral Securities plus or minus the mark to market values of the Swap Agreement as determined by the Calculation Agent *For the avoidance of doubt, the mark to market value of the Swap Agreement shall take into account any amounts due to be paid to the Swap Counterparty as a result of the occurrence of one or more Credit Events*
Calculation Agent/ Swap Counterparty	XYZ Bank plc

135

Final Price	As As determined by the Calculation Agent, in accordance with the Valuation Method on the basis of the Relevant Quotations (exclusive of any accrued interest and expressed as a percentage) for the relevant Reference Obligation as determined on the Valuation Date by the Calculation Agent. Final Price may be determined after the Valuation Date as more fully described in the final documentation.
Potential Failure to Pay	Applicable
Valuation Method	Market
Valuation Time	Any time determined in the sole discretion of the Calculation Agent on the Valuation Date
Quotation Amount	Any amount not greater than the Credit Position multiplied by the Implicit Portfolio Size, as selected in the sole discretion of the Calculation Agent
Relevant Quotation	Bid
Additional Specified Currencies	None
Additional Public Sources	None
Denominations	EUR 50,000
Business Days	Target
Listing	Application for listing will be made to an EU exchange after the Issue Date
Rating	Yes
Governing Law	English

Selling Restrictions   Investors are required to inform
                                       themselves of, and comply with, the
                                       restrictions on sales of the Notes set out in
                                       the Programme Documents which include:
                                       US, UK and the jurisdiction of the Issuer

Defined terms

The terms of the Notes are based on the definitions and provisions contained
in the 2000 ISDA Definitions and the 2003 ISDA Credit Derivatives
Definitions as supplemented by the May 2003 Supplement (as published by
the International Swaps and Derivatives Association, Inc.) (the
"Definitions"), subject to amendment as set out herein and in the Credit
Provisions Annex (the "Credit Annex") attached. In the event of any
inconsistency between the Definitions, the Credit Annex and this termsheet,
this termsheet will govern.

Portfolio CLN Reference assets ("Schedule")

#	Reference entities	Credit positions	Benchmark Obligation	Applicable trading standards
1	3i GROUP PLC	2.00%		Europe
2	ACCOR	2.00%	Primary Obligor: ACCOR SA, Maturity: 5-Jul-2006, Coupon: 5.75, CUSIP/ISIN: FR0000486409, Original Issue Amount: EUR 800,000,000	Europe
3	ACOM CO LTD	2.00%	Primary Obligor: ACOM CO LTD, Maturity: 10-May-2010, Coupon: 2.56, CUSIP/ISIN: JP310860B055, Original Issue Amount: JPY 10,000,000,000	Japan
4	ADECCO SA	2.00%	Primary Obligor: ADECCO FINANCIAL SERVICE, Guarantor: ADECCO SA, Maturity: 15-Mar-2006, Coupon: 6 CUSIP/ISIN: XS0126005429, Original Issue Amount: EUR 400,000,000	Europe
5	AIFUL CORPORATION	2.00%	Primary Obligor: AIFUL CORPORATION, Maturity: 28-Jun-2010, Coupon: 2.93, CUSIP/ISIN: JP310504A069, Original Issue Amount: JPY 10,000,000,000	Japan
6	ALLIANZ AG	2.00%	Primary Obligor: ALLIANZ FINANCE II B.V., Guarantor: ALLIANZ AG, Maturity: 13-Jan-2025, Coupon: 6.5, CUSIP/ISIN: XS0159527505, Original Issue Amount: EUR 1,000,000,000	Europe
7	ALTRIA GROUP INC	2.00%	Primary Obligor: PHILIP MORRIS, Maturity: 15-Jan-2027, Coupon: 7.75, CUSIP/ISIN: US718154CF28, Original Issue Amount: USD 750,000,000	North America
8	AMBAC ASSURANCE CORPORATION	2.00%	Primary Obligor: LAFAYETTE SOVEREIGN CDO LTD, Maturity: 30-Oct-2011, Coupon: LIBOR06M + 0.54%, CUSIP/ISIN: 506759AA7, Original Issue Amount: USD 145,100,000	North American Monoline
9	AMERICAN EXPRESS COMPANY	2.00%	Primary Obligor: AMERICAN EXPRESS, Maturity: 12-Sep-2006, Coupon: 5.5, CUSIP/ISIN: US025816AN95, Original Issue Amount: USD 1,000,000,000	North America
10	AMERICAN INTERNATIONAL GROUP INCORPORATED	2.00%	Primary Obligor: AMERICAN INTL GROUP, Maturity: 9-Nov-2031, Coupon: 0, CUSIP/ISIN: US026874AP25, Original Issue Amount: USD 1,519,734,000	North America
11	ARROW ELECTRONICS INCORPORATED	2.00%	Primary Obligor: ARROW ELECTRONICS INCORPORATED, Maturity: 21-Feb-2021, Coupon: 0, CUSIP/ISIN: US042735AY61, Original Issue Amount: USD 1,523,750,000	North America
12	ARVINMERITOR INCORPORATED	2.00%	Primary Obligor: ARVINMERITOR, Maturity: 1-Mar-2012, Coupon: 8.75, CUSIP/ISIN: US043353AA92, Original Issue Amount: USD 400,000,000	North America

Reference assets ("Schedule")

#	Reference entities	Credit positions	Benchmark Obligation	Applicable trading standards
13	ASHLAND INCORPORATED	2.00%		North America
14	ASSICURAZIONI GENERALI SPA	2.00%	Primary Obligor: ASSICURAZIONI GENERALI SPA, Maturity: 20-Jul-2022, Coupon: 6.9, CUSIP/ISIN: XS0114165276, Original Issue Amount: EUR 750,000,000	Europe
15	AT&T WIRELESS SERVICES INCORPORATED	2.00%	Primary Obligor: AT&T WIRELESS SVCS INC, Maturity: 1-Mar-2011, Coupon: 7.875, CUSIP/ISIN: USU0027MAB38, Original Issue Amount: USD 3,000,000,000	North America
16	AVIVA PLC	2.00%	Primary Obligor: AVIVA PLC, Maturity: 14-Nov-2021, Coupon: 5.75, CUSIP/ISIN: XS0138717953, Original Issue Amount: EUR 800,000,000	Europe
17	AVNET INCORPORATED	2.00%	Primary Obligor: AVNET INCORPORATED, Maturity: 15-Feb-2005, Coupon: 7.875, CUSIP/ISIN: US053807AF07, Original Issue Amount: USD 360,000,000	Europe
18	AXA	2.00%	Primary Obligor: AXA, Maturity: 15-Dec-2020, Coupon: 6.75, CUSIP/ISIN: XS0122029548, Original Issue Amount: EUR 1,100,000,000	Europe
19	BANCO DI NAPOLI SPA	2.00%		Europe
20	BAYER AKTIENGESELLSCHAFT	2.00%	Primary Obligor: BAYER AG, Maturity: 10-Apr-2012, Coupon: 6, CUSIP/ISIN: XS0145758040, Original Issue Amount: EUR 2,000,000,000	Europe
21	BAYERISCHE HYPO-UND VEREINSBANK AG	2.00%	Primary Obligor: BAYER HYPO-VEREINSBANK, Maturity: 12-Oct-2010, Coupon: 6.625, CUSIP/ISIN: DE0001025856, Original Issue Amount: EUR 500,000,000	Europe
22	BAYERISCHE MOTOREN WERKE AG	2.00%	Primary Obligor: BMW FINANCE NV, Guarantor: BAYERISCHE MOTOREN WERKE AG, Maturity: 9-Jan-2006, Coupon: 5.25, CUSIP/ISIN: XS0124494708, Original Issue Amount: EUR 750,000,000	Europe
23	BOMBARDIER INC	2.00%	Primary Obligor: BOMBARDIER INC, Maturity: 1-May-2012, Coupon: 6.75, CUSIP/ISIN: US097751AG66, Original Issue Amount: USD 550,000,000	North America
24	BRISTOL-MYERS SQUIBB CO.	2.00%	Primary Obligor: BRISTOL-MYERS SQUIBB, Maturity: 1-Oct-2011, Coupon: 5.75, CUSIP/ISIN: US110122AG36, Original Issue Amount: USD 2,500,000,000	North America

Reference assets ("Schedule")

#	Reference entities	Credit positions	Benchmark Obligation	Applicable trading standards
25	BRITISH AMERICAN TOBACCO PLC	2.00%	Primary Obligor: BAT INTERNATIONAL FINANCE PLC, Guarantor: BRITISH AMERICAN TOBACCO PLC, Maturity: 25-Feb-2009, Coupon: 4.875, CUSIP/ISIN: XS0094703799, Original Issue Amount: EUR 1,700,000,000	Europe
26	CARNIVAL CORP	2.00%	Primary Obligor: CARNIVAL CORP, Maturity: 15-Apr-2008, Coupon: 6.15, CUSIP/ISIN: CCLLN 7 1/8 06/12, Original Issue Amount: USD 200,000,000	North America
27	CENTERPOINT ENERGY RESOURCES CORP	2.00%		North America
28	CIT GROUP INC	2.00%	Primary Obligor: CIT GROUP INC, Maturity: 2-Apr-2012, Coupon: 7.75, CUSIP/ISIN: US125581AB41, Original Issue Amount: USD 1,250,000,000	North America
29	CNA FINANCIAL CORPORATION	2.00%	Primary Obligor: CNA FINANCIAL CORP, Maturity: 15-Dec-2008, Coupon: 6.6, CUSIP/ISIN: US126117AK66, Original Issue Amount: USD 200,000,000	North America
30	COMMERZBANK AG	2.00%	Primary Obligor: COMMERZBANK AG, Maturity: 2-May-2011, Coupon: 6.125, CUSIP/ISIN: DE0006288921, Original Issue Amount: EUR 500,000,000	Europe
31	COMPAGNIE DE SAINT-GOBAIN	2.00%	Primary Obligor: SAINT-GOBAIN NEDERLAND B.V., Guarantor: COMPAGNIE DE SAINT-GOBAIN, Maturity: 7-Sep-2009, Coupon: 4.75, CUSIP/ISIN: FR0000494973, Original Issue Amount: EUR 1,000,000,000	Europe
32	COMPUTER ASSOCIATES INTERNATIONAL INC	2.00%	Primary Obligor: COMPUTER ASSOCIATES INTERNATIONAL INC, Maturity: 15-Apr-2008, Coupon: 6.5, CUSIP/ISIN: US204912AG49, Original Issue Amount: USD 350,000,000	Europe
33	CREDIT SUISSE FIRST BOSTON INTERNATIONAL	2.00%		North America
34	DAIMLERCHRYSLER AG	2.00%	Primary Obligor: DAIMLERCHRYSLER NORTH AMERICA HOLDING CORPORATION Guarantor: DAIMLERCHRYSLER AG, Maturity: 18-Jan-2011, Coupon: 7.75, CUSIP/ISIN: US233835AP25, Original Issue Amount: USD 1,500,000,000	Europe
35	DELPHI CORPORATION	2.00%	Primary Obligor: DELPHI CORPORATION, Maturity: 1-May-2009, Coupon: 6.5 CUSIP/ISIN: US247126AB11, Original Issue Amount: USD 500,000,000	North America

Reference assets ("Schedule")

#	Reference entities	Credit positions	Benchmark Obligation	Applicable trading standards
36	DEUTSCHE LUFTHANSA AG	2.00%	Primary Obligor: DEUTSCHE LUFTHANSA AG, Maturity: 25-Jul-2006, Coupon: 2.25, CUSIP/ISIN: XS0131446055, Original Issue Amount: EUR 250,000,000	Europe
37	DEUTSCHE TELEKOM AG	2.00%	Primary Obligor: DEUTSCHE TELEKOM INTERNATIONAL FINANCE BV, Guarantor: DEUTSCHE TELEKOM AG, Maturity: 20-May-2008, Coupon: 5.25, CUSIP/ISIN: DE0002317807, Original Issue Amount: EUR 2,000,000,000	Europe
38	DPL INC	2.00%	Primary Obligor: DPL INC, Maturity: 1-Sep-2011, Coupon: 6.875, CUSIP/ISIN: US233293AH20, Original Issue Amount: USD 400,000,000	North America
39	DUKE CAPITAL CORPORATION	2.00%	Primary Obligor: DUKE CAPITAL CORPORATION, Maturity: 1-Oct-2009, Coupon: 7.5, CUSIP/ISIN: 26439RAF3, Original Issue Amount: USD 500,000,000	North America
40	EASTMAN KODAK COMPANY	2.00%	Primary Obligor: EASTMAN KODAK CO, Maturity: 15-Nov-2013, Coupon: 7.25, CUSIP/ISIN: US277461BD00, Original Issue Amount: USD 500,000,000	North America
41	ELECTRONIC DATA SYSTEMS CORPORATION	2.00%	Primary Obligor: ELECTRONIC DATA SYSTEMS, Maturity: 15-Oct-2009, Coupon: 7.125, CUSIP/ISIN: US285659AE88, Original Issue Amount: USD 700,000,000	Norh America
42	EMI GROUP PLC	2.00%	Primary Obligor: CAPITAL RECORDS INC, Guarantor: EMI GROUP PLC, Maturity: 15-Aug-2009, Coupon: 8.375, CUSIP/ISIN: US14063RAB15, Original Issue Amount: USD 500,000,000	North America
43	EUROPEAN AERONAUTIC DEFENCE AND SPACE COMPANY EADS N.V.	2.00%	Primary Obligor: EADS FINANCE B.V., Guarantor: EADS NV, Maturity: 3-Mar-2010, Coupon: 4.625, CUSIP/ISIN: XS0163822488, Original Issue Amount: EUR 1,000,000,000	Europe
44	FEDERAL HOME LOAN MORTGAGE CORPORATION	2.00%		North America
45	FINANCIAL SECURITY ASSURANCE INCORPORATED	2.00%		North America Monoline
46	BRITISH AIRWAYS PLC	2.00%	Primary Obligor: British Airways plc Maturity 15 May 2008 Coupon: 7.25% ISIN XS02052365324	North America

Reference assets ("Schedule")

#	Reference entities	Credit positions	Benchmark Obligation	Applicable trading standards
47	FKI PLC	2.00%	Primary Obligor: FKI PLC, Maturity: 22-Feb-2010, Coupon: 6.625, CUSIP/ISIN: XS0107657222, Original Issue Amount: EUR 600,000,000	Europe
48	FORD MOTOR COMPANY	2.00%	Primary Obligor: FORD MOTOR COMPANY, Maturity: 16-Jul-1931, Coupon: 7.5, CUSIP/ISIN: US345370CA64, Original Issue Amount: USD 4,800,000,000	Europe
49	FORTIS NV	2.00%	Primary Obligor: FORTFINLUX S.A., Maturity: 5-Jul-2049, Coupon: FRN, CUSIP/ISIN: XS0147484314, Original Issue Amount: EUR 1,250,000,000	Europe
50	GATX FINANCIAL CORPORATION	2.00%		North America

In my life, why do I give valuable time,
To people who don't care if I live or die ... ?

— The Smiths, *Heaven Knows I'm Miserable Now*
(Rough Trade Records) 1984

4

Credit Derivatives: Basic Applications

As derivative instruments are over-the-counter contracts, credit derivatives are very flexible products with a wide range of applications. It was their introduction that enabled synthetic structured products to be developed, which are now a major part of the debt capital markets. In Part II of this book we look in detail at synthetic securitisation, in this chapter we present an overview of some basic applications.

Managing Credit Risk

Credit derivatives were introduced initially as tools to hedge credit risk exposure, by providing insurance against losses suffered due to "credit events". At market inception in 1994, commercial banks were using them to protect against losses on their corporate loan books. The principle behind credit derivatives is straightforward and this makes them useful equally for both protection buyers and sellers. For instance, while commercial banks were offloading their loan book risk, investors who may have previously been unable to gain exposure to this sector (because of the lack of a "market" in bank loans) could now take it on synthetically. The flexibility of credit derivatives provides users with a number of advantages precisely because they are OTC products and can be designed to meet specific user requirements.

We focus on credit derivatives as instruments that may be used to manage risk exposure inherent in a corporate or non-AAA sovereign bond portfolio. They may also be used to manage the credit risk of commercial loan books. The intense competition amongst commercial banks, combined with rapid disintermediation, has meant that banks have been forced to evaluate their lending policy, with a view to improving profitability and return on capital. The use of credit derivatives assists banks with restructuring their businesses, because they allow banks to repackage and transfer credit risk, while retaining assets on balance sheet (when required) and thus maintain client relationships. As the instruments isolate certain aspects of credit risk from the underlying loan or bond and transfer them to another entity, it becomes possible to separate the ownership and management of credit risk from the other features of ownership associated with the assets in question. This means that illiquid assets such as bank loans, and illiquid bonds, can have their credit risk exposures transferred and the bank owning the assets can protect against credit loss even if it cannot transfer the physical assets themselves.

The same principles apply to the credit risk exposures of portfolio managers. For fixed income portfolio managers, some of the advantages of credit derivatives include the following:

- they can be tailor-made to meet the specific requirements of the entity buying the risk protection, as opposed to the liquidity or term of the underlying reference asset;
- they can be "sold short" without risk of a liquidity or delivery squeeze, as it is a specific credit risk that is being traded. In the cash market it is not possible to "sell short" a bank loan for example, but a credit derivative can be used to establish synthetically the economic effect of such a position;
- as they theoretically isolate credit risk from other factors such as client relationships and interest rate risk, credit derivatives introduce a formal pricing mechanism to price credit issues only. This means a market can develop in credit only, allowing more efficient pricing, and it becomes possible to model a term structure of credit rates;
- they are off-balance sheet instruments[1] and as such incorporate tremendous flexibility and leverage, exactly like other financial derivatives. For example, bank loans are not particularly attractive investments for certain investors because of the administration required in managing and servicing a loan portfolio. However an exposure to bank loans and their associated return can be achieved by say, a total return swap while simultaneously avoiding the

---

[1] When credit derivatives are embedded in certain fixed income products, such as structured notes and credit-linked notes, they are then off-balance sheet, but part of a structure that may have on-balance sheet elements.

administrative costs of actually owning the assets. Hence credit derivatives allow investors access to specific credits while allowing banks access to further distribution for bank loan credit risk.

Thus credit derivatives can be an important instrument for bond portfolio managers as well as commercial banks, who wish to increase the liquidity of their portfolios, gain from the relative value arising from credit pricing anomalies, and enhance portfolio returns. Some key applications are summarised below.

Diversifying the credit portfolio

A bank or portfolio manager may wish to take on credit exposure by providing credit protection on assets that it already owns, in return for a fee. This enhances income on their portfolio. They may sell credit derivatives to enable non-financial counterparties to gain credit exposures, if these clients do not wish to purchase the assets directly. In this respect, the bank or asset manager performs a credit intermediation role.

Reducing credit exposure

A bank can reduce credit exposure either for an individual loan or a sectoral concentration, by buying a credit default swap. This may be desirable for assets in their portfolio that cannot be sold for client relationship or tax reasons. For fixed income managers, a particular asset or collection of assets may be viewed as favorable holdings in the long-term, but at risk from short-term downward price movements. In this instance, a sale would not fit in with long-term objectives, however short-term credit protection can be obtained via a credit swap.

Acting as a credit derivatives market maker

A financial entity may wish to set itself up as a market-maker in credit derivatives. In this case, it may or may not hold the reference assets directly, and depending on its appetite for risk and the liquidity of the market, it can offset derivative contracts as and when required.

Applications of Total Return Swaps

There are a number of reasons why portfolio managers may wish to enter into TRS arrangements. One of these is to reduce or remove credit risk. Using TRSs as a credit derivative instrument, a party can remove exposure to an asset without having to sell it. In a vanilla TRS, the total return payer retains rights to the reference asset, although in some cases servicing and voting rights may be transferred. The total return receiver gains an exposure to the reference asset without having to pay out the cash proceeds that would be required to purchase it. As the maturity of the swap rarely matches that of the asset, the swap receiver may gain from the positive funding or *carry* that derives from being able to roll over short-term funding of a longer-term asset.[2] The total return payer, on the other hand, benefits from protection against market and credit risk for a specified period of time, without having to liquidate the asset itself. On maturity of the swap, the total return payer may reinvest the asset if it continues to own it, or it may sell the asset in the open market. Thus the instrument may be considered a synthetic repo. A TRS agreement entered into as a credit derivative is a means by which banks can take on unfunded off-balance sheet credit exposure. Higher-rated banks that have access to LIBID funding can benefit by funding on-balance sheet assets that are credit protected through a credit derivative such as a TR swap, assuming the net spread of asset income over credit protection premium is positive.

A TRS conducted as a synthetic repo is usually undertaken to effect the temporary removal of assets from the balance sheet. This may be desired for a number of reasons, for example, if the institution is due to be analysed by credit rating agencies or if the annual external audit is due shortly. Another reason a bank may wish to temporarily remove lower credit-quality assets from its balance sheet is if it is in danger of breaching capital limits in between the quarterly return periods. In this case, as the return period approaches, lower quality assets may be removed from the balance sheet by means of a TR swap, which is set to mature after the return period has passed.

We look now at some more applications of TRS instruments.

Capital structure arbitrage

A capital structure arbitrage describes an arrangement whereby investors exploit mispricing between the yields received on two different loans by the same issuer. For example, assume that the reference entity has both a commercial bank loan and a subordinated bond issue outstanding, but that the former pays LIBOR plus 330 basis points, while the latter pays LIBOR

---

[2] This assumes a positively-sloping yield curve.

plus 230 basis points. An investor enters into a total return swap in which it effectively is purchasing the bank loan and selling short the bond. The nominal amounts will be at a ratio, for argument's sake let us say 2:1, as the bonds will be more price-sensitive to changes in credit status than the loans.

This trade is illustrated in Figure 4.1 The investor receives the "total return" on the bank loan, while simultaneously paying the return on the bond in addition to LIBOR plus 30 basis points, which is the price of the TR swap. The swap generates a net spread of 175 basis points, given by [(100 bps × 0.5) + (250 bps × 0.5)].

Figure 4.1   Total return swap in capital structure arbitrage.

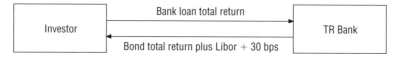

Synthetic repo

Total return swaps are increasingly used as synthetic repo instruments, most commonly by investors that wish to purchase the credit exposure of an asset without purchasing the asset itself. This is conceptually similar to what happened when interest rate swaps were introduced, which enabled banks and other financial institutions to trade interest rate risk without borrowing or lending cash funds.

Under a TRS, an asset such as a bond position may be removed from the balance sheet. As stated previously, a bank may use TRSs to reduce the amount of lower-quality assets on the balance sheet in order to avoid an adverse impact on regular internal and external capital and credit exposure reporting. This can be done by entering into a short-term TRS with say, a two-week term that straddles the reporting date. Bonds are removed from the balance sheet if they are part of a sale plus TRS transaction. This is because, legally, the bank selling the asset is not required to repurchase bonds from the swap counterparty, nor is the total return payer obliged to sell the bonds back to the counterparty (or indeed sell the bonds at all on maturity of the TRS).

Let us assume then, that a portfolio manager believes that a particular bond that it does not hold is about to decline in price. To reflect this view, the portfolio manager may do one of the following:

Sell the bond in the market and cover the resulting short position in repo: The cash flow out is the coupon on the bond, with capital gain if the bond falls in price. Assume that the repo rate is floating, say LIBOR plus a spread. The manager must be aware of the funding costs of the trade, so that unless the bond can be covered in repo at *general collateral* rates[3], the funding will be at a loss. The yield on the bond must also be lower than the LIBOR plus spread received in the repo.

As an alternative, enter into a TRS: the portfolio manager pays the total return on the bond and receives LIBOR plus a spread. If the bond yield exceeds the LIBOR spread, the funding will be negative, however the trade will gain if the trader's view is proved correct and the bond falls in price by a sufficient amount. If the breakeven funding cost (which the bond must exceed as it falls in value) is lower in the TR swap, this method will be used rather than the repo approach. This is more likely if the bond is special.

The TRS as off-balance sheet funding tool

The TRS may be used as a funding tool, as a means of securing off-balance sheet financing for assets held (for example) on a market making book. It is most commonly used in this capacity by broker-dealers and securities houses that have little or no access to unsecured or Libor-flat funding. When used for this purpose the TRS is similar to a repo transaction, although there are detail differences. Often a TRS approach is used instead of classic repo when the assets that require funding are less liquid or indeed not really tradeable. These can include lower-rated bonds, illiquid bonds such as certain ABS, MBS and CDO securities and assets such as hedge fund interests.

Bonds that are taken on by the TRS provider must be acceptable to it in terms of credit quality. If no independent price source is available the TRS provider may insist on pricing the assets itself.

As a funding tool the TRS is transacted as follows:

- the broker-dealer swaps out a bond or basket of bonds that it owns to the TRS counterparty (usually a bank), who pays the market price for the security or security;

---

[3] That is, the bond cannot be *special*. A bond is special when the repo rate payable on it is significantly (say, 20–30 basis points or more) below the *general collateral* repo rate, so that covering a short position in the bond entails paying a substantial funding premium.

- the maturity of the TRS can be for anything from one week to one year or even longer. For longer-dated contracts, a weekly or monthly re-set is usually employed, so that the TRS is re-priced and cashflows exchanged each week or month;
- the funds that are passed over by the TRS counterparty to the broker-dealer have the economic effect of being a loan to cover the financing of the underlying bonds. This loan is charged at Libor plus a spread;
- at the maturity of the TRS, the broker-dealer will owe interest on funds to the swap counterparty, while the swap counterparty will owe the market performance of the bonds to the broker-dealer if they have increased in price. The two cashflows are netted out;
- for a longer-dated TRS that is re-set at weekly or monthly intervals, the broker-dealer will owe the loan interest plus any decrease in basket value to the swap counterparty at the reset date. The swap counterparty will owe any increase in value.

By entering into this transaction the broker-dealer obtains Libor-based funding for a pool of assets it already owns, while the swap counterparty earns Libor plus a spread on funds that are in effect secured by a pool of assets. This transaction takes the original assets off the balance sheet of the broker-dealer during the term of the trade, which might also be desirable.

The broker-dealer can add or remove bonds from or to the basket at each re-set date. When this happens the swap counterparty re-values the basket and will hand over more funds or receive back funds as required. Bonds are removed from the basket if they have been sold by the broker-dealer, while new acquisitions can be funded by being placed in the TRS basket.

We illustrate a funding TRS trade using an example. Table 4.1 shows a portfolio of five hypothetical convertible bonds on the balance sheet of a broker-dealer. The spreadsheet also shows market prices. This portfolio has been swapped out to a TRS provider in a six-month, one-week re-set TRS contract. The TRS bank has paid over the combined market value of the portfolio at a lending rate of 1.141250%. This represents one-week Libor plus 7 basis points. We assume the broker-dealer usually funds at above this level, hence the attraction of this TRS contract.

We see from Table 4.2 that the portfolio has a current market value of USD 151,080,000. This value is lent to the broker-dealer in return for the bonds.

One week later the TRS is re-set. We see from Table 4.3 that the portfolio has increased in market value since the last re-set. Therefore the swap counterparty pays this difference over to the broker-dealer. This

Table 4.1 Spreadsheet showing basket of hypothetical bonds used in TRS funding trade.

Market Rates

EUR/USD FX Rate	1.266550
US$ 1W Libor	1.07125

Name	Currency	Nominal Value	Price	Accrued	Amount	FX Rate	ISIN/CUSIP Code	Market Price	Accrued Interest
ABC Telecom	EUR	16,000,000	111.671%	0.8169%	22,795,534.57	1.2666		111.6713875	0.8169989
XYZ Bank	USD	17,000,000	128.113%	1.7472%	22,076,259.03	1.0000		128.113125	1.7472222
XTC Utility	EUR	45,000,000	102.334%	0.3135%	58,845,000.00	1.2666		102.3337875	0.31352459
SPG Corporation	EUR	30,000,000	100.32500%		30,000,325.00	1.2666		100.325	0
Watty Exploited	USD	15,000,000	114.997%	0.7594%	17,363,503.13	1.0000		114.9973125	0.759375
					151,080,621.72				

Payments

Interest ($)

Rate	0.000000%
Principle	151,080,000.00

Interest Payable	+0.00

Performance ($)

New Portfolio Value	151,080,621.72
Old Portfolio Value	n/a
Performance Payment	n/a

Net Payment ($)

Broker-Dealer receives from swap counterparty	+0.00

New Loan

Portfolio Additions ($)	0.00	
New Loan Amount ($)	151,080,621.72	
New Interest Rate	1.141250%	1w Libor + 7 bps

Table 4.2 Spreadsheet showing basket of bonds at TRS re-set date plus performance and interest payments due from each TRS counterparty.

EUR/USD 1.2431

Bond	Curr	Nominal Value	Price	Accrued	Amount	FX	ISIN/CUSIP	Market Price	Accrued Interest
ABC Telecom	EUR	16,000,000	111.5000 %	0.78%	22,331,239	1.2431		111.5	0.77595628
XYZ Bank	USD	17,000,000	125.0000 %	1.58%	21,518,931	1		125	1.58194444
XTC Utility	EUR	45,000,000	113.0000000%	0.28%	63,369,825	1.2431		113	0.28278689
SPG Corporation	EUR	30,000,000	100.75		30,225,000	1.2431		100.75	
Watty Exploited	USD	15,000,000	113.0620 %	0.63%	17,053,518.2	1		113.0619965	0.628125
					154,498,511.95				

payments
interest
  rate   1.14125%   1W LIBOR + 7bps
  amount   151,080,000.00   151,113,526.12
interest payable **33,526.12**   interest payable by broker-dealer   old portfolio value: +151,080,951.67 US$
      interest rate: 1.14125%
      +33,526.33 US$

performance
  old portfolio value 151,080,000.00
  new portfolio value 154,498,511.95
performance payment **−3,418,511.95**

Swap ctpy pays − 3,384,985.83 [if negative, swap counterparty pays, if positive, broker-dealer pays] new portfolio value: +154,498,511 US$
      performance: 3,418,511 US$
      Net payment

new loan
  additions —
  new loan amount 154,498,511.95
  new interest rate 1.14875%

Table 4.3   TRS basket value after addition of new bond.

EUR/USD 1.228

Bond	Curr	Nominal Value	Price		Accrued	Amount	FX	ISIN/CUSIP	Market Price	Accrued Interest
ABC Telecom	EUR	16,000,000	111.5000	%	0.78%	22,331,239	1.2431		111.5	0.77595628
XYZ Bank	USD	17,000,000	125.0000	%	1.58%	21,518,931	1		125	1.5819444
XTC Utility	EUR	45,000,000	113.0000000%	%	0.28%	63,369,825	1.2431		113	0.28278689
SPG Corporation	EUR	30,000,000	100.75			30,225,000	1.2431		100.75	
Watty Exploited	USD	15,000,000	113.0620	%	0.00628125	17,053,518	1		113.061996	0.628125
Lloyd Cole Funding	USD	15,000,000	112.0923	%	0.57%	16,899,628.1	1		112.092313	0.571875
						171,398,140.07				

payments

interest		
rate	1.14875%	1W LIBOR + 7bps
amount	154,498,511.95	
interest payable	34,510.03	

performance

old portfolio value	154,498,511.95
new portfolio value	171,398,140.07
performance payment	−16,899,628.13

Swap ctpy pays | −16,865,118.09

new loan

additions	16,899,628.13
new loan amount	171,398,140.07
new interest rate	1.22750%

payment is netted out with the interest payment due from the broker-dealer to the swap counterparty. The interest payment is shown as USD 34,510.

Table 4.3 shows the basket after the addition of a new bonds, and the resultant change in portfolio value.

Applications for Portfolio Managers

Credit derivatives have allowed market participants to separate and disaggregate credit risk, and therefore to trade this risk in a secondary market.[4] Initially portfolio managers used them to reduce credit exposure, subsequently they have been used in the management of portfolios, to enhance portfolio yields and in the structuring of synthetic collateralised debt obligations. We summarise portfolio managers' main uses of credit derivatives below.

Enhancing portfolio returns

Asset managers can derive premium income by trading credit exposures in the form of derivatives issued with synthetic structured notes. The multi-tranching aspect of structured products enables specific credit exposures (credit spreads and outright default), and their expectations, to be sold to specific areas of demand. By using structured notes such as credit-linked notes, tied to the assets in the reference pool of the portfolio manager, the trading of credit exposures is crystallised as added yield on the asset manager's fixed income portfolio. In this way, the portfolio manager has enabled other market participants to gain an exposure to the credit risk of a pool of assets but not to any other aspects of the portfolio, and without the need to hold the physical assets themselves.

Reducing credit exposure

Let us consider a portfolio manager that holds a large portfolio of bonds issued by a particular sector (say, utilities) and they believe that spreads in this sector will widen in the short-term. Previously, in order to reduce its credit exposure, it would have to sell bonds, however this may crystallise a mark-to-market loss and may conflict with its long-term investment strategy. An alternative approach would be to enter into a credit default swap, purchasing protection for the short-term. If spreads do widen these swaps

---

[4] For example, see Satyajit Das, *Credit Derivatives and Credit Linked Notes*, (Singapore: John Wiley and Sons Ltd, 2000, 2nd edition, Chapters 2–4)

will increase in value and may be sold at a profit in the secondary market. Alternatively, the portfolio manager may enter into total return swaps on the desired credits. It pays the counterparty the total return on the reference assets, in return for Libor. This transfers the credit exposure of the bonds to the counterparty for the term of the swap, in return for the credit exposure of the counterparty.

Let us consider now the case of a portfolio manager wishing to mitigate credit risk from a growing portfolio (say, one that has just been launched). Figure 4.2 shows an example of an unhedged credit exposure to a hypothetical credit-risky portfolio. It illustrates the manager's expectation of credit risk building up to $250 million as the portfolio is built up, and then declining to a more stable level as the credits become more established. A three-year credit default swap entered into shortly after provides protection on half of the notional exposure, shown as the broken line. The net exposure to credit events has been reduced by a significant margin.

Figure 4.2   Reducing credit exposure.

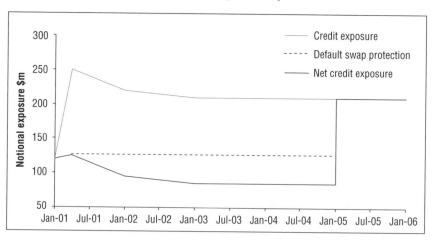

Credit switches and zero-cost credit exposure

Protection buyers utilising credit default swaps must pay premium in return for transferring their credit risk exposure. An alternative approach for an asset manager involves the use of credit switches for specific sectors of the portfolio. In a credit switch, the portfolio manager purchases credit protection on one reference asset or pool of assets, and simultaneously sells protection on another asset or pool of assets.[5] So for example, the portfolio manager would purchase protection for a particular fund and sell protection on another. Typically the entire transaction would be undertaken with one investment bank, which would price the structure so that the net cash flows would be zero. This has the effect of synthetically diversifying the credit exposure of the portfolio manager, enabling it to gain and/or reduce exposure to sectors it desires.

Exposure to market sectors

Investors can use credit derivatives to gain exposure to sectors for which they do not wish a cash market exposure. This can be achieved with an *index* swap, which is similar to a TRS, with one counterparty paying a total return that is linked to an external reference index. The other party pays a LIBOR-linked coupon or the total return of another index. Indices that are used may include the government bond index, a high-yield index or a technology stocks index. Assume that an investor believes that the bank loan market will outperform the mortgage-backed bond sector and in order to reflect this view the investor enters into an index swap in which they pay the total return of the mortgage index and receive the total return of the bank loan index.

Another possibility is synthetic exposure to foreign currency and money markets. Again we assume that an investor has a particular view on an emerging market currency. The investor can purchase a short-term (say one-year) domestic coupon-bearing note, with the principal redemption linked to a currency factor. This factor is based on the ratio of the spot value of the foreign currency on issue of the note to the value on maturity. Such currency-linked notes can also structured so that they provide an exposure to sovereign credit risk. The downside of currency-linked notes is that if the exchange rate goes the other way, the note will have a zero return, in effect a negative return once the investor's funding costs have been taken into account.

---

[5] A pool of assets would be concentrated on one sector, such as utility company bonds.

Credit spreads

Credit derivatives can be used to trade credit spreads. Let us assume that an investor has negative views on a certain emerging market government bond credit spread relative to UK gilts. The simplest way to reflect this view would be to go long a credit default swap on the sovereign, paying X basis points. Assuming that the investor's view is correct and the sovereign bonds decrease in price as their credit spread widens, the premium payable on the credit swap will increase. The investor's swap can then be sold into the market at this higher premium.

Walking down the street, feet beating the pavement,
Kingston looks dead in the dead-grey rain.
But I like the rain, this English day,
And I don't care, if no one else does....

— The New English, *This English Day*
(Jackfruit Music) 1986

5

Credit Derivatives Pricing and Valuation[1]

In this chapter we look at the various approaches used in the pricing and valuation of credit derivatives. We consider generic techniques and compare prices obtained using different pricing models. We also present an intuitive look at pricing to illustrate the basic concept behind pricing a credit default swap.

Introduction

The pricing of credit derivatives should aim to provide a 'fair value' for the credit derivative instrument. In the sections below, we discuss the pricing models currently used in the industry. The effective use of pricing models requires an understanding of the models' assumptions, the key pricing parameters and a clear understanding of the limitations of a pricing model. Issues to consider when carrying out credit derivative pricing include:

- Implementation and selection of appropriate modeling techniques;
- Parameter estimation;
- Quality and quantity of data to support parameters and calibration;
- Calibration to market instruments for risky debt.

For credit derivative contracts in which the payout is on credit events other than default, the modelling of the credit evolutionary path is critical. If, however, a credit derivative contract does not payout on intermediate stages between the current state and default, then the important factor is the

---

[1] This chapter was co-authored with Richard Pereira at Dresdner Kleinwort Wasserstein and Rod Pienaar at Deutsche Bank AG. The views and opinions contained herein represent those of the authors in their individual private capacity.

probability of default from the current state. An introduction to default probabilities is given at Appendix 5.6.

Before continuing with this chapter, you may wish to look at the section that discusses the asset swap pricing method, part of our discussion on the *basis*, in Chapter 8. This was commonly used at the inception of the credit derivatives market, but is rarely used today due to the inherent differences between asset swaps and other credit derivatives. In the following chapter, we look specifically at CDS pricing.

We now consider a number of pricing models as used in the credit derivative markets.

Pricing Models

Pricing models for credit derivatives fall into two classes:

- structural models and;
- reduced form models.

We discuss these models below.

Structural models

Structural models are characterised by modelling the firm's value in order to provide the probability of firm default. The Black-Scholes-Merton option pricing framework is the foundation of the structural model approach. The default event is assumed to occur when the firm's assets fall below the book value of the debt.

Merton applied option pricing techniques to the valuation of corporate debt.[2] By extension, the pricing of credit derivatives based on corporate debt may, in some circumstances, be treated as an option on debt (which is therefore analogous to an option on an option model).

Merton models have the following features:

- default events occur predictably when a firm has insufficient assets to pay its debt;
- a firm's assets evolve randomly. The probability of firm default is determined using the Black-Scholes-Merton option pricing theory.

Some practitioners argue that Merton models are more appropriate than reduced form models when pricing default swaps on high yield bonds, due

---

[2]   Merton, R. C., "On the pricing of corporate debt: the risk structure of interest rates", *Journal of Finance*, 1974, pp. 449–470.

to the higher correlation of high yield bonds with the underlying equity of the issuer firm.

The constraint of structural models is that the behavior of the value of assets and the parameters used to describe the process for the value of the firm's assets are not directly observable and the method does not consider the underlying market information for credit instruments.

Reduced form models

Reduced form models are a form of no-arbitrage model. These models can be fitted to the current term structure of risky bonds to generate no arbitrage prices. In this way, the pricing of credit derivatives using these models is consistent with the market data on the credit risky bonds traded in the market. These models allow the default process to be separated from the asset value and are more commonly used to price credit derivatives.

Some of the key features of reduced form models include:

- Complete and arbitrage-free credit market conditions are assumed;
- Recovery rate is an input into the pricing model;
- Credit spread data to estimate the risk neutral probabilities is used.
- Transition probabilities from credit agencies can be accommodated in some of these models. The formation of the risk neutral transition matrix from the historical transition matrix is a key step;
- Default can take place randomly over time and the default probability can be determined using the risk neutral transition matrix;

When implementing reduced form models it is necessary to consider issues such as the illiquidity of the underlying credit risky assets. Liquidity is often assumed to be present when we develop pricing models. However in practice there may be problems when calibrating a model to illiquid positions, and in such cases the resulting pricing framework may be unstable and provide the user with spurious results. Another issue is the relevance of using historical credit transition data, in order to project future credit migration probabilities. In practice it is worthwhile reviewing the sensitivity of price to the historical credit transition data when using the model.

The key reduced form models which provide a detailed modelling of default risk include those presented by Jarrow, Lando and Turnbull (1997),[3]

---

[3]   Jarrow, R., and Lando, D., "A Markov model for the term structure of credit spreads", *Review of Financial Studies*, Volume 10, 1997, pp. 481–523.

Das and Tufano (1996)[4] and Duffie and Singleton (1995).[5] We consider these models in this section.

Jarrow, Lando and Turnbull (JLT) model

This model focuses on modeling default and credit migration. Its data and assumptions include the use of:

- a statistical rating transition matrix which is based on historic data;
- risky bond prices from the market used in the calibration process;
- a constant recovery rate assumption. The recovery amount is assumed to be received at the maturity of the bond;
- a credit spread assumption for each rating level.

It also assumes that there is no correlation between interest rates and credit rating migration.

The statistical transition matrix is adjusted by calibrating the expected risky bond values to the market values for risky bonds. The adjusted matrix is referred to as the risk neutral transition matrix. The risk neutral transition matrix is key to the pricing of several credit derivatives.

The JLT model allows the pricing of default swaps, as the risk neutral transition matrix can be used to determine the probability of default. The JLT model is sensitive to the level of the recovery rate assumption and the statistical rating matrix. It has a number of advantages, as the model is based on credit migration, it allows the pricing of derivatives for which the payout depends on such credit migration. In addition, the default probability can be explicitly determined and may be used in the pricing of credit default swaps.

The disadvantages of the model include the fact that it depends on the selected historical transition matrix. The applicability of this matrix to future periods needs to be considered carefully, for example, whether or not it adequately describes future credit migration patterns. In addition, it assumes all securities with the same credit rating have the same spread, which is restrictive. For this reason, the spread levels chosen in the model are a key assumption in the pricing model. Finally, the constant recovery rate is another practical constraint, as in practice the level of recovery will vary.

---

[4]   Sanjiv Das and Peter Tufano: "Pricing Credit Sensitive Debt when Interest Rate, Credit Ratings and Credit Spreads Are Stochastic", *Journal of Financial Engineering*, 1996.
[5]   Duffie, D and K. Singleton: "Modelling Term Structures of Defaultable Bonds," Review of Financial Studies (1997).

The Das-Tufano model

The Das Tufano (DT) model is an extension of the JLT model. The model aims to produce the risk neutral transition matrix in a similar way to the JLT model, however this model uses stochastic recovery rates. The final risk neutral transition matrix should be computed from the observable term structures. The stochastic recovery rates introduce more variability in the spread volatility. Spreads are a function of factors that may not only be dependent on the rating level of the credit, as in practice credit spreads may change even though credit ratings have not changed. Therefore, to some extent, the DT model introduces this additional variability into the risk neutral transition matrix.

Various credit derivatives may be priced using this model. For example, credit default swaps, total return swaps and credit spread options. The pricing of these products requires the generation of the appropriate credit dependent cash flows at each node on a lattice of possible outcomes. The fair value may be determined by discounting the probability weighted cash flows. The probability of the outcomes is determined by reference to the risk neutral transition matrix.

The Duffie-Singleton model

The Duffie Singleton model approach considers the three components of risk for a credit risky product, namely the risk-free rate, the hazard rate and the recovery rate.

The *hazard rate* characterizes the instantaneous probability of default of the credit risky underlying exposure. As each of the components above may not be static over time, a pricing model may assume a process for each of these components of risk. The process may be implemented using a lattice approach for each component. The constraint on the lattice formation is that this lattice framework should agree to the market pricing of credit risky debt. Here we demonstrate that the credit spread is related to risk of default (as represented by the hazard rate) and the level of recovery of the bond. Let us assume that a zero-coupon risky bond maturing in a small time element Δt where

λ is the annualised hazard rate;
φ is the recovery value;
r is the risk free rate;
s is the credit spread.

and where its price P is given by:

$$P = e^{-r\Delta t} ((1 - \lambda \Delta t) + (\lambda \Delta t)\varphi).$$ (5.1)

Alternatively P may be expressed as:

$$P \cong e^{-\Delta t(r + \lambda(1 - \varphi))}$$ (5.2)

However as the usual form for a risky zero-coupon bond is:

$$P = e^{-\Delta t(r + s)}$$ (5.3)

Therefore we have shown that:

$$s \cong \lambda(1 - \varphi)$$ (5.4)

This implies that the credit spread is closely related to the hazard rate (that is, the likelihood of default) and the recovery rate.

This relationship between the credit spread, the hazard rate and recovery rate is intuitively appealing. The credit spread is perceived to be the extra yield (or return) that the investor requires for the credit risk assumed. For example:

- as the hazard rate (or instantaneous probability of default) rises, the credit spread increases; and
- as the recovery rate decreases, the credit spread increases.

A "hazard rate" function may be determined from the term structure of credit. The hazard rate function has its foundation in statistics and may be linked to the instantaneous default probability.

The hazard rate function ($\lambda(s)$) can then be used to derive a probability function for the survival function $S(t)$:

$$S(t) = \exp^{-\int_0^t \lambda(s)ds}$$ (5.5)

The hazard rate function may be determined by using the prices of risky bonds. The lattice for the evolution of the hazard rate should be consistent with the hazard rate function implied from market data. An issue when performing this calibration is the volume of relevant data available for the credit.

Recovery rates

The recovery rate usually takes the form of the percentage of the par value of the security recovered by the investor.

The key elements of the recovery rate include the:

- level of the recovery rate;
- uncertainty of the recovery rate based on current conditions specific to the reference credit;
- time interval between default and the recovery value being realized.

Generally, recovery rates are related to the seniority of the debt. Therefore if the seniority of debt changes, the recovery value of the debt may change. Also recovery rates exhibit significant volatility.

Credit Spread Modelling

Although spreads may be viewed as a function of default risk and recovery risk, spread models do not attempt to break down the spread into its default risk and recovery risk components.

The pricing of credit derivatives which payout according to the level of the credit spread require that the credit spread process is adequately modelled. In order to achieve this, a stochastic process for the distribution of outcomes for the credit spread is an important consideration.

An example of the stochastic process for modeling credit spreads, which may be assumed, includes a mean reverting process such as:

$$ds = k(\mu - s)dt + \sigma s dw \tag{5.6}$$

where

ds is the change in the value of the spread over an element of time (dt);
dt is the element of time over which the change in spread is modeled;
s is the credit spread;
k is the rate of mean reversion;
μ is the mean level of the spread;
dw is Wiener increment (sometimes written dW, dZ or dz);
σ is the volatility of the credit spread.

In this model, when s rises above a mean level of the spread, the drift term $(\mu - s)$ will become negative and the spread process will drift towards (revert) to the mean level. The rate of this drift towards the mean is dependent on k the rate of mean reversion.

The pricing of a European spread option requires the distribution of the credit spread at the maturity (T) of the option. The choice of model affects the probability assigned to each outcome. The mean reversion factor reflects the historic economic features overtime of credit spreads, to revert to the average spreads after larger than expected movements away from the average spread.

Therefore the European option price may be reflected as:

$$\text{Option price} = E[e^{-rT}(\text{Payoff}(s, X)] = e^{-rT} \int_0^\infty f(s, X)p(s)ds \quad (5.7)$$

where

X is the strike price of the spread option;

$p(s)$ is the probability function of the credit spread;

$E[\ ]$ denotes the expected value;

$f(s,X)$ is the payoff function at maturity of the credit spread.

More complex models for the credit spread process may take into account factors such as the term structure of credit and possible correlation between the spread process and the interest process.

The pricing of a spread option is dependent on the underlying process. For example, let us compare the pricing results for a spread option model including mean reversion to the pricing results from a standard Black-Scholes model in Tables 5.1 and 5.2 on the following page:

Table 5.1 Comparison of model results.

Expiry in 6 months Risk free rate = 10% Strike = 70bps Credit spread = 60bps Volatility = 20%	Mean reversion model price	Standard Black Scholes price	% difference between standard Black Scholes and mean revision model price
Mean level = 50 bps K = .2			
Put	0.4696	0.5524	17.63%
Call	10.9355	9.7663	11.97%
Mean level = 50 bps K = .3			
Put	0.3510	0.5524	57.79%
Call	11.2031	9.7663	14.12%
Mean level = 80 bps K = .2			
Put	0.8729	0.5524	58.02%
Call	8.4907	9.7663	15.02%
Mean level = 80 bps K = .3			
Put	0.8887	0.5524	60.87%
Call	7.5411	9.7663	29.51%

Table 5.2   Comparison of model results.

Expiry in 6 months Risk free rate = 10% Strike = 70bps Credit spread = 60bps Volatility = 20%	Mean reversion model price	Standard Black Scholes price	% difference between standard Black Scholes and mean revision model price
Mean level = 50bps *K = .2*			
Put	0.8501	1.4331	68.58%
Call	11.2952	10.4040	8.56%
Mean level = 50 bps *K = .3*			
Put	0.7624	1.4331	87.97%
Call	12.0504	10.4040	15.82%
Mean level = 80 bps *K = .2*			
Put	1.9876	1.4331	38.69%
Call	7.6776	10.4040	35.51%
Mean level = 80 bps *K = .3*			
Put	2.4198	1.4331	68.85%
Call	6.7290	10.4040	54.61%

Tables 5.1 and 5.2 illustrate the sensitivity of the pricing of a spread option to changes to the underlying process. Comparing Tables 5.1 to 5.2 illustrates the impact of time to expiry increasing by six months. In a mean reversion model, the mean level and the rate of mean reversion are important parameters which may significantly affect the probability distribution of outcomes for the credit spread, and hence the price.

Credit Spread Products

The forward credit spread

The forward credit spread can be determined by considering the spot prices for the risky security and risk-free benchmark security, while the forward yield can be derived from the forward price of these securities. The forward credit spread is the difference between the forward risky security yield and the forward yield on a risk free security. The forward credit spread is calculated by using yields to the forward date and the yield to the maturity of the risky assets.

Example 5.1 Determining the forward credit spread:

Current Date:	1/2/98
Forward Date:	1/8/98
Maturity:	1/8/06
Time period from current date to maturity:	8 years and 6 months
Time period from current date to forward date:	6 months

Yield to forward date:

Risk-free security	6.25%
Risky security	6.50%

Yield to maturity:

Risk-free security	7.80%
Risky security	8.20%

Forward yields (calculated from inputs above — see below for detail derivation)

Risk-free security	7.8976 %
Risky security	8.3071%

The details of the calculation of forward rates are:

Risk-free security: $(1.0780)^{8\,6/12} = (1.0625)^{6/12} * (1 + rf_{risk\,free})^8$

where

$rf_{risk/free}$ is the forward risk-free rate implied by the yields on a risk-free security. This equation implies that $rf_{risk/free}$ is 7.8976 %. Similarly for the risky security we have:

$$(1.082)^{8\,6/12} = (1.065)^{6/12} * (1 + rf_{risky})^8$$

where

rf_{risky} is the forward risky rate implied by the yields on a risky security. This equation implies that rf_{risky} is 8.3071%.

Therefore, the forward credit spread is the difference between the forward rate implied by the risky security less the forward rate implied by the yields on a risk-free security. In the example above, this is $rf_{risky} - rf_{risk\,free} = 8.3071 - 7.8976 = 0.4095\%$

> The current spread is equal to 8.20 − 7.80 = 0.40% = 40 bps. The difference between the forward credit spread and the current spread is 0.4095 − 0.40 = 0.0095% = 0.95 basis points.

The calculation of the forward credit spread is critical to the valuation of credit spread products. The payoff of spread forwards is highly sensitive to the implied forward credit spread.

Credit spread options

First generation pricing models for credit spread options may use models as described in the section on spread models. The key market parameters in a spread option model include the forward credit spread and the volatility of the credit spread.

The volatility of the credit spread is a difficult parameter to determine. It may be approached in different ways including:

- the historical volatility of the difference between the reference asset yield and the yield on a risk-free benchmark;
- estimation of the historical volatility by considering the components: historic volatility of the reference asset yield, historic volatility of the benchmark yield, correlation of the returns between the reference asset yield and the benchmark yield;
- the estimate of the volatility of the spread by using the implied volatility of the reference asset yield, implied volatility of the benchmark yield and a suitable forward looking estimate of the correlation between the returns on the reference asset yield and benchmark asset yield.

If the model incorporates mean reversion, then other key inputs include the mean reversion level and the rate of mean reversion. These inputs cannot be observed directly and the choice should be supported by the model developers and constantly reviewed to ensure that they remain relevant. Other inputs include:

- the strike price;
- the time to expiry and;
- the risk-free rate for discounting.

A key issue with credit spread options is ensuring that the pricing models used will calibrate to the market prices of credit risky reference assets. The recovery of forward prices of the reference asset is a constraint to the evolution of the credit spread. More complex spread models may allow for the correlation between the level of the credit spread and the interest rate level. The reduced form models described earlier are a new generation of credit derivative pricing models that are now increasingly being used to price spread options.

Asset swaps

Assume that an investor holds a bond and enters into an asset swap with a bank. The value of an asset swap is the spread the bank pays over or under LIBOR. This is based on the following components:

(i) the value of the coupons of the underlying asset compared to the market swap rate;

(ii) the accrued interest and the clean price premium or discount compared to par value. Thus when pricing the asset swap it is necessary to compare the par value and to the underlying bond price;

The spread above or below LIBOR reflects the credit spread difference between the bond and the swap rate.

The Bloomberg asset swap calculator pricing screens shown in Chapters 2 and 3 show these components in the analysis of the swapped spread details.

Example 5.2   Asset swap terms

Let us assume that we have a credit risky bond with the following details:

Currency:	EUR
Issue date:	31 March 2000
Maturity:	31 March 2007
Coupon:	5.5 % per annum
Price (Dirty):	105.3%
Price (Clean):	101.2%
Yield:	5%
Accrued interest:	4.1%
Rating:	A1

The investor pays 105.3% of par value to buy this bond and receives the fixed coupons of 5.5% of par value. Let us assume that the swap rate is 5%. The investor of this bond enters into an asset swap with a bank in which the investor pays the fixed coupon and receives LIBOR +/− spread.

The asset swap price (i.e. spread) on this bond has the following components:

(i) the value of the excess value of the fixed coupons over the market swap rate is paid to the investor. Let us assume that in this case this is approximately 0.5% when spread into payments over the life of the asset swap;

(ii) the difference between the bond price and par value is another factor in the pricing of an asset swap. In this case the price premium, which is expressed in present value terms, should be spread over the term of the swap and treated as a payment by the investor to the bank (if a dirty price is at a discount to the par value then the payment is made from the bank to the investor). For example, in this case let us assume that this results in a payment by the investor to the bank of approximately 0.23%, when spread over the term of the swap.

These two elements result in a net spread of 0.5% − 0.23% = 0.27%. Therefore the asset swap is quoted as LIBOR + 0.27% (or LIBOR plus 27 bps).

Total return swap (TRS) pricing

The present value of the two legs of the TRS should be equivalent. This implies that the level of the spread is dependent on the following factors:

- credit quality of the underlying asset;
- credit quality of the TRS counterparty;
- capital costs and target profit margins;
- funding costs of the TRS provider, as they will hedge the swap by holding the position in the underlying asset.

The fair value for the TRS will be the value of the spread for which the present value of the LIBOR +/− spread leg equals the present value of the returns on the underlying reference asset. The present value of the returns on the underlying reference asset may be determined by evolving the underlying reference asset. The expected value of the TRS payoff at maturity should be discounted to the valuation date.

The reduced form models described earlier are a new generation of credit derivative pricing models that are now increasingly being used to price total return swaps.

Anson *et al* (2004) present an intuitive and straightforward method of valuing TRS contracts, which we summarise with permission here.

Bearing in mind that the basic TRS is an instrument that swaps a regular Libor-based interest payment against the economic performance of an asset, we can set a formula for pricing the floating-leg Libor side, or rather, the spread over Libor paid on the floating leg. We use the following notation:

L_t is Libor at time t

s is the spread over Libor

R_t is the total return at time t

$L_t + s$ Cashflow payout by swap payer

Under risk-neutral pricing both legs of the contract must net-present-value to zero. That is, the spread payable under the TRS must be such that payoff from both legs of the contract must net to zero. Therefore, as stated in Anson (*ibid*) we can state

$$E_0\left\{\sum_{j=1}^{n}\exp\left(-\int_0^{T_j}r(t)dt\right)[R_j-(L_j+s)]\right\}=0 \qquad (5.1)$$

where r is the risk-free discount rate.

If we assume that r, R and L are three distinctly separate and random variables, we can re-arrange (5.1) above to give us

$$E_0\left\{\sum_{j=1}^{n}\exp\left(-\int_0^{T_j}r(t)dt\right)[R_j-L_j]\right\}=E_0\left\{\sum_{j=1}^{n}\exp\left(-\int_0^{T_j}r(t)dt\right)\right\}s \qquad (5.2)$$

which can be transformed into

$$E_0\left\{\sum_{j=1}^{n}\exp\left(-\int_0^{T_j}r(t)dt\right)\right\}=E_0\sum_{j=1}^{n}E_0\left[\exp\left(-\int_0^{T_j}r(t)dt\right)\right]=\sum_{j=1}^{n}P(0,T_j).$$

$$(5.3)$$

This expression gives the value of the sum of credit-risk-free zero-coupon bond prices. It therefore implies

$$E_0 \sum_{j=1}^{n} E_0 \left[\exp\left(-\int_0^{T_j} r(t)dt \right) R_j - L_j \right] = \sum_{j=1}^{n} P(0, T_j)s. \qquad (5.4)$$

From this we can simplify the left-hand side of (5.4) above to give us

$$\sum_{j=1}^{n} P(0, T_j)E_0^{Fj}[R_j - L_j] = \sum_{j=1}^{n} P(0, T_j)s. \qquad (5.5)$$

The left-hand side of the expression above can be used to obtain the forward price of an asset, and hence is used to generate forward curves for R the total return leg of the TRS as well as for L the Libor leg. This expression is

$$\sum_{j=1}^{n} P(0, T_j)[f_j^R - f_j^L] = \sum_{j=1}^{n} P(0, T_j)s.$$

where f_j^i is the forward rate of i with i being applicable to both R and L. Using this, we are now in a position to solve for the TRS spread s using the expression

$$s = \frac{\displaystyle\sum_{j=1}^{n} P(0, T_j)[f_j^R - f_j^L]}{\displaystyle\sum_{j=1}^{n} P(0, T_j)} \qquad (5.6)$$

In fact what the expression above is what we would have guessed intuitively from our knowledge of interest-rate swaps; the spread s is the weighted-average of the expected difference between the two legs. The weight is given by

$$\frac{P(0, T_j)}{\displaystyle\sum_{j=1}^{n} P(0, T_j)}$$

with the weights summing to one.

The reason the two legs in a TRS do not give identical cashflows and forward values is because of the perceived difference in credit risk of each leg (otherwise they would have the same value). It is the measure of this credit risk that is key to credit derivative valuation.

For a detailed coverage of the various model approaches used in determining the forward curves, see Anson (*ibid*), chapter 5.

Credit Curves

The credit curves (or default swap curves) reflect the term structure of spreads by maturity (or tenor) in the credit default swap markets. The shape of the credit curves are influenced by the demand and supply for credit protection in the credit default swaps market and reflect the credit quality of the reference entities (both specific and systematic risk). The changing levels of credit curves provide traders and arbitragers with the opportunity to measure relative value and establish credit positions.

In this way, any changes of shape and perceptions of the premium for CDS protection are reflected in the spreads observed in the market. In periods of extreme price volatility, for example as seen in the middle of 2002, the curves may invert to reflect the fact that the cost of protection for shorter-dated protection trades at wider levels than the longer- dated protection. This is consistent with the pricing theory for credit default swaps. The probability of survival of a credit may be viewed as a decreasing function against time. The survival probabilities for each traded reference credit can be derived from its credit curve. The survival probability is a decreasing function because it reflects the fact that the probability of survival of a credit reduces over time. For example, the probability of survival to year three is higher than the probability of survival to year five. Under non-volatile market conditions, the shape of the survival probability and the resulting credit curve assume a different form to the shape implied in volatile market conditions, that is the graphs may change to reflect the higher perceived likelihood of default.

For example, the shape of the survival probability may take the form as shown in Figure 5.1.

The corresponding credit curves that are consistent with these survival probabilities take the form shown in Figure 5.2.

This shows that the credit curve inversion is consistent with the changes in the survival probability functions.

In this analysis, we assumed that the assumed recovery rate for the "cheapest to deliver" bond remained the same at 35% of notional value.

Figure 5.1   Probability of survival of credit.

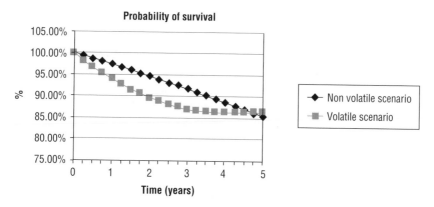

Figure 5.2   Credit curves corresponding to survival probabilities.

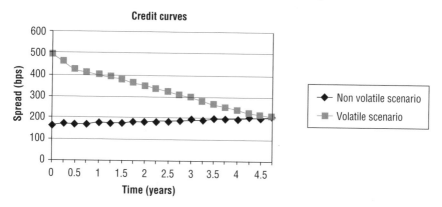

Bibliography

Anson, M., Fabozzi, F., Choudhry, M., Chen, R-R, *Credit Derivatives: Instruments, Applications and Pricing*, John Wiley 2004.

John C Hull, *Options, Futures and Other Derivaties*, Fifth edition, Prentice Hall.

J.C. Hull and A. White, "Valuing credit default swaps I:No counterparty default risk", *Journal of Derivatives*, 8 No.1 (Fall 2000) 29–40.

Appendix 5.1

Default Probabilities[6]

Default probabilities are one of the most important factors to take into account when pricing credit derivatives. What makes one credit derivative cheaper than the other (assuming constant maturity periods and recovery rates)? The answer is the default probability of the underlying reference asset. To understand how default probabilities affect the price of a say credit default swap let us use the following analogy. Let us say that one is currently residing in a financially risky country and has a certain amount of money placed in this countries' bank. As the investor is worried about the bank defaulting he wants to 'insure' his loan so that if a default happens he will receive the notional amount of the loan. If a potential 'insurer' is found he will be most interested in gauging what the chances of default are for the bank. The higher the default probability the higher the insurance premium. The same principle is found when pricing a credit default swap. The CDS seller is interested in estimating the default probability of the reference asset. The higher this probability will be the higher the premium demanded.

How does a CDS seller estimate the default probability of the reference asset?

The most common approach taken is to measure the difference between the risk-free rate (usually the risk free government benchmark yield or the Libor swap curve rate) and the risky rate which is taken either as the yield of the risky bond or the yield curve which the bonds credit rating and industry is mapped to. Once we have this available raw data we can use a number of analytical procedures to calculate default probabilities.

Figure A5.1   Default probabilities by calculating the expected default loss.

maturity	risk free zero	corp bond yield	expected default loss % of no default value
1	4.00%	4.25%	0.24969%
2	4.00%	4.50%	0.99502%
3	4.00%	4.70%	2.07810%
4	4.00%	4.85%	3.34285%
5	4.00%	4.95%	4.63895%

---

[6] This section was co-authored with Aaron Nematnejad when he was at Bloomberg L.P. in London. He is now with Daiwa USA. The views remain thosed of the authors in their individual private capacity.

The simplest method used to estimate default probabilities is the expected default loss method. The assumption here is that increased amount of the corporate bond yield from the yield of the risk free rate is due to the probability of default. Figure A5.1 shows displays a set of risk free rates as well as corporate bond risky rates for a term structure of five years.

Here the default probabilities are calculated by working out the percentage difference between the risky and the risk free discount factors. For example the value for maturity one year is obtained by

$$1\text{-exp(-(corp bond yield-risk fee yield)*time to maturity)}. \qquad (1)$$

Note that the probabilities above are cumulative.[2] To obtain marginal default probabilities between two points on the term structure, take one rate and minus from the other. For example the default probability between year 2 and 3 is 1.08309%.

The above analysis is however an unrealistic model for default probabilities. When bonds are defaulted they do not become worthless, rather there is a recovery rate associated with a bond depending the amount of assets that are recovered from the underlying reference entity of the bond. This recovery rate is conventionally defined by R. It represents the proportion of the face value of the bond which is recovered. We need to adjust equation (1) to take into account of this recovery rate in the following manner

$$\frac{[1-\exp(-(\text{corp bond yield} - \text{risk fee yield}) * \text{time to maturity})]}{1-R} \qquad (2)$$

Hull and White(2000) use a more sophisticated approach to modelling default probabilities. In their analysis they take into account the bonds face value and accrued interest. Hull and White also use coupon bearing bonds, which are easily observable to obtain default probabilities.

To understand this process we need to use Hull and Whites approach to of evaluating the cost of default. The PV of the cost of default is assigned as

$$\beta = v(t)[F(t) - R(t)C(t)]$$

---

[2] For a full derivation of how this formula is derived please see Hull (2002).

where $v(t)$ is the discount factor at time t, $F(t)$ is the forward price of a risk-free bond maturing at time t. $R(t)$ is the recovery rate of the risky bond at time t and $C(t)$ is the claim made by the holders of the bond. β is the present value from the loss of the bond. As there is a probability associated with β occurring the total present value of the jth bond is

$$G - B = \Sigma p\beta$$

where G is the price of a risk free bond, B is the price of the risky bond.

The above equation allows p to be derived inductively. Rearranging the formula we obtain

$$\frac{(G - B - \Sigma p\beta)}{\beta = p}$$

There is one other limitation in the above analysis. We assumed that default can only happen at maturity. To extend the analysis for default to happen any time up to the maturity

We set β = integral (between t(i) and t(i-1) (β = v(t)[F(t)-R(t)C(t)]) dt

Above we represented different methods of computing default probabilities, starting with the simplest case and ending with the most sophisticated. In practise all models are used in CDS pricing. The simplest case is used when practitioners manually calculate these values for a quick estimate. The Hull and White model is used when complex compuational process are available.

Jackie Wilson Said (I'm in Heaven When You Smile)

— Van Morrison

6

Credit Default Swap Pricing[1]

In this chapter, we concentrate specifically on the credit default swap (CDS), and a market approach for pricing these instruments. We consider the plain vanilla structure, in which a protection buyer pays a regular premium to a protection seller, up to the maturity date of the CDS, unless a credit event triggers termination of the CDS and a contingent payment from the protection seller to the protection buyer. If such a triggering event occurs, the protection buyer only pays a remaining fee for accrued protection from the last premium payment up the time of the credit event. The settlement of the CDS then follows a pre-specified procedure, which was discussed in Chapter 2.

Theoretical Pricing Approach

A default swap, like an interest rate swap, consists of two legs, one corresponding to the premium payments and the other to the contingent default payment. The present value (PV) of a default swap can be viewed as the algebraic sum of the present values of its two legs. The market premium is similar to an interest rate swap in that the premium makes the current aggregate PV equal to zero. That is, for a par interest rate swap, the theoretical net present value of the two legs must equal zero; the same principle applies for the two cash flow legs of a CDS.

---

[1] This chapter was co-authored with Abukar M Ali. The views and opinions expressed herein represent those of the authors in their individual private capacity.

The cash flows of a CDS are illustrated in Figure 6.1:

Figure 6.1   Illustration of cash flows in a default swap.

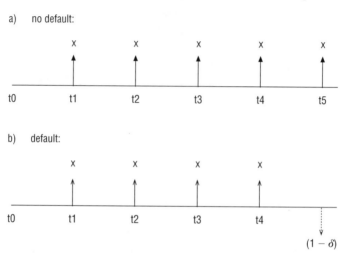

Normally, the default payment on a credit default swap will be $(1 - \delta)$ times its notional amount, where δ is defined as the recovery rate of the reference security. The reason for this payout is clear — it allows a risky asset to be transformed into a risk-free asset by purchasing default protection referenced to this credit. For example, if the expected recovery rate for a given reference asset is 30% of its face value, upon default the remaining 70% will be paid by the protection seller. Credit agencies such as Moody's provide recovery rate estimates for corporate bonds with different credit ratings using historical data.

The valuation of each leg of the cash flows is considered below. As these cash flows may terminate at an unknown time during the life of the deal, their values are computed in a probabilistic sense, using the discounted expected value as calculated under the risk neutral method and assumptions.

The theoretical pricing of credit derivatives has attracted some attention in academic literature, as we discussed in the previous chapter. Longstaff and Schwartz (1995) present the pricing of credit spread options based on an exogenous mean-reverting process for credit spreads. Duffie (1999) presents a simple argument for the replication of a simple reduced form model of the instrument. Here we introduce a reduced form-type pricing model developed by Hull and White (2000). Their approach was to calibrate their model based on the traded bonds of the underlying reference name on a time series of credit default swap prices.

Like most other approaches, their model assumes that there is no counterparty default risk. Default probabilities, interest rates and recovery rates are independent.

Finally, they also assume that the claim in the event of default is the face value plus accrued interest. Consider the valuation of a plain vanilla credit default swap with $1 notional principal. First, we introduce the notation below:

T : Life of credit default swap in years;

$q(t)$: Risk neutral probability density at time t;

R : Expected recovery rate on the reference obligation in a risk neutral world (independent of the time of default);

$u(t)$: Present value of payments at the rate of $1 per year on payment dates between time zero and time t;

$e(t)$: Present value of an accrual payment at time t equal to $t - t^*$ where t^* is the payment date immediately preceding time t;

$v(t)$: Present value of $1 received at time t;

w : Total payment per year made by credit default swap buyer;

s : Value of that causes the value of the credit default swap to have a value of zero;

π : The risk neutral probability of no credit event during the life of the swap;

$A(t)$: Accrued interest on the reference obligation at time t as a percent of face value.

The value π is one minus the probability that a credit event will occur by time T. This is also referred to as the *survival probability* and can be calculated from $q(t)$:

$$\pi = 1 - \int_0^T q(t)dt .\qquad(6.1)$$

The payments last until a credit event or until time T, whichever happens sooner. If default occurs at $t(t < T)$, the present value of the payment is $w[u(t) + e(t)]$. If there is no default prior to time T, the present value of the payment is $wu(T)$. The expected present value of the payment is, therefore:

$$w\int_0^T q(t)[u(t) + e(t)]dt + w\pi u(T) .\qquad(6.2)$$

Given the assumption about the claim amount, the risk neutral expected payoff from the credit default swap (CDS) contract is derived as follows:

$$1 - R[1 + A(t)] \text{ multiplying } -R \text{ by } [1 + A(t)]$$
$$1 - R[1 + A(t)] = 1 - R - A(t)R.$$

The present value of the expected payoff from the CDS is given as:

$$\int_0^T [1 - R - A(t)R]q(t)v(t)dt \tag{6.3}$$

The value of the credit default swap to the buyer is the present value of the expected payoff minus the present value of the payments made by the buyer, or:

$$\int_0^T [1 - R - A(t)R]q(t)v(t)dt - w\int_0^T q(t)[u(t) + e(t)]dt + w\pi u(T) \tag{6.4}$$

In equilibrium, the present value of each leg of the above equation should be equal. We can now calculate the credit default swap spread s which is the value of w that makes the equation equal to zero by simply rearranging the equation, as shown below:

$$s = \frac{\displaystyle\int_0^T [1 - R - A(t)R]q(t)v(t)dt}{\displaystyle\int_0^T q(t)[u(t) + e(t)]dt + \pi u(T)} \tag{6.5}$$

The variable s is referred to as the credit default swap spread or CDS spread.

The formula at (6.5) is simple and intuitive for developing an analytical approach for pricing credit default swaps because of the assumptions used. For example, the model assumes that interest rates and default events are independent; also, the possibility of counterparty default is ignored. The spread s is the payment per year, as a percentage of notional principal, for a newly issued credit default swap.

Market Approach

We now present a discrete form pricing approach that is used in the market, using market-observed parameter inputs.

We stated earlier, a CDS has two cash flow legs, the fee premium leg and the contingent cash flow leg. We wish to determine the par spread or premium of the CDS, remembering that for a par spread valuation — in accordance with no-arbitrage principles — the net present value of both legs must be equal to zero (that is, they have the same valuation).

The valuation of the fee leg is given by the following relationship:

PV of No-default fee payments = $s_N \times Annuity_N$

which is given by:

$$PV = s_N \sum_{i=1}^{N} DF_i \cdot PND_i \cdot A_i \qquad (6.6)$$

where

s_N is the par spread (CDS premium) for maturity N;
DF_i is the risk-free discount factor from time T_0 to time T_i;
PND_i is the no-default probability from T_0 to T_i;
A_i is the accrual period from T_{i-1} to T_i.

Note that the value for *PND* is for the specific reference entity for which a CDS is being priced.

If the accrual fee for the CDS is paid upon default and termination, then the valuation of the fee leg is given by the relationship:

PV of No-default fee payments + PV of Default accruals
= $s_N \times Annuity_N + s_N \times Default\ Accrual_N$

which is given by:

$$PV_{NoDefault+DefaultAccrual} = s_N \sum_{i=1}^{N} DF_i \cdot PND_i \cdot A_i + s_N \sum_{i=1}^{N} DF_i \cdot (PND_{i-1} - PND_i) \cdot \frac{A_i}{2}$$

$$(6.7)$$

where

$(PND_{i-1} - PND_i)$ is the probability of a credit event occurring during period T_{i-1} to T_i.

$\dfrac{A_i}{2}$ is the average accrual amount from T_{i-1} to T_i.

The valuation of the contingent leg is approximated by:

PV of Contingent $=$ Contingent$_N$

which is given by:

$$PV_{Contingent} = (1 - R) \sum_{i=1}^{N} DF_i \cdot (PND_{i-1} - PND_i) \tag{6.8}$$

where

R is the recovery rate of the reference obligation.

For a par credit default swap, we know that:

Valuation of fee leg $=$ Valuation of Contingent leg.

Therefore we can set:

$$s_N \sum_{i=1}^{N} DF_i \cdot PND_i \cdot A_i + s_N \sum_{i=1}^{N} DF_i \cdot (PND_{i-1} - PND_i) \cdot \frac{A_i}{2}$$

$$= 1 - R) \sum_{i=1}^{N} DF_i \cdot (PND_{i-1} - PND_i) \tag{6.9}$$

which may be rearranged to give us the formula for the CDS premium s as follows:

$$s_N = \frac{1 - R) \sum\limits_{i=1}^{N} DF_i \cdot (PND_{i-1} - PND_i)}{\sum\limits_{i=1}^{N} DF_i \cdot PND_i \cdot A_i + DF_i \cdot (PND_{i-1} - PND_i) \cdot \dfrac{A_i}{2}} \tag{6.10}$$

In Figure 6.2 we illustrate an application of the expression at (6.10) for a CDS of varying maturities, assuming a recovery rate of the defaulted reference asset of 30%, using actual/360 day-count convention. Default probabilities are taken from Moody's published data for the reference entity's credit rating group.

Figure 6.2   Example of CDS spread premium pricing.

Period	Yield %	DF_i	PN_i	Annuity$_N$	Default accrual$_N$	Contingent leg$_N$	s_N
0.5	2.33	0.9884	93.05%	0.47	0.008	0.048	988
1	2.52	0.9763	86.56%	0.901	0.016	0.093	998
1.5	2.87	0.9638	81.51%	1.3	0.022	0.127	945
2	3.22	0.9478	77.30%	1.673	0.028	0.155	896
2.5	3.52	0.9317	74.32%	2.024	0.032	0.175	837
3	3.82	0.9144	71.45%	2.355	0.036	0.193	794
3.5	4.02	0.8964	69.90%	2.672	0.038	0.203	737
4	4.22	0.8779	68.37%	2.975	0.040	0.213	695
4.5	4.37	0.8591	68.06%	3.269	0.040	0.215	639
5	4.52	0.8407	67.76%	3.555	0.040	0.217	594

Source: Author notes.

Market Illustration

By way of example, we see in Figure 6.3 that the mid-market value of s for the Daimler-Chrysler name as at October 2002, for a five-year CDS was 148/158 basis points, or 0.0148/0.0158 (bid and ask) per dollar of principal value, as at October 2002.

Figure 6.3   Credit default swap quotes for US and European auto-maker reference credits.

Credit	Rating	Autos & transport — 5 year protection		
		Bid	Ask	Change
BMW	A1/NR	38	48	2
DaimlerChrysler	A3/BBB1	148	158	24.5
Fiat	NR/NR	675	775	25
Renault	Baa2/BBB	100	115	2.5
Volvo	A3*2/NR	72	82	2
VW	A1/A1	68	78	0

Source: Bloomberg LP.

The implementation of the above pricing methodology is frequently carried out by market participants using the Bloomberg credit default swap analytics page, which is accessed on Bloomberg by typing:

[Ticker] [Coupon] [maturity year] [CORP] CDSW <go>.

Figure 6.4 shows the CDSW page using the modified Hull and White model, with certain default parameter inputs, as selected for the Daimler-Benz five-year CDS, as at October 2002. This implementation links the rates observed in the credit protection market and the corporate bond market, via probabilities of default of the issuer. The input used to price the CDS contract is selected from a range of market-observed yield curves, and includes:

- a curve of CDS spreads;
- an issuer (credit-risky) par yield curve;
- a default probability curve (derived from the default probabilities of the underlying reference for each maturity implied by the par credit default swap spreads).

Figure 6.4   Bloomberg page CDSW using modified Hull-White pricing on selected Credit Default Swap.

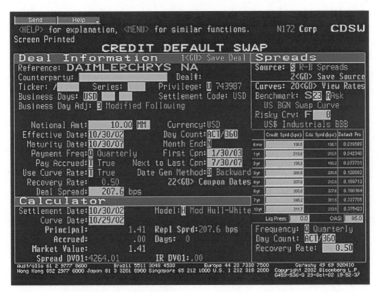

© Bloomberg L.P. Used with permission.

The assumptions based on the independence of recovery rates, default probabilities, and interest rates may not hold completely in practice, since high interest rates may cause companies to experience financial difficulties and default or administration. As a result, default probabilities will increase. Therefore, a positive relationship between interest rates and default probabilities may be associated with high discount rates for the CDS payoffs. This has the effect of reducing the credit default swap spread.

Nevertheless, the modified Hull-White approach presents a neat and intuitive approach that allows for a closed-form pricing approach for credit default swaps, using parameter inputs from the market.

Description of Bloomberg screen CDSW[2]

Screen CDSW on Bloomberg, shown in Figure 6.4, is an implementation of the procedure for pricing a CDS described in Hull and White (2000). The input used in the model to price the CDS contract is one of the three described above. The Bloomberg implementation links the market in CDS prices and the cash bond market with issuer default probabilities.

To calculate the present value of the CDS fee leg (premium leg), the Bloomberg system uses the curve of probabilities of default of the reference entity. To calculate the expected present value of the CDS contingent leg, it also requires an assumption on the payoff in the case of default, for this it uses [(par − R) + Accrued], where R is the recovery rate. The theoretical value of the CDS is then the difference in the expected present values of the two legs.

Calculating the default probability default curve

Given a curve of par CDS spreads (spreads of CDSs's of various maturities, each with a net present value of zero), the system calculates an implied default probability curve by using a bootstrap procedure. Thus, it finds a default probability curve, such that all given CDS contracts have a zero value. An alternative procedure is, given a curve of risky par coupon rates (bond yields), the system calculates the default probability curve implied by this curve, again using a bootstrap process. The assumption is made that in the case of default of a bond, its value drops to a fraction R of par.

---

[2] This section summarises (with permission) the notes behind Bloomberg page CDSW.

Calculating an implied issuer par coupon curve (the "risky curve")

If a default probability curve is known, the system can compute a corresponding curve of par coupon rates, corresponding to the size of the coupons an issuer of bonds will have to pay, in order to compensate investors for the default risk they are taking on. In other words, given one of the following curves, the system transforms it into the other two curves:

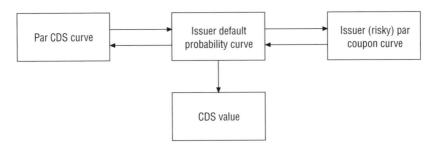

Liquidity premium

The observed spread between an issuer par curve and the risk-free par curve reflects a liquidity premium as well as default risk. The Liquidity Premium field is a flat spread and selected measure of liquidity. This spread is deducted from the spread between the risky and the risk-free curves before calculation of the default probabilities. A market convention for the liquidity premium is the spread between AAA rates and the interbank swap rate. This spread is generally within a 0 to 25 basis point magnitude. The screen defaults to 0 bps.

Issuer spread-to-fair value

The Bloomberg system assigns a relevant fair market curve to each bond in accordance with its currency, industry sector and credit rating (for example, USD A-rated utilities). It also assigns an option-adjusted spread to each issuer, so that the default probability analysis becomes issuer-specific rather than industry specific.[3]

---

[3] See Choudhry (2001) for more information on option-adjusted spreads.

The Bloomberg generic CDS price page[4]

Chapter 2 illustrated examples of CDS price pages that are contributed by individual market-making banks. The Bloomberg system also has a generic pricing page that makes use of all contributors' prices to present a CDS pricing curve for any selected market. The main menu screen is CDSD, shown at Figure 6.5. From this page, we select a market sector and reference entity. For example, we select "Communications" and then Telefonica SA, a telecommunications company. We then select three specific price providers (if none are available a default "generic" contributor will apply), as shown at Figure 6.6. By then selecting <GO> we see the generic curve for this company, shown at Figure 6.7.

The CDSD menu also enables users to select a range of reference names within a market sector, so that CDS prices can be compared. The menu page for this is shown at Figure 6.8.

Figure 6.5   Bloomberg screen CDSD, menu page for generic CDS prices, as at July 2003.

<HELP> for explanation, <MENU> for similar functions.   N219 Curncy **CDSD**

CREDIT DEFAULT SWAP SPREAD CURVES

Enter the corporate ticker, currency and debt type to search.
Corporate Ticker:▮▮▮   Currency:▮▮   Debt Type:▮   99) Search

MARKET SECTOR

1) Basic Materials	7) Financial
2) Communications	8) Government
3) Consumer, Cyclical	9) Industrial
4) Consumer, Non-cyclical	10) Technology
5) Diversified	11) Utilities
6) Energy	

12) **CDS Indices**

13) Custom Curves
14) User Defaults
15) Pricing Source Defaults
16) Supported References / CDS Curves
17) Supported CDS Tickers
18) Contributed Curve by CDS Ticker

Australia 61 2 9777 8600   Brazil 5511 3048 4500   Europe 44 20 7330 7500   Germany 49 69 920410
Hong Kong 852 2977 6000 Japan 81 3 3201 8900 Singapore 65 6212 1000 U.S. 1 212 318 2000 Copyright 2004 Bloomberg L.P.
G926-802-3 14-Apr-04 14:35:46

© Bloomberg L.P. Used with permission.

---

[4]   The author would like to thank Peter Jones at Bloomberg L.P for his assistance with this section.

Figure 6.6   Bloomberg screen CDSD, search results.

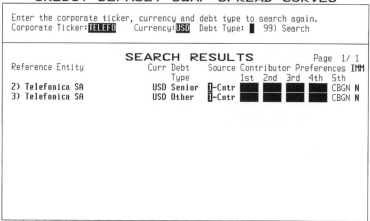

<HELP> for explanation.   N219 **Curncy** **CDSD**
1<GO> to update, <Menu> to return
CREDIT DEFAULT SWAP SPREAD CURVES

Enter the corporate ticker, currency and debt type to search again.
Corporate Ticker:`TELEFO`   Currency:`USD` Debt Type: ▮ 99) Search

	SEARCH RESULTS			Page 1/ 1
Reference Entity	Curr Debt	Source Contributor Preferences **IMM**		
	Type	1st 2nd 3rd 4th 5th		
2) Telefonica SA	USD Senior	▮-Cntr ▮ ▮ ▮ ▮	CBGN	N
3) Telefonica SA	USD Other	▮-Cntr ▮ ▮ ▮ ▮	CBGN	N

Australia 61 2 9777 8600   Brazil 5511 3048 4500   Europe 44 20 7330 7500   Germany 49 69 920410
Hong Kong 852 2977 6000 Japan 81 3 3201 8900 Singapore 65 6212 1000 U.S. 1 212 318 2000 Copyright 2004 Bloomberg L.P.
                                                             G926-802-3 14-Apr-04 14:37:23

© Bloomberg L.P. Used with permission.

Figure 6.7   Bloomberg screen CDSD, contributed CDS spreads for
Telefonica SA reference entity, as at July 2003.

<HELP> for explanation.   N219 **Curncy** **CDSD**
1<GO> to save source and contributors, <Menu> to return
CONTRIBUTED CDS SPREADS

Enter the corporate ticker, currency and debt type to search again.
Corporate Ticker:`TELEFO`   Currency:`USD` Debt Type: ▮ 99) Search

▮ Contributed Par CDS Spreads

	Term	Ticker	Contributor	Bid	Ask	Update
				(bps)		Time
2)	6 mo		*	40.00	45.50	
3)	1 yr	CTLFO1U1	*	40.00	45.50	
4)	2 yr		*	40.00	45.50	
5)	3 yr	CTLFO1U3	*	40.00	45.50	
6)	4 yr		*	40.00	45.50	
7)	5 yr	CTLFO1U5	CBGN	40.00	45.50	4/ 8 Day Count: ACT/360
8)	7 yr		*	40.00	45.50	Frequency: Q
9)	10 yr		*	40.00	45.50	Recovery Rate: 0.40

* Piecewise linear, Flat extrapolation

Contributor Preferences: ▮ ▮ ▮ ▮ CBGN

Australia 61 2 9777 8600   Brazil 5511 3048 4500   Europe 44 20 7330 7500   Germany 49 69 920410
Hong Kong 852 2977 6000 Japan 81 3 3201 8900 Singapore 65 6212 1000 U.S. 1 212 318 2000 Copyright 2004 Bloomberg L.P.
                                                             G926-802-3 14-Apr-04 14:39:05

© Bloomberg L.P. Used with permission.

Figure 6.8   Bloomberg screen CDSD, CDS spread curves menu page for banking sector.

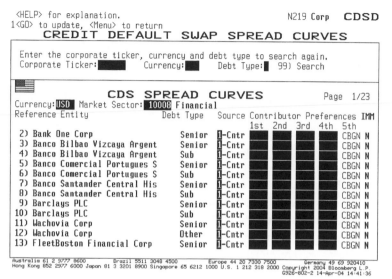

<HELP> for explanation.   N219 Corp   **CDSD**
1<GO> to update, <Menu> to return
    CREDIT DEFAULT SWAP SPREAD CURVES

Enter the corporate ticker, currency and debt type to search again.
Corporate Ticker:▓▓▓▓▓   Currency:▓▓   Debt Type:▓ 99) Search

            CDS SPREAD CURVES   Page 1/23
Currency:USD Market Sector: 10008 Financial
Reference Entity   Debt Type   Source Contributor Preferences IMM
                                                1st 2nd 3rd 4th 5th
  2) Bank One Corp   Senior ▯-Cntr   CBGN N
  3) Banco Bilbao Vizcaya Argent Senior ▯-Cntr   CBGN N
  4) Banco Bilbao Vizcaya Argent Sub   ▯-Cntr   CBGN N
  5) Banco Comercial Portugues S Senior ▯-Cntr   CBGN N
  6) Banco Comercial Portugues S Sub   ▯-Cntr   CBGN N
  7) Banco Santander Central His Senior ▯-Cntr   CBGN N
  8) Banco Santander Central His Sub   ▯-Cntr   CBGN N
  9) Barclays PLC   Senior ▯-Cntr   CBGN N
 10) Barclays PLC   Sub   ▯-Cntr   CBGN N
 11) Wachovia Corp   Senior ▯-Cntr   CBGN N
 12) Wachovia Corp   Other   ▯-Cntr   CBGN N
 13) FleetBoston Financial Corp   Senior ▯-Cntr   CBGN N

Australia 61 2 9777 8600   Brazil 5511 3048 4500   Europe 44 20 7330 7500   Germany 49 69 920410
Hong Kong 852 2977 6000 Japan 81 3 3201 8900 Singapore 65 6212 1000 U.S. 1 212 318 2000 Copyright 2004 Bloomberg L.P.
                                                          G926-802-2 14-Apr-04 14:41:36

© Bloomberg L.P. Used with permission.

Equity Default Swap Valuation

We introduced equity default swaps in Chapter 2. In this section, we describe an approach to pricing them. As we have already discussed, the key difference between an EDS and a CDS is that instead of a "credit event", the former incorporates a trigger event that applies if the reference stock falls in price by a pre-specified percentage amount. In our example in Chapter 2, we used a 50% sell-off level. Hence, the key to valuing the EDS in our example is our view of how likely it is for the reference entity to fall in price by 50%. One possible approach is to look at historical data on the stock in determining this likelihood. Another approach is an implied equity event probability. We introduce these concepts in the next section.

Historical equity event probability

A logical way to approach the pricing of an EDS is to consider the reference stock price movement in the past, and use this analysis to determine an equity event probability. As an example, let us use an un-named corporate entity, which we shall call XYZ plc, and chart its share price from 1993. For each day from 1993 to 2003, we plot the end-of-day closing price as the reference price and then check to see if during the next three years the stock price closed at or below 50% of the reference price. We use three years because this is the term of our example EDS. (We can conduct the check for whatever period the EDS has been contracted for.) For starting dates during the last three years, we consider the price history from the starting date up to the current date.

Figure 6.9 shows the historical data for XYZ plc, with the distribution of three-year prices. We show the distribution of the lowest stock price of each of the three-year periods, expressed as a percentage of the starting price. Using actual prices for XYZ plc, the greatest amount the stock sold off over any three-year period was 47%. At no time during our ten-year period did the stock sell off to 50% of its starting price within three years. So an EDS written with a 50% equity event would not have been triggered at any time during the ten-year period we examined. From this analysis then, the historical equity event probability is 0%.

As long as we are prepared to accept the limitations of using historical data as an input to valuation, we have an equity event probability that we can use and compare to the CDS prices, which are often calculated from default probabilities obtained using default rates.

Figure 6.9   XYZ plc: distribution of three-year price minima.

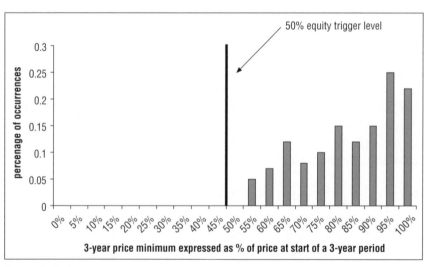

Source: Author's notes.

Implied equity event probability

An approximate market probability of an EDS equity event occurring is given by:

$$\text{Implied Probability} \cong \frac{\text{EDS Spread} \times \text{Number of Years}}{100\% - R} \qquad (6.11)$$

where R is the recovery rate as before but in the special pre-set case used for EDS contracts.

This calculation divides the amount paid by the protection buyer, assuming the swap runs to term, by the amount paid by the protection seller on occurrence of the equity event. From the values shown in our British Aerospace plc example (Example 2.3 in Chapter 2), which was a three-year EDS trading at 240 bps, with a 30% recovery rate, we have:

$$\text{Implied Probability} \cong \frac{2.40\% \times 3}{70\%} = 10.3\%$$

In other words, from this EDS price, we can see that the market estimates a 10.3% chance that BAE plc stock will reach 50% of its current level within the next three years. An investor who disagreed with this view, for example, if they thought the real probability was lower, could sell EDS protection to earn a yield pick-up. An investor with the opposite view may buy protection using the EDS contract at this price.

References and Bibliography

Choudhry, Moorad, *The Bond and Money Markets: Strategy, Trading, Analysis*, Butterworth-Heinemann 2001.

Choudhry, Moorad, "Some Issues in the Asset-Swap Pricing of Credit Default Swaps," in Fabozzi, F., (editor), *Professional Perspectives on Fixed Income Portfolio Management*, volume 4, New York: John Wiley and Sons 2003.

Duffie, D., and M. Huang, "Swap Rates and Credit Quality," *Journal of Finance*, 51, No. 3 (July 1996).

Hogg, R. and A. Craig, 1970, *Introduction to Mathematical Statistics*, 3rd edition, New York: Macmillan.

J. Hull and A. White, "Valuing Credit Default Swaps I: No Counter-party Default Risk," *Journal of Derivatives*, 8 (1), Fall 2000.

Jarrow, R.A., and S.M. Turnbull, "Pricing Options on Derivative Securities Subject to Credit Risk," *Journal of Finance*, 50 (1995), 53–58.

Melchiori, M., "Credit Derivative Models: Which Archimedean Copula is the right one?", *YieldCurve.Com*, October 2003.

Yekutieli, Iddo. "With Bond Stripping, the Curve's the Thing," Internal Bloomberg report (1999).

Don't get lost in all that Stock Exchange stuff … keep the faith, the bass guitar and the Fred Perry.

— Phil Broadhurst, *The Mighty Utterance* 1989

7

The Asset Swap – Credit Default Swap Basis I: the asset-swap pricing of credit default swaps[1]

Introduction

As discussed in Chapter 2, asset swaps, although pre-dating the credit derivative market, are viewed as a form of credit derivative. They are viewed as cash market instruments. However because an asset swap is a structure that explicitly prices a credit-risky bond in terms of its spread over Libor (inter-bank credit risk), it can be viewed as a means by which to price credit derivatives. In fact in the early days of the credit derivatives market, the most common method of pricing credit default swaps was by recourse to the asset swap spread of the reference credit, as the credit default swap premium should (in theory) be equal to the asset swap spread of the reference asset. Therefore we can say that the asset swap provides an indicator of the minimum returns that would be required for specific reference credits, as well as a mark-to-market reference. It is also a hedging tool for a CDS position.

We first consider the use of this technique, before observing how these two spread levels differ. The next chapter will look in detail at the factors that cause this difference in spread, which is known as the *credit default swap basis*.

---

[1] This chapter is a slightly modified version of what first appeared in Choudhry (2001).

Asset Swap Pricing

Basic concept

Credit derivatives are sometimes valued using the asset swap pricing technique. The asset swap market is a reasonably reliable indicator of the returns required for individual credit exposures, and provides a mark-to-market framework for reference assets as well as a hedging mechanism. As we saw in Chapter 2, a par asset swap typically combines the sale of an asset such as a fixed-rate corporate bond to a counterparty, at par and with no interest accrued, with an interest rate swap. The coupon on the bond is paid in return for Libor, plus a spread if necessary. This spread is the asset swap spread and is the price of the asset swap. In effect, the asset swap allows market participants that pay Libor-based funding to receive the asset-swap spread. This spread is a function of the credit risk of the underlying bond asset, which is why it may be viewed as equivalent to the price payable on a credit default swap written on that asset.

The generic pricing is given by:

$$Y_a = Y_b - ir$$

where

Y_a is the asset swap spread;
Y_b is the asset spread over the benchmark;
ir is the interest rate swap spread.

The asset spread over the benchmark is the bond (asset) redemption yield over that of the government benchmark. The interest rate swap spread reflects the cost involved in converting fixed-coupon benchmark bonds into a floating-rate coupon during the life of the asset (or default swap), and is based on the swap rate for that maturity.

The theoretical basis for deriving a default swap price from the asset swap rate can be illustrated by looking at a basis-type trade involving a cash market reference asset (bond) and a default swap written on this bond. This is similar in concept to the risk-neutral or *no-arbitrage* concept used in derivatives pricing. The theoretical trade involves:

* a long position in the cash market floating-rate note (FRN) priced at par, which pays a coupon of Libor + X basis points;

- a short position (bought protection) in a default swap written on the same FRN, of identical term to maturity and at a cost of Y basis points;

Assume that the buyer of the bond is able to fund the position at LIBOR. In other words, the bondholder has the following net cash flow:

$$(100 - 100) + [(\text{Libor} + X) - (\text{Libor} + Y)]$$

or $X - Y$ basis points.

In the event of default, the bond is delivered to the protection seller in return for payment of par, enabling the bondholder to close out the funding position. During the term of the trade, the bondholder has earned $X - Y$ basis points while assuming no credit risk. For the trade to meet the no-arbitrage condition, we must have $X = Y$. If $X \neq Y$ the investor would be able to establish the position and generate a risk-free profit.

This is a logically tenable argument as well as a reasonable assumption. The default risk of the cash bondholder is identical in theory to that of the default seller. In the next section, we illustrate an asset swap pricing example, before looking at why, in practice, there exist differences in pricing between default swaps and cash market reference assets.

Asset-swap pricing example

XYZ plc is a Baa2-rated corporate. The seven-year asset swap for this entity is currently trading at 93 basis points; the underlying seven-year bond is hedged by an interest rate swap with an Aa2-rated bank. The risk-free rate for floating-rate bonds is LIBID minus 12.5 basis points (assume the bid-offer spread is 6 basis points). This suggests that the credit spread for XYZ plc is 111.5 basis points. The credit spread is the return required by an investor for holding the credit of XYZ plc. The protection seller is conceptually long the asset, and so would short the asset to hedge its position. This is illustrated in Figure 7.1. The price charged for the default swap is the price of shorting the asset, which works out as 111.5 basis points each year.

Therefore we can price a credit default written on XYZ plc as the present value of 111.5 basis points for seven years, discounted at the interest rate swap rate of 5.875%. This computes to a credit swap price of 6.25%.

Reference:	XYZ plc
Term:	Seven years
Interest rate swap rate:	5.875%
Asset swap:	LIBOR plus 93 bps
Default swap pricing	
Benchmark rate:	LIBID minus 12.5 bps
Margin:	6 bps
Credit default swap:	111.5 bps
Default swap price:	6.252%

Figure 7.1   Credit default swap and asset swap hedge.

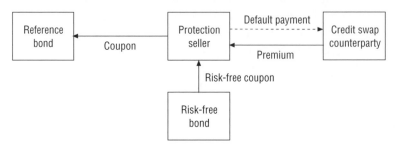

Pricing differentials

Market observation tells us that, contrary to what theory predicts, the prices of asset swaps and CDS contracts written on the same corporate entity differ, sometimes by a considerable extent. This should not surprise us, as the two instruments actually cover different things. A number of factors observed in the market serve to make the price of credit risk that has been established synthetically using default swaps to differ from its price as traded in the cash market. In fact, identifying (or predicting) such differences gives rise to arbitrage opportunities that may be exploited by basis trading in the cash and derivative markets.[2] These factors include the following:

- bond identity: the bondholder is aware of the exact issue that they are holding in the event of default, however default swap sellers may receive potentially any bond from a basket of deliverable instruments that rank *pari passu* with the cash asset — this is the delivery option afforded the long swap holder;

---

[2]   This is known as trading the credit default basis and involves either buying the cash bond and buying a default swap written on this bond, or selling the cash bond and selling a default swap written on the bond.

- the borrowing rate for a cash bond in the repo market may differ from LIBOR if the bond is to any extent *special* — this does not impact the default swap price which is fixed at inception;
- certain bonds rated AAA (such as US agency securities) sometimes trade below LIBOR in the asset swap market, however, a bank writing protection on such a bond will expect a premium (i.e. positive spread over LIBOR) for selling protection on the bond;
- depending on the precise reference credit, the default swap may be more liquid than the cash bond, resulting in a lower default swap price, or less liquid than the bond, resulting in a higher price;
- default swaps may be required to pay out on credit events that are technical defaults, and not the full default that impacts a cash bondholder; protection sellers may demand a premium for this additional risk;
- the default swap buyer is exposed to counterparty risk during the term of the trade, unlike the cash bondholder.

For these and other reasons the default swap price usually differs from the cash market price for the same asset. We examine them again, in greater detail in the next chapter. In any case, the existence of the basis means that banks generally use credit pricing models, based on the same models used to price interest rate derivatives, when pricing credit derivatives.

Illustration using Bloomberg

Observations from the market show the difference in price between asset swaps on a bond and a credit default swap written on that bond, reflecting the factors stated in the previous section. We illustrate this now using a euro-denominated corporate bond.

The bond is the Air Products & Chemicals 6.5% bond due July 2007. This bond is rated A3/A as shown in Figure 7.2, the description page from Bloomberg. The asset swap price for that specific bond to its term to maturity as at 18 January 2002 was 41.6 basis points. This is shown in Figure 7.3. The relevant swap curve used as the pricing reference is indicated on the screen as curve 45, which is the Bloomberg reference number for the euro swap curve and is shown in Figure 7.4.

We now consider the credit default swap page on Bloomberg for the same bond, which is shown in Figure 7.5. For the similar maturity range, the credit default swap price would be approximately 115 basis points. This differs significantly from the asset swap price.

Figure 7.2 Bloomberg DES page for Air Products & Chemicals bond.

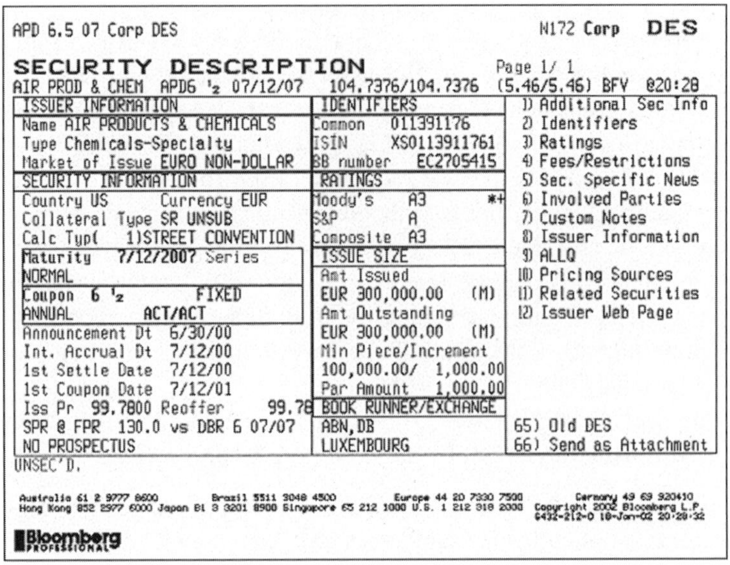

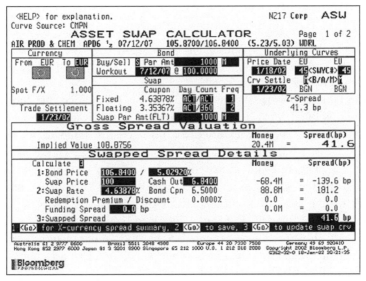

APD 6.5 07 Corp DES N172 Corp DES
SECURITY DESCRIPTION Page 1/ 1
AIR PROD & CHEM APD6 ½ 07/12/07 104.7376/104.7376 (5.46/5.46) BFV @20:28

ISSUER INFORMATION
Name AIR PRODUCTS & CHEMICALS
Type Chemicals-Specialty
Market of Issue EURO NON-DOLLAR
SECURITY INFORMATION
Country US Currency EUR
Collateral Type SR UNSUB
Calc Typ(1)STREET CONVENTION
Maturity 7/12/2007 Series
NORMAL
Coupon 6 ½ FIXED
ANNUAL ACT/ACT
Announcement Dt 6/30/00
Int. Accrual Dt 7/12/00
1st Settle Date 7/12/00
1st Coupon Date 7/12/01
Iss Pr 99.7800 Reoffer 99.78
SPR @ FPR 130.0 vs DBR 6 07/07
NO PROSPECTUS
UNSEC'D.

IDENTIFIERS
Common 011391176
ISIN XS0113911761
BB number EC2705415
RATINGS
Moody's A3 *+
S&P A
Composite A3
ISSUE SIZE
Amt Issued
EUR 300,000.00 (M)
Amt Outstanding
EUR 300,000.00 (M)
Min Piece/Increment
100,000.00/ 1,000.00
Par Amount 1,000.00
BOOK RUNNER/EXCHANGE
ABN,DB
LUXEMBOURG

1) Additional Sec Info
2) Identifiers
3) Ratings
4) Fees/Restrictions
5) Sec. Specific News
6) Involved Parties
7) Custom Notes
8) Issuer Information
9) ALLQ
10) Pricing Sources
11) Related Securities
12) Issuer Web Page
65) Old DES
66) Send as Attachment

© Bloomberg L.P. Used with permission.

Figure 7.3 Asset swap calculator page ASW on Bloomberg, 18 January 2002.

<HELP> for explanation. N217 Corp ASW
Curve Source: CMPN
ASSET SWAP CALCULATOR Page 1 of 2
AIR PROD & CHEM APD6 ½ 07/12/07 105.8700/106.8400 (5.23/5.03) WDRL

Currency: From EUR To EUR
Spot F/X 1.000
Trade Settlement 1/23/02
Bond: Buy/Sell S Par Amt 1000 M
Workout 7/12/07 @ 100.0000
Swap: Coupon Day Count Freq
Fixed 4.63878% ACT/ACT 1
Floating 3.35367% ACT/360 2
Swap Par Amt(FLT) 1000 M
Underlying Curves: Price Date EU EU
1/18/02 45<SWYC#> 45
Crv Settle I<B/A/M> M
1/23/02 BGN BGN
Z-Spread 41.3 bp

Gross Spread Valuation
Implied Value 108.8756 Money 20.4M = Spread(bp) 41.6

Swapped Spread Details
Calculate 3 Money Spread(bp)
1:Bond Price 106.8400 / 5.02920%
Swap Price 100 Cash Out 6.8400 -68.4M = -139.6 bp
2:Swap Rate 4.63878% Bond Cpn 6.5000 88.8M = 181.2
Redemption Premium / Discount 0.0000% 0.0 = 0.0
Funding Spread 0.0 bp 0.0M = 0.0
3:Swapped Spread 41.6 bp
1 <Go> for X-currency spread summary, 2 <Go> to save, 3 <Go> to update swap crv

© Bloomberg L.P. Used with permission.

Figure 7.4   Euro swap curve on Bloomberg as at
18 January 2002.

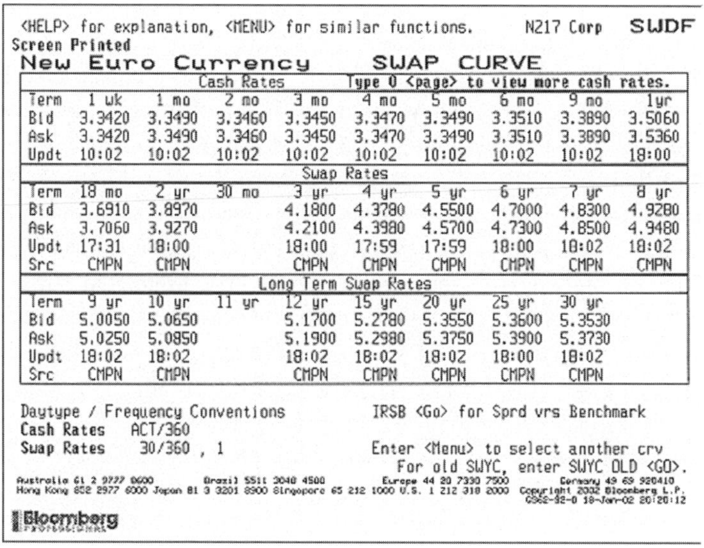

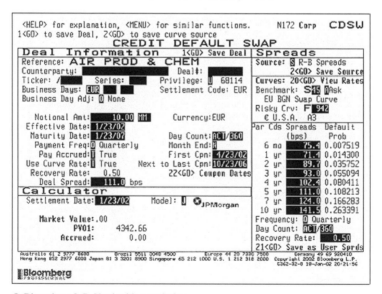

© Bloomberg L.P. Used with permission.

Figure 7.5   Default swap page CDSW for Air Products &
Chemicals bond, 18 January 2002.

© Bloomberg L.P. Used with permission.

From the screen we can see that the benchmark curve is the same as that used in the calculation shown in Figure 7.3. However, the corporate curve used as the pricing reference is indicated as the euro-denominated US-issuer A3 curve, and this is shown in Figure 7.6. This is page CURV on Bloomberg, and is the fair value corporate credit curve constructed from a basket of A3 credits. We can view the list of bonds that are used to construct the curve on following pages of the same screen. For comparison, we also show the Bank A3 rated corporate credit yield curve, in Figure 7.7.

Prices observed in the market invariably show this pattern of difference between the asset swap price and the credit default swap price. The page CDSW on Bloomberg uses the generic risky curve to calculate the default swap price, and adds the credit spread to the interest rate swap curve (shown in Figure 7.4). However, the ASW page is the specific asset swap rate for that particular bond, to the bond's term to maturity and this is another reason why the prices of the two instruments differ significantly.

Using Bloomberg, we can select either the JPMorgan credit default swap pricing model or a generic discounted credit spreads model. These are indicated by "J" or "D" in the box marked "Model" on the CDSW page. Figure 7.8 shows this page with the generic model selected. Although there is no difference in the swap prices, as expected, the default probabilities have changed under this setting.

Figure 7.6   Fair market curve, euro A3 sector.

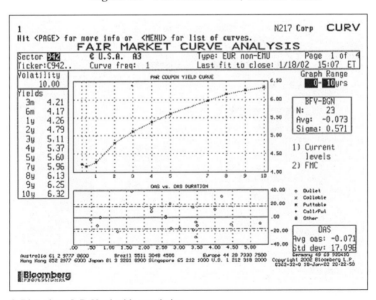

Figure 7.7   Fair market curve, euro Banks A3 sector.

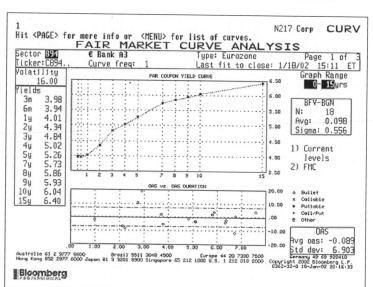

© Bloomberg L.P. Used with permission.

Figure 7.8   CDSW page with discounted spreads model selected.

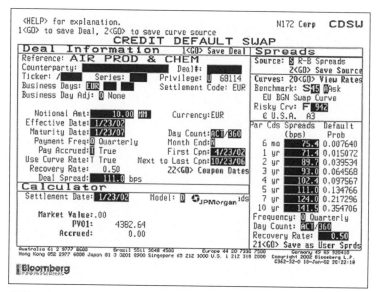

© Bloomberg L.P. Used with permission.

Our example illustrates the difference in swap price that we discussed earlier, and can be observed for any number of corporate credits across sectors. This suggests that middle office staff and risk managers that use the asset swap technique to independently value default swap books are at risk of obtaining values that differ from those in the market. This is an important issue for credit derivative market-making banks.

References

Choudhry, M., "Some Issues in the Asset-Swap Pricing of Credit Default Swaps", in *Derivatives Week*, Euromoney Publications, 2 December 2001.

There are some days in the early spring when the weather is such that, no matter where you are, either in town or countryside, England is at her best and it's good to be alive.

— Geoffrey Wellum, *First Light*
(Penguin Books) 2002

8

The Credit Default Swap Basis II: analysing the relationship between cash and synthetic markets

The most commonly executed credit derivative instrument is the credit default swap. The rapid growth of the credit derivative market has produced a highly liquid market in credit default swaps across the credit curve. This liquidity in turn has helped to generate further growth in the market. For a large number of corporate and certain sovereign names the liquidity of the credit derivative market frequently exceeds that available for the same reference names in the cash market.[1] It is this feature that has enabled fund managers to exploit their expertise in credit trading by originating so-called *synthetic CDO* vehicles that enable them to arbitrage between cash and synthetic markets. For example, see Goodman and Fabozzi (2002) and Choudhry (2002). As well as greater liquidity, the synthetic market also offers investors the opportunity to access any part of the credit term structure, and not just those parts of the term structure where corporate borrowers have issued paper. The liquidity of the synthetic market has resulted in many investors accessing both the credit derivative and the cash bond markets to meet their investment requirements. As well as greater liquidity, the synthetic market also offers other potential advantages to investors who would generally consider only the cash markets. For illustration, we list some potential advantages in Figure 8.1, which builds on what we first considered in Table 2.2.

---

[1] For instance, see *RISK*, Robeco CSO, May 2002. The asset swap market is part of the cash market, despite the fact that an interest rate derivative (the swap element) is part of an asset swap.

Figure 8.1 Comparing cash and derivatives markets for investors.

	Cash bonds	Credit derivatives
Corporate (issuer) names available	Existing issuers only	Any reference name can be traded
Liquidity	Variable liquidity	No limit to size and term of trade
Bid-offer spread	Greater below AAA names	Smaller
Maturity	Fixed dates	Any date required
Principal guaranteed	Not common	Available if reuqired
Coupon	Typcially fixed	Fixed or floating
Yield	Lower	Higher

In this chapter, we consider the close relationship between the synthetic and cash markets in credit. This relationship manifests itself most clearly in the shape of the credit default swap *basis*. First, we consider briefly why the synthetic market price spread will necessarily differ from the cash spread. We then look in further detail at the factors that drive the basis and the implications this has for market participants. Finally, from market observation, we look at the dynamics of the credit default swap basis.

The Asset Swap Price

A well-established risk management technique in the market combines an interest rate swap to transform the coupon base of a corporate bond. This produces an asset swap. This is an agreement that converts the cash flows of a bond from a fixed-rate to a floating-rate (or vice-versa). The coupon on the bond is paid in return for LIBOR, plus a spread if necessary. This spread is the asset swap spread and is the price of the asset swap. On the basis that the swap rate payable by a bank in the inter-bank market is LIBID, this asset swap spread is a function of the credit risk of the underlying bond.[2] As we saw in Chapter 7, this is why it may be viewed as equivalent to the price payable on a credit default swap written on the same asset, because it reflects the credit risk of the asset over and above the interbank credit risk. In the previous chapter, we described the no-arbitrage argument that indicates why this should be the case. As we noted however, there are a

---

[2] Or, to put it another way, the Libor-flat asset swap rate is the rate payable for firms of roughly AA-rating quality, this being the accepted credit quality of the interbank market.

number of reasons why the asset swap spread will differ from the same-reference asset credit default swap premium.[3] This is also noted in Bomfim (2002), who illustrates the divergence of asset swap (ASW) and credit default swap (CDS) spreads using financial entity and industrial entity reference names. The divergence is greatest with the industrial names considered in Bomfin's article.

During the initial phase of the CDS market, the asset swap price was frequently used in CDS valuation, and is still used as such in certain applications, particularly by support staff in banks. However, as noted in Choudhry (*ibid*), middle office desks and risk managers that use the asset swap technique to independently value default swap books are at risk of obtaining values that differ from those in the market. This is an important issue for credit derivative market-making banks. In practice, the CDS spread will differ from the ASW spread, and this has important implications for market participants in both cash and synthetic credit markets.

The Credit Default Swap Basis

While the theoretical case can be made as to why the CDS price should be equal to the ASW price, market observation tells us that this is not the case. This difference in pricing between the cash and synthetic markets was noted in the previous chapter and results from the impact of a combination of factors. In essence, it is because credit derivatives isolate and trade credit as their sole asset, separately from any funding consideration, that they are priced at a different level than the asset swap on the same reference asset. However, there are other important factors that must be considered, which we consider shortly.

The difference between the CDS and the ASW price is known as the *basis*. The basis is given by:

credit default spread (D) – the asset swap spread (S).[4]

Where $D - S > 0$, we have a *positive basis*. A positive basis occurs when the credit derivative trades higher than the asset swap price, and is common. Where $D - S < 0$, we have a *negative basis*. A negative basis occurs when the credit derivative trades tighter than the cash bond asset swap spread.

---

[3] Or from the same reference name.

[4] We may state the formal definition of the credit default swap-bond basis as being the difference between the credit default spread and the par bond floating-rate spread of the same reference asset, the latter as expressed for an asset swap on the bond.

Figure 8.2 shows the basis for a sample of reference credits during May 2003. We use mid-prices for five-year CDS and ASW for each name. The sample reflects the customary market state, with a positive basis for all but one of the names.

Figure 8.2   Selected reference name credit default swap and asset swap spreads, May 2003.

Reference credit	Credit rating	CDS spread	Asset swap spread (Libor plus)	Basis
Financials				
Ford Motor Credit	A2/A	59.3	51.1	+ 8.2
Household Finance	A2/A	72.2	57.2	+15.0
JPMorgan Chase	Aa3/AA−	89.0	66.9	+22.1
Merrill Lynch	Aa3/AA−	108.1	60.4	+47.7
Industrials				
AT & T Corp	Baa2/BBB+	224.0	217.6	+ 6.4
FedEx Corp	Baa2/BBB+	499.0	481.2	+17.8
General Motors	A3/BBB	205.1	237.7	−32.6
IBM (6-yr callable bond)	A1/A+	27.2	8.2	+19.0
IBM (4-yr callable bond)	A1/A+	33.3	11.0	+22.3

Bonds used are 5-year conventional bullet bonds
CDS is five-year maturity
AT&T is 4-year maturity
FedEx is 3-year maturity

(*Source:* Bloomberg L.P., CSFB, JPMorgan Chase, Bank of America)

We illustrate further the different trading levels by looking at two issuer names in the Euro-markets, Telefonica and FIAT. Figure 8.3 shows the yield spread levels for a selection of US dollar and euro bonds issued by Telefonica, as at November 2002. We can see that the credit default swap price is at levels comparable with the cheapest bond in the group, the 7.35% 2005 bond, issued in US dollars.

A similar picture emerges when looking at a group of FIAT bonds, also from November 2002, as shown at Figure 8.4. Note that the credit curve given by the credit default swap prices inverts. This is because a year earlier FIAT had issued a very large size "exchangeable" bond that had a July 2004 put date. The basis, previously flat, widened to over 100 basis points due to market-makers hedging this bond with convertible bonds of the same name.

Figure 8.3   Telefonica bond asset swap and credit default swap spread levels, November 2002.

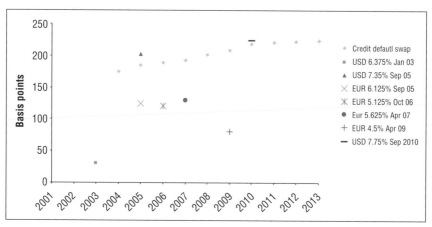

(*Source:* Bloomberg LP)

Figure 8.4   FIAT bond asset swap and credit default swap spread levels, November 2002.

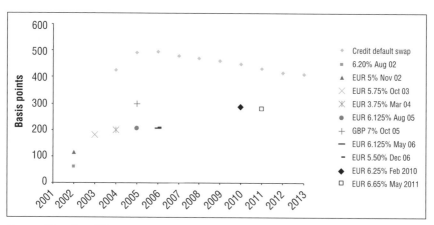

(*Source:* Bloomberg LP)

The basis will fluctuate in line with market sentiment on the particular credit. For instance, for a worsening credit, the basis can become positive quickly. This is illustrated in Figure 8.5 which shows the widening in spread between the five-year credit default swap levels with the similar maturity May 2006 bond of the same name (in this case, British Airways plc). The

Figure 8.5   British Airways plc, credit default swap versus bond spread levels.

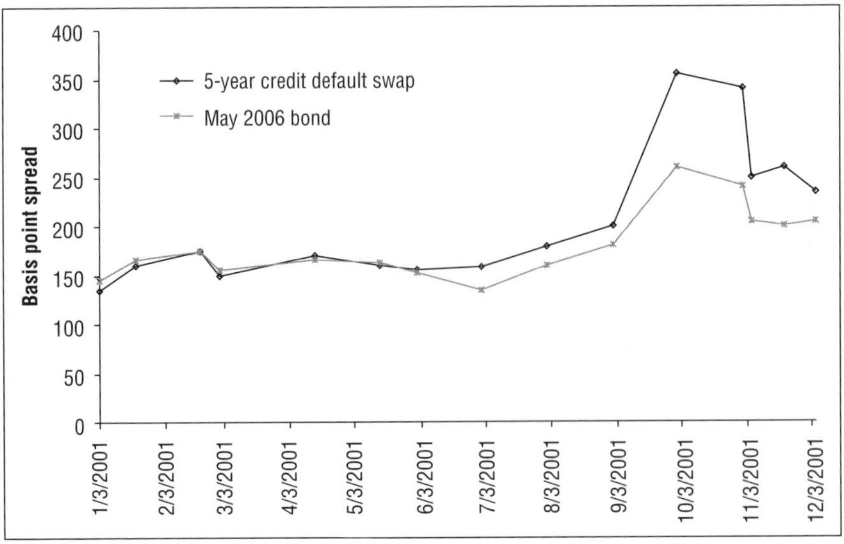

(*Source:* Bloomberg LP)

impact of the deteriorating business outlook in the last quarter of 2001 is prevalent, with the improving situation also illustrated towards the end of the year.

Factors behind the basis

The basis arises from a combination of factors, which we may group into:

- technical factors;
- market factors.

Technical factors, which are also referred to in the market variously as *fundamental* or *contractual* factors, are issues related to the definition or specification of the reference asset and of the CDS contract. *Market* factors, which are also referred to as *trading* factors, relate to issues connected with the state of the market in which credit swap contracts and reference assets are traded. Each factor exerts an influence on the basis, forcing it wider or tighter — the actual market basis at any one time will reflect the impact of all these factors together. We consider them in detail next.

Technical factors

Technical factors that influence the size and direction of the basis include the following:

CDS premiums are above zero: the price of a CDS represents the premium paid by the protection buyer to the protection seller — in effect an insurance premium. As such it is always positive. Certain bonds rated AAA (such as US agency securities, World Bank bonds or German Pfandbriefe) frequently trade below LIBOR in the asset swap market; this reflects the market view of credit risk associated with these names as being very low and also above bank quality. However, a bank writing protection on such a bond will expect a premium (positive spread over LIBOR) for selling protection on the bond. This will lead to a positive basis.

Greater protection level of the CDS contract: credit default swaps are frequently required to pay out on credit events that are technical defaults, and not the full default that impacts a cash bondholder. Protection sellers therefore demand a premium for this additional risk that results in the CDS trading above the ASW spread.

Bond identity and the delivery option: many CDS contracts that are physically settled name a reference *entity* rather than a specific reference asset. On occurrence of a credit event, the protection buyer often has a choice of deliverable assets with which to effect settlement. The looser the definition of deliverable asset is in the CDS contract documents, the larger the potential delivery basket: as long as the bond meets pre-specified requirements for seniority and maturity, it may be delivered. We can contrast this with the position of the bondholder in the cash market, who is aware of the exact issue that they are holding in the event of default. Default swap sellers on the other hand, may receive potentially any bond from the basket of deliverable instruments that rank *pari passu* with the cash asset — this is the delivery option afforded the long swap holder.

In practice therefore, the protection buyer will deliver the *cheapest-to-deliver* bond from the delivery basket, exactly as it would for an exchange-traded futures contract. This delivery option has questionable value in theory, but significant value in practice. For example, the bonds of a specific obligor that might be trading cheaper in the market include:

- the bond with the lowest coupon;
- a convertible bond;
- an illiquid bond;
- an ABS bond compared to a conventional fixed-coupon bond;
- a very long-dated bond.

Following experience in the US market (see Tolk 2001), the US adopted "modified restructuring" as one of the definitions of a credit event, which specifically restricts the delivery of long-dated bonds where restructuring is the credit event that triggers a contract payout. Nevertheless, the last named item is still relevant in the European market.

We can therefore see that the delivery option does carry value in the market. Similarly for an option contract, this value increases the closer the contract holder gets to the "strike price", which for a CDS is a credit event. Market sentiment on the particular reference name drives the basis more or less positive, depending on how favourably the name is viewed. As the credit quality of the reference name worsens, protection sellers quote higher CDS premiums. The basis also widens as the probability of a credit event increases. This is illustrated at Figure 8.6, the basis graph for AT&T. In March 2002, the firm was rated A2/A. By October, the CDS spread had widened considerably, and similarly to other firms in its sector whose telecommunications customers had reduced expenditure, its rating has been downgraded to Baa2/BBB+. Where the opposite has occurred, and firms are upgraded as credit quality improves, the market has observed a narrowing basis.

Figure 8.6   AT&T basis: increasing as perceived credit quality worsens.

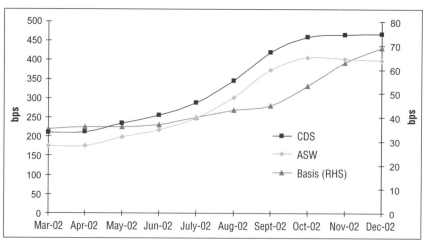

(*Yield source:* Bloomberg LP)

As a consequence of all these factors, protection sellers demand a higher premium for taking on a long position synthetically, compared to a cash position.

Accrued coupon: this factor may be associated with cash- or physically-settled contracts. In certain cases, the reference bond accrued coupon is also delivered to the protection buyer in the event of default. This has the effect of driving the CDS premium (and hence the basis) higher.

Assets trading above or below par: unlike a long cash bond position, a CDS contract provides protection on the entire par value of the reference asset. On occurrence of a credit event, the CDS payout is par minus the recovery value (or minus the asset price at the time of default). If the asset is not trading at par, this payout will either over- or under-compensate the protection buyer, depending on whether the asset is trading at a premium or discount to par. Therefore if the bond is trading at a discount, the protection seller will experience a greater loss than that suffered by an investor who is holding the cash bond. For example, an investor who pays $90 per $100 nominal to buy a cash bond has less value at risk than an investor who has written CDS protection on the same bond. If the bond obligor defaults, and a recovery value for the bond is set at $30, the cash investor will have lost $60 while the CDS seller will have lost $70. As a result, the CDS price will trade at a higher level than the ASW price for the same asset where this is trading below par, leading to a larger basis.

The reverse applies for assets trading above par. If the reference asset is trading at a premium to par, the loss suffered by a CDS seller will be lower than that of the cash bondholder. This has the effect of driving the basis lower.

Funding versus LIBOR:[5] the funding cost of a bond plays a significant part in any trading strategy associated with it in the cash market. As such, it is a key driver of the ASW spread. A cash bond investor needs to fund the position, and we take the bond's repo rate as its funding rate.[6] The funding rate, or the bond's *cost-of-carry*, determines if it is worthwhile for the investor to buy and hold the bond. A CDS contract, however, is an unfunded credit derivative that assumes a LIBOR funding cost. Therefore an investor

---

[5] It is a moot point if this is a technical factor or a market factor. *Funding risk* exists in the cash market, and does not exist in the CDS market — the risk that, having bought a bond for cash, the funding rate at which the cost of funds is renewed rises above the bond's cost-of-carry. This risk, if it is to be compensated in the cash (asset swap) market, demands a higher asset swap spread and hence drives the basis lower.

[6] This being market practice, even if the investor is a fund manager who has bought the bond outright as the bondholder, it can repo out the bond, for which it will pay the repo rate on the borrowed funds. Therefore the funding rate is always the bond's repo rate for purposes of analysis.

that has a funding cost of LIBOR plus 25 basis points will view the following two investments as theoretically identical:

- buying a floating-rate note priced at par and paying LIBOR plus 125 bps;
- selling a CDS contract on the same FRN at a premium of 100 bps.

Therefore the funding cost in the market influences the basis. If it did not, the above two strategies would no longer be identical and arbitrage opportunities would result. Hence a LIBOR-plus funding cost will drive the basis higher. Equally, the reverse applies if the funding costs of an asset are below LIBOR (or if the investor can fund the asset at sub-LIBOR). This factor was discussed earlier.

Another factor to consider is the extent of any "special-ness" in the repo market.[7] The borrowing rate for a cash bond in the repo market differs from LIBOR if the bond is to any extent *special*. This does not impact the default swap price, which is fixed at inception. This is more a market factor however, which we consider in the next section.

Counterparty risk: the protection buyer in a CDS contract takes on the counterparty risk of the protection seller, which does not occur in the cash market. This exposure lasts for the life of the contract, and is significant if, on occurrence of a credit event, the protection seller is unable to fulfill its commitments. This feature has the effect of driving down the basis, because to offset against this risk, the buyer will look to a CDS premium that is *below* the cash asset swap spread. In addition, the protection buyer will wish to look for protection seller counterparties that have a low default correlation to the reference assets being protected, to further reduce counterparty risk exposure. For example, the counterparty risk exposure of a protection buyer in a CDS contract increases when the contract has been written by an investment bank on a bank that is also a CDS market-maker.

On the other hand, the protection seller is exposed to counterparty risk of the protection buyer. Should the latter default, the CDS contract will terminate. The protection seller will suffer a mark-to-market loss if the CDS premium has widened since trade inception.

Legal risk associated with CDS contract documentation: this risk has been highlighted in a number of high-profile cases, where a (unintended) broad definition of "credit event" as stated in the contract documents has

---

[7]   If the repo rate for a specific bond is more than 25–30 bps lower than the "general collateral" rate for that asset class's repo rate, it is deemed "special". The cost of funds payable by the holder of a special bond that is repo'ed out will be lower than LIBOR.

exposed the protection seller to unexpected risks. Typically this will be where a "credit event" has been deemed to occur beyond what might be termed a default or technical default. This occurred, for example, with Conseco in the United States, as first discussed in Tolk (2001).

Associated with legal risk is documentation risk, the general risk that credit events and other terms of trade, as defined in the CDS documentation, may be open to dispute or arguments over interpretation. We can expect documentation risk to decrease as legal documentation is standardised across a larger number of shares. The 2003 ISDA definitions also seek to address this issue.

Market factors

Market factors that influence the size and direction of the basis include the following:

Market demand: strong demand from protection buyers such as commercial banks protecting loan books, or insurance companies undertaking synthetic short selling trades, will drive the basis wider. Equally, strong market demand from protection sellers will drive the basis tighter.

Liquidity premium: the CDS for a particular reference asset may reflect a liquidity premium for that name. An investor seeking to gain exposure to that name can buy the bond in the cash market or sell protection on it in the CDS market. For illiquid maturities or terms, the protection seller may charge a premium. At the two- to five-year maturities, the CDS market is very liquid (as is the cash market). For some corporate names, however, cash market liquidity dries up towards the ten-year area. In addition, depending on the precise reference credit, the default swap may be more liquid than the cash bond, resulting in a lower default swap price, or less liquid than the bond, resulting in a higher price.

Liquidity in the cash market can be quite restricted for below investment-grade names, and secondary market trading is usually confined to "current" issues. Similarly to the repo market, the relationship flows both ways and liquid names in the cash market are usually liquid names in the CDS market. However for corporate names for which no bonds exist, CDS contracts are the only way for investors to gain an exposure (see below).

Relative liquidity is also related to the next item on our list.

Shortage of cash assets: in some markets it is easier to source a particular reference name or reference asset in the CDS market than in the cash market. This has always been the case in the loan market. While there has been a secondary market in loans in the US for some time, it is relatively illiquid in Europe. In the bond market, it can be difficult to short some corporate bonds due to problems in covering the position in repo, and also there is the risk that the bonds go special in repo. When cash assets are difficult to short, traders and speculators can buy protection in the CDS market. This does not involve any short covering or repo risk, and also fixes the cost of "funding" (the CDS premium) at trade inception. The demand for undertaking this in CDS has a positive impact on the basis.

The structured finance market: the rapid growth of the market in synthetic collateralised debt obligations (CDO) has both arisen out of, and driven, the liquidity of the CDS market. These products are considered in detail in Goodman and Fabozzi (2002) and Choudhry (2002). Synthetic CDOs use CDS contracts to source reference credits in the market and frequently make use of basket CDS and a portfolio of credits. As investment vehicles, they sell protection on reference names. The counterparty to the CDO vehicle will hedge out its exposure in the CDS market. Large demand in the CDS market, arising from hedging requirements of CDO counterparties, impacts the basis and frequently drives it lower.

New market issuance: the impact of new bond and loan issues on the CDS basis illustrates the rapid acceptance of this instrument in the market, and its high level of liquidity. Where previously market participants would hedge new issues using interest rate derivatives and/or government bonds, they now use CDS as a more exact hedge against credit risk. However the impact on the basis flows both ways and may increase or decrease it, depending on specific factors. For example, new issues of corporate bonds enlarge the delivery basket for physically-settled CDS contracts. This should widen the basis, but the cash market may also widen as well as investors move into the new bonds. For loans, a new issue by banks is often hedged in the CDS market, and this should cause the basis to widen. Convertible bond issuance also tends to widen the basis. We noted earlier the impact of the issue of an exchangeable bond by Fiat on the CDS basis for that name.

The Basis "smile"

If plotted graphically, the CDS-cash basis tends to exhibit a "smile". This is illustrated in Figure 8.7 and is known as the *basis smile*. This reflects a number of the features we have discussed above. The main reasons for the smile effect is that highly-rated reference names, such as AA or higher, fund in the asset swap market at sub-LIBOR. However, if an entity is buying protection on such a name, it will pay above LIBOR premiums. The basis therefore tends to increase with better quality names and results in the smile effect. Other factors that impact the smile are the cheapest-to-deliver option for lower-rated credits.

Figure 8.7   Basis smile for industrial names, November 2002.

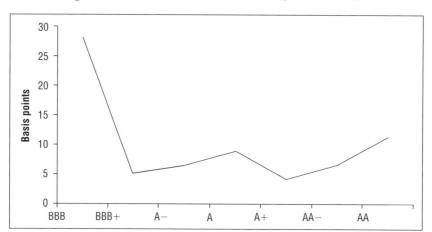

The dynamics of the default swap basis

Positive and negative basis situations

At any time, the CDS basis reflects the combined impact of all the above factors. Some of these will affect the basis with positive bias, whereas others will have a negative bias. Generally, technical and market factors that tend to drive the basis wider include:

- CDS premiums above zero;
- The delivery option;
- Accrued coupon;
- Bond price below par;
- Funding below LIBOR;
- Legal and documentation risk;
- Market liquidity;
- New bond issuance;
- Difficulty of shorting cash bonds.

The factors that tend to drive the basis lower include:

- Counterparty risk;
- Bonds priced above par;
- Funding above LIBOR;
- Impact of the structured finance market.

However a reversal of the market circumstances can lead to the same factor having a reverse impact. For instance, if a credit is viewed in the market as being of decreasing quality, factors such as the delivery option, bonds trading below par, difficulty in shorting the cash bond and worsening liquidity all push the basis wider. However if the credit is viewed as improving in terms of quality, the impact of these factors diminishes (for example, the delivery option has decreasing value as the probability of a credit event occurring decreases).

The market norm is a positive basis, for all the reasons that we have discussed. While some of the factors above do influence the basis towards a negative value, observation tells us that the market norm is a positive basis. The combination of all the various factors tends to result in a negative basis usually only for reference names that are highly rated in terms of credit quality. This is because those factors that drive the basis lower carry greater influence for highly-rated names. Specifically:

• the cash bond price is generally closer to par for high-quality credits;
• the value of the delivery option is less, as there is less chance of default or credit event for AAA and AA-rated names;

In addition, compared to sub-investment grade names, highly-rated names are more often selected as reference credits in synthetic CDOs. All these factors combine to drive the basis lower for good-quality names, and this sometimes leads to negative values.

As well as being relatively uncommon, a negative basis is usually temporary. They usually reflect a particular set of circumstances, which disappear over (short periods of) time. They also represent an arbitrage opportunity for market participants that can trade across cash and synthetic markets, which returns the basis to positive territory as soon as it is exploited in the market. We illustrate the temporary nature of the negative basis at Figure 8.8. This shows how the basis had reverted to positive for those sectors that had exhibited it, within three months.

Market observation of the basis trend

To illustrate the interplay between cash and synthetic markets, and the influence of all the above factors acting together, we show at Figure 8.9 the ASW and CDS spreads for a sample of 100 investment-grade US dollar-denominated corporate bonds, during June 2002 to January 2003. This shows the default swap basis trend during this period, with the overall basis staying positive on the whole but moving between positive and negative.

Figure 8.8   Basis values compared across sectors, September–December 2002.

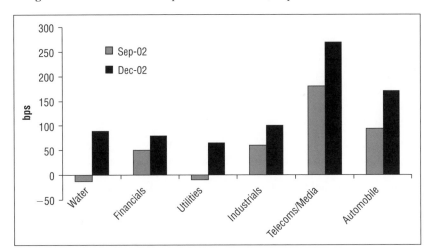

Source: Bloomberg LP, JPMorgan Chase Bank, Bank of America.

Figure 8.9   The dynamics of the default swap basis, 2002–2003.

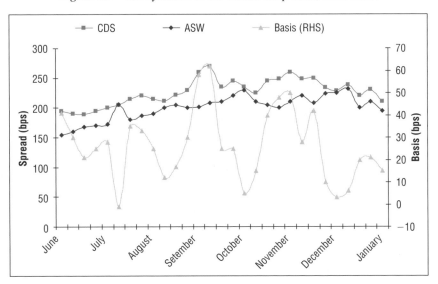

Source: Bloomberg LP, CSFB, JPMorgan Chase Bank.

We conclude from this observation that:

- the overall default swap basis was essentially positive;
- the CDS spread volatility at least matches that of the cash market, and sometimes exceeds it;
- at times the basis moved with the cash spread, but not to the same extent, thus widening as the cash spread widened;
- there is a high degree of correlation between the two markets, as we would expect;
- the basis itself moves in the direction of the market; in other words, we observe that the basis widens as cash and synthetic spreads widen.

We may conclude that the basis acts much as the repo rate acts in the cash bond market. The relationship between special rates in repo and bond prices moves both ways, and one can lead the other depending on circumstances (see Bank of England 1992). The CDS market has a two-way relationship with the cash asset swap market, and each will lead the other according to circumstance.

The impact of the basis on trading strategy

From the inception of trading in CDS, market participants have known that inefficiencies in pricing can result in arbitrage opportunities. Using CDS, the basic market neutral strategy (credit risk-free) is to buy the cash bond and swap it in the asset swap market, and buy protection using CDS. The trader receives the bond coupon as floating coupon, and pays the CDS premium. To match payment and receipt bases, the bond is a floating-rate bond with the coupon swapped out to fixed-rate.

The existence of the basis enables us to quantify the theoretical gain for the arbitrageur. As with other basis type trades, typified by the government bond basis, the existence of a non-zero basis implies a risk-free arbitrage opportunity. If the basis is non-zero, a trader can put on a credit risk-free arbitrage trade across the cash and synthetic markets. The two scenarios are:

- Positive basis: sell the cash bond and sell protection on that bond;
- Negative basis: buy the bond and buy protection using a CDS. In this trade, the investor has the value of the delivery option (we assume a physically-settled CDS).

The first trade requires short-covering in the repo market, which exposes the investor to funding risks if the bond goes special. The latter trade is easier to implement as there are no short-cover issues to consider, but it must be funded on the balance sheet. Therefore, the investor's funding costs also impact the profitability of the trade. If it is sub-LIBOR, the trade looks attractive and the investor will profit by the amount of the basis. If the funding cost is above LIBOR, it must be below the negative basis value for the trade to work. However, because the basis trade for a negative basis is easier to implement, negative basis values rarely stay negative for long and revert to positive once arbitragers get to work.

The basis can also be used to identify ways to enhance portfolio returns for a fund manager that is able to switch from cash to synthetic markets and vice versa. As the basis moves, it indicates which sector is experiencing widening spreads into which fund managers can switch. Alternatively, a fund manager that has a view on which corporate sectors are likely to experience significant moves in the basis can move into that sector and undertake a basis trade to benefit from this move.

Conclusion

From this study of the credit default swap basis we can conclude that the CDS market is very liquid and very closely correlated to the movements of the cash bond market. Although the theoretical argument can be made, using the no-arbitrage principal, that the CDS premium must equal the asset swap premium, market observation tells us that a non-zero credit default swap-bond basis always exists between the CDS and asset swap markets. A non-zero basis arises from the influence of a number of technical and market factors, the impact of which varies with market conditions.

The basis moves closely with the markets as a whole. The relationship between the synthetic and cash markets, which is measured by the basis, is a two-way one, and the synthetic market will often lead the cash market. This experience, which mirrors the relationship in the interest rate market between cash bonds and interest rate derivatives, is a clear indicator of the liquid market that now prevails in credit default swaps.

References

Anson, M., *Credit Derivatives*, FJF Associates 1999.

Bank of England, "Review of the Gilt Repo Market", *Quarterly Bulletin*, Bank of England, February 1997.

Bomfim, A., "Credit Derivatives and their potential to synthesize risk-less assets", *Journal of Fixed Income*, Vol 12, No 3, December 2002, pp. 6–16.

British Bankers' Association, *Credit Derivatives Report 2002/2003*, British Bankers' Association 2003.

Choudhry, M., "Some issues in the asset-swap pricing of credit default swaps", *Derivatives Week,* Euromoney Publications, 2 December 2001.

Choudhry, M., *The Repo Handbook,* Butterworth Heinemann 2002 (a), Chapter 10.

Choudhry, M., "Combining securitisation and trading in credit derivatives: an analysis of the managed synthetic collateralised debt obligation", *Euromoney Debt Capital Markets Handbook,* Euromoney Publications 2002 (b).

Francis, J., J. Frost, and J. Whittaker, *The Handbook of Credit Derivatives,* McGraw-Hill 1999.

Goodman, L., and Fabozzi, F., *Collateralised Debt Obligations,* Wiley 2002.

Tolk, J., "Understanding the risks in Credit Default Swaps", *Moody's Special Report,* Moody's Investors Service, 16 March 2001.

II

Structured Credit Products and Synthetic Securitisation

Structured products is the generic term used to refer to a wide variety of capital market instruments. They include bonds issued as part of a securitisation, such as asset-backed securities (ABS) and mortgage-backed securities (MBS), which are well-established and were first introduced during the 1970s. A more recent product is the collateralised debt obligation (CDO), which is also well-established, the first such deal being introduced in 1988. Structured products also include various classes of instruments that are also called *hybrid products*, combinations of two or more basic products such as vanilla bonds and interest rate swaps, or vanilla bonds linked to external references or benchmarks. The existing literature on this subject is large and in-depth.

In this part of the book, we examine *structured credit products*. These are products that combine securitisation technology with credit derivative instruments. As such, they are also examples of *synthetic securitisation*: synthetic because they replicate the economic effects of securitisation without the actual "true sale" event, which is the building block of traditional securitisation.

For background information, we present an introduction to traditional securitisation. This is then followed by a detailed look at the main synthetic securitisation products, which are

229

synthetic collateralised debt obligations (also known as *collateralised synthetic obligations* or *CSOs*) and synthetic MBS transactions. We also look at synthetic conduits and repack structures.

I'll never forget the first day I met her,
That September morning was clear and fresh,
The way she spoke, and laughed at my jokes ...
She became a magic mystery to me, and we'd sit together in
double-History twice a week ...
In the end it took me a dictionary,
To find out the meaning of unrequited ...

— Billy Bragg, "This Saturday Boy",
from *Brewing Up With Billy Bragg* (Go! Discs) 1984

An Introduction to Securitisation[1]

The second part of this book examines *synthetic securitisation*. This is a generic term covering structured financial products that use credit derivatives in their construction. In fact another term for the products we discuss in Part II could be "hybrid structured products". However, because the economic impact of these products mirrors some of those of traditional securitisation instruments, we use the term "synthetic securitisation". To fully understand this, we need to be familiar with traditional or *cash flow* securitisation as a concept, and this is what we discuss now. Readers who are familiar with the subject may wish to proceed directly to Chapter 10.

The motivations behind the origination of synthetic structured products sometimes differ from those of cash flow ones, although sometimes they are straight alternatives. Both product types are aimed at institutional investors, who may or may not be interested in the motivation behind their origination (although they will — as prudent portfolio managers — be interested in the name and quality of the originating institution). Both techniques aim to create disintermediation and bring the seekers of capital, and/or risk exposure, together with providers of capital and risk exposure.

In this chapter we introduce the basic concepts of securitisation and look at the motivation behind their use, as well as their economic impact. We illustrate the process with a brief hypothetical case study. We then move on to discuss a more advanced synthetic repackaging structure.

---

[1] This chapter was co-authored with Anuk Teasdale of YieldCurve.com.

The Concept of Securitisation

Securitisation is a well-established practice in the global debt capital markets. It refers to the sale of assets, which generate cash flows from the institution that owns the assets, to another company that has been specifically set up for the purpose of acquiring them, and the issuing of notes by this second company. These notes are backed by the cash flows from the original assets. The technique was introduced initially as a means of funding for US mortgage banks. Subsequently, the technique was applied to other assets such as credit card payments and equipment leasing receivables. It has also been employed as part of asset/liability management, as a means of managing balance sheet risk.

Securitisation allows institutions such as banks and corporations to convert assets that are not readily marketable — such as residential mortgages or car loans — into rated securities that are tradeable in the secondary market. The investors that buy these securities gain exposure to these types of original assets that they would not otherwise have access to. The technique is well established and was first introduced by mortgage banks in the United States during the 1970s. The synthetic securitisation market was established much more recently, dating from 1997. The key difference between cash and synthetic securitisation is that in the former market, as we have already noted, the assets in question are actually sold to a separate legal company known as a special purpose vehicle (SPV).[2] This does not occur in a synthetic transaction, as we shall see.

Sundaresan (1997) defines securitisation as,

> " ... a framework in which some illiquid assets of a corporation or a financial institution are transformed into a package of securities backed by these assets, through careful packaging, credit enhancements, liquidity enhancements and structuring."
>
> (page 359)

The process of securitisation creates *asset-backed bonds*. These are debt instruments that have been created from a package of loan assets on which interest is payable, usually on a floating basis. The asset-backed market was developed in the US and is a large, diverse market containing a wide range of instruments. Techniques employed by investment banks today enable an

---

[2]   An SPV is also referred to as a Special Purpose Entity (SPE) or a Special Purpose Company (SPC). See the box on page 235 for more information on SPVs.

entity to create a bond structure from any type of cash flow. Assets that have been securitized include loans such as residential mortgages, car loans, and credit card loans. The loans form assets on a bank or finance house balance sheet, which are packaged together and used as backing for an issue of bonds. The interest payments on the original loans form the cash flows used to service the new bond issue. Traditionally, mortgage-backed bonds are grouped in their own right as mortgage-backed securities (MBS), while all other securitisation issues are known as asset-backed bonds or ABS.

Example 9.1   Special Purpose Vehicles

The key to undertaking securitisation is the Special Purpose Vehicle or SPV. They are also known as Special Purpose Entities (SPE) or Special Purpose Companies (SPC). They are distinct legal entities that act as the "company" through which a securitisation is undertaken. They act as a form of repackaging vehicle, used to transform, convert or create risk structures that can be accessed by a wider range of investors. Essentially they are legal entity to which assets such as mortgages, credit card debt or synthetic assets such as credit derivatives are transferred, and from which the original credit risk/reward profile is transformed and made available to investors. An originator will use SPVs to increase liquidity and to make liquid risks that cannot otherwise be traded in any secondary market.

An SPV is a legal trust or company that is not, for legal purposes, linked in any way to the originator of the securitisation. As such it is *bankruptcy-remote* from the sponsor. If the sponsor suffers financial difficulty or is declared bankrupt, this will have no impact on the SPV, and hence no impact on the liabilities of the SPV with respect to the notes it has issued in the market. Investors have credit risk exposure only to the underlying assets of the SPV.[3]

To secure favourable tax treatment SPVs are frequently incorporated in offshore business centres such as Jersey or the Cayman Islands, or areas that have set up SPV-friendly business legislation such as Ireland or the Netherlands. The choice of

---

[3] In some securitisations, the currency or interest-payment basis of the underlying assets differs from that of the overlying notes, and so the SPV will enter into currency and/or interest-rate swaps with a (bank) counterparty. The SPV would then have counterparty risk exposure.

location for an SPV is dependant on a number of factors as well as taxation concerns, such as operating costs, legal requirements and investor considerations.[4] The key issue is taxation however; the sponsor will wish all cashflows both received and paid out by the SPV to attract low or no tax. This includes withholding tax on coupons paid on notes issued by the SPV.

SPVs are used in a wide variety of applications and are an important element of the market in structured credit products. An established application is in conjunction with an asset swap, when an SPV is used to securitise the asset swap so that it becomes available to investors who cannot otherwise access it. Essentially the SPV will purchase the asset swap and then issue notes to the investor, who gain an exposure to the original asset swap albeit indirectly. This is illustrated in Figure 9.1.

Figure 9.1   Asset swap package securitised and economic effect sold on by SPV.

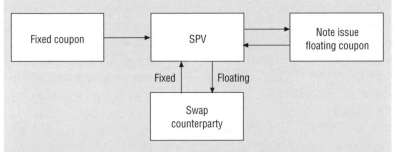

The most common purpose for which an SPV is set up is a cashflow securitisation, in which the sponsoring company sells assets off its balance sheet to the SPV, which funds the purchase of these assets by issuing notes. The revenues received by the assets are used to pay the liability of the issued overlying notes. Of course, the process itself has transformed previously un-tradeable assets such as residential mortgages into tradeable ones, and freed up the balance sheet of the originator.

---

[4]   For instance investors in some European Union countries will only consider notes issued by an SPV based in the EU, so that would exclude many offshore centres.

SPVs are also used for the following applications:

- converting the currency of underlying assets into another currency more acceptable to investors, by means of a currency swap
- issuing credit-linked notes. Unlike CLNs issued by originators direct, CLNs issue dby SPVs do not have any credit-linkage to the sponsoring entity. The note is linked instead to assets that have been sold to the SPV, and its performance is dependent on the performance of these assets. Another type of credit-linked SPV is when investors select the assets that (effectively) collateralise the CLN and are held by the SPV. The SPV then sells credit protection to a swap counterparty, and on occurrence of a credit event the underlying securities are sold and used to pay the SPV liabilities
- they are used to transform illiquid into liquid ones. Certain assets such as trade receivables, equipment lease receivables or even more exotic assets such as museum entry-fee receipts are not tradeable in any form, but can be made into tradeable notes via securitisation.

For legal purposes an SPV is categorised as either a Company or a Trust. The latter is more common in the US market, and its interests are represented by a Trustee which is usually the Agency services department of a bank such as JPMorgan Chase or Citibank, or a specialist Trust company such as Wilmington Trust. In the Euromarkets SPVs are often incorporated as companies instead of Trusts.

Reasons for Undertaking Securitisation

The driving force behind securitisation has been the need for banks to realize value from the assets on their balance sheet. Typically these assets are residential mortgages, corporate loans, and retail loans such as credit card debt. Let us consider the factors that might lead a financial institution to securitize part of its balance sheet. These might be the following:

- if revenues received from assets remain roughly unchanged but the size of assets has decreased, there will be an increase in the return on equity ratio;

- the level of capital required to support the balance sheet will be reduced, which again can lead to cost savings or allow the institution to allocate the capital to other, perhaps more profitable, business;
- to obtain cheaper funding: frequently the interest payable on asset-backed securities is considerably below the level payable on the underlying loans. This creates a cash surplus for the originating entity.

In other words, the main reasons that a bank securitises part of its balance sheet is for one or all of the following reasons:

- funding the assets it owns;
- balance sheet capital management;
- risk management and credit risk transfer.

We shall now consider each of these in turn.

Funding

Banks can use securitisation to: (i) support rapid asset growth; (ii) diversify their funding mix, and reduce cost of funding and; (iii) reduce maturity mismatches.

The market for asset-backed securities is large, with an estimated size of US$1,000 billion invested in ABS issues worldwide annually, of which US$150 billion is in the European market alone.[5] Access to this source of funding enables a bank to grow its loan books at a faster pace than if they were reliant on traditional funding sources alone. For example, in the UK a former building society-turned-bank, Northern Rock plc, has taken advantage of securitisation to back its growing share of the UK residential mortgage market. Securitising assets also allows a bank to diversify its funding mix. Banks generally do not wish to be reliant on a single or a few sources of funding, as this can be high-risk in times of market difficulty. Banks aim to optimise their funding between a mix of retail, interbank and wholesale sources. Securitisation has a key role to play in this mix. It also enables a bank to reduce its funding costs. This is because the securitisation process de-links the credit rating of the originating institution from the credit rating of the issued notes. Typically, most of the notes issued by SPVs will be higher-rated than the bonds issued directly by the originating bank itself.

---

[5] Source: CSFB, *Credit Risk Transfer*, 2 May 2003.

While the liquidity of the secondary market in ABS is frequently lower than that of the corporate bond market, and this adds to the yield payable by an ABS, it is frequently the case that the cost to the originating institution of issuing debt is still lower in the ABS market because of the latter's higher rating. Finally, there is the issue of maturity mismatches. The business of bank asset-liability management (ALM) is inherently one of maturity mismatch, since a bank often funds long-term assets such as residential mortgages, with short-term asset liabilities such as bank account deposits or interbank funding. This can be removed via securitisation, as the originating bank receives funding from the sale of the assets, and the economic maturity of the issued notes frequently matches that of the assets.

Balance sheet capital management

Banks use securitisation to improve balance sheet capital management. This provides: (i) regulatory capital relief; (ii) economic capital relief and; (iii) diversified sources of capital.

As stipulated in the Bank for International Settlements (BIS) capital rules,[6] also known as the Basel rules, banks must maintain a minimum capital level for their assets, in relation to the risk of these assets. Under Basel I, for every $100 of risk-weighted assets, a bank must hold at least $8 of capital, however the designation of each asset's risk-weighting is restrictive. For example, with the exception of mortgages, customer loans are 100% risk-weighted regardless of the underlying rating of the borrower or the quality of the security held. The anomalies that this raises, which need not concern us here, is being addressed by the Basel II rules which become effective from 2008. However, the Basel I rules, which have been in place since 1988 (and effective from 1992), are another driver of securitisation. As an SPV is not a bank, it is not subject to Basel rules and it therefore only needs such capital that is economically required by the nature of the assets they contain. This is not a set amount, but is significantly below the 8% level required by banks in all cases. Although an originating bank does not obtain 100% regulatory capital relief when it sells assets off its balance sheet to an SPV, because it will have retained a "first-loss" piece out of the issued notes, its regulatory capital charge will be significantly reduced after the securitisation.[7]

---

[6] For further information on this see Choudhry (2001).
[7] We discuss first-loss later on.

To the extent that securitisation provides regulatory capital relief, it can be thought of as an alternative to capital raising, compared with the traditional sources of Tier 1 (equity), preferred shares, and perpetual loan notes with step-up coupon features. By reducing the amount of capital that has to be used to support the asset pool, a bank can also improve its return-on-equity (ROE) value. This is received favourably by shareholders.

Risk management

Once assets have been securitised, the credit risk exposure on these assets for the originating bank is reduced considerably and, if the bank does not retain a first-loss capital piece (the most junior of the issued notes), it is removed entirely. This is because assets have been sold to the SPV. Securitisation can also be used to remove non-performing assets from banks' balance sheets. This has the dual advantage of removing credit risk and removing a potentially negative sentiment from the balance sheet, as well as freeing up regulatory capital. Further, there is a potential upside from securitizing such assets, if any of them start performing again, or there is a recovery value obtained from defaulted assets, the originator will receive any surplus profit made by the SPV.

Benefits of securitisation to Investors

Investor interest in the ABS market has been considerable from the market's inception. This is because investors perceive asset-backed securities as possessing a number of benefits. Investors can:

- diversify sectors of interest;
- access different (and sometimes superior) risk-reward profiles;
- access sectors that are otherwise not open to them.

A key benefit of securitisation notes is the ability to tailor risk-return profiles. For example, if there is a lack of assets of any specific credit rating, these can be created via securitisation. Securitised notes frequently offer better risk-reward performance than corporate bonds of the same rating and maturity. While this might seem peculiar (why should one AA-rated bond perform better in terms of credit performance than another just because it is asset-backed?), this often occurs because the originator holds the first-loss piece in the structure.

A holding in an ABS also diversifies the risk exposure. For example, rather than invest $100 million in an AA-rated corporate bond and be exposed to "event risk" associated with the issuer, investors can gain exposure to, say, 100 pooled assets. These pooled assets will clearly have lower concentration risk.

The Process of Securitisation

We now look at the process of securitisation, the nature of the SPV structure and issues such as credit enhancements and the cash flow "waterfall".

The securitisation process involves a number of participants. In the first instance there is the *originator*, the firm whose assets are being securitised. The most common process involves an *issuer* acquiring the assets from the originator. The issuer is usually a company that has been specially set up for the purpose of the securitisation, which is the SPV and is usually domiciled offshore. The creation of an SPV ensures that the underlying asset pool is held separate from the other assets of the originator. This is done so that in the event that the originator is declared bankrupt or insolvent, the assets that have been transferred to the SPV will not be affected. This is known as being bankruptcy-remote. Conversely, if the underlying assets begin to deteriorate in quality and are subject to a ratings downgrade, investors have no recourse to the originator.

By holding the assets within an SPV framework, defined in formal legal terms, the financial status and credit rating of the originator becomes almost irrelevant to the bondholders. The process of securitisation often involves *credit enhancements*, in which a third-party guarantee of credit quality is obtained, so that notes issued under the securitisation are often rated at investment grade and up to AAA-grade.

The process of structuring a securitisation deal ensures that the liability side of the SPV — the issued notes — carries a lower cost than the asset side of the SPV. This enables the originator to secure lower cost funding that it would not otherwise be able to obtain in the unsecured market. This is a tremendous benefit for institutions with lower credit ratings.

Figure 9.1 illustrates the process of securitisation in simple fashion.

Figure 9.1   The securitisation process.

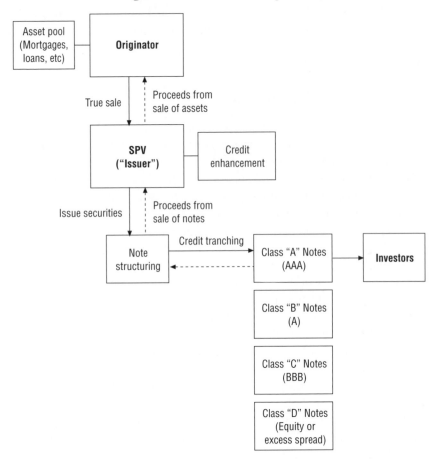

Mechanics of securitisation

Securitisation involves a "true sale" of the underlying assets from the balance sheet of the originator. This is why a separate legal entity, the SPV, is created to act as the issuer of the notes. The assets being securitized are sold onto the balance sheet of the SPV. The process involves:

- undertaking "due diligence" on the quality and future prospects of the assets;
- setting up the SPV and then effecting the transfer of assets to it;
- underwriting of loans for credit quality and servicing;

- determining the structure of the notes, including how many tranches are to be issued, in accordance with originator and investor requirements;
- the rating of notes by one or more credit rating agencies;
- placing of notes in the capital markets.

The sale of assets to the SPV needs to be undertaken so that it is recognised as a true legal transfer. The originator obtains legal counsel to advise it in such matters. The credit rating process considers the character and quality of the assets, and also whether any enhancements have been made to the assets that will raise their credit quality. This can include *over-collateralisation,* which is when the principal value of notes issued is lower than the principal value of assets, and a liquidity facility provided by a bank.

A key consideration for the originator is the choice of the underwriting bank, which structures the deal and places the notes. The originator awards the mandate for its deal to an investment bank on the basis of fee levels, marketing ability and track record with assets being securitised.

SPV structures

There are essentially two main securitisation structures, amortising (pass-through) and revolving. A third type, the master trust, is used by frequent issuers.

Amortising structures

Amortising structures pay principal and interest to investors on a coupon-by-coupon basis throughout the life of the security, as illustrated in Figure 9.2. They are priced and traded based on expected maturity and weighted-average life (WAL), which is the time-weighted period during which principal is outstanding. A WAL approach incorporates various pre-payment assumptions, and any change in this pre-payment speed will increase or decrease the rate at which principal is repaid to investors. Pass-through structures are commonly used in residential and commercial mortgage-backed deals (MBS), and consumer loan ABS.

Figure 9.2   Amortising cashflow structure.

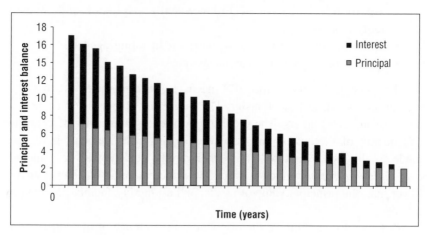

Revolving structures

Revolving structures revolve the principal of the assets; that is, during the revolving period, principal collections are used to purchase new receivables which fulfill the necessary criteria. The structure is used for short-dated assets with a relatively high pre-payment speed, such as credit card debt and auto-loans. During the amortisation period, principal payments are paid to investors either in a series of equal installments (*controlled amortisation*) or principal is "trapped" in a separate account until the expected maturity date and then paid in a single lump sum to investors (*soft bullet*).

Master trust

Frequent issuers under US and UK law use *master trust* structures, which allow multiple securitisations to be issued from the same SPV. Under such schemes, the originator transfers assets to the master trust SPV. Notes are then issued out of the asset pool based on investor demand. Master trusts are used by MBS and credit card ABS originators.

Securitisation note tranching

As illustrated in Figure 9.1, in a securitisation the issued notes are structured to reflect specified risk areas of the asset pool, and thus are rated differently. The senior tranche is usually rated AAA. The lower-rated notes usually have an element of *over-collateralisation* and are thus capable of absorbing losses. The most junior note is the lowest-rated or non-rated. It is often referred to as the *first-loss piece*, because it is impacted by losses in the underlying asset pool first. The first-loss piece is sometimes called the *equity piece* or equity note (even though it is a bond) and is usually held by the originator.

Credit enhancement

Credit enhancement refers to the group of measures that can be instituted as part of the securitisation process for ABS and MBS issues so that the credit rating of the issued notes meets investor requirements. The lower the quality of the assets being securitised, the greater the need for credit enhancement. This is usually by some or all of the following methods:

- *Over-collateralisation*: where the nominal value of the assets in the pool are in excess of the nominal value of issued securities;
- *Pool insurance*: an insurance policy provided by a composite insurance company to cover the risk of principal loss in the collateral pool. The claims paying rating of the insurance company is important in determining the overall rating of the issue.
- *Senior/Junior note classes*: credit enhancement is provided by subordinating a class of notes ("class B" notes) to the senior class notes ("class A" notes). The class B note's right to its proportional share of cash flows is subordinated to the rights of the senior noteholders. Class B notes do not receive payments of principal until certain rating agency requirements have been met, specifically satisfactory performance of the collateral pool over a pre-determined period, or in many cases until all of the senior note classes have been redeemed in full.
- *Margin step-up*: a number of ABS issues incorporate a step-up feature in the coupon structure, which typically coincides with a call date. Although the issuer is usually under no obligation to redeem the notes at this point, the step-up feature was introduced as an added incentive for investors, to convince them from the outset that the economic cost of paying a higher coupon is unacceptable and that the issuer would seek to refinance by exercising its call option.
- *Excess spread*: this is the difference between the return on the underlying assets and the interest rate payable on the issued notes (liabilities). The monthly excess spread is used to cover expenses and any losses. If any surplus is left over, it is held in a reserve account to cover against future losses or (if not required for that), as a benefit to the originator. In the meantime the reserve account is a credit enhancement for investors.

All securitisation structures incorporate a *cash waterfall* process, whereby all the cash that is generated by the asset pool is paid in order of payment priority. Only when senior obligations have been met can more junior obligations be paid. An independent third party agent is usually employed to run "tests" on the vehicle to confirm that there is sufficient cash available to pay all obligations. If a test is failed, then the vehicle will start to pay off the notes, starting from the senior notes. The waterfall process is illustrated in Figure 9.3.

Figure 9.3 Cashflow waterfall (priority of payments).

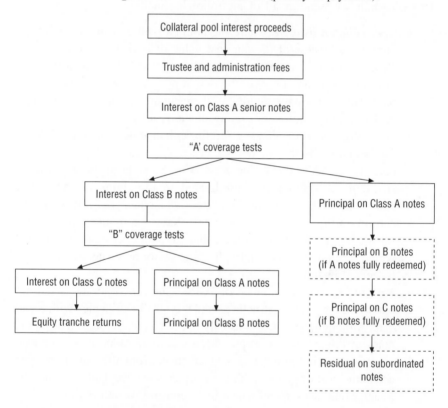

Impact on balance sheet

Figure 9.4 illustrates, by way of an hypothetical example, the effect of a securitisation transaction on the liability side of an originating bank's balance sheet. Following the process, selected assets have been removed from the balance sheet, although the originating bank will usually have

Figure 9.4   Regulatory capital impact of securitisation.

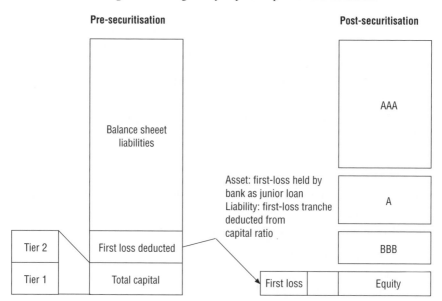

retained the first-loss piece. With regard to the regulatory capital impact, this first-loss amount is deducted from the bank's total capital position. For example, assume a bank has $100 million of risk-weighted assets and a target Basel ratio of 12%,[8] and it securitises all $100 million of these assets. It retains the first-loss tranche that forms 1.5% of the total issue. The remaining 98.5% will be sold on to the market. The bank will still have to set aside 1.5% of capital as a buffer against future losses, but it has been able to free itself of the remaining 10.5% of capital.

Illustrating the process of securitisation

To illustrate the process of securitisation, we consider an hypothetical airline ticket receivables transaction, originated by a fictitious company called ABC Airways plc and arranged by the equally fictitious XYZ Securities Limited. The following illustrates the kind of issues that are considered by the investment bank that is structuring the deal.

---

[8] The minimum is 8% but many banks prefer to set aside an amount well in excess of this minimum required level.

Originator: ABC Airways plc
Issuer: "Airways No 1 Ltd"
Transaction: Ticket receivables airline future flow securitisation bonds
€200m three-tranche floating-rate notes, legal maturity 2010
Average life 4.1 years
Tranches: Class "A" note (AA), Libor plus [ ] bps[9]
Class "B" note (A), Libor plus [ ] bps
Class "E" note (BBB), Libor plus [ ] bps
Arranger: XYZ Securities plc

Due diligence

XYZ Securities undertakes due diligence on the assets to be securitized. In this case, it examines the airline performance figures over the last five years, as well as modelling future projected figures, including:

* total passenger sales;
* total ticket sales;
* total credit card receivables;
* geographical split of ticket sales.

It is the future flow of receivables, in this case credit card purchases of airline tickets, that is being securitised. This is a higher-risk asset class than say, residential mortgages, because the airline industry has a tradition of greater volatility of earnings than mortgage banks.

Marketing approach

The present and all future credit card ticket receivables generated by the airline are transferred to an SPV. The investment bank's syndication desk seeks to place the notes with institutional investors across Europe. The notes are first given an indicative pricing ahead of the issue, to gauge investor sentiment. Given the nature of the asset class, during November 2002 the notes are marketed at around three-month LIBOR plus 70–80 basis points (AA note), 120–130 basis points (A note) and 260–270 basis points (BBB note). The notes are "benchmarked" against recent issues with similar asset classes, as well as the spread level in the unsecured market of comparable issuer names.

---

[9]   The price spread is determined during the marketing stage, when the notes are offered to investors during a "roadshow".

Deal structure

The deal structure is shown at Figure 9.5.

Figure 9.5   Airways No 1 Limited deal structure.

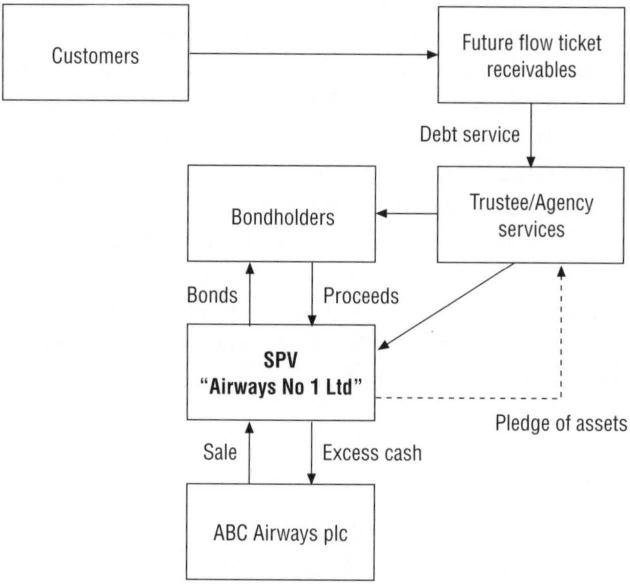

The process leading to the issue of notes is as follows:

- ABC Airways plc sells its future flow ticket receivables to an offshore SPV set up for this deal, incorporated as Airways No 1 Ltd;
- the SPV issues notes in order to fund its purchase of the receivables;
- the SPV pledges its right to the receivables to a fiduciary agent, the Security Trustee, for the benefit of the bondholders;
- the Trustee accumulates funds as they are received by the SPV;
- the bondholders receive interest and principal payments, in the order of priority of the notes, on a quarterly basis.

In the event of default, the Trustee will act on behalf of the bondholders to safeguard their interests.

Financial guarantors

The investment bank decides whether or not an insurance company, known as a monoline insurer, should be approached to "wrap" the deal by providing a guarantee of backing for the SPV in the event of default. This insurance is provided in return for a fee.

Financial modelling

XYZ Securities constructs a cash flow model to estimate the size of the issued notes. The model considers historical sales values, any seasonal factors in sales, credit card cash flows, and so on. Certain assumptions are made when constructing the model, for example growth projections, inflation levels and tax levels. The model considers a number of different scenarios, and also calculates the minimum asset coverage levels required to service the issued debt. A key indicator in the model is the debt service coverage ratio (DSCR). The more conservative the DSCR, the more comfort there is for investors in the notes. For a residential mortgage deal, this ratio may be approximately 2.5–3.0, however for an airline ticket receivables deal, the DSCR is unlikely to be lower than 4.0. The model therefore calculates the amount of notes that can be issued against the assets, whilst maintaining the minimum DSCR.

Credit rating

It is common for securitisation deals to be rated by one or more of the formal credit ratings agencies such as Moody's, Fitch or Standard & Poor's. A formal credit rating makes it easier for XYZ Securities to place the notes with investors. The methodology employed by the ratings agencies takes into account both qualitative and quantitative factors, and differs according to the asset class being securitized. The main issues in a deal such as our hypothetical Airways No 1 deal would be expected to include:

- corporate credit quality: these are risks associated with the originator, and are factors that affect its ability to continue operations, meet its financial obligations, and provide a stable foundation for generating future receivables. This might be analysed according to the following:
  (i) ABC Airways' historical financial performance, including its liquidity and debt structure;
  (ii) its status within its domicile country, for example whether or not it is state-owned;
  (iii) the general economic conditions for industry and for airlines, and;

(iv) the historical record and current state of the airline, for instance its safety record and age of its aeroplanes;

• the competition and industry trends: ABC Airways' market share, the competition on its network;

• regulatory issues, such as the need for ABC Airways to comply with forthcoming legislation that will impact its cash flows;

• legal structure of the SPV and transfer of assets;

• cash flow analysis.

Based on the findings of the ratings agency, the arranger may re-design some aspect of the deal structure so that the issued notes are rated at the required level.

This is a selection of the key issues involved in the process of securitisation. Depending on investor sentiment, market conditions and legal issues, the process from inception to closure of the deal may take anything from three to 12 months or more. After the notes have been issued, the arranging bank no longer has anything to do with the issue, however the bonds themselves require a number of agency services for their remaining life until they mature or are paid off (see Procter and Leedham, 2004). These agency services include paying the agent, cash manager and custodian.

References and Bibliography

Bhattacharya, A., Fabozzi, F., (eds.), *Asset-Backed Securities*, FJF Associates, 1996.

Choudhry, M., *The Bond and Money Markets: Strategy, Trading, Analysis*, Butterworth-Heinemann 2001.

Fabozzi, F., Choudhry, M., *The Handbook of European Structured Financial Products*, John Wiley 2004.

Hayre, L., (editor), *The Salomon Smith Barney Guide to Mortgage-Backed and Asset-Backed Securities*, John Wiley and Sons 2001.

Martellini, L., P., Priaulet, S., Priaulet, *Fixed Income Securities*, John Wiley and Sons 2003.

Morris, D., *Asset Securitisation: Principles and Practices*, Executive Enterprise 1990.

Procter, N., and Leedham, E., "Trust and Agency Services in the Debt Capital Market", in Fabozzi, F., and Choudhry, M., *The Handbook of European Fixed Income Securities*, John Wiley 2004.

Sundaresan, S., *Fixed Income Markets and Their Derivatives*, South-Western Publishing 1997, chapter 9.

Where's the love that we once had,
The one we thought would last and last ... ?

— Joe Diffie, *Life's So Funny*
(Sony Music) 1995

10

Synthetic Collateralised Debt Obligations[1]

In the previous chapter we looked at the basic concepts of traditional cash flow securitisation. Combining certain aspects of this technique with credit derivatives technology gives rise to so-called *synthetic securitisation*, also known as unfunded securitisation. In a synthetic transaction, the credit risk of a pool of assets is transferred from an originator to investors, but the assets themselves are not sold.[2] In certain jurisdictions, it may not be possible to undertake a cash securitisation due to legal, regulatory, cross-border or other restrictions. Or, it may be that the process simply takes too long under the prevailing market conditions. In such cases, originators use synthetic transactions, which employ some part of the traditional process allied with credit derivatives. However, if the main motivation of the originator remains funding concerns, then the cash flow approach must still be used. Synthetic transactions are mainly used for credit risk and regulatory capital reasons, and not funding purposes.

This chapter is an analysis of the synthetic collateralised debt obligation, or collateralised synthetic obligation (CSO). We focus on the key drivers of this type of instrument, from an issuer and investor point of view, before assessing the mechanics of the structures themselves. This takes the form of a case study-type review of selected innovative transactions. Finally, we

---

[1] The author thanks Katul Tanna at JPMorgan Chase Bank and Dr Chee Hau at Standard & Poors, for review comments on an earlier draft of this chapter.

[2] Although the first synthetic transactions were "balance sheet" deals, in which the originating bank transferred the credit risk of a pool of assets it held without actually selling them off its balance sheet, the fact that assets are not actually transferred means that the originator does actually have to own them in the first place. It may wish to transfer the credit risk for portfolio trading reasons. We look at this development of CSOs in this chapter too.

propose a new structure that combines the advantages of existing deal types to date, which presents features of interest to a wide group of investors and issuers alike. We begin with a brief introduction to the concept of the collateralised debt obligation, a progressive development of well-established securitisation techniques.

Securitisation and the Collateralised Debt Obligation (CDO)

A *cash flow* CDO is a structure that is represented by an issue of notes which has interest and principal payments linked to the performance of the underlying assets of the vehicle. These underlying assets act as the *collateral* for the issued notes, hence the name. There are many similarities between CDOs and other asset-backed securities (ABS), which pre-dated them. The key difference between CDOs and other ABS and multi-asset repackaged securities is that the collateral pool is generally (though not always) actively managed by a collateral portfolio manager. This pool can be either bank loans, bonds, or a mixture of both loans and bonds. Pure loan structures are known as collateralised loan obligations (CLOs) and pure bond structures are known as collateralised bond obligations (CBO). A mixed pool of assets would be a CDO.

Generally CDOs feature a multi-tranche overlying note structure, with most or all of the notes being rated by one or more of the public credit ratings agencies. The priority of payment of the issued securities reflects the credit rating for each note, with the most senior note being the highest rated. In Europe, issued securities may pay a fixed or floating coupon, usually on a semi-annual, quarterly or monthly basis[3], with senior note issues rated from AAA to A and junior and mezzanine notes rated BBB to B. There may be unrated subordinated and *equity* pieces issued. The equity note is actually a bond, and represents the shareholding interest in the vehicle, its return is variable and linked to the performance of the collateral pool. Investors in the subordinated notes receive coupon after payment of servicing fees and the coupon on senior notes. The equity and subordinated note are the first-loss pieces and, as they carry the highest risk, have a higher expected return compared to that of the underlying collateral. In a CDO, the cash flows of

---

[3] Hence proving once and for all that Eurobonds, defined as international securities issued by a syndicate of banks and clearing in Euroclear and Clearstream, may pay coupon on frequencies other than an annual basis!

the underlying assets are used to fund the liabilities of the overlying notes. As the notes carry different ratings, there is a *priority of payment* that must be followed, which is the cash flow waterfall. The waterfall was explained in Chapter 9.

In other words, cash flow CDOs are quite similar to traditional ABS, with the key difference being the nature of the underlying asset pool. Banks and financial institutions use CDOs to diversify their sources of funding, to manage portfolio risk and to obtain regulatory capital relief. Investors are attracted to the senior notes in a transaction because these allow them to earn relatively high yields compared to other asset-backed bonds of a similar credit rating. Other advantages for investors include:

- exposure to a diversified range of corporate credit names;
- access to the fund management and credit analysis skills of the portfolio manager;
- generally, a lower level of uncertainty and risk exposure compared to a single bond of similar rating.

A recommended reading on cash flow CDOs is Fabozzi and Goodman (2001).

The Synthetic CDO

Synthetic CDOs were introduced to meet differing needs of originators, where credit risk transfer is of more importance than funding considerations. Compared with conventional cash flow deals, which feature an actual transfer of ownership or *true sale* of the underlying assets to a separately incorporated legal entity, a synthetic securitisation structure is engineered so that the credit risk of the assets is transferred by the sponsor or originator of the transaction, from itself, to the investors by means of credit derivative instruments. The originator is therefore the credit protection buyer and investors are the credit protection sellers. This credit risk transfer may be undertaken either directly or via an SPV. Using this approach, underlying or *reference* assets are not moved off the originator's balance sheet, so it is adopted whenever the primary objective is to achieve risk transfer rather than balance sheet funding. The synthetic structure enables removal of credit exposure without asset transfer, so may be preferred for risk management and regulatory capital relief purposes. For banking institutions it also enables loan risk to be transferred without selling the loans themselves, thereby allowing customer relationships to remain unaffected.

The first synthetic deals were observed in the US market, while the first deals in Europe were observed in 1998. Figure 10.1 illustrates market growth in Europe.

Figure 10.1   CDO market growth in Europe.

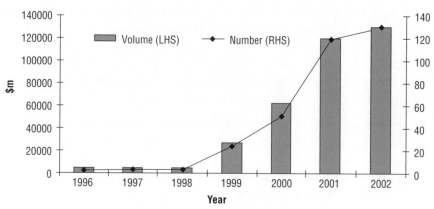

Volume includes rated debt and credit default swap tranches and unrated super-senior tranches for synthetic CDOs, and excludes equity tranches.

Source: Moodys

Assessing the genesis of the synthetic CDO

The original cash flow-style CDO was a tool for intermediation. In this respect, it can be viewed as a (mini-) bank, albeit a more efficient tool for intermediation than a bank. Where a CDO-type structure differs from a bank is in the composition of its asset pool: unlike a bank, its asset pool is not diverse, but is tailored to meet the specific requirements of both the originator and the customer (investor). It is this tailoring that generates the economic efficiencies of the CDO. In an institutional scenario, as exists in a bank, assets are, in effect, priced at their lowest common denominator. Hence, a bank that has 10% of its assets held in the form of emerging market debt would be priced at a lower value than an equivalent institution that does not hold such risky assets. The CDO-structure's liabilities are also more tailored to specific needs, with a precise mix of equity holders, AAA-liabilities and so on.

We may view the CDO-type entity as similar to a banking institution and a tool for the intermediation of risk. A synthetic CDO may be viewed in similar terms, but in its case the analogy is more akin to that of an insurance company rather than a bank. This reflects the separation of funding from credit risk that is facilitated by the synthetic approach, and the resulting ability to price pure credit — a risk management mechanism that is analogous to how an insurance company operates in comparison to a bank. The investors in a synthetic CDO do not purchase the assets that are referenced in a vehicle, they merely wish an economic exposure to it. This is made possible through the use of credit derivatives in the CDO structure.

Combining securitisation technology with credit derivatives, into synthetic structures, was particularly suited to the European market, with its myriad of legal and securitisation jurisdictions. The traditional method of securitisation, involving selling assets into a special purpose vehicle and used for balance sheet and risk management purposes, was viewed as less efficient than it had proved in the North American market. This was due to the differing circumstances prevailing in each market:

- In the US market, commercial banks were traditionally lower-rated than their counterparts in Europe. Hence the funding element of a cash flow securitisation was a key motivating factor behind a deal, as the originator could secure lower funding costs by means of the securitisation;
- European banks, being higher-rated than US banks, had less need of the funding side in a securitisation deal — compared to US banks, they obtained a greater share of their funding from their retail customer base. A significant portion of their funding was obtained at LIBOR-minus, compared to the LIBOR-flat funding of US banks.

So although European banks had an interest in transferring risk from their balance sheet, they had less need of the funding associated with traditional securitisation. A cash flow CDO was not as economic for originators in the European market because they did not have a need for funding, and so this approach had little or no benefit for them. However, banks still needed to reduce regulatory capital requirements and transfer credit risk. This led to the first static balance sheet synthetic CDO, known as BISTRO, which was originated by JPMorgan in 1997.[4]

The first synthetic CDOs were balance sheet driven; banks structured deals for regulatory capital management purposes. These deals reflected a desire by banks to shift their credit risk and by so doing, manage capital more efficiently. Later deals followed an arbitrage model: they were originated by fund managers, who were perceived by investors as being

---

[4]   See the exhibit on the BISTRO deal.

more professional at managing risk. Hence the "second generation" of CDO structures, which reflected the comparative advantage generated as insurance companies were able to split up an overall "pool" of risk and break this into separate pieces. These pieces were tailored to specific investor preferences. Compared to cash flow structures, synthetic structures separate the risk transfer element from the funding element. This mirrors what occurred in the early 1980s with interest rate swaps, shortly after these were introduced. Interest rate swaps also split the interest rate risk from the funding risk, as they were off-balance sheet instruments with no exchange of principal. This is the same case with credit derivatives and is precisely what has happened in the credit derivatives market.

Deal motivations

Differences between synthetic and cash CDOs are perhaps best reflected in the different cost-benefit economics of issuing each type. The motivations behind the issue of each type usually also differ. A synthetic CDO is constructed out of the following:

- a short position in a credit default swap (bought protection), by which the sponsor transfers its portfolio credit risk to the issuer;
- a long position in a portfolio of bonds or loans, the cash flow from which enables the sponsor to pay liabilities of overlying notes.

The originators of the first synthetic deals were banks that wished to manage the credit risk exposure of their loan books, without having to resort to the administrative burden of true sale cash securitisation. They are a natural progression in the development of credit derivative structures, with single name credit default swaps being replaced by portfolio default swaps. Synthetic CDOs can be "de-linked" from the sponsoring institution, so that investors do not have any credit exposure to the sponsor itself. The first deals were introduced (in 1998) at a time when widening credit spreads and the worsening of credit quality among originating firms meant that investors were sellers of those cash CDOs that had retained a credit linkage to the sponsor. A synthetic arrangement also means that the credit risk of assets that are otherwise not suited to conventional securitisation may be transferred, while assets are retained on the balance sheet. Such assets include bank guarantees, letters of credit or cash loans that have some legal or other restriction on being securitised. For this reason, synthetic deals are more appropriate for assets that are described under multiple legal jurisdictions.

The economic advantage of issuing a synthetic versus a cash CDO can be significant. Put simply, the net benefit to the originator is the gain in regulatory capital cost, minus the cost of paying for credit protection on the credit default swap side. In a partially funded structure, which combines cash notes and credit derivatives, a sponsoring bank obtains full capital relief when note proceeds are invested in 0% risk-weighted collateral such as Treasuries or gilts. The "super-senior" swap portion carries a 20% risk weighting.[5] A synthetic deal would be cheaper — where credit default swaps are used, the sponsor pays a basis point fee, which for a AAA-rated security might be in the range of 10–30 bps, depending on the stage of the credit cycle. In a cash structure where bonds are issued, the cost to the sponsor is the benchmark yield plus the credit spread, which would be considerably higher when compared to the default swap premium. This is illustrated in the example shown at Figure 10.2, where we assume certain spreads and premiums in comparing a partially funded synthetic deal with a cash deal. The assumptions are:

- that the super-senior credit swap cost is 15 bps, and carries a 20% risk weight;
- the equity piece retains a 100% risk-weighting;
- the synthetic CDO invests note proceeds in sovereign collateral that pays sub-LIBOR.

Synthetic deals can be *unfunded, partially funded* or *fully funded*. An unfunded CDO is comprised wholly of credit default swaps, while fully funded structures are arranged so that the entire credit risk of the reference portfolio is transferred through the issue of credit-linked notes. We discuss these shortly.

Within the European market, static synthetic balance sheet CDOs are the most common structure. The reasons that banks originate them are two-fold:

- *capital relief*: banks can obtain regulatory capital relief by transferring lower-yield corporate credit risk such as corporate bank loans off their balance sheet. Under Basel I rules, all corporate debt carries an identical 100% risk-weighting; therefore with banks having to assign 8% of capital for such loans, higher-rated (and hence lower-yielding) corporate assets require the same amount of capital but

---

[5]   This is as long as the counterparty is an OECD bank, which is invariably the case. It is called 'super-senior' because the swap is ahead of the most senior of any funded (note) portion.

Figure 10.2   Hypothetical generic cash flow and synthetic CDO comparative deal economics.

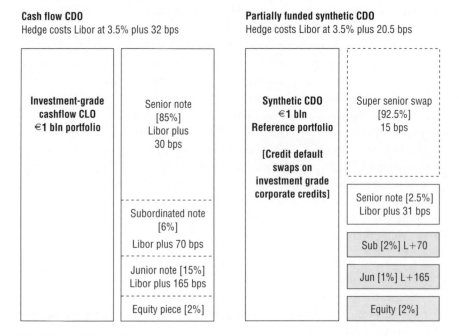

Cash flow CDO
Hedge costs Libor at 3.5% plus 32 bps

Partially funded synthetic CDO
Hedge costs Libor at 3.5% plus 20.5 bps

Investment-grade cashflow CLO €1 bln portfolio

Senior note [85%] Libor plus 30 bps

Subordinated note [6%] Libor plus 70 bps

Junior note [15%] Libor plus 165 bps

Equity piece [2%]

Synthetic CDO €1 bln Reference portfolio

[Credit default swaps on investment grade corporate credits]

Super senior swap [92.5%] 15 bps

Senior note [2.5%] Libor plus 31 bps

Sub [2%] L+70

Jun [1%] L+165

Equity [2%]

Regulatory capital relief

Cash CDO
Capital charge on assets reduces from 8% (100% RW) to 2% (equity piece only now 100% RW)
Regulatory capital relief is 6%

Synthetic CDO
Capital charge on assets reduces from 8% (100% RW) to 3.48% (equity piece plus super senior swap at 20% RW)
Regulatory capital relief is 4.52%

generate a lower return on that capital. A bank may wish to transfer such higher-rated, lower-yield assets from its balance sheet, and this can be achieved via a CDO transaction. The capital requirements for a synthetic CDO are lower than for corporate assets. For example, the funded segment of the deal is supported by high quality collateral such as government bonds, and via a repo arrangement with an OECD bank, carries a 20% risk weighting, as does the super-senior element;

- *transfer of credit risk*: the cost of servicing a fully funded CDO, and the premium payable on the associated credit default swap, can be prohibitive. With a partially funded structure, the issue amount is typically a relatively small share of the asset portfolio. This substantially lowers the default swap premium. Also, as the CDO investors suffer the first loss element of the portfolio, the super-senior default swap can be entered into at a considerably lower cost than that on a fully funded CDO.

Deal mechanics

A synthetic CDO is so-called because the transfer of credit risk is achieved "synthetically" via a credit derivative, rather than by a "true sale" to an SPV. Thus in a synthetic CDO, the credit risk of the underlying loans or bonds is transferred to the SPV using credit default swaps and/or total return swaps (TRS). However, the assets themselves are not legally transferred to the SPV, and they remain on the originator's balance sheet. Using a synthetic CDO, the originator can obtain regulatory capital relief[6] and manage the credit risk on its balance sheet, but it will not receive any funding. In other words, a synthetic CDO structure enables originators to separate credit risk exposure and asset funding requirements. The credit risk of the asset portfolio, now known as the reference portfolio, is transferred, directly or to an SPV, through credit derivatives. The most common credit contracts used are credit default swaps. A portion of the credit risk may be sold on as credit-linked notes. Typically, a large majority of the credit risk is transferred via a super senior credit default swap[7], which is dealt with a swap counterparty but usually sold to monoline insurance companies at a significantly lower spread over LIBOR compared with the senior AAA-rated tranche of cash flow CDOs. This is a key attraction of synthetic deals for originators. Most deals are structured with mezzanine notes sold to a wider set of investors, the proceeds of which are invested in risk-free collateral such as Treasury bonds or Pfandbriefe securities. The most junior note, known as the "first-loss" piece, may be retained by the originator. On occurrence of a credit event among the reference assets, the originating bank receives funds remaining from the collateral after they have been used to pay the principal on the issued notes, less the value of the junior note.

---

[6] This is because reference assets that are protected by credit derivative contracts, and which remain on the balance sheet, attract a lower regulatory capital charge under Basel rules.

[7] So called because the swap is ahead of the most senior of any funded (note) portion, which latter being "senior" means the swap must be "super-senior".

A generic synthetic CDO structure is shown in Figure 10.3. In this generic structure, the credit risk of the reference assets is transferred to the issuer SPV and ultimately the investors, by means of the credit default swap and an issue of credit-linked notes. In the default swap arrangement, the risk transfer is undertaken in return for the swap premium, which is then paid to investors by the issuer. The note issue is invested in risk-free collateral rather than passed on to the originator, in order to de-link the credit ratings of the notes from the rating of the originator. If the collateral pool is not established, a downgrade of the sponsor may result in a downgrade of the issued notes. Investors in the notes expose themselves to the credit risk of the reference assets, and if there are no credit events they will earn returns to at least equal the collateral assets and the default swap premium. If the notes are credit-linked, they will also earn excess returns based on the performance of the reference portfolio. If there are credit events, the issuer will deliver the assets to the swap counterparty and will pay the nominal value of the assets to the originator out of the collateral pool. Credit default

Figure 10.3   Generic synthetic CDO structure.

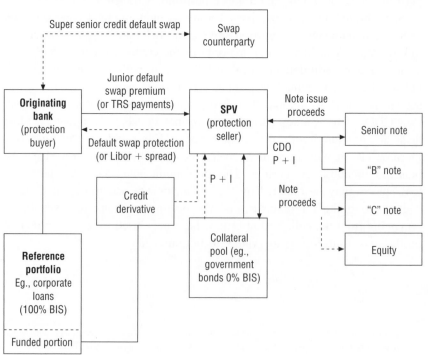

swaps are unfunded credit derivatives, while CLNs are funded credit derivatives where the protection seller (the investors) fund the value of the reference assets up-front, and receive a reduced return on occurrence of a credit event.

Funding mechanics

As the super-senior piece in a synthetic CDO does not need to be funded, there is a key advantage of the synthetic mechanism compared to a cash flow arbitrage CDO. During the first half of 2002, the yield spread for the AAA note piece averaged 45–50 basis points over LIBOR[8], while the cost of the super-senior swap was around 10–12 basis points. This means that the CDO manager can reinvest in the collateral pool risk-free assets at LIBOR minus 5 basis points, and it is able to gain from a saving of 28–35 basis points on each nominal $100 of the structure that is not funded. This is a considerable gain. If we assume that a synthetic CDO is 95% unfunded and 5% funded, this is equivalent to the reference assets trading at approximately 26–33 basis points cheaper in the market. There is also an improvement to the return on capital measure for the CDO manager. Since typically the manager retains the equity piece, if this is 2% of the structure and the gain is 33 basis points, the return on equity is improved by [0.36/0.02] or 16.5%.

Another benefit of structuring CDOs as synthetic deals is their potentially greater attraction for investors (protection sellers). Often, selling credit default swap protection on a particular reference credit generates a higher return than "going long" the underlying cash bond. In general this is because the credit default swap price is greater than the asset swap price for the same name, for a number of reasons as discussed in Chapter 8. For example, during 2001 the average spread of the synthetic price over the cash price was 15 basis points in the five-year maturity area for BBB-rated credits.[9] The main reasons why default swap spreads tend to be above cash spreads were discussed earlier.

---

[8] Averaged from the yield spread on 7 synthetic deals closed during January–June 2002, yield spread at issue, rates data from Bloomberg.

[9] Source: JPMorgan, *CDO Research*, September 2002.

Example 10.1 Credit Risk Transfer

In simple terms, the protection buyer, which is usually the collateral manager of the CDO, enters into a credit default swap with the SPV, which is the junior default swap labeled in Figure 10.3. By buying protection on the reference entities, the CDO manager transfers the credit risk on these entities to the CDO investors, who are protection sellers. In return for taking on this risk, investors receive a premium from the protection buyer. Therefore, as shown in Figure 10.3, the return for investors is the coupon on the collateral securities together with the credit default swap premium.

The super-senior piece is unfunded and typically sold to a swap counterparty or monoline insurer as a basket credit default swap, called the super-senior credit default swap. The credit risk on this piece is statistically very low, because it represents the most senior piece of the portfolio and is usually comprised of high quality investment grade credits. There is thus a very low probability that loss due to default will exceed the portion of the CDO that is funded, thereby eating into the super-senior piece, so this represents a very low risk, termed "catastrophe risk" in an insurance company. Because the senior note is often AAA-rated, and the super-senior piece ranks above this, it is a higher quality risk than AAA risk.

Advantages of synthetic structures

The introduction of synthetic securitisation vehicles was in response to specific demands of sponsoring institutions, and they present certain advantages over traditional cash flow structures. These include:

- speed of implementation: a synthetic transaction can, in theory, be placed in the market sooner than a cash deal, and the time from inception to closure can be as low as four weeks, with an average execution time of 6–8 weeks compared to 3–4 months for the equivalent cash deal. This reflects the shorter ramp-up period noted above;
- banking relationships can be maintained with clients whose loans need not be sold off the sponsoring entity's balance sheet;
- no requirement to fund the super-senior element;
- for many reference names the credit default swap is frequently cheaper than the same name underlying cash bond;

- transaction costs such as legal fees can be lower, as there is no necessity to set up an SPV;
- the range of reference assets that can be covered is wider, and includes undrawn lines of credit, bank guarantees and derivative instruments that give rise to legal and true sale issues in a cash transaction;
- the use of credit derivatives introduces greater flexibility to provide tailor-made solutions for credit risk requirements;
- the cost of buying protection is usually lower as there is little or no funding element and the credit protection price is below the equivalent-rate note liability.

This does not mean that the cash transaction is now an endangered species. It retains certain advantages of its own over synthetic deals, which include:

- no requirement for an OECD bank (the 20% BIS risk-weighted entity) to act as the swap counterparty to meet capital relief requirements;
- lower capital relief available compared to the 20% risk-weighting on the OECD bank counterparty;
- larger potential investor base, as the number of counterparties is potentially greater (certain financial and investing institutions have limitations on the degree of usage of credit derivatives);
- lower degree of counterparty exposure for originating entity. In a synthetic deal the default of a swap counterparty means cessation of premium payments or more critically, a credit event protection payment, and termination of the credit default swap.

Investment banking advisors structure the arrangement for their sponsoring client that best meets the latter's requirements. Depending on the nature of these, this can be either a synthetic or cash deal.

Synthetic CDO Deal Structures

We now look in further detail at the various types of synthetic CDO structures.

Generic concept

Synthetic CDOs have been issued in a variety of forms, labelled in generic form as arbitrage CDOs or balance sheet CDOs. Structures can differ to a considerable degree from one another, having only the basics in common with each other. The latest development is the *managed synthetic* CDO.

A synthetic arbitrage CDO is originated generally by collateral managers who wish to exploit the difference in yield between that obtained on the underlying assets and that payable on the CDO, both in note interest and servicing fees. The generic structure is as follows: an especially-created SPV enters into a total return swap with the originating bank or financial institution, referencing the bank's underlying portfolio (the reference portfolio). The portfolio is actively managed and is funded on the balance sheet by the originating bank. The SPV receives the "total return" from the reference portfolio, and in return it pays LIBOR plus a spread to the originating bank. The SPV also issues notes that are sold into the market to CDO investors, and these notes can be rated as high as AAA as they are backed by high-quality collateral, which is purchased using the note proceeds. A typical structure is shown in Figure 10.4.

Figure 10.4   Synthetic arbitrage CDO structure.

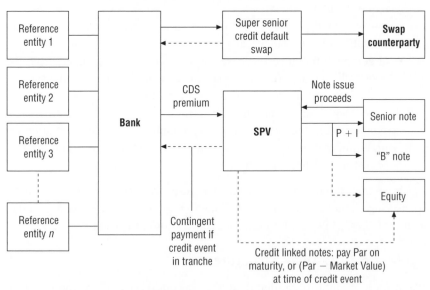

A balance sheet synthetic CDO is employed by banks that wish to manage regulatory capital. As before, the underlying assets are bonds, loans and credit facilities originated by the issuing bank. In a balance sheet CDO, the SPV enters into a credit default swap agreement with the originator, with the specific collateral pool designated as the reference portfolio. The SPV receives the premium payable on the default swap, and thereby provides credit protection on the reference portfolio. There are three types of CDO within this structure. A fully synthetic CDO is a completely *unfunded* structure, which uses credit default swaps to transfer the entire credit risk of the reference assets to investors who are protection sellers. In a *partially funded* CDO, only the highest credit risk segment of the portfolio is transferred. The cash flow that is needed to service the synthetic CDO overlying liability is received from the AAA-rated collateral that is purchased by the SPV with the proceeds of an overlying note issue. An originating bank obtains maximum regulatory capital relief by means of a partially funded structure, through a combination of the synthetic CDO and a super-senior swap arrangement with an OECD banking counterparty. A super-senior swap provides additional protection to that part of the portfolio, the senior segment, which is already protected by the funded portion of the transaction. The sponsor may retain the super-senior element or may sell it to a monoline insurance firm or credit default swap provider.

Some commentators categorize synthetic deals using slightly different terms. For instance Boggiano, Waterson and Stein (2002) define the following types:

- balance sheet static synthetic CDO;
- managed static synthetic CDO;
- balance sheet variable synthetic CDO;
- managed variable synthetic CDO.

As described by Boggiano *et al*, the basic structure is similar to that for a partially funded synthetic CDO. In fact there is essentially little difference between the first two types of deal, in the latter an investment manager rather than the credit swap counterparty selects the portfolio. However, the reference assets remain static for the life of the deal in both cases. For the last two deal types, the main difference is that an investment manager, rather than the originator bank, trades the portfolio of credit swaps under specified guidelines. This is arguably not a structural difference and so for the purposes of this book we consider them both as managed CDOs, which are described later.

Synthetic deals may be either static or managed. Static deals have the following advantages:

- there are no ongoing management fees to be borne by the vehicle;
- the investor can review and grant approval to credits that are to make up the reference portfolio.

The disadvantage is that if there is a deterioration in credit quality of one or more names, there is no ability to remove or offset this name from the pool and the vehicle continues to suffer from it. During 2001, a number of high profile defaults in the market meant that static pool CDOs performed below expectation. This explains partly the rise in popularity of the managed synthetic deal, which we discuss later.

Funded and unfunded deals

Synthetic deal structures are arranged in a variety of ways, with funded and unfunded elements to meet investor and market demand. A generic partially funded synthetic transaction is shown in Figure 10.5. It shows an arrangement whereby the issuer enters into two credit default swaps — the first with an SPV that provides protection for losses up to a specified amount

Figure 10.5 Partially funded synthetic CDO structure.

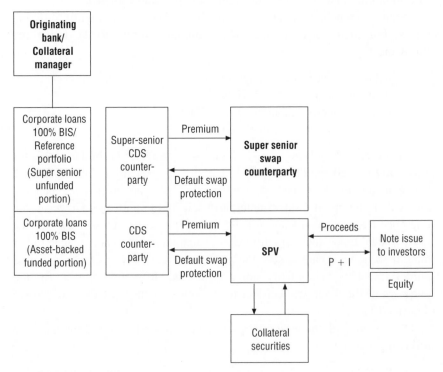

of the reference pool[10], while the second swap is set up with the OECD bank or, occasionally, an insurance company.[11]

A *fully funded* CDO is a structure where the credit risk of the entire portfolio is transferred to the SPV via credit linked notes. In a fully funded (or just "funded") synthetic CDO, the issuer enters into the credit default swap with the SPV, which itself issues credit-linked notes (CLNs) to the value of the assets on which the risk has been transferred. The proceeds from the notes are invested in risk-free government or agency debt such as gilts, bunds or Pfandbriefe, or in senior unsecured bank debt. Should there be a default on one or more of the underlying assets, the required amount of the collateral is sold and the proceeds from the sale are paid to the issuer to recompense for the losses. The premium paid on the credit default swap must be sufficiently high to ensure that it covers the difference in yield between that on the collateral and that on the notes issued by the SPV. The generic structure is illustrated in Figure 10.6.

Figure 10.6 Fully funded synthetic balance sheet CDO structure.

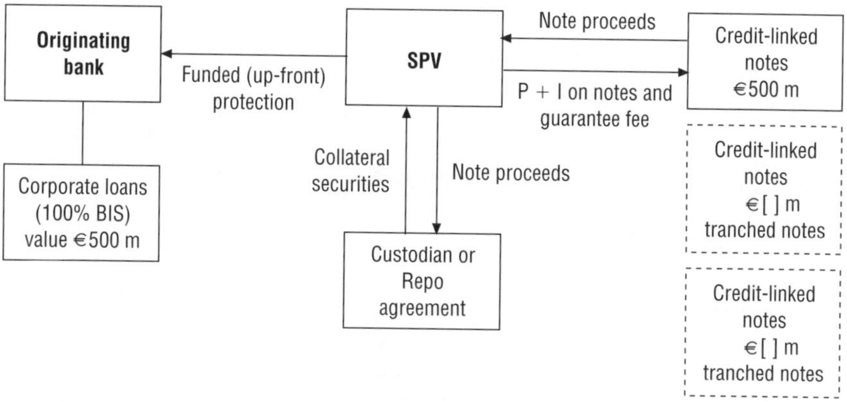

Fully funded CDOs are relatively uncommon. One of the advantages of the partially funded arrangement is that the issuer pays a lower premium compared to a fully funded synthetic CDO, because it is not required to pay the difference between the yield on the collateral and the coupon on the note issue (the unfunded part of the transaction). The downside is that the issuer

---

[10] In practice, to date this portion has been between 5% and 15% of the reference pool.
[11] An "OECD" bank, thus guaranteeing a 20% risk-weighting for capital ratio purposes, under Basel I rules.

receives a reduction in risk-weighting for capital purposes to 20% for the risk transferred via the super-senior default swap.

The fully *unfunded* CDO uses only credit default swaps in its structure. The swaps are rated in a similar way to notes, and there is usually an "equity" piece that is retained by the originator. The reference portfolio is again commercial loans, usually 100% risk-weighted, or other assets. The credit rating of the swap tranches is based on the rating of the reference assets, as well as other factors such as the diversity of the assets and ratings performance correlation. The typical structure is illustrated in Figure 10.7. As well as the equity tranche, there is one or more junior tranches, one or more senior tranches and super senior tranche. The senior tranches are sold on to AAA-rated banks as a portfolio credit default swap, while the junior

Figure 10.7   The fully synthetic or unfunded CDO.

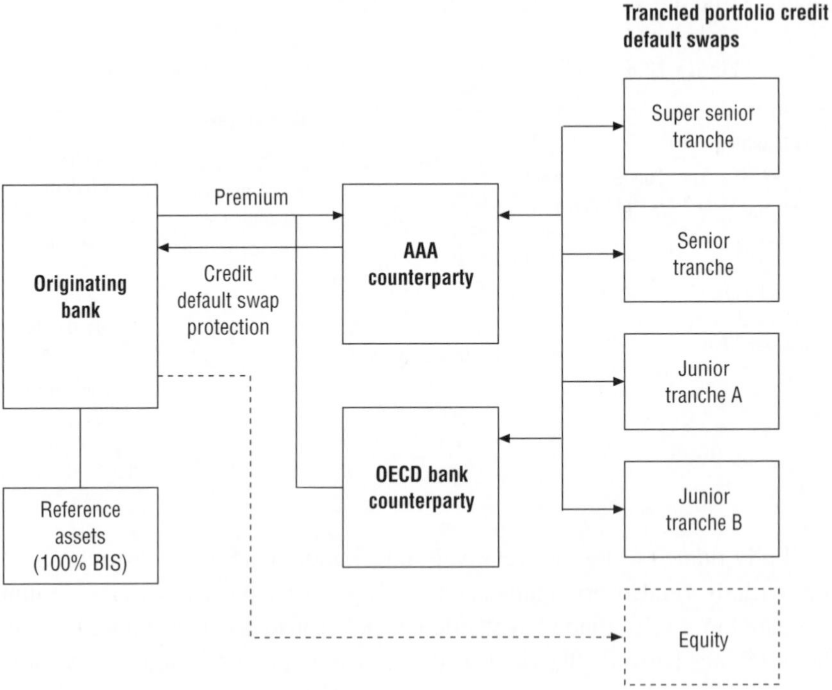

tranche is usually sold to an OECD bank. The ratings of the tranches are typically:

* super-senior: AAA;
* senior: AA to AAA;
* junior: BB to A;
* equity: unrated.

The credit default swaps are not single-name swaps, but are written on a class of debt. The advantage for the originator is that it can name the reference asset class to investors without having to disclose the name of specific loans. Default swaps are usually cash-settled and not physically-settled, so that the reference assets can be replaced with other assets if desired by the sponsor.

Deal term sheet

In the markets, the first description of a transaction is usually provided in the deal term sheet, produced by the arranging bank. For illustrative purposes, we show at Appendix 10.3, a sample term sheet for a hypothetical deal, which we have called Scarab CDO I Limited. This term sheet is representative of what may be encountered in the market, although there is a wide discrepancy among these, with some being just one side of A4 paper, while others my be 40 or 50 pages long. The full legal description of the deal is given in the deal offering circular (OC). For full details of the legal and documentation aspects of a securitisation, see Garcia and Patel (2004).

Example 10.2 **The Fully Unfunded Synthetic CDO**

This example illustrates a fully unfounded deal, which can be either on balance sheet or source reference assets externally. Because it is fully unfunded, the liabilities of the deal structure are comprised purely of credit default swaps (CDS), and so it can also be structured with or without an SPV. Our example is of a hypothetical deal structure with the following terms:

Originator: Banking institution
Reference Portfolio: €900 m notional
                       80–100 corporate names sourced in the market

---

CDS tranching: Super-senior CDS €815 m notional

         "Class A" CDS €35 m notional

         "Class B" CDS €15 m notional

         "Class C" CDS €20 m notional

         "Class D" or Equity CDS €15 m notional

The structure is illustrated in Figure 10.8.

Figure 10.8 Fully unfunded synthetic CDO, structure diagram.

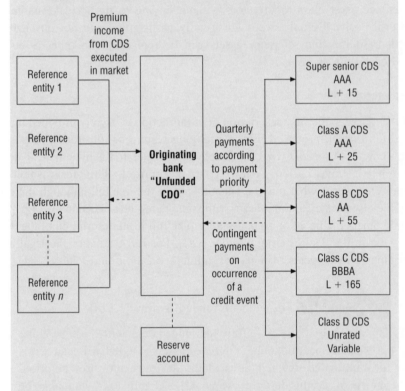

The key difference with this structure is that it can be arranged directly by the originating institution. There is no need to set up an SPV. In fact, this is also an on-balance sheet deal. The rating of the tranches is based on the loss allocation, with credit events among reference assets being set up so that the junior note suffers losses first. This follows traditional structured finance technology.

However unlike traditional structures, the interest payments on the liability side are not subject to a waterfall; instead, they are guaranteed to investors. This increases the attraction of the deal. Thus, on occurrence of a credit event, interest payments are still received by investors. It is the notional amount, on which interest is calculated, that is reduced, thereby reducing the interest received. Losses of notional value above the Class D threshold eat into the Class C swap notional amount.

This is a version of an arbitrage deal, with the originating bank taking the role of a fund manager. It features the following:

- the bank selects the initial portfolio, using its credit skills to select credits in the market, which are referenced via credit default swaps. The bank sells protection on these assets; the premium received exceeds the premium paid on the liability side, which creates the arbitrage gain for the bank. The reduced premium payable on the liability side reflects the tranches arrangement of the liaibilities;
- the reference assets are sourced by the bank on its own balance sheet, before the CDO itself is closed in the market;
- the bank has freedom to dynamically manage the portfolio during the life of the deal, taking a view on credits in line with its fundamental analysis of the market;
- trading profits are trapped in a "reserve account", which is also available to cover trading losses and losses suffered due to credit events.

As part of the rating requirements for the deal, the originating bank follows certain eligibility constraints on which exposures it can take on. This can include restrictions on:

- reference entities being rated at investment grade by the ratings agencies;
- no single reference credit to have a total exposure of more than 10 million;
- the reference entity is incorporated in a specified list of countries;
- geographical and industrial concentration;

- a trading turnover limit of 20% of notional value per annum;
- a Moody's diversity score of at least 45 on closing and no lower than 42 during life of deal.[12]

In addition to the "guaranteed" nature of interest payments for investors (subject to level of credit events), the principal advantage of this structure is that it may be brought to market very quickly. There is no requirement for the originator to set up an SPV, and no need to issue and settle notes. The originator can therefore take advantage of market conditions and respond quickly to investor demands for return enhancement and diversification.

The Managed Synthetic CDO

Managed synthetic CDOs are the latest variant of the synthetic CDO structure.[13] They are similar to the partially funded deals we described earlier, except that the reference asset pool of credit derivatives is actively traded by the sponsoring investment manager. It is the maturing market in credit default swaps, resulting in high liquidity in a large number of synthetic corporate credits, that has facilitated the introduction of the managed synthetic CDO. With this structure, originators can use credit derivatives to arbitrage cash and synthetic liabilities, as well as leverage off their expertise in credit trading to generate profit. The advantages for investors are the same as the advantages of earlier generations of CDOs, except that with active trading they are gaining a larger exposure to the skills of the investment manager. The underlying asset pool is again, a portfolio of credit default swaps. However, these are now dynamically managed and actively traded, under specified guidelines. Thus, there is greater flexibility afforded to the sponsor, and the vehicle records trading gains or losses as a result of credit derivative trading. In most structures, the investment manager can only buy protection (short credit) in order to offset an existing sold protection default swap. For some deals, this restriction is removed and the investment manager can buy or sell credit derivatives to reflect its view.

---

[12] See Appendix 10.1 for an introduction to the concept of the diversity score.

[13] These are also commonly known as collateralised synthetic obligations or CSOs within the market. *RISK* magazine has called them collateralised swap obligations, which handily also shortens to CSOs. Boggiano *et al* (2002) refer to these structures as managed variable synthetic CDOs, although the author has not come across this term in other literature.

Structure

The structure of the managed synthetic is similar to the partially funded synthetic CDO, with a separate legally incorporated SPV.[14] On the liability side, there is an issue of notes, with note proceeds invested in collateral or *eligible investments* that are made up of one or a combination of the following:

- a bank deposit account or guaranteed investment contract (*GIC*) which pays a pre-specified rate of interest;[15]
- risk-free bonds such as US Treasury securities, German Pfandbriefe or AAA-rated bonds such as credit-card ABS securities;
- a repo agreement with risk-free collateral;
- a liquidity facility with a AA-rated bank;
- a market-sensitive debt instrument, often enhanced with the repo or liquidity arrangement described above.

On the asset side, the SPV enters into credit default swaps and/or total return swaps, selling protection to the sponsor. The investment manager (or "collateral manager") can trade in and out of credit default swaps after the transaction has closed in the market.[16] The SPV enters into credit derivatives via a single basket credit default swap to one swap counterparty, written on a portfolio of reference assets, or via multiple single-name credit swaps with a number of swap counterparties. The latter arrangement is more common and is referred to as a *multiple dealer* CDO. A percentage of the reference portfolio is identified at the start of work on the transaction, with the remainder of the entities being selected during the ramp-up period ahead of closing. The SPV enters into the other side of the credit default swaps by selling protection to one of the swap counterparties on specific reference

---

[14] We use the term SPV for *special purpose vehicle*. This is also referred to as a special purpose entity (SPE) or special purpose company (SPC).

[15] A GIC has been defined either as an account that pays a fixed-rate of interest for its term, or more usually an account that pays a fixed spread below LIBOR or EURIBOR, usually three-month floating rolled over each interest period.

[16] This term is shared with other securitisation structures. When notes have been priced, and placed in the market, and all legal documentation signed by all named participants, the transaction has *closed*. In effect, this is the start of the transaction, and the noteholders should receive interest payments during the life of the deal and principal repayment on maturity.

entities. Thereafter, the investment manager can trade out of this exposure in the following ways:

- buying credit protection from another swap counterparty on the same reference entity. This offsets the existing exposure, but there may be residual risk exposure unless premium dates are matched exactly or if there is a default in both the reference entity and the swap counterparty;
- unwinding or terminating the swap with the counterparty;
- buying credit protection on a reference asset that is outside the portfolio. This is uncommon as it leaves residual exposures and may affect premium spread gains.

The SPV actively manages the portfolio within specified guidelines, the decisions being made by the investment manager. Initially the manager's opportunity to trade may be extensive, but this will be curtailed if there are losses. The trading guidelines will extend to both individual credit default swaps and at the portfolio level. They may include:

- parameters under which the investment manager (in the guise of the SPV) may actively close out, hedge or substitute reference assets using credit derivatives;
- guidelines under which the investment manager can trade credit derivatives to maximise gains or minimise losses on reference assets that have improved or worsened in credit quality or outlook.

Credit default swaps may be cash settled or physically settled, with physical settlement being more common in a managed synthetic deal. In a multiple dealer CDO, the legal documentation must be in place with all names on the counterparty dealer list, which may add to legal costs as standardisation may be difficult.

Investors who are interested in this structure are seeking to benefit from the following advantages compared to vanilla synthetic deals:

- active management of the reference portfolio and the trading expertise of the investment manager in the corporate credit market;
- a multiple dealer arrangement, so that the investment manager can obtain the most competitive prices for credit default swaps;
- under physical settlement, the investment manager (via the SPV) has the ability to obtain the highest recovery value for the reference asset.

A generic managed synthetic CDO is illustrated at Figure 10.9.

Figure 10.9 Generic managed synthetic CDO.

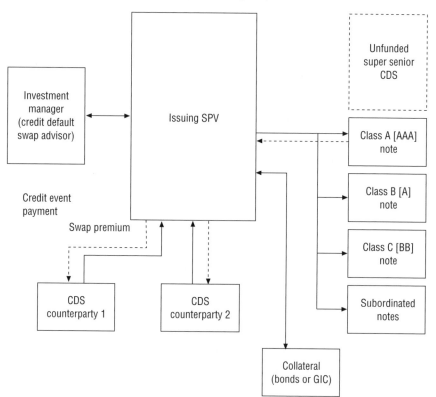

Originators generally appoint third-party portfolio administrators for managed synthetic CDOs to look after the deal during its life, because they are the most complex CSOs. The portfolio administrator is responsible for running (among other things) the rating agency compliance tests, such as the waterfall tests, and reporting on the quality of the reference portfolio to investors.

A schematic diagram of the roles performed by the portfolio administrator on a hypothetical managed CSO is shown in Appendix 10. 2.

Example 10.3 The AAA-rated Reference Portfolio CDO

This illustration is of an hypothetical managed synthetic CSO that generates value from low-risk reference assets. The deal structure is shown in Figure 10.10. During a period of economic downturn and widening spreads, higher yields on AAA-rated securities enable synthetic CDOs to be structured that are backed by a pool of AAA- rated collateral. Thus a very low-risk CDO vehicle can be created, providing investors with favorable risk/reward profiles. In this structure, investors are exposed to ratings downgrade risk rather than default risk, since it is extremely unlikely that an AAA-rated entity will experience default during the life of the deal.

The transaction features:

- a reference portfolio comprised solely of AAA credits: this can be a mixture of conventional bullet bonds, ABS and MBS securities and credit default swaps;
- a liability notes structure tranched so that the junior note is BBB-rated, however its effective risk is actually lower than this rating suggests. Thus a favorable risk/reward profile is created for investors;
- a return on a note that is BBB-rated (and hence paying BBB-note interest spread over LIBOR) but which is, in effect, AAA-rated given the nature of the collateral backing;
- all notes paying a fixed spread over LIBOR.

The proceeds of the note issues are held in a reserve account that is authorised to invest in "eligible investments". These are typically a cash account (or "GIC" account), Treasury bills and Treasury securities or other AAA-rated sovereign bonds. This reserve account is used to pay for any losses incurred by the reference portfolio; surplus reserves are for the benefit of the originating bank.

The risk/reward profile of the issued notes is possible because the reference assets are all AAA-rated. Investors in this deal are being exposed to spread risk rather than default risk (because a AAA-rated asset can be downgraded). Nevertheless, BBB noteholders are able to earn an attractive return at what is, for practical purposes, a risk exposure considerably lower than BBB-rated risk.

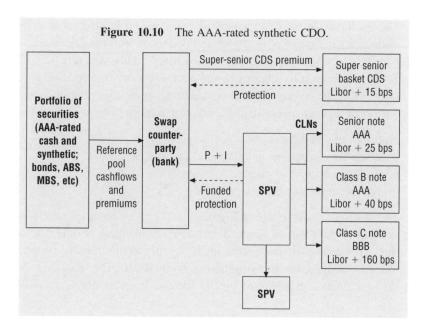

Figure 10.10   The AAA-rated synthetic CDO.

The Single-Tranche Synthetic CDO

One of the advantages offered to investors in the synthetic market is the ability to invest at maturities required by the investor, rather than at maturities selected by bond issuers. For example, Figure 10.11 illustrates that while the bond market provides assets at only selected points on the credit curve, synthetic products allow investors to access the full curve.

Figure 10.11   Hypothetical credit term structure.

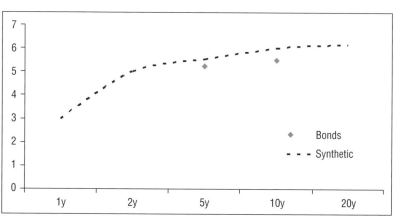

The flexibility of the CSO, enabling deal types to be structured to meet the needs of a wide range of investors and issuers, is well illustrated with the tailor-made or "single-tranche CDO" structure.[17] This structure has been developed in response to investor demand for exposure to a specific part of a pool of reference credits. With this structure, an arranging bank creates a tailored portfolio that meets specific investor requirements with regard to:

* portfolio size and asset class;
* portfolio concentration, geographical and industry variation;
* portfolio diversity and rating;
* investment term-to-maturity.

The structure is illustrated in Figures 10.12 and 10.13, respectively with and without an SPV issuer. Under this arrangement, there is only one note tranche. The reference portfolio, made up of credit default swaps, is dynamically hedged by the originating bank itself. The deal has been arranged to create a risk/reward profile for one investor only (or possibly

Figure 10.12   Single Tranche CDO I: issue direct from arranging bank.

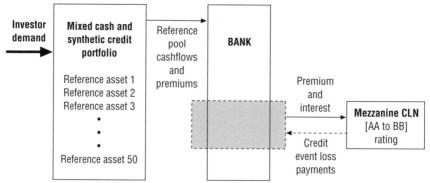

No credit event: 100% par value on due maturity date
Credit event: [Par − market value] of defaulted reference entitles exceeding the subordination

---

[17] These deals have been arranged by a number of investment banks, including JPMorgan Chase, Bank of America, UBS Warburg and Credit Agricole Indosuez. They are known variously as *tailor-made CDOs, tranche-only CDOs, on-demand CDOs, iCDOs* and *investor-driven CDOs* as well as single-tranche CDOs. The author prefers the last one!

Figure 10.13   Single Tranche CDO II: issue via SPV.

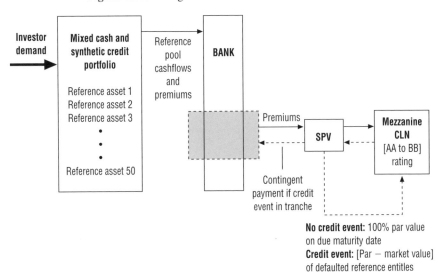

No credit event: 100% par value on due maturity date
Credit event: [Par − market value] of defaulted reference entitles exceeding the subordination

multiple investors with identical requirements), who buys the single tranche note. This also creates an added advantage that the deal can be brought to market very quickly. The key difference with traditional CSOs is that the arranging bank does not transfer the remainder of the credit risk of the reference pool. Instead, this risk is dynamically managed, and hedged in the market using derivatives.

Deal structure

The investor in a single-tranche CDO makes a decision on the criteria of assets in the portfolio, and the subordination of the issued tranche. Typically this will be at the mezzanine level, that is, covering the 4% to 9% loss level in the portfolio. This enables a favorable risk/return profile to be set up because a CDO tranche that is exposed to 4–9% losses has a very low historical risk of default (approximately equivalent to a Moody's A2 rating) and a high relative return given its tranching, around LIBOR plus 200 basis points as at May 2003. This is the risk/retrun profile of the mezzanine piece.

Figure 10.14 illustrates the default probability distribution for credit events in a CDO. Figure 10.15 shows the more specific distribution as applicable to the mezzanine tranche. We clarify this further with some hypothetical values for a capital structure and default distribution in Figure 10.16.

Figure 10.14 Credit loss distribution.

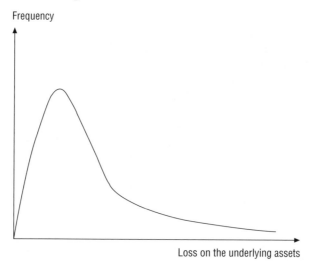

Frequency

Loss on the underlying assets

Figure 10.15 Expected loss distribution for tranched notes.

Probability

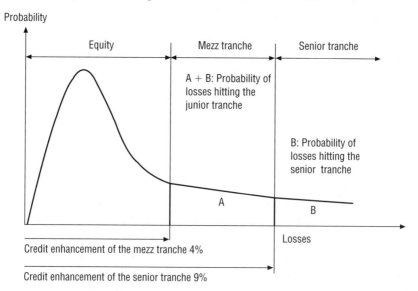

Equity | Mezz tranche | Senior tranche

A + B: Probability of losses hitting the junior tranche

B: Probability of losses hitting the senior tranche

A

B

Losses

Credit enhancement of the mezz tranche 4%

Credit enhancement of the senior tranche 9%

Figure 10.16   Capital structure and default distribution for single-tranche (mezzanine note) synthetic CDO.

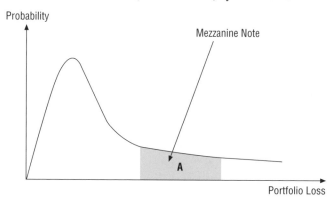

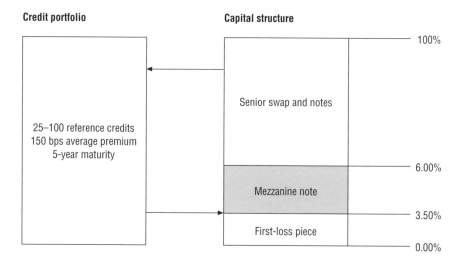

Unlike a traditional CDO, a single-tranche CDO has a very simple cash flow "waterfall". Compared with Figure 9.3, which showed the waterfall for a cash CDO, a single-tranche waterfall will consist of only agency service and hedge costs, and the coupon of the single tranche itself.

Some of the issues the investor should consider when working with the arranging bank to structure the deal include:

- the number of names in the credit portfolio, usually this ranges from 50 to 100 names;
- the geographical split of the reference names;

- the required average credit rating and average interest spread of the portfolio;
- the minimum credit rating required in the portfolio.

If the deal is being rated, as with any CDO type, the mix of assets needs to meet ratings agency criteria for diversity and average rating. The *diversity score* of a portfolio is a measure of the diversity of a portfolio based on qualities such as industrial and geographical concentration. It can be defined as the number of equivalent uncorrelated assets in the pool.[18] We illustrate an hypothetical portfolio at Figure 10.17, which shows the composition of a generic portfolio for a single-tranche CDO.

Figure 10.17   Hypothetical portfolio composition for generic single-tranche CDO.

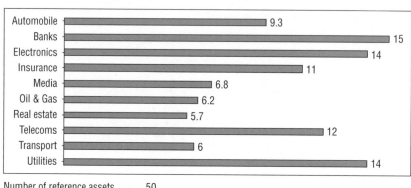

Number of reference assets	50
Moodys diversity score	46
Average rating	A2
Average maturity	5 years

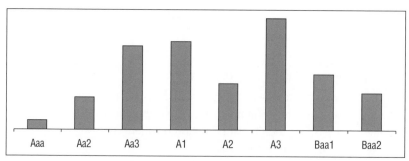

---

[18] Further background on Moody's diversity score is given at Appendix 10.1.

The position and rating of the issued single-tranche is as required by the investor. The subordination of the note follows from the required rating of the investor. For instance, the investor may require an A2 rating for the note. The process followed involves:

- targeting the required rating on the issued tranche;
- setting the required return on the note, and hence determining where the tranche will lie;
- defining the percentage of first loss that must occur before the issued tranche is impacted by further losses;
- setting the size of the note issue, in line with investor requirements. For instance, if the investor wishes to place $20 million in the note, and the reference pool is $800 million nominal value, this implies a 2.5% tranche.

As with the previous synthetic CDOs, a single-tranche CDO can be either a static or a managed deal. In a managed deal, the investor can manage the portfolio and effect substitutions if this is part of its requirement. To facilitate this, the deal may be set up with one or more fund managers in place to deal when substitutions are required by the investor. Alternatively, an investor may leave trading decisions to a fund manager.

Advantages of the single-tranche structure

For certain investors, the single-tranche CDO presents a number of advantages over the traditional structure. These include:

- flexibility: the features of the investment can be tailor-made to suit the investor's needs. The investor can select the composition of the portfolio, the size of the tranche and its subordination level;
- note terms exactly as required: the coupon and maturity of the note are tailor-made for the investor;
- shorter time frame: the deal can be brought to market relatively quickly, and in as little as four weeks compared to anything from two months to one year for a conventional CSO;
- lower cost of issue: including lower legal costs because of the short time to issue and no protracted marketing effort by the arranger.

The flexibility of the single-tranche structure means that the market can expect to see more variations in their arrangement, as more investors evaluate it as an asset class. The market has seen both "static" and "managed" single-tranche CDOs, following experience with traditional CSOs. Figure 10.19 is a summary of the differences between traditional and single-tranche synthetic CDOs.

Hypothetical pricing example

Figure 10.18 is a simplified illustration of a pricing example for a single-tranche CDO, with market rates as observed on Bloomberg during April 2003. We assume the portfolio is constituted in the following way:

Number of credits: 80
Nominal size: €800 million
Diversity score: 48
Average rating: BBB+/Baa1
Minimum rating: BBB−/Baa3
Maturity: 5 years

The originating bank structures a single-tranche CDO following investor interest with the following terms:

Subordination level: 3.90% (this means that five defaults are supported, assuming a 35% recovery rate)
Tranche size: €25 million
Expected rating: A/A2
Spread: EURIBOR + 220 basis points

Figure 10.18   Single tranche CDO illustrative pricing example.

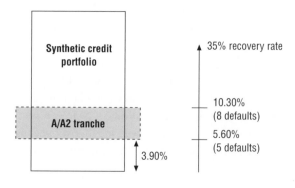

Figure 10.19   Differences between traditional and single-tranche synthetic CDOs.

Characteristic	Single tranche	Traditional CSO
Type	Static, substitution, managed	Static, substitution, managed
Structure	A portfolio of reference credits, for which protection sold via a basket credit default swap	A portfolio of reference credits, for which protection sold via a basket credit default swap
	A specific tranche of the portfolio credit risk is transferred to a sole investor. Remaining risk stays with originator, and is delta-hedged	The portfolio risk is transferred in its entirety, through a tranched CDS and/or CLN arrangement, to market investors
	A bilateral arrangement	A syndicated securitisation arrangement
Portfolio	Between 20–100 reference credits diversified across geography, industry	Between 100–150 reference credits, diversified across geography, industry
	Typically investment-grade	Can include investment-grade, high-yield, emerging market, special situations (sole AAA-rated, etc)
	Can be customised to meet specific credit rating, foreign-exchange and interest-rate requirements of investor	Can be customised at structuring stage but to meet needs of a wider group of investors. Will be marketed once general structure is known.
Deal economies	Shorter time scale, increased deal volume	Longer time-scale to bring to market
	Greater opportunity to react to specific market conditions and capture arbitrage	Decreased ability to capture arbitrage opportunities as they arise

Example 10.4   CDO Equity Note

Equity is the most junior note in the capital structure of a CDO. For this reason it is also known as the "first-loss" piece of the CDO, carrying the highest risk of payment delays and losses due to credit events or default. The equity, which is actually issued as a "bond" with an international security number (known as an ISIN), receives any cash that is left over after all other liabilities and claims have been paid from the asset cash flows. These include management and servicing fees plus the senior debt liabilities. In a cash flow structure, the return to the equity holder is a function of defaults and payment delays of assets in the collateral portfolio. The level of trading or credit rating downgrades does not have an impact on the equity unless they affect the cash flows of the structure. The equity piece receives the residual cash flows generated by the structure, but there is a distinction between coupon cash flows and principal cash flows. The residual coupon is paid out as it is received, while the residual principal cash flows are not paid out until after all debt notes are paid off.

Given all this, we can see that CDO equity is a "leveraged" exposure to credit risk, taken on by the equity investor. The holder of CDO equity, which is frequently the collateral manager or sponsor of the deal, will have a view that the cash flows generated by the underlying assets will be sufficient to bear expected credit losses and provide enough surplus to pay on the equity note. When assessing the expected returns therefore, the investor considers the expected level of defaults and how this will impact on the structure. This assessment must also take into account the leveraged nature of the structure, because of the large amount of the debt in the vehicle.

The timing, as well as extent, of defaults is critical to equity return. With a cash flow CDO the initial size of the excess net spread of assets over liabilities means that there is a "front-loaded" pattern to equity cash receipts. Equity holders receive a significant part of return early in the deal, because the initial excess spreads are high, since defaults are unlikely to occur at the start of the deal and will not peak until later on in the deal's life. The later in life that defaults do occur, the greater will be the return to the equity holder.

CDO equity is not a straightforward bond and must be assessed carefully by investors due to their complexity. The structure of the CDO and the quality of the collateral pool are very important issues for consideration, as is the extent of secondary market trading of the note (which will be low to start with). In addition, potential investors must consider what benchmark should be used as a comparison when assessing the return on the note, and what product can be used to hedge the equity note if needed.

Example 10.5   CDO of Equity Default Swaps

We introduced equity default swaps (EDS) in chapter 2. We saw that the EDS was an equity version of the standard CDS, with a barrier level for the price of the equity acting as the "credit event", now termed the equity event. In effect this makes an EDS similar to an out-of-the-money barrier option.

The latest development in structured credit is the CDO of EDS, or *Equity Collateralised Obligation*. This is identical to a conventional synthetic CDO whose reference portfolio was a static pool of CDS, except that the portfolio is now comprised of EDS, or a mixture of CDS and EDS. Typically the portfolio is made up of between 30 and 100 reference entities, with a similar exposure to each reference entity. Investors can gain exposure to the reference pool at the risk-reward level they desire, as the structure will issue tranched notes just like a conventional CDO.

Although the two structures have much in common, there are detail differences. EDS contracts are generally written with a trigger level of 30% and quoting a fixed recovery rate (usually 50%), although there are sometimes provisions for a variable rate depending on the stock price. Corporate events such as merger, acquisition, or delisting will have greater impact. Under certain circumstances, a reference entity may need to be substituted, if this is allowed for in the documentation. The credit ratings agencies consider the different characteristics of equity versus debt in their ratings approach, although they still evaluate a reference portfolio for reference entity correlation, industry concentration, and geographical concentration, just as they would for a CDS portfolio. So a CDO of EDS would have a diversity score. The unique aspects include having a weighed average trigger probability, rather than weighted average default probability, but these are describing essentially the same thing. When rating the CDO, the ratings agencies will set portfolio criteria that dictate the shape and content of the reference portfolio, such as a maximum percentage share in one stock market or a maximum percentage share in one industrial sector.

The behaviour of equities is often idiosyncratic compared to that of debt. A Standard & Poor's research document[1] has noted that two corporate entities with the same credit rating can demonstrate very different risk-return profiles. For example, consider the following observations, stated in the S&P report:

Company	Rating	Industry	Domicile	Sharpe ratio
Iberdrola SA	A+	Utilities	Spain	55.31%
SanPaolo IMI SpA	A+	Financial	Italy	18.07%
Assicurazio Generali	A+	Financial	Italy	22.94%

(Source: S&P)

The first two companies have the same credit rating but widely differing Sharpe ratios.[2] However the second and third companies not only share the same credit rating, they also share the same domicile and the same industrial sector, but also show slightly different Sharpe ratios. Investors will want to note this performance behaviour when analysing CDOs of EDS.

Case Studies

Let us now consider a number of specific deals to illustrate the progressive development of the synthetic CDO market since inception. These are:

- BISTRO: the first static synthetic balance sheet CDO;
- ALCO1: a balance sheet deal arranged for credit risk management and regulatory capital purposes;
- Blue Chip Funding: a managed synthetic CDO;
- Jazz I CDO: a managed synthetic "hybrid" CDO;
- Dynaso 2002-1 Limited: a dynamic synthetic CSO;
- Leonardo Synthetic Plc: synthetic aviation securities CDS.

The latest manifestation of synthetic securitisation technology is the managed synthetic CDO or CSO. In Europe, these were originated by fund managers, with the first example issued in 2001. Although they are, in effect,

---

1 *Global Methodology for CDOs of Equity and Credit Default Swaps*, Standard & Poor's, 17 February 2004
2 The Sharpe ratio is a measure of return after allowing for the level of volatility of the asset and its return over and above the risk-free return. There are numerous references available on it.

investment vehicles, the disciplines required to manage what is termed a "structured credit product" is not necessarily identical to those required for a corporate bond fund. Investment bank arrangers suggest that a track record in credit derivatives trading is an essential pre-requisite to being a successful CSO manager. There is an element of reputational risk at stake if a CDO suffers a downgrade. For example, during 2001 Moody's downgraded elements of 83 separate CDO deals, across 174 tranches, as underlying pools of investment-grade and high-yield corporate bonds experienced default.[19] Thus managing a CDO presents a high-profile record of a fund manager's performance.

In Europe, fund managers that have originated managed synthetic deals include Robeco, Cheyne Capital Management, BAREP Asset Management and AXA Investment Managers. In the second part of this chapter we look at three specific deals as case studies, issued in the European market during 2001 and 2002.

The deals discussed are innovative structures and a creative combination of securitisation technology and credit derivatives. They show how a portfolio manager can utilise vehicles of this kind to exploit its expertise in credit trading as well as provide attractive returns for investors. Managed synthetic CDOs also present fund managers with a vehicle to build on their credit derivatives experience.

BISTRO: the first synthetic securitisation

Generally viewed as the first synthetic securitisation, BISTRO was a JP Morgan vehicle brought to the market in December 1997. The transaction was designed to remove the credit risk on a portfolio of corporate credits held on JP Morgan's books, with no funding or balance sheet impact. The overall portfolio was $9.7 billion, with $700 million of notes issued, in two tranches, by the BISTRO SPV. The proceeds of the note issue were invested in US Treasury securities, which in turn were used as collateral for the credit default swap entered into between JP Morgan and the vehicle. This was a five-year swap written on the whole portfolio, with JP Morgan as the protection buyer. BISTRO, the protection seller, paid for the coupons on the issued notes from funds received from the collateral pool and the premiums on the credit default swap. Payments on occurrence of credit events were paid out from the collateral pool.

---

[19] Source: CreditFlux, April 2002.

Under this structure, JP Morgan transferred the credit risk on $700 million of its portfolio to investors, and retained the risk on a first-loss piece and the residual piece. The first-loss piece was not a note issue, but a $32 million reserve cash account held for the five-year life of the deal. First losses were funded out of this cash reserve, which was held by JP Morgan. This is shown in Figure 10.20.

Figure 10.20 BISTRO deal structure.

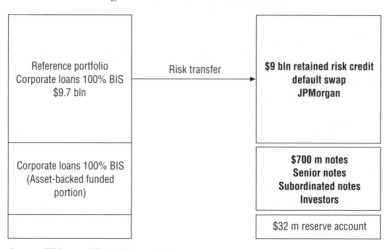

Source: JPMorgan. Used with permission.

The asset pool is static for the life of the deal. The attraction of the deal for investors included a higher return on the notes compared to bonds of the same credit rating and a bullet-maturity structure, compared to the amortising arrangement of other ABS asset classes.

The BISTRO deal featured:

- the credit risk exposure of a pool of assets being transferred without moving the assets themselves from the balance sheet;
- a resultant reduction of the credit exposure for the originator;
- no funding element for the originator: in other words, a securitisation deal that separated the liquidity feature from the risk transfer;
- the application of structured finance rating technology;
- unfunded liabilities which were nevertheless tranched, as in a traditional cash flow securitisation, so that these liabilities could be rated.

Investors in the deal, who were effectively taking on the credit risk of the assets on the originator's balance sheet, were attracted to the deal because:

- the deal provided exposure to particular credits and a credit risk/ return profile, but without a requirement for this exposure to be funded;
- the deal economics were aimed at a precise transfer of specifically-packaged segments of risk, enabling the investor to realize greater value;
- the equity holder gained from a leveraged exposure, which meant the cost of this exposure was lowered.

The originating bank retained a comparative advantage on the funding, while the investor gained the required exposure to the credit risk. The investor, in effect, provided the comparative advantage because it is not subject to regulatory capital requirements. In summary, the deal was a "win-win" transaction for both the bank and the investor. The investor — here typically a fund manager or insurance company — can price the risk very efficiently because it is an expert in the market. It also benefits from the cheap(er) funding that the bank is able to source.

ALCO 1 Limited

The ALCO 1 CDO is described as the first Asian market rated synthetic balance sheet CDO from a non-Japanese bank.[20] It is a S$2.8 billion structure sponsored and managed by the Development Bank of Singapore (DBS). The structure diagram is shown in Figure 10.21.

The structure allows DBS to transfer the credit risk on a S$2.8 billion reference portfolio of mainly Singapore corporate loans to a special purpose vehicle, ALCO 1, using credit default swaps. As a result, DBS can reduce the risk capital it has to hold on the reference loans, without physically moving the assets from its balance sheet. The structure is a S$2.45 billion super-senior tranche — unfunded credit default swap — with a S$224 million notes issue and S$126 million first-loss piece retained by DBS. The notes are issued in six classes, collateralised by Singapore government T-bills and a reserve bank account, the "GIC" account. There is also a currency and interest rate swap structure in place for risk hedging, and

---

[20] Source: Moody's.

Figure 10.21 ALCO 1 deal structure

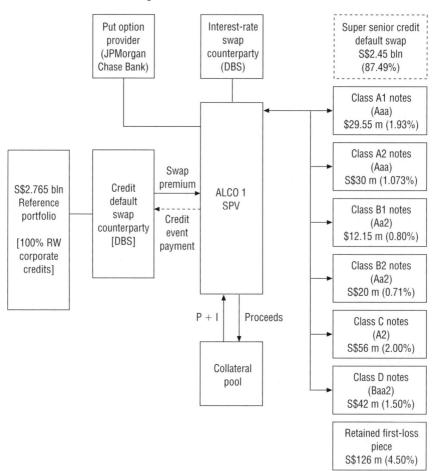

Source: Moody's. Used with permission.

Figure 10.22 ALCO 1 note tranching

Class	Amount	Per cent	Rating	Interest rate
Super senior swap	S$2.450 m	87.49%	NR	14 bps
Class A1	US$29.55 m	1.93%	AAA	3m USD LIBOR + 50 BPS
Class A2	S$30 m	1.07%	Aaa	3m SOR + 45 bps
Class B1	US$12.15 m	0.80%	Aa2	3m USD Libor + 85 bps
Class B2	S$20 m	0.71%	Aa2	3m SOR + 80 bps
Class C	S$56 m	2.00%	A2	5.20%
Class D	S$42 m	1.50%	Baa2	6.70%

Source: Moody's. Used with permission.

a put option that covers the purchase of assets by the arranger if the deal terminates before expected maturity date. The issuer enters into credit default swaps with a specified list of counterparties. The default swap pool is static, but there is a substitution facility for up to 10% of the portfolio. This means that under certain specified conditions, up to 10% of the reference loan portfolio may be replaced by loans from outside the vehicle. Other than this though, the reference portfolio is static.

Name	ALCO 1 Limited
Originator:	Development Bank of Singapore Ltd
Arrangers:	JPMorgan Chase Bank
	DBS Ltd
Trustee:	Bank of New York
Closing date:	15 December 2001
Maturity:	March 2009
Portfolio:	S$2.8 billion of credit default swaps
Reference assets:	199 reference obligations (136 obligors)
Portfolio Administrator:	JPMorgan Chase Bank Institutional Trust Services

As the first rated synthetic balance sheet deal in Asia, ALCO 1-type structures have subsequently been adopted by other commercial banks in the region. The principal innovation of the vehicle is the method by which the reference credits are selected. The choice of reference credits on which swaps are written must, as expected with a CDO, follow a number of criteria set by the ratings agency, including diversity score, rating factor, weighted average spread, geographical and industry concentration, among others.

Structure and mechanics

The issuer enters into a portfolio credit default swap with DBS as the CDS counterparty to provide credit protection against losses in the reference portfolio. The credit default swaps are cash-settled. In return for protection premium payments, after aggregate losses exceeding the S$126 million "threshold" amount, the issuer is obliged to make protection payments to DBS. The maximum obligation is the S$224 million note proceeds value. As per market convention with securitized notes, further losses above the threshold amount are allocated to overlying notes in their reverse order of seniority. The note proceeds are invested in a collateral pool comprised initially of Singapore Treasury bills.

During the term of the transaction, DBS, as the CDS counterparty, is permitted to remove any eliminated reference obligations that are fully paid, terminated early or otherwise no longer eligible. In addition, DBS has the option to remove up to 10% of the initial aggregate amount of the reference portfolio, and substitute new or existing reference names.

For this structure, credit events are defined specifically as:

- failure to pay;
- bankruptcy.

Note how this differs from European market CDOs where the list of defined credit events is invariably longer, frequently including restructuring and credit rating downgrades.

The reference portfolio is an Asian corporate portfolio, but with a small percentage of loans originated in Australia. The portfolio is concentrated in Singapore (80%). The weighted average credit quality is Baa3/Ba1, with an average life of three years. The Moody's diversity score is low (20), reflecting the concentration of loans in Singapore. There is a high industrial concentration. The total portfolio at inception was 199 reference obligations amongst 136 reference entities (obligors). By structuring the deal in this way, DBS obtains capital relief on the funded portion of the assets, but at lower cost and less administrative burden than a traditional cash flow securitisation, and without having to undertake a true sale of the assets.

Blue Chip Funding 2001–1 plc

Blue Chip Funding is a managed synthetic CDO originated by Dolmen Securities, which closed in December 2001. The deal has a 1 billion reference portfolio, with the following terms:

Name	Blue Chip Funding 2001-1 plc
Manager:	Dolmen Securities Limited
Arranger:	Dolmen Securities Limited
	Dresdner Kleinwort Wasserstein
Closing date:	17 December 2001
Portfolio:	€1 billion of credit default swaps
Reference assets:	80 investment-grade entities
Portfolio Administrator:	Bank of New York

The structure is partially funded, with 80 million of notes issued, or 8% of the nominal value. The share of the unfunded piece is comparatively high.

The proceeds from the notes issue are invested in AAA securities, which are held in custody by the third-party agency service provider, which must be rated at AA− or higher. The diversity of the structure is reflected in there being 80 different credits, with a weighted average rating of A−, with no individual asset having a rating below BBB−.
The structure is illustrated in Figure 10.23.

Figure 10.23 Blue Chip Funding managed synthetic CDO.

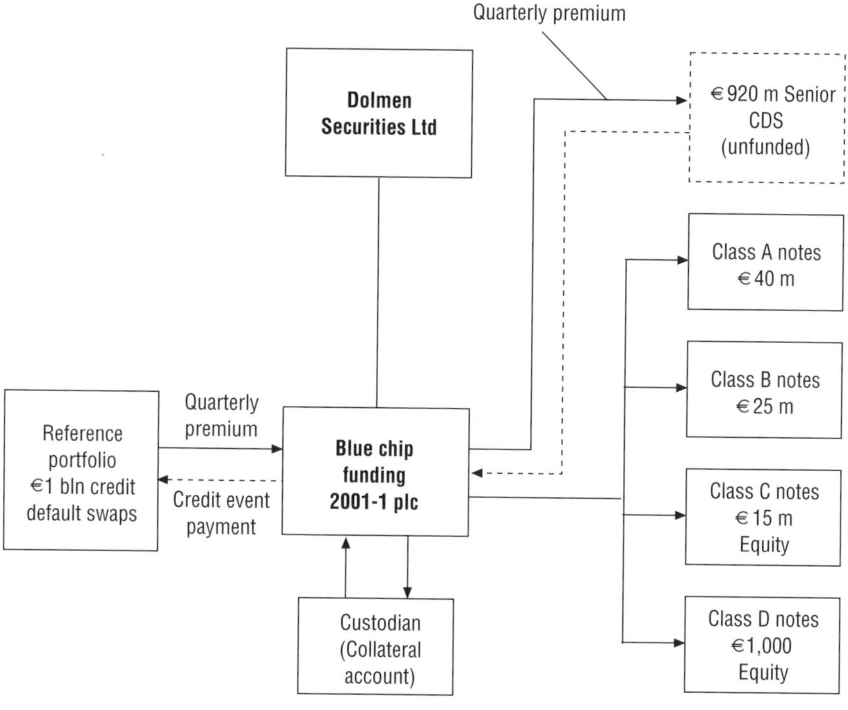

Source: S&P. Used with permission.

With this deal, the managers have the ability to trade the credit default swaps with a pre-specified panel of dealers. The default swap counterparties must have a short-term rating of A−1+ or better. Trading will result in trading gains or losses. This contrasts with a static synthetic deal, where investors have not been affected by trading gains or losses that arise from pool substitutions. The deal was rated by Standard & Poor's, which in its rating report described the management strategy as "defensive trading" to avoid acute credit deteriorations. There are a number of guidelines that the manager must adhere to, such as:

- the manager may both sell credit protection and purchase credit protection, however the manager may only short credit (purchase credit protection) in order to close out or offset an existing previous sale of protection;
- there is a discretionary trading limit of 10% of portfolio value;
- a minimum weighted-average premium of 60 bps for swaps must be maintained;
- a minimum reinvestment test must be passed at all times: this states that if the value of the collateral account falls below 80 million, interest generated by the collateral securities must be diverted from the equity (Class C and D notes) to the senior notes until the interest cover is restored.

The issuer has sold protection on the reference assets. On occurrence of a credit event, the issuer will make credit protection payments to the swap counterparty. If the vehicle experiences losses as a result of credit events or credit default swap trading, these are made up from the collateral account. An interesting feature of this structure is the existence of two equity pieces, the C and D notes. The C note ranks above the D note in terms of payment priority. It also exhibits a fixed coupon, compared to the more traditional variable floating return paid by the D note.

Jazz CDO I B.V.

Jazz CDO I BV is an innovative CDO structure and one of the first *hybrid* CDOs introduced in the European market. A hybrid CDO combines elements of a cash flow arbitrage CDO and a managed synthetic CDO. Therefore, the underlying assets are investment grade bonds and loans, and synthetic assets such as credit default swaps and total return swaps. The Jazz vehicle comprises a total of 1.5 billion of referenced assets, of which 210 million is made up of a note issue. Its hybrid arrangement enables the portfolio manager to take a view on corporate and bank credits in both cash and synthetic markets. Therefore a structure like Jazz bestows the greatest flexibility for credit trading on CDO originators. The vehicle is illustrated in Figure 10.24.

Figure 10.24   Jazz CDO I B.V. structure diagram.

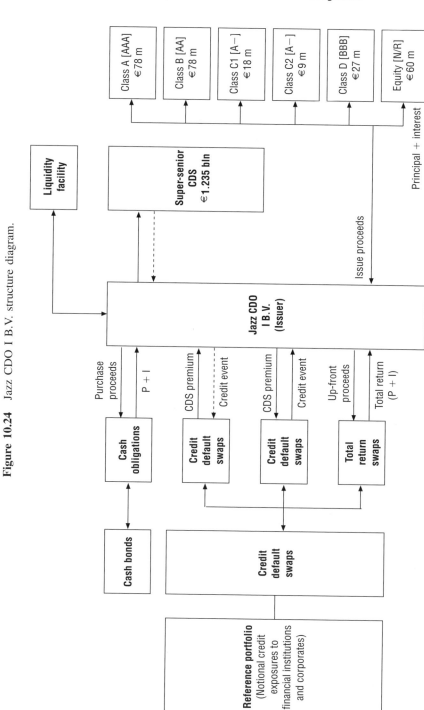

The main innovation of the structure is a design that incorporates both funded and unfunded assets as well as funded and unfunded liabilities. This arrangement means that the portfolio manager is free to trade both cash and derivative instruments, thereby exploiting its experience and knowledge across the markets. At a time of increasing defaults in CDOs, during 2001 and 2002, static pool deals began to be viewed unfavorably by certain investors, because of the inability to offload deteriorating or defaulted assets. Jazz CDO I is an actively managed deal, and its attraction reflects to a great extent the perception with which the portfolio manager is viewed by investors. So the role of the portfolio manager is critical to the ratings analysis of the deal. This covered:

- experience in managing cash and synthetic assets;
- its perceived strength in credit research;
- previous experience in managing CDO vehicles;
- infrastructure arrangements, such as settlement and processing capability.

These factors, together with the traditional analysis used for static pool cash CDOs, were used by the ratings agencies when assessing the transaction.

Name:	Jazz CDO I B.V.
Manager:	Axa Investment Managers S.A.
Arranger:	Deutsche Bank AG
Closing date:	8 March 2002
Maturity:	February 2011
Portfolio:	€1.488 billion
Reference assets:	Investment grade synthetic and cash securities
Portfolio Administrator:	JP Morgan Chase Bank

Structure

The assets in Jazz CDO I may be comprised of credit default swaps, total return swaps, bonds and loans, at the manager's discretion. The asset mix is set up by:

- purchase of cash assets, funded by the proceeds of the note issue and the liquidity facility;
- selling protection via credit default swaps;
- buying protection via credit default swaps;

- entering into total return swaps, whereby the total return of the reference assets is received by the vehicle in return for a payment of LIBOR plus spread (on the notional amount). This is funded via the liquidity facility.

The liability side of the structure is a combination of:

- the super-senior credit default swap;
- issued notes and equity piece (see Figure 10.24).

However, the asset and liability mix can be varied by the portfolio manager at its discretion, and can be expected to change over time. In theory the asset pool can comprise 100% cash bonds or 100% credit default swaps, in practice we should expect to see a mixture as shown in Figure 10.24.

The total return swap and the Jazz I CDO

As noted in Chapter 3, the TRS used as part of the Jazz I CDO structure is a funded TRS. The generic TRS is an unfunded credit derivative. The TRS arrangement was shown at Figure 3.16 and we have reproduced it here in Figure 10.25.

Figure 10.25   Total return swap as used in Jazz I CDO BV.

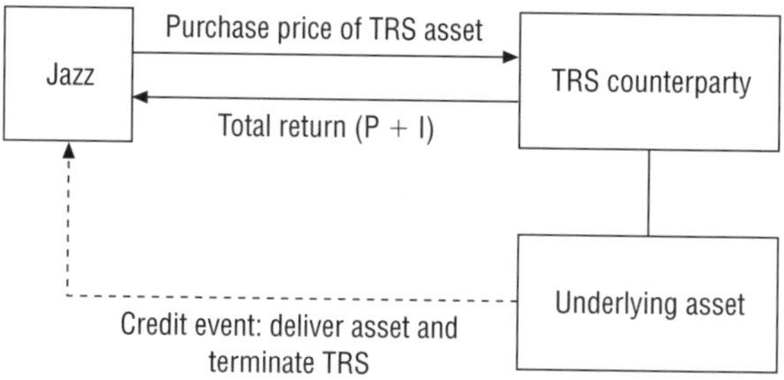

Liquidity facility

A liquidity facility of €1.7 billion is an integral part of the structure. It is used as a reserve to cover losses arising from credit default swap trading, occurrence of credit events, and to fund any purchases when the mix of cash versus synthetic assets is altered by the manager. This includes the purchase of bonds and the funding of total return swaps. The facility is similar to a revolving credit facility and is provided by the arrangers of the transaction.

If the manager draws on the liquidity facility, this is viewed as a funded liability, similar to an issue of notes, and is in fact senior in the priority of payments to the overlying notes and the super-senior credit default swap.

Trading arrangements

Hybrid CDOs are the latest development in the arena of managed synthetic CDOs. The Jazz CDO structure enables the portfolio manager to administer credit risk across cash and synthetic markets. The cash market instruments that may be traded include investment- grade corporate bonds, structured finance securities such as ABS or MBS, and corporate loans. The portfolio manager may buy and sell both types of assets, that is, it may short credit in accordance with its view. In other words, the restriction that exists with the Blue Chip deal is removed in Jazz CDO. Therefore, the portfolio manager can buy protection in the credit derivative market as it wishes, and not only to offset an existing long credit position (sold protection). The only rules that must be followed when buying protection are that:

* the counterparty risk is of an acceptable level;
* there are sufficient funds in the vehicle to pay the credit derivative premiums.

The manager may trade where existing assets go into default, or where assets have either improved or worsened in credit outlook (to take or cut a trading profit/loss). Another significant innovation is the ability of the vehicle to enter into *basis trades* in the credit market. An example of such a trade is to buy a cash bond and simultaneously purchase protection on that bond in the credit default swap market. Similar to trades undertaken in the exchange-traded government bond futures market, this is an arbitrage-type strategy where the trader seeks to exploit price mismatches between the cash and synthetic markets.

The various combinations of trades that may be entered into are treated in different ways for counterparty risk and regulatory capital. For an offsetting position in a single name, the options are to use:

* only credit default swaps to cancel out an exposure, when both credit default swaps are traded with the same counterparty: this is netted out for risk purposes;
* credit default swaps only, but with different counterparties: there will be a set-aside for counterparty risk requirement exposure;
* a credit default swap and cash bond: regarded as a AAA-rated asset for capital purposes.

The Offering Circular for the deal lists a number of trading guidelines that must be followed by the manager. These include a limit of 20% by volume annual turnover level.

Dynaso 2002–1 Limited

The Dynaso CSO is a managed synthetic CDO that presents features of interest because of the way the excess spread in the vehicle impacts the way the note tranches are rated. It also has other distinguishing structural features. The originator of the deal is DZ Bank in Germany. The terms of the deal are:

Issuer:	Dynaso 2002-1 Limited, Jersey SPV
Effective date:	6 November 2002
Schedule maturity:	6 November 2007
Arranger:	DZ Bank
Co-arranger:	The Bank of Nova Scotia, London branch
Trustee:	JP Morgan Chase Bank
Reference portfolio:	Notional credit exposure on 100 corporate credits
Amount:	€1 billion
Minimum diversity score:	55
Weighted average rating:	A3

The transaction structure is shown in Figure 10.26 and the note tranching in Figure 10.27.

This deal was originated to provide investors with exposure to corporate credits. Investors were among DZ Bank's network of co-operative banks in Germany. The key feature of interest in this structure concerns the Class E note (see Figure 10.26). Any excess spread that remains in the vehicle after the senior liabilities have been paid is paid into an excess spread account. The Class E note differs from the Class A, B and C notes in that on maturity, the balance of the excess spread account may be used to restore the Class E note to par value. The remaining residual balance is then available to pay Class D noteholders. This structure has resulted in the Class E note being rated Aaa by Moody's, which is a unique arrangement. The E note also has a fixed coupon, a rare feature in European deals.

The deal structure is based around the super-senior CDS, which forms 85% of the liabilities side. The remaining 15% is split into the five classes of notes. The note proceeds are held in a cash deposit account. In the event of any defaults in the reference portfolio, the notes are written off in order

Figure 10.26 Dynaso 2002–1 CSO structure diagram.

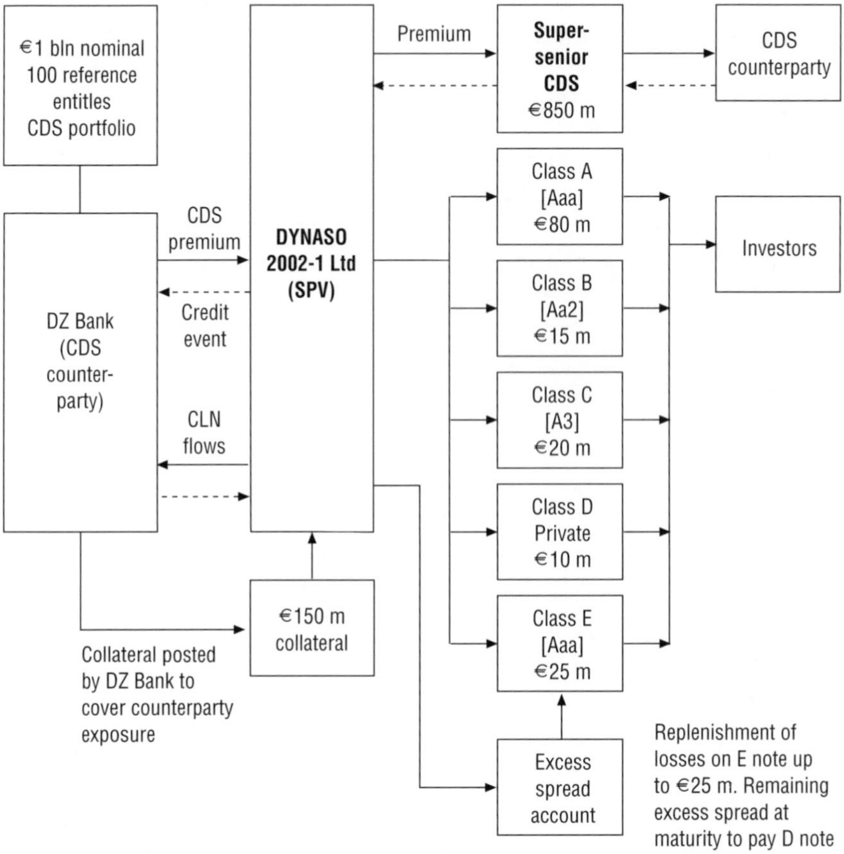

Source: Moody's. Used with permission.

Figure 10.27 Dynaso 2002–1 CSO note tranching.

Class	Nominal size €m	Per cent	Rating	Coupon
Senior CDS	850	85.00%	NR	n/a
Class A	80	8.00%	Aaa	3m Euribor + 100 bps
Class B	15	1.50%	Aa2	3m Euribor + 125 bps
Class C	20	2.00%	A3	3m Euribor + 250 bps
Class D	10	1.00%	Private	n/a
Class E	25	2.50%	Aaa	5.00%

Source: Moody's. Used with permission.

of priority. The portfolio CDS does not amortise. The reference pool is managed dynamically by DZ Bank as portfolio advisor, although as the substitution is limited to 10% of the pool in any one year, this is not a fully "managed" synthetic CDO.

Credit events are defined as (i) bankruptcy (ii) failure to pay and (iii) restructuring, with "modified restructuring" applying to US reference credits and "old restructuring" to any other reference credits.

Leonardo Synthetic CDO

The Italian capital market witnessed a number of innovative transactions early in the development of synthetic structured products. The Leonardo Synthetic plc deal is one such transaction. Closing in June 2001, it was an early example of a balance sheet synthetic CDO, as well as the first synthetic securitisation of aircraft financing and aviation industry loans and letters of credit. The originator, IntesaBCI, sought to transfer the credit risk on a revolving pool of loans made to clients in connection with aircraft purchases and leases. This transfer was effected partly by a credit default swap between the originator and a swap counterparty (Merrill Lynch), and partly by a combination of funded and unfunded credit derivatives issued by the SPV for the transaction.

The terms of the deal are summarised below:

Originator (and Servicer):	IntesaBCI
Issuer:	Leonardo Synthetic plc
Structure:	Credit default swaps and credit-linked notes
Trustee:	Deutsche Bankers Trust
Reference portfolio:	Aviation industry loans and letters of credit
Notional value:	US$ 1 billion
Secured liability proportion:	97%
Unsecured liability proportion:	3%
Collateral (Classes "A" and "B"):	Italian government bonds
Collateral (Class "C"):	Cash deposit at account bank

The transaction structure is shown at Figure 10.28 below, while the note tranching is shown at Figure 10.29.

Figure 10.28 Leonardo synthetic CDO.

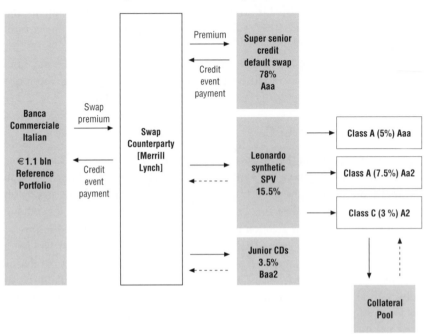

Figure 10.29 Leonardo Synthetic CDO tranche summary.

Class	Amount USD m	Percent	Issue price	Rating	Coupon Euribor 3m1
Senior swap	[780]	78	n/a	Aaa	Premium 12 bps
A	55	5.0	100	Aaa	[26]
B	82.5	7.5	100	Aa2	[35]
C	33	3.0	100	A2	[67]
Junior CDS	[35]	3.5	n/a	Baa2	Premium 124 bps
[First loss]	33	3.0	100	NR	Excess

(*Source:* Moody's. *Yields source:* Bloomberg)

The proceeds of the CLN issue was invested in Italian government bonds, which act as collateral to support the Class "A" and "B" notes. The junior Class "C" notes are collateralised by a bank account deposit.

A feature of the structure is that a credit event is described as being related specifically to the reference obligations of the named corporates. Investors therefore acquire an exposure only to the corporate obligors themselves, mainly airlines, and not to the Issuer SPV. They do not have an exposure to the Issuer itself. A credit event. Credit events are defined as bankruptcy of a reference entity, and failure to pay, only. There is a five-year revolving period during which loans can be replaced, as they drop out of the reference portfolio for redemption, prepayment and other reasons. Substitute loans must meet pre-specified criteria. The first 3% of losses in the portfolio are covered by the equity holder, losses beyond this threshold level are allocated first to the junior CDS, and then to the Class "C" CLN, and so on.

The transaction was designed to remove the credit risk of an initial pool of 127 reference loans and letters of credit, made to 32 borrowers by IntesaBCI. It also resulted in lowering of regulatory capital. It was a ground-breaking deal in the European market, and was typical of the innovation in the market for structured credit pioneered in Italy.

Conclusions

The case studies we have considered here are innovative structures and a creative combination of securitisation technology and credit derivative instruments. We have seen that more recent structures have been introduced into the market that make use of total return swaps as well as credit default swaps, and also remove the restriction on shorting credit. Analysis of these vehicles shows how a portfolio manager can utilise the arrangement to exploit its expertise in credit trading, and its experience of the credit derivatives market, to provide attractive returns for investors. The most flexible vehicles, such as Jazz CDO I, in theory allow more efficient portfolio risk management when compared to static or more restrictive deals. As the market in synthetic credit, in Europe at least, is frequently more liquid than the cash market for the same reference names, it is reasonable to expect more transactions of this type in the near future.

Appendices

Appendix 10.1

The Moody's Diversity Score

The diversity score for a CDO is Moody's measure for the number of uncorrelated assets in a portfolio. A CDO portfolio must meet a minimum diversity score for its required credit rating. The strict definition of diversity score is " the number of independent assets with identical nominal amount which as a portfolio have the same total notional amount, expected loss and variance as the portfolio itself. Moody's divides assets in accordance with their industry sector and assigns a default correlation among assets in each industry.

The diversity score D is given by:

$$D = \frac{\left\{\sum_{j=1}^{T}(N_j * P_j)\right\} * \left\{\sum_{j=1}^{T}(N_j \ (1 - P_j)\right\}}{\sum_{j=1}^{T}\left\{\left(\sum_{k=1}^{T}(r_{jk} * N_k * \sqrt{(p_k * (1 - P_j))})\right) * N_j * \sqrt{(p_j * (1 - P_j))}\right\}}$$

where

N_j is the outstanding principal balance of collateral debt security j;
N_k is the outstanding principal balance of collateral debt security k;
p_j is the default probability of security j;
p_k is the default probability of security k;
T is the total number of collateral debt securities in the portfolio;
r_{jk} is the correlation of security j with security k.

The default correlations are assigned by Moody's to each industry sector that it classifies. The default probability is the cumulative probability that a collateral debt security defaults during its life. It is given by:

$$P_j = \frac{E}{(1 - R)}$$

where

E is the expected loss
R is the Moody's recovery rate.

The expected loss is assigned to a security based as shown on a standard table supplied by Moody's, and is based on its credit rating and term to maturity. The recovery rate is assigned to each class of security by Moody's, in accordance with its credit rating.

Appendix 10.2

The roles of the Trustee and portfolio administrator on a CSO.

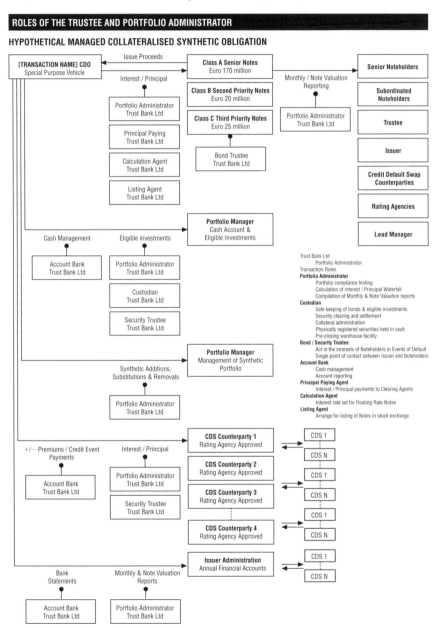

ROLES OF THE TRUSTEE AND PORTFOLIO ADMINISTRATOR

HYPOTHETICAL MANAGED COLLATERALISED SYNTHETIC OBLIGATION

© Dr Chee Hau 2002. Reproduced with permission.

Appendix 10.3

Hypothetical deal term sheet

Scarab CSO Limited

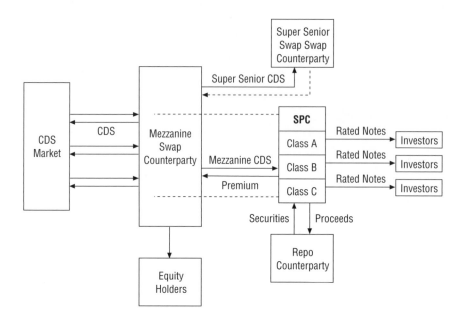

Transaction indicative terms and conditions

The Issuer   [Scarab CSO Ltd] is a special purpose, bankruptcy remote, company (SPV). The company will be registered in [Jersey/Ireland/ Luxembourg]. It is set up in order to acquiring securities through a **Repurchase Agreement**, selling credit protection through a **Mezzanine Credit Default Swap Agreement,** refinancing through the issuance of **Collateralised Debt Obligations** ("the Notes"), and charging its assets as security for its obligations under the Mezzanine Credit Default Swap Agreement and the Notes

The Issuer is required to produce annual audited accounts and annual management reports.

The SPV shares will be held on trust (or equivalent in Netherlands/Luxembourg) under a Charitable Trust Agreement

Trustee   [Trust Bank of London plc]

Auditors   [ ]

SPV Administrator   [ ]

The Mezzanine Credit Default Swap Agreement

The Issuer will enter into a Mezzanine Credit Swap Agreement with the Mezzanine Swap Counterparty under which the Issuer agrees to provide up to _[ ] of credit protection in respect of the Portfolio, provided aggregated losses on such Portfolio exceed _[ ]

Premium: on each Interest Payment Dates, the Mezzanine Swap Counterpart will pay to the Issuer a premium defined as follow:

[A*Ma + B*Mb + C*Mc + Spd*(A + B + C)]*(Nd/360) + OpEx

where

A: average daily principal amount outstanding on Class A Notes

B: average daily principal amount outstanding on Class B Notes

C: average daily principal amount outstanding on Class C Notes

Ma: [ ]% per annum (Class A Notes spread over EURIBOR)

Mb: [ ]% per annum (Class B Notes spread over EURIBOR)

Mc: [ ]% per annum (Class C Notes spread over EURIBOR)

Spd: [ ]%

Nd: Actual number of days of the Interest Period

OpEx: the Operating Expenses payable by the Issuer on the Interest Payment Date

Credit Events: means the occurrence of any of the following, each of which has the meaning given to it by the 2003 ISDA Credit Derivatives Definitions:

- Failure to pay
- Modified Restructuring
- Obligation Acceleration
- Bankruptcy
- Repudiation/Moratorium

The Mezzanine Swap Counterpart

XYZ Bank plc

The Repurchase Agreement

On the Issue Date, the Issuer will enter into the Repurchase Agreement with the Repo Counterpart pursuant to which, both parties agree to enter into a series of repurchase transactions in respect of Collateral Securities. Each transaction will begin on an Interest Payment Date (Issue Date for the first transaction) and end on the following Interest Payment Date. The Issuer receives the Collateral Securities against the payment of the **Purchase Price** by the Repo Counterpart in the beginning and receives the **Repurchase Price** against delivery of the Collateral Securities at the end of the repurchase transaction.

Collateral Securities to be chosen by the Repo Counterpart, they must be Government Securities or ABS Securities as described thereafter:

Government Securities: bonds issued by a government of a country of European Union with a maturity below 10 years and a rating of at least AA+ by S&P's/Aa1 by Moody's and denominated in Euro.

ABS Securities: floating rate asset backed securities and fixed rate covered bonds (pfandbriefe) with an expected maturity below 10 years, rated AAA S&P's/Aaa Moody's and denominated in Euro (or any former currency of the member states of the European Union that have adopted the Euro)

Price Differential: the difference between the Repurchase Price and the Purchase Price on each Repurchase transaction will be the following:

(3M EURIBOR −Spd)*(Nd/360)*N

where
Spd: [ ]% per annum
Nd: the actual number of days of the Repo Transaction
N: the average principal outstanding amount of the Notes during that Transaction

Haircut and Margin call

Haircut: Agreed Collateralisation Level: [to be checked with the rating agencies]
Margin call: bilateral
Frequency: daily
Threshold Amount: _100,000
Delivery: within 3 Business Days

Credit Settlement Amounts
Notice: within 6 Business Days
Collateral Securities concerned: the highest bid price

Substitution

Option for the Repo Counterpart to make any substitution in the composition of the Collateral Securities whithin the agreed constraints without any prior consent from the Issuer.

Downgrade

- In case of downgrade of any ABS Securities, the Repo Counterpart will have to replace the affected ABS Securities by eligible Collateral Securities (within 10 Business Days)
- If the short term senior unsecured debt of the Repo Counterpart ceased to be rated at least A−1+/P−1, the Repo Counterpart should switch all ABS Securities for Government Securities
- If the short term senior unsecured debt of the Repo Counterpart ceased to be rated at least A−1+/P−1, the Repo Counterpart should within 10 Business Days (a) procure credit support under conditions satisfactory to Rating Agencies in order to avoid the current rating of the Notes, or (b) procure that a third party having such rating substitutes itself to the Repo Counterpart in the Repurchase Agreement

The Repo Counterpart	XYZ Bank plc
The Security Trustee	[Trust Bank of London plc]
The Arranger	XYZ Bank plc
The Lead Manager	XYZ Bank plc
The Principal Paying Agent	[ ]
The Agent Bank and Listing Agent	[ ]

The Class A Notes

The Class B Notes

The Class C Notes

Use of Proceeds	The Issuer will use the net proceeds of the Notes to purchase the Collateral Securities under the Repurchase Agreement

Status of the Notes

Interest on the Notes

Mandatory Redemption	In case of termination of the Repurchase Agreement or the Mezzanine Credit Default Swap Agreement for any reason
Optional Redemption	For tax reasons
Final Redemption	The Notes will be redeemed on the **Scheduled Maturity Date**, unless a Credit Event Notice is served to the Issuer less than [ ] Business Days before the Scheduled Maturity Date, in which case the redemption may be postponed until at most [ ] Business Days after the Schedule Maturity Date, which is expected to be [ ] (the "**Final Maturity Date**").
Cash Management	On each Interest Payment Date, the Cash Manager will use the Price Differential received under the Repurchase Agreement and the Premium received under the Mezzanine Credit Default Swap to pay in order • The Operating Expenses due to the Trustee • The Operating Expenses due to the other creditors

- The termination payment under the Mezzanine Swap Agreement (provided that credit event has been verified ...)
- Any interest due on Class A Notes
- Any interest due on Class B Notes
- Any interest due on Class C Notes

Security for the Notes   The notes will be secured by first ranking fixed security interest over the Issuer rights against its counterparts and the balance standing to the credit of the Issuer's Account. The Issuer will also pledge in favor of the Trustee its securities and bank account

In case of enforcement of the security, the Trustee will use the proceeds to make payment in the following order of priority:

1. The Repurchase Price due to the Repo Counterpart
2. Any Operating Expense due to the Trustee
3. Operating Expenses due to the Operating Creditors
4. The aggregate amounts in respect of the Cash Settlement Amounts due to the Mezzanine Swap Counterpart
5. Accrued and unpaid interest to Class A Notes
6. Unpaid principal due to Class A Notes
7. Accrued and unpaid interest to Class B Notes
8. Unpaid principal due to Class B Notes
9. Accrued and unpaid interest to Class C Notes
10. Unpaid principal due to Class C Notes
11. Termination payment to the Mezzanine Swap Counterpart

Limited Recourse	The Notes will be limited recourse obligations of the Issuer. If the net proceeds of the Security after it has been enforced liquidated are not sufficient to cover all payments due under the Notes, no other assets of the Issuer will be available to pay any shortfall, and all the liabilities of the Issuer will be extinguished
Rating	AAA/Aaa for class A Notes A/A1 for Class B Notes BBB/Baa1 for Class C Notes
Listing	Luxembourg Stock Exchange

Further documentation for review

The Offering Circular
The Deed of Charge
The Articles of Incorporation
The List of Relevant Agreements
The Investor Reports
The Subscription Agreement
The Agency Agreement
The Trust Deed
The Deed of Charge
The Repurchase Agreement
The Mezzanine Credit Default Swap Agreement
The Pledge Agreement
The Cash Management Agreement
The Domiciliation Agreement
The Bank Agreement

References and Bibligraphy

Anson M., *Credit Derivatives*, FJF Associates 1999, Chapter 3.
Boggiano, K., Waterson, and Stein, C., "Four forms of synthetic CDOs", *Derivatives Week*, Euromoney Publications, Volume XI, No 23, 10 June 2002.
Bomfim, A., "Credit Derivatives and Their Potential to Synthesize Riskless Assets", *Journal of Fixed Income*, December 2002, pp. 6–16.
Choudhry, M., "Some issues in the asset-swap pricing of credit default swaps", *Derivatives Week*, Euromoney Publications, 2 December 2001.

Choudhry, M., "Trading credit spreads: the case for a specialised exchange-traded credit futures contract", *Journal of Derivatives Use, Trading and Regulation*, Volume 8, No 1, June 2002.

Choudhry, M., "Combining securitisation and trading in credit derivatives: an analysis of the managed synthetic collateralised debt obligation", *Euromoney Debt Capital Markets Yearbook*, London: Euromoney Publications 2002.

Das, S., *Structured Products and Hybrid Securities*, John Wiley 2001, chapter 12.

Fabozzi, F., Goodman, L., (editors), *Investing in Collateralised Debt Obligations*, FJF Associates 2001.

Garcia, L., Patel, T., "Legal Documentation on Bond Issuances," in Fabozzi, F., and Choudhry, M., (editors), *Handbook of European Fixed Income Securities*, John Wiley and Sons 2004.

Gregory, J., *Credit Derivatives: The Definitive Guide*, RISK Books 2003.

Kasapi, A., *Mastering Credit Derivatives*, FT Prentice Hall 1999.

McPherson, N., H. Remeza, and D. Kung, *Synthetic CDOs and Credit Default Swaps*, CSFB 2002.

"Education never ends, Watson. It's a series of lessons, with the greatest for the last."

— *The Adventure of the Red Circle*
His Last Bow
Sir Arthur Conan Doyle
(1859–1930)

11

Integrating Cash and Synthetic Markets: The Multi-SPV Credit Hybrid CDO Structure[1]

The synthetic collateralised debt obligation (CDO) is well-established as a vehicle used to facilitate balance sheet capital management, credit risk transfer and credit trading. In this chapter, we propose an innovative new structure that combines a multi-Special Purpose Vehicle (SPV) arrangement, together with a hybrid cash and synthetic element that splits the vehicle into stand-alone pieces to suit specific investor requirements. The structure uses existing technology, packaged together in a way that integrates cash and synthetic markets. This results in a product offering greater flexibility than has been issued in the market before now, and enables financial institutions that already originate cash or synthetic CDOs to benefit from this flexibility.

The new structure may be used to achieve one or a combination of the following:

- credit risk transfer and/or regulatory capital management of assets already on the balance sheet;
- exploiting arbitrage opportunities between cash and synthetic credits;
- obtaining funding for acquiring assets subsequently used in an arbitrage synthetic transaction;
- a significant increase in potential deal size, due to the benefits arising from the multi-SPV structure;
- any combination of conventional bonds, structured financial products (ABS, MBS and CDO), loans and synthetic assets such as credit default swaps in the reference portfolio;

---

[1] This chapter was co-written with Ketul Tanna of JPMorgan Chase Bank. The views represent those of the authors in their individual private capacity.

- leveraging the credit expertise of a fund manager to deliver gains for the equity participants in the vehicle;
- meeting the requirements of a varied class of investors by means of the multi-SPV structure, including multi-currency requirements and specific fund management styles.

We describe here the proposed structure. We begin first by assessing the origins and efficacy of the synthetic CDO structure and its use of credit derivatives. We then describe the proposed new structure, and how originators would benefit from adopting this approach when bringing new transactions to the market.

Since the inception of the first synthetic deals the market has evolved, with continuing development of newer structures to meet differing originator and investor requirements. The proposed multi-SPV may be considered the "fourth-generation" of such products, following the structures introduced previously (see Choudhry [2003]). This is illustrated in Figure 11.1.

Figure 11.1   Four generations in the development of synthetic CDOs.

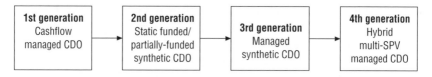

| 1st generation
Cashflow
managed CDO | 2nd generation
Static funded/
partially-funded
synthetic CDO | 3rd generation
Managed
synthetic CDO | 4th generation
Hybrid
multi-SPV
managed CDO |

As we have seen in the previous chapter, the first European synthetic deals were balance sheet CLOs, with underlying reference assets being commercial loans on the originator's balance sheet. Originators were typically banking institutions. Arbitrage synthetic CDOs have also been introduced, typically by fund management institutions, and involve sourcing credit derivative contracts in the market and then selling these on to investors in the form of rated notes, at the arbitrage profit. Within the synthetic market, arbitrage deals were the most frequently issued during 2001, reflecting certain advantages they possess over cash CDOs (see McPherson *et al* [2002]).

The Multi-SPV Credit Hybrid Vehicle

We now describe a structure that is designed to integrate the cash and synthetic credit markets in one vehicle. By arranging a CDO deal in this way, originators will be able to attract wider investor interest. The vehicle we describe combines a cash funded element as well as a synthetic element, hence the term "hybrid". The active management of the vehicle will be similar to that we have described in the previous section on managed synthetic CDOs.

Deal structure

The structure diagram is shown at Figure 11.2, and the deal terms are explained in Figure 11.3. The note tranching and funding is shown at Figure 11.4.

The structure is comprised of the following:

- a reference portfolio sourced in the market or on originator's balance sheet;
- a total return swap (TRS) set up for funding purposes;
- a back-to-back TRS;
- a second-loss credit protection credit default swap;
- a funded element of credit-linked notes issued by SPV 2;
- if required, a managed arbitrage-element of credit default swap trading undertaken out of SPV 1.

The TRS is a funded total rate-of-return swap of the form shown in Figure 10.25 in Chapter 10.

Deal arrangement

The reference portfolio may be comprised of conventional bonds, asset-backed securities (ABS), loans or synthetic assets such as credit default swaps. The type of assets that can be placed in the portfolio are dictated by the deal terms and conditions. The portfolio is actively managed by the fund manager, which retains an equity participation in the deal. Assets can be substituted by the fund manager acting under portfolio guidelines.

The funding stage of the transaction, indicated by SPV 3 in Figure 11.2, is executed first. This enables the deal to acquire assets. This SPV enters into a back-to-back TRS with the originator that transfers the total return of assets to the originator and eventually on to a swap counterparty via SPV 1. The fund manager can execute credit derivatives in the market via SPV 1, and a multi-dealer arrangement that would be conducted in a managed arbitrage synthetic deal (see Choudhry [2002]).

The cash CDO element of the structure is executed by SPV 2, which issued credit-linked notes. This SPV provides the "second-loss" protection for the originator. Proceeds of the note issue are invested in risk-free assets such as T-bills, or placed in a reserve cash account or structured deposit. If

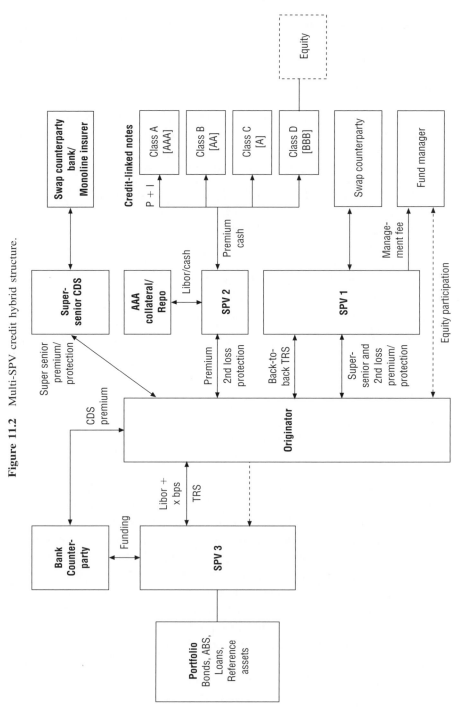

Figure 11.2   Multi-SPV credit hybrid structure.

Figure 11.3 Deal terms.

Multi-SPV credit hybrid structure	
Portfolio-size	1 bln – 7 bln
Trade date	Month 1 Year 1
Ramp-up end date	Month 1 Year 2
Call date	Month 1 Year 7
Final maturity	Month 1 Year 20

Figure 11.4 Possible note tranching and funding costs.

Class	Amount	Suggested percentage	Rating	Funding cost
Super senior swap	[ ]	86.00%	N/R	12–14 bps
Class A	[ ]	4.95%	AAA	Libor + 20–24 bps
Class B	[ ]	3.20%	AA	Libor + 40–50 bps
Class C	[ ]	2.80%	A	Libor + 80–90 bps
Class D	[ ]	1.05%	BBB	Libor + 180–200 bps
[Equity]	[ ]	2.00%	N/R	Retained spread

Funding cost 25 bps
Regulatory capital 3.6% [1.6% + 2.00%]
Funding cost per unit of equity 7.25 bps
No interest mis-match (pay and receive Libor)

proceeds are invested in eligible investments, these are placed in a repo with a counterparty bank. The return on the issued notes is linked to the return from the collateral pool and the premium payments received by the SPV from the originator for taking on the second-loss risk protection.

The originator retains equity participation in the structure to benefit from gains made by the fund manager in running the portfolio and in entering into credit default swap trading.

Deal highlights

For a balance-sheet-type transaction, the originator is able to transfer credit risk of assets held on its balance sheet. It can also benefit from the arbitrage gain from sourcing credit protection on these assets in the credit default swap market compared to the return received on these assets in the cash market. As we have seen from the previous chapter, there is significant saving in regulatory capital charge from the partially-funded structure. In addition, the managed element of the deal, which is undertaken via SPV 1 and a multi-dealer counterparty arrangement, will allow the originator to undertaken credit trading in the market.

The multi-SPV structure enables the originator to benefit from being able to undertake the following:

- structure and close large volume deals by placing risk across a wide range of investors, both cash bond investors and credit derivative counterparties;
- provide a vehicle that enables each investor an opportunity to tailor the SPV to meet their specific investment requirements and criteria; for instance, specific requirements in terms of currency requirements, market sector and particular fund management style;
- allows the Portfolio Manager to leverage experience from different areas of their firm to blend skills into the management of the overall deal;
- using existing market familiarity with credit derivatives, cash and synthetic CDOs and managed arbitrage synthetic CDOs to introduce a more complex product across a wider range of investors and markets;
- retain flexibility in the deal structure so that risk exposure of any asset class can be transferred, and any asset class targeted in the market for credit trading;
- securitise both cash and synthetic assets as required.

Due to the familiarity with existing CDO product across US and European legal jurisdictions, it will be possible to bring the new structure to the market under existing legislation.

Summary

The synthetic CDO structure is well-established in the debt capital markets. In its different variants, financial institutions have employed the product for balance sheet management, credit risk transfer and credit trading. We have shown how the deal mechanics can be advantageous for commercial banks wishing to effectively control regulatory capital. The greater liquidity of the synthetic credit market, compared to the cash market, has made synthetic CDO accessible for investors.

The next generation of this product will be designed to integrate cash and synthetic markets. By engineering one transaction that can generate interest across a wider range of investors, the originator will benefit from a greater deal flexibility. This has significant implications for efficient balance sheet management.

Sunrise doesn't last all morning,
The cloudburst doesn't last all day,
Seem's my love is up and has left you with no warning,
It's not always going to be this grey.

— George Harrison, *All Things Must Pass*
(Apple Records) 1970

12

Synthetic CDOs: Risk and Return[1]

Following our brief interlude where we presented an idea for a new hybrid structure, we return to CSO analysis with a look at the returns profile of a "typical" structure. The rapid growth of the CSO market reflects its capacity for flexibility and innovation, therefore it is not really appropriate to speak of a "typical" structure, because all deals have detail differences. However it is possible to get a good idea of the main principles of interest to investors.

Investor Risks and Return

Fund managers consider investing in CDO-type products because they represent a diversification in the European bond markets, with yields that are comparable to credit card or auto-loan ABS assets. A CDO also gives investors exposure to sectors in the market that may not otherwise be accessible to most investors, for example credits such as small- or medium-sized corporate entities that rely on entirely bank financing. Also, the extent of credit enhancement and note tranching in a CDO means that they may show better risk/reward profiles than that of straight conventional debt, with a higher yield but incorporating asset backing and insurance backing. In cash and synthetic CDOs, the issue notes are often bullet bonds, with a fixed term to maturity, whereas other ABS and MBS product are amortizing securities with only average (expected life) maturities. This may suit certain longer-dated investors.

---

[1] The author would like to thank Ketul Tanna at JPMorgan Chase in London for his assistance with preparing this chapter.

An incidental perceived advantage of cash CDOs is that they are typically issued by financial institutions, such as higher-rated banks. This usually provides comfort to investors on the credit side, but also on the administration and servicing side with regard to underlying assets, compared to consumer receivables securitisations.

CDO yield spreads

To illustrate yields, Figure 12.1 shows the spreads on a selected range of CDO notes during January 2002 over the credit spectrum. Figure 12.2 shows a comparison of different asset classes in European structured products during February 2002. In Figure 12.3 we show the note spread at issue for a selected number of synthetic CDOs closed during 2001–2002. The regression of these and selected other AAA-rated note spreads against maturity shows an adjusted R^2 of 0.802, shown at Figure 12.4, which suggests that for a set of AAA-rated securities, the term to maturity is not the only consideration.[2] Other factors that may explain the difference in yields include perception of the asset manager, secondary market liquidity and the placing power of the arranger of the transaction.

Figure 12.1   CDO note spreads, January 2002.

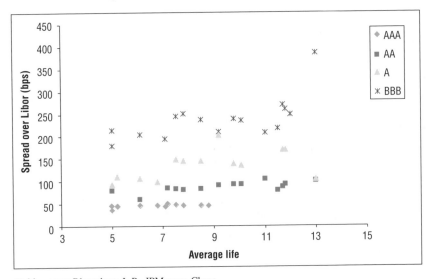

Yield source: Bloomberg L.P., JPMorgan Chase.

---

2 Calculated from 12 synthetic CDO senior (AAA-rated) notes issued in Europe during Jan–Jun 2002, yields obtained from Bloomberg.

Figure 12.2   Comparing CDO yields to other securitisation asset classes, average spreads over LIBOR as at February 2002.

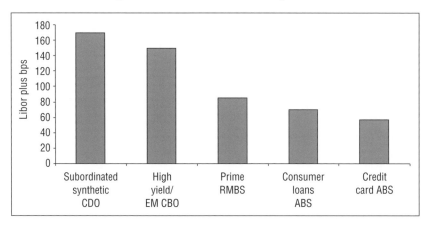

Source: Bloomberg L.P. Unamed investment banks.

Figure 12.3   Selected synthetic deal spreads at issue.

Deal name plus close date	Moodys	S&P	Fitch	Spread bps	Index
Jazz CDO Mar-02					
Class A	Aaa	AAA		47	6 m Libor
Class B	Aa2	AAA		75	6 m Libor
Class C-1		A−		135	6 m Libor
Class D		BBB		240	6 m Libor
Robecco III CSO Dec-01					
Class A	Aaa			55	3 m Euribor
Class B	Aa2			85	3 m Euribor
Class C	Baa1			275	3 m Euribor
Marylebone Road CBO III Oct-01					
Class A-1	Aaa	AAA		45	3 m Libor
Class A-2	Aa1	AAA		65	3 m Libor
Class A-3	A2	AAA		160	3 m Libor
Brooklands referenced linked notes Jul-01					
Class A	Aaa		AAA	50	3 m Libor
Class B	Aa3		AA−	80	3 m Libor
Class C	Baa2		BBB−	250	3 m Libor
Class D-1	n/a		BBB	500	3 m Libor
North Street Ref. Linked Notes 2002-2 Oct-00					
Class A			AAA	70	6 m Libor
Class B			AA	105	6 m Libor
Class C			A	175	6 m Libor

Yield source: Bloomberg L.P., JPMorgan Chase.

Figure 12.4   AAA spreads as at February 2002 (selected European CDO deals).

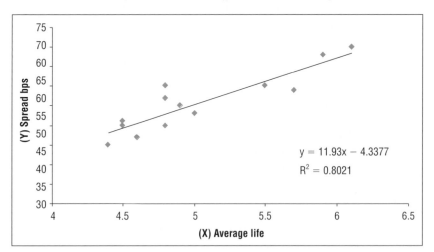

Investor risk considerations

The key structural differences between synthetic and conventional securitisation are the absence of a true sale of assets and the use of credit derivatives. Investors must therefore focus on different aspects of risk that the former instrument represents. Although it might be said that each securitisation — irrespective of it being cash or synthetic — is a unique transaction with its own characteristics, synthetic deals are very transaction-specific because they can be tailor-made to meet very specific requirement. Such requirements can be with regard to reference asset type, currency, underlying cash flows, credit derivative instrument, and so on.

Investor risk in a synthetic deal centers on the credit risk inherent in reference assets and the legal issues associated with the definition of credit events. The first risk is closely associated with securitisation in general, but synthetic securitisation in particular. Remember that the essence of the transaction is credit risk transfer, and investors (protection sellers) desire exposure to the credit performance of reference assets. So investors are taking on the credit risk of these assets, be they conventional bonds, ABS securities, loans or other assets. The primary measure of this risk is the credit rating of the assets, taken together with any credit enhancements, as well as their historical ratings performance.

The second risk is more problematic and open to translation issues. In a number of deals the sponsor of the transaction must also determine when a credit event has taken place; as the sponsor is also buying protection there is scope for a conflict of interest here. The more critical concern, and one which has given rise to litigation in past cases, is what exactly constitutes a credit event. A lack of clear legal definition can lead to conflict if the protection buyer believes that a particular occurrence is a credit event and therefore the trigger for a protection payout, however this is disputed by the protection seller. Generally the broader the definition of "credit event", the greater the risk there is of dispute. Trigger events should therefore be defined in the governing legal documentation as precisely as possible.

Most descriptions of events defined as trigger events, including those listed in the 1999 ISDA *Credit Derivatives Definitions*, include circumstances that fall short of a general default, so that payouts can be enforced when the reference asset obligor is not in default. This means that the risk taken on by investors in synthetic deals is higher than that taken on in a conventional cash deal. It is important for investors to be aware of this — credit ratings for a bond issue do not reflect all the credit events that are defined by ISDA. This means that the probability of loss for a synthetic note of a specific rating may be higher than for a conventional note of the same reference name.

Portfolio Considerations

We saw in Chapter 10 that the CSO market, having begun as "static" deals originated for credit risk management and regulatory capital reasons, quickly produced "managed" deals that were brought out for slightly different reasons. The originator of a managed synthetic deal, usually a portfolio manager, has some flexibility in the daily running of the CSO. For example, it can:

- decide on the timing of delivered obligations so as to maximize recovery value;
- substitute reference credits, or trade out of them, if they look like they might have a negative impact on the vehicle;
- take a view on credit-risky assets through trading them in the credit derivative market.

The static CSO vehicle, on the other hand, does not have such flexibility, or it only has a limited substitution ability for a small percentage of the portfolio. For example, in a static deal, delivered obligations are usually required to be automatically liquidated with a pre-specified time period.

Trading patterns

The flexibility afforded the originator of a managed CSO, compared to a static one, reflects the different motivations behind its issue. Most managed CSOs are structured so that the deal sponsor has a trading ability and the synthetic market equivalent of a "ramp up" period during which reference assets may be sourced. This period may extend for a long time after deal closure. This trading flexibility means (in theory, providing the fund manager is doing a good job) that the equity holders should benefit from trading gains and therefore a higher return. They should also (in theory) suffer lower losses as the fund manager can limit negative impact of deteriorating credits by removing or replacing them.

A managed CSO may have the following trading guidelines written into its governing legal documentation:

- the freedom to terminate CDS positions that have deteriorated and are causing, or will cause, losses. This can be done by putting on a trade in the opposite direction on the same name (bought protection to cancel out a previous sold protection position), or by terminating the original position for a fee;
- closing out CDS positions that have improved in credit quality, and so crystallise a profit. The cash generated by so doing can then be held in the reserve account or used to invest in a new CDS position;
- undertaking trading in the CDS market (and cash market for a hybrid CSO) on a discretionary basis, in accordance with the fund manager's views.

Generally the governing documentation will set limits on the type of trading that can be undertaken, for example there may be restrictions on the geographical location and industrial sector of a reference entity, or the trading volume may be set at no more than 20% of the nominal value of the portfolio each year.

Hypothetical return profile

We now illustrate the main issues in investors' return analysis using a hypothetical CSO trade. We have not covered over-collateralisation tests (OC), which are very common in cash CDOs and CSOs, and so let us assume that in this hypothetical transaction there are no OC tests. The note tranching of our CSO is shown in Figure 12.5. The capital structure

Figure 12.5   Hypothetical CSO transaction, note tranching.

Class	Note nominal m	Per cent of deal	Rating	Coupon
Super senior CDS	850	85.00%	n/r	12 bps
Class A	60	6.00%	AAA	E + 55 bps
Class B	25	2.50%	AA	E + 90 bps
Class C	20	2.00%	A	E + 175 bps
Class D	10	1.00%	BBB	E + 350 bps
Equity	35	3.50%	n/r	Variable

Average expected maturity 5 years
E = 3 m euribor
The CSO reference pool has average rating of BBB1 and pays average 130 bps CDS premium

presented would not look unusual in the CSO market, with the equity piece paying the vehicle's excess spread and therefore stated as a "variable" return.

By making certain assumptions about the reference pool and using default probability data from Moody's, we can generate the internal rate of return (IRR) for each of the note classes across a number of default scenarios. This is shown in Figure 12.6. In our selected circumstances, we can see that the Class A and B notes do not experience any loss even when the five-year cumulative default rate reaches 7%. The Class C note is impacted by credit deterioration and suffers loss when the cumulative default rate reaches 5%. For the Class D note, this point is reached at the 3% level. Compared to the long-term historical average five-year cumulative default rate, which is approximately 1.9% for BBB-rated corporate names for the period 1970–1998,[3] we can see that all classes of notes lie above this figure and should not, based on historical data, experience losses during their five-year life.[4]

This analysis may appeal to certain investors. Of course we have kept it simplistic deliberately, but this helps make the illustration. A number of factors can cause the notes to experience loss earlier, mostly associated with our assumptions not turning out be accurate. The most obvious factor is if there is a higher than expected level of defaults or other credit events, or if

---

3 This figure is quoted from Moody's, *"Default and Recovery Rates of Corporate Bond Issuers"*, February 2002

4 The five-year cumulative default rate for BBB-rated names in individual years does reach considerably higher than 1.9%, for example it was over 5% in 1986 and over 3% for most of 1981–1988. However it was also lower than 1% during the first half of the 1990s.

the recovery rate is lower than 35%. However, as a relative value proposition, especially for investors looking to diversify out of traditional asset classes, it may be worth some attention. In this regard, we also present Figure 12.7 which compares the IRR expected performance of the Class D note and a BBB-rated corporate bond fund. The corporate bond fund used is (an un-named) investment bank's fund, which publishes its return regularly. This fund is comprised of 120 BBB-rated corporate bonds, all equally-weighted. To compare this to our CSO, which has a CDS premium of 130 bps, we assume that the fund pays a return of Euribor plus 110 basis points (the asset swap spread over Euribor is invariably at a level below the CDS spread, the positive basis we discussed in Chapter 8). Applying the same cumulative default rates we obtain Figure 12.7.

The key conclusion to make is that the CSO note can experience higher cumulative default rates before it suffers loss, compared to the corporate bond fund. In fact we may expect this, because the CSO note is part of a vehicle in which there is a first-loss piece that will absorb the first 3.50% of losses. The corporate bond fund will suffer losses as soon as the first default occurs. Equally, the higher IRR is expected, because CSO notes (and cash CDO notes) are invariably priced to pay a higher spread than straight debt of the same rating and industrial sector. This reflects the secondary market

Figure 12.6   Hypothetical CSO, IRR profiles.

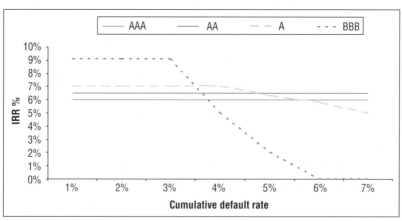

Assumptions of the analysis
Defaults occurr evenly over time
Recovery rate is 35%
CDS spread is 130 bps
Euribor curve as at January 2003

Figure 12.7   Comparing expected return performance of hypothetical CSO Class D note and (unspecified) BBB-rated corporate bond fund.

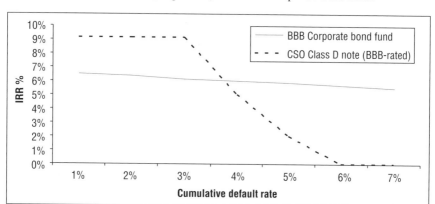

liquidity, or lack thereof, of the CSO note market as well as the relative unfamiliarity of the market for investors. On the other hand, the CSO note will suffer greater loss during a period of high corporate default, once losses exceed the nominal value of the equity note.

Impact of Correlation on CDO Return

CDO note tranches and their corresponding returns are sensitive to the structure's underlying asset correlation. As we saw in chapter 10, each note tranche in a CDO represents specific risk/return profiles, and a particular slice of a portfolio of credits that have been pooled together. Each tranche is also placed in order of seniority in the capital structure of the CDO. Equity tranche investors are exposed to the first losses in the portfolio, followed by the mezzanine note investors and finally the senior note investors.[1] Because senior and super-senior note investors are the last to suffer loss, they are, statistically, very unlikely to actually experience any losses. Hence the term "catastrophic risk" to describe their risk exposure.

---

[1] This is why it is so common for originators or sponsors to hold the equity piece themselves. By being exposed to portfolio losses before anyone else, they tempt external investors into holding the more senior pieces. Without this application of securitisation technology, the originator would not have been able to get investors to hold any parcel of the pool of assets.

Each note tranche is exposed, to different degrees, to the performance of all the names in the portfolio. This sensitivity is measured in the following ways:

- tranche delta: the credit risk of the note to each of the names in the portfolio, that is, the change in value of the note for a change in the credit spread of each reference credit;
- gamma: the second-order sensitivity of the value of a note to changes in the credit spread of each reference name in the portfolio ("idiosyncratic gamma"), or the second-order sensitivity of a note to a change in spread of the entire portfolio ("systemic gamma").

The key aspect of this note sensitivity is correlation. This is a measure of how each of the reference credits perform with respect to each other. Positive correlation indicates a pool of credits that behave in the same way, that is, their credit spread will generally move in the same direction whether widening or narrowing. Negative correlation indicates a pool of credits whose spreads tend to move in opposite direction. Although it is rare to observe, a zero correlation suggests that the reference credits behave in an independent manner.

The investment decision

Since each CDO note tranche represents a different risk/return profile, investors will seek to build a portfolio that is tailored to their desired risk profile and market view. In many, if not most, cases investors will hold part of one tranche of a CDO issue, and this was the main focus of the chapter until now. More sophisticated investors hold combinations of notes in one or more CDO(s). For instance consider the following alternative strategies:

- holding the equity note and being short of the mezzanine note: this creates a leveraged credit exposure, and also all but eliminates catastrophic risk exposure. It reduces total expected return however;
- holding the equity note and delta-hedging credit risk exposure using a basket CDS contract for the whole portfolio: this creates systemic gamma and short idiosyncratic gamma;
- holding the equity note and delta hedging specific names in the portfolio: this creates a leveraged credit risk exposure and eliminates idiosyncratic gamma exposure on specific names.

The last strategy, in particular, is sensitive to the impact of correlation in the portfolio. We can illustrate this with one of our hypothetical CDO structures.

Assume we structure a synthetic CDO issue comprised of 100 reference names. Following the rating agency review the portfolio characteristics are as shown in Table 12.1.

Table 12.1   Hypothetical synthetic CDO portfolio characteristics.

Average tenor	4.5 years
Average recovery rate	40%
Diversity score	65
Average credit rating	A3/Baa1
Average spread	65 basis points

During the pre-close marketing phase, the CDO is stated as being expected to have a capital structure around the following ranges:

Equity note	0.5%–2.50%
Mezzanine note Baa3	2.50%–5.50%
"B" note A3	5.50%–7.50%
"A" note Aaa	7.50%–10.00%

The remainder is of course comprised of the super-senior swap.

The CDO notes are priced in accordance with their correlation sensitivity. On closing, the portfolio correlation will be calculated as a final value and the notes priced in line with that value. However during the structuring phase, the notes are priced at the spread corresponding to a particular correlation value. Assume that these alternative spreads are as shown in Table 12.2. Note spreads are basis points over Libor, assuming act/360 day-count basis and quarterly coupon. The statistical expected loss for the portfolio is a fixed figure based on a constant recovery rate.[2]

Table 12.2   Hypothetical synthetic CDO, note spreads in accordance with portfolio correlation

Correlation	20%	35%	50%
Equity note	14.50%	11.90%	8.70%
Mezzanine note	320	305	248
B Note	60	95	110
A Note	35	55	80

---

2 This exercise was conducted around February-March 2004, and so indicative credit spreads reflect those observed in the market at that time.

The results we calculate and which are shown in Table 12.2 provide a very interesting observation on the impact of correlation on return. We see that investors in the Equity note are long of correlation risk, while those holding the Mezzanine note are short correlation risk. Why is this?

A lower level of correlation means that the names in the portfolio do not act in concert with each other. This implies that portfolio losses are more at the expected average level, and that the probability of catastrophic loss in the portfolio is lower. In other words, the Equity noteholder is more likely to experience loss, and so the return on the note will be higher. A higher level of correlation means that the portfolio names are more likely to act in the same way, that is their credit performance will be similar. In other words, if one name in the portfolio suffers default, it is highly likely that other names will also default. This translates into a higher probability of catastrophic loss, which will impact more senior noteholders. This means that holders of these notes will demand a higher return the greater the positive correlation in the portfolio.

The price of each tranche, and its subsequent mark-to-market after issue, is therefore sensitive to portfolio correlation.

Combo note structures

The capital structure of a CDO is sometimes adjusted shortly prior to issue to take account of correlation sensitivities. This involves linking part of the return of a tranche to that of the Equity note or another note, so-called "combination structures" or Combo note structures, which was first observed with the Robeco III CSO underwritten by JPMorgan Chase and closed in December 2001 (see Choudhry 2002). The main principle behind a Combo note structure involves restructuring the coupon of a tranche so that a part of the return is linked to the Equity note. This reduces the correlation sensitivity of the Combo note while also increasing the coupon. The Combo note may pay either a Libor spread plus a variable return based on the performance of the Equity note, or a fixed coupon. The greater the share of the Combo note return that is linked to the Equity note, the lower its sensitivity to correlation.

A Combo note structure offers an alternative investment strategy for investors. We have seen how higher-rated note tranches in a CSO carry correlation risk, while lower-rated tranches are long of correlation risk. A Combo note retains a higher credit rating, but by linking part of its return to a lower-rated note, its correlation risk is reduced.

References and Bibliography

Choudhry, M., "Combining securitisation and trading in credit derivatives: an analysis of the managed synthetic CDO", *Euromoney International Debt Capital Markets Handbook 2003*, Euromoney Publications 2002

Nothing lasts forever, son.

— Benton Fraser's father, *Due South* 1997

13

Basic Principles in CDO Valuation and Cashflow Waterfall Models

To complete our discussion of CDOs, this chapter presents an overview of the main principles in CDO valuation. To assist understanding we will consider cash as well as synthetic CDOs. We do not discuss one common approach, Moody's Binomial Expansion technique, because that is covered in existing literature that is readily accessible, and made available by Moody's. However we present some key concepts that should set the scene satisfactorily for practitioners.

Overview

The valuation of note tranches in a CDO structure is a function of a number of factors, an important one of which is the credit quality of the underlying portfolio. This is measured by aggregating individual securities' default probabilities, and also considering their default correlation and diversity. If the portfolio experiences a deterioration in credit quality, this has the biggest impact on the equity tranche, because this has a leveraged exposure to the portfolio and is the first-loss piece. Other factors that impact the valuation of the tranches include:

- changes in the level of portfolio diversification, which increase concentration risk and may have a negative impact;
- if the underlying assets are viewed as being risky relative to a more recent CDO issue;
- if any of the rating agency guidelines are ignored or compliance tests are breached;

- if the cost of funding on the liabilities side is variable but the return on assets is fixed, any negative move regarding the former will reduce value.

Another important factor is the perception in the market of the portfolio manager.

Common valuation approaches methods include the following:

- Cash flow value: the net present value (NPV) of the cash flows through to maturity;
- Liquidation value: the value of the underlying assets should the CDO be unwound;
- Secondary market value: the actual market price at which already-issued notes will trade.

We consider these briefly now.

Valuation approaches

Cash flow method

The future cash flows approach involves modelling the cash flows under certain assumptions. It provides a reasonable expected value that is to be received on a particular note tranche, if held to maturity. A computer simulation is run to determine the expected cash flows and the expected loss for each tranche. The average of all scenarios is used to arrive at an NPV for each tranche.

The simulation uses the following parameter inputs:

- the par value of the underlying assets, assuming they are not in default;
- assumed rate of recovery;
- the amortisation profile of all assets and assumptions on rate of reinvestment;
- cash held in vehicle bank accounts.

Liquidation value method

The liquidation value approach to pricing CDO note tranches is based on calculating the most realistic minimum value for each tranche in the event of liquidation, based on the market value of the assets. This is undertaken by establishing the mark-to-market value of the underlying assets, whatever these are. In theory it should be possible to obtain these values for bonds, loans and CDSs. Once the value of the underlying is confirmed, this is offset against the principal and interest accrued on all the CDO note tranches (the liabilities).

This approach is viewed as being a tractable and transparent one and is often used by investors.

Secondary market value method

This is a market observation method, which may not be applicable if the notes under consideration are particularly illiquid. The reasoning is that the secondary market provides an explicit valuation for any CDO tranche because it clears the price at which buyers and sellers for the tranche will deal. This approach is highly effective where a price can be obtained, however many notes are not priced and there are relatively few market-makers for many issues (often a price can only be obtained from the bank that underwrote and arranged the issue).

Correlation products and valuation

We now explore further the different approaches to pricing CDO tranches.

Basket CDS

The synthetic CDO is a correlation product, in effect an extension of a basket CDS or basket CLN. A common approach to valuing these is via a Monte Carlo simulation. This involves generating the expected time to default from the simulation, and then calculating a basket spread as follows:

- simulate the expected time-to default of the assets in the basket, in order of default; the nth time to default is stated as $p_n(i)$ where i is the defaulted asset;
- calculate the present value of the premium or coupon stream paid up to time $p = \min[p_n(i), T]$ where T is the basket maturity date;
- where $p_n(i) < T$ then the present value is given by $M(p_n(i))(1 - r(i))$ where M is the Libor rate expressed as a discount factor and r is the recovery rate for defaulted asset i. If $p_n(i) > T$ then the present value is zero.
- calculate the average of the present value for the protection premium (the basket PV01) and the protection leg present value over all simulated paths;
- finally, divide the average value of this protection premium by the PV01 and this provides the premium spread.

This approach is used in practice for basket CDS of up to 100 assets although the Monte Carlo simulation takes longer the greater the number of assets.

Synthetic CDO tranches

The above approach can also be used to price a synthetic CDO note tranche. The simulation is run this time to generate a time-to-default for each asset in the reference portfolio and then the note tranche spread over Libor calculated as before. Another approach is to price a note from its loss distribution. We will describe this qualitatively here.

Consider a basket CDS linked to a note tranche, where the tranche is described by upper and lower values Pu and Pd, which are percentages of the notional value of the reference portfolio. This value is given by

$$N_{Tranche} = N_{Portfolio} \ (P_u - P_d).$$

The basket CDS has expiry date of T and for the period $t < T$ the cumulative loss in the portfolio up to time t is denoted by $L(t)$. The loss amount of the tranche is given by

$$L_{Tranche}(t) = \max[L(t) - P_d.0] - \max[L(t) - P_u,o].$$

This is actually the payoff profile that one would use to describe an option. Infact Picone (2001) describes CDO note tranches as options on the reference portfolio, and we look at his analysis in the next section.

We then proceed to price the note using the same approach to price a CDS, which requires us to calculate or obtain a probability of default for the tranche. This is given by

$$\text{Probability}(t) = \frac{E_0^T[L_{Tranche}(t)]}{N_{Tranche}}$$

where E is the risk-neutral expectation operator.

Carrying on the CDS analogy, we now price the "contingent payment leg" of the note as follows

$$PV = N_{Tranche} \int_0^T M(0, \ u)dP(u)$$

where $M(0, \ u)$ is the Libor discount factor for the period from t to T.

The value of the payment premium leg is denoted by the premium spread s and we wish the value at time of default of asset i. We introduce a factor for the accrued payments at I denoted by a_i, and so the premium value present value is given by

$$PV = sN_{Tranche} \sum_{j=1}^{n} a_i(1 - \text{Prob}(T_i))M(0, T_i).$$

The investor therefore values the note tranche as follows:

$$PV_{Tranche} = \text{Premium Leg PV} - \text{Protection Leg PV}.$$

Thus the synthetic CDO note can be valued provided we generate a loss distribution for the note applicable to the valuation period t to T.

CDO viewed as an option

Picone (2001) describes a recent technique that values a cash flow CDO as an option instrument, with the collateral portfolio as the underlying asset. We summarise his approach here.

Under this method, the CDO is viewed as simple balance sheet, as shown in Figure 13.1.

Figure 13.1   Simple CDO balance sheet.

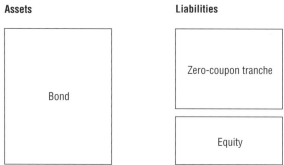

The asset side of the balance sheet is assumed to hold only one asset, a corporate bond, and the liability side is made up of a zero-coupon bond tranche and the equity tranche. From this, we can state that the value of the asset side is given by:

$$\text{Assets} = \text{Zero-coupon tranche} + \text{Equity} \quad (13.1)$$

The portfolio manager realizes the asset on maturity. From the sale proceeds the manager redeems the zero-coupon bond and then distributes remaining funds to equity holders. This follows the priority of payments.

Under company law the equity holders have the right, but not the obligation, to pay off bondholders and assume control over the asset's remaining value. If on maturity the asset value is greater than the value of debt, then the equity holders will exercise this "option" and pay off the bondholders. If the value of the asset is lower than that of the bond, then equity holders are more likely to default and transfer the residual asset value to the bondholders (in accordance with priority of payment).

Under this scenario, the equity holders' position is analogous to that of a holder of a call option on the same asset. The strike price of the asset is the nominal value of the zero-coupon bond tranche, above this value the option becomes in-the-money. The position of the bondholders is that of investors who have purchased a debt obligation that is default-free and pays a risk-free rate. They are also, in effect, short a put option to the equity holders. So if the equity holders choose not to pay off their debt (not exercise their option), they will deliver the asset to the bondholders at a strike price equal to the debt amount.

Following this we can now write the value of the asset as:

$$A = PV_Z - \max(Z - A, 0) + \max(A - Z, 0) \qquad (13.2)$$

where

A is the value of the asset at maturity;
Z is the nominal value of the zero-coupon bond tranche;
PV_Z is the present value of the zero-coupon tranche.

Equation (13.2) is actually the put-call parity of the famous Black-Scholes option pricing model. By using this, we can view the zero-coupon tranche as a combination of a zero-coupon bond plus a short position on a put option on the underlying asset, with a strike price equal to the nominal value of the bond itself.

We can rationalise that the probability of default is the same as the probability of exercising the put option. If this probability rises, the value of the put option also rises, and so lowers the investment value of bondholders. The probability of exercising the option can be calculated from standard option pricing models. Exactly as with equity options, the volatility of the asset price is the most important model parameter. We use the same volatility value to obtain the probability of default.

We have to modify (13.2) to make it more applicable to a multi-tranche CDO. It is common for CDOs to issue three or more note tranches. The notes are rated at different levels by the rating agencies because they represent different risk exposures to the asset pool and also because they are ranked in a priority of payments. For our purposes however, we view all tranches as zero-coupon bonds with an embedded put option. The key difference is that each tranche represents a different strike price and different probability of default.

We now re-assess Figure 13.1 and assume that our CDO is structured into a senior note, a mezzanine note and a junior note. The payoff for the junior noteholder given by:

$$
\begin{aligned}
P_E &= E - \min(E, L) \\
&= \max(E - L, 0) \\
&= Put(E, L)
\end{aligned}
\tag{13.3}
$$

where

L	is the realised loss on the collateral;
E	is the size of the equity piece, expressed as a percentage of the liability;
$Put(E, L)$	is written on the equity piece E.

So if losses are greater than E, the junior piece is completely absorbed and further losses are paid for by the Mezzanine noteholder.

We can use (13.3) to extract the equity piece as the call option in (13.2) as follows:

$$
\begin{aligned}
P_E &= A - Z - \min(A - Z, A - L) \\
&= A - Z + \max[A - Z, L - A] \\
&= A - Z + \max[Z, L] - A \\
&= A - Z + \max[A - Z, L - A] \\
&= \max[A - Z, 0]
\end{aligned}
\tag{13.4}
$$

The payoff for the senior noteholder is given by:

$$
\begin{aligned}
P_S &= A - E - \max(L - E, 0) \\
&= A - E - Call(E, L)
\end{aligned}
\tag{13.5}
$$

where

$Call(E, L)$ is written on the equity piece E.

The payoff for the mezzanine noteholder is given by:

$$
\begin{aligned}
P_M &= \max[\min(M - E, M - L), 0]P \\
&= \max[(M - E) + \min(E - L, 0), 0] \\
&= (M - E) + \max[\min(E - L, 0), -(M - E)] \\
&= (M - E) + \min(E - L, 0) + \max[0, -(L - E) - \min(E - L, 0)] \\
&= (M - E) - \max(L - E, 0) + \max[0, E - L - \min(E - L, 0)].
\end{aligned}
$$

$$(13.6)$$

We can note further that:

$$(E - L) - \min(E - L, 0) = \alpha > 0 \qquad (13.7)$$

if;

$$L = M + \alpha.$$

With (13.7) we can formulate:

$$\max[(0, E - L - \min(E - L, 0)]\max(L - M, 0) \qquad (13.8)$$

Therefore from (13.6) we have:

$$
\begin{aligned}
P_M &= (M - E) - \max(L - E, 0) + \max[L - M, 0) \\
&= (M - E) + \textstyle\prod(M, E)
\end{aligned}
$$

$$(13.9)$$

where

$$\textstyle\prod(M - E) = \max(L - M, 0) - \max[L - E, 0) \qquad (13.10)$$

and

M is the size of the mezzanine piece, expressed as a percentage of the liability.

Therefore from (13.9), the mezzanine note payoff is equal to the portfolio of a zero-coupon bond, together with a portfolio of two call options, which are a long call option on the exercise price M and a short call option on the exercise price E.

Applying this approach to more complex structures, we see that the call and put options are written on a pool of assets that might comprise bonds, loans and CDS.

Hypothetical Case Study

For illustration, let us examine the valuation of a cash flow CDO that has been "structured" for this book, using the cashflow approach.

ABC 2003-1 CDO

Assets: Bank loans
Close date: June 2003
Maturity: June 2013

The capital structure and extract of the portfolio is shown in Figure 13.2. We aggregate the cash flows and apply the cash flow valuation method, a summary for which is shown in Figure 13.3. This enables us to obtain the values for the note tranches, which are shown below.

	IRR	Original Coupon
AAA/Aaa	0.40%	0.40%
AA/Aa2	0.91%	0.80%
BBB/Baa2	1.15%	1.50%
BB/Ba2	−4.29%	2.80%

Figure 13.2   Capital structure and extract from portfolio.

Class	Principal	WAM years per cent	Coupon	Issue price	Proceeds
Class A	400,000,000	4.05	80 L + 40	100	400,000,000
Class B	50,000,000	5.65	10 L + 80	100	50,000,000
Class C	25,000,000	6.08	5 L + 150	100	25,000,000
Class D	10,000,000	6.95	2 L + 280	100	10,000,000
Equity	15,000,000	1.85	3 Excess spread	100	15,000,000
	500,000,000				500,000,000

Portfolio summary

Number of issuers	80
Notional €m	485,250,000
Price	94.75
Average spread	192.5
Average maturity	Oct 08
Average rating	BBB−
Aggregate principal balance	458,251,000
Cash reserve	13,252,125
Average loan price	91.55

Extract of portfolio

Issue	Security	Country	Seniority	Amount €m	Price	Spread	Maturity	Average life	Sector
Airco Ltd	Loan	UK	Senior secured	2,939,451	89.55	355	13-Aug-08	5.49	Aviation
BriTel	Loan	UK	Senior secured	4,791,258	93.25	289	25-Jun-08	5.65	Telecoms
Brosnan	Loan	Germany	Senior secured	6,000,000	45.25	855	1-Dec-07	4.95	Utilities

Figure 13.3   Cashflow valuation.

Period	AAa/Aaa	AA/Aa2	BBB/Baa2	BB/Ba2
Jun-04	−400000000	−500000000	−25000000	−15000000
Jun-05	8,498,562	385,256	325,252	1,254,145
Jun-06	48,259,784	504,215	441,520	1,428,525
Jun-07	98,586,987	558,625	445,251	1,427,525
Jun-08	59,868,524	579,452	417,852	1,427,852
Jun-09	895,652	39,254,181	1,524,584	1,426,875
Jun-10			456,825	1,434,582
Jun-11			20,125,415	852,541
Jun-12			125,485	1,434,589
Jun-13			1,548,528	115,215
IRR	1.78%	2.75%	2.84%	−1.69%
Libor spread	0.40%	0.91%	1.15%	−4.29%

We then compare these values to the secondary market values for notes of comparable quality and structure, to obtain a reasonable valuation for the tranches.

Cashflow Waterfall Model: Static Synthetic CDO[1]

For illustrative purposes we show the basic breakdown of a cashflow model for a static synthetic CDO. This is done via Excel spreadsheets.

Cashflow model

This is a working cashflow waterfall model for an hypothetical static synthetic collateralised debt obligation, "Synthetic CDO Ltd", with issue size USD 115 million. It is a partially funded CSO, with super senior portfolio CDS and tranched CLNs. The liabilities of the CDO reference a portfolio of 100 corporate reference assets. The proceeds of the CLN issue are invested in collateral securities of German Bunds, which are then repo'd out to a repo counterparty and act as collateral for the CLN issue. The return on the collateral securities represents the protection for the CLN investors,

---

[1] This section was co-authored with Suleman Baig of Deutsche Bank AG, during the time he was with JPMorgan, who is also the author of the waterfall model. The authors are writing in their individual private capacity and this material does not represent in any way the authors' respective employers.

who can expect a minimum return based on return on collateral. However the excess return to CLN noteholders is made up of the credit-linked return, linked to reference assets.

The definitions refer to an hypothetical "Offering Circular" (OC) for this transaction.

The note tranching to this transaction is given at Figure 13.4 below, which also shows the terms of the deal. It also shows the calculation of interest at the time this snapshot is taken. The amounts calculated here are shown on the summary sheets that appear later.

Figure 13.5 is the inputs to the model, showing the various types of fees and payments that make up cashflows of the waterfall. Figure 13.6 shows receipts of cash to the vehicle beginning with note proceeds on issue and then subsequent items such as repo interest. It also shows results of the "Par Coverage Test" which shows if the vehicle has sufficient cash to cover liabilities at par, as well as cash flows resulting from credit events of any assets in the portfolio. These are marked "A" and "B" on Figure 13.6 for readers' reference.

Figure 13.7 shows the waterfall itself. We reference at "A" where the value for the Class B-1 note interest distribution amount will fall, this amount is the payment of excess interest, after the application of interest and principal payments of A3 and Par coverage tests. The bottom half of the spreadsheet shows the remaining calculations required, for the junior note liabilities.

Finally Figure 13.8 shows the cashflow movements in the vehicle's bank accounts at the time the calculation is made on the model.

Figure 13.4   "Synthetic CDO", terms of deal and note tranching.

Static data

Closing Date	8/9/02
Scheduled Maturity Redemption Date	8/9/12
Final Payment Date	10/9/13
Period Start Date	11/25/02
Period End Date	2/24/03
Period (days)	91
Pay Method	360
Three Month EURIBOR	0.03045
Repurchase Date	Y
Maturity or Redemption Date	N
Repo Termination Event	N
Unsettled Credit Events	N
Denomination	50,000

Note class	Price	Original value	Period start principal amount	Deferred interest (b/f)	Principal amount adjusted for Intra period events*	Principal reduction	Period end principal amount	Deferred interest (c/f)	Denom. O/S (start)	Denom. O/S (end)	Number of shares	interest per EUR 1k note	Margin	Interest due	Interest paid
A-1	100%	38,250,000	38,250,000	—	38,250,000	—	38,250,000		50,000.00	50,000.00	765.00	441.73	0.0045	337,923.45	337,923.45
A-2	100%	21,250,000	21,250,000	—	21,250,000	—	21,250,000		50,000.00	50,000.00	425.00	467.01	0.0065	198,479.25	198,479.25
A-3	100%	29,750,000	29,750,000	—	29,750,000	—	29,750,000	—	50,000.00	50,000.00	595.00	587.08	0.0160	349,312.60	349,312.60
B-1	100%	20,400,000	10,656,875	—	10,656,875	—	2,985,625		26,119.79	7,317.71	408.00	—	—	—	—
B-2	100%	5,100,000	—	—	—	—	—		0.00	0.00	102.00	—	—	—	—

*Cash Settlement Amounts & Deferred interest outstanding at such time
© Suleman Baig 2003

Figure 13.5 Inputs to waterfall model.

	Inputs	Fees	Accounts	Events	Static data	Note amount O/S (b/f)	Credit events	Terms
Static Data								
Period Start Date	11/25/02							
Period End Date	2/24/03							
Three Month EURIBOR	0.03045							
Events								
Maturity or Redemption Date	N							
Repo Termination Event	N							
Unsettled Credit Events	N							
Aggregate Amount Outstanding (b/f)								
Class A-1 Note	38,250,000							
Class A-2 Note	21,250,000							
Class A-3 Note	29,750,000							
A-3 Notes Deferred Interest	—							
Class B-1 Note	10,656,875							
Class B-2 Note	—							
Accounts								
Collateral Account (24437301)								
Opening Balance (bf)	31,717							
Net Proceeds of the Notes	99,906,875							
Market Value of the Repo Securities	105,027,176							
Payment Account (24437303 — Balance at Pay Date)								
Opening Balance	—							
Expense Account (24437304)								
Opening Balance	60,640							
Unpaid Issuer Expenses	—							
Other Net Movements	—							

Figure 13.5 (Cont'd)

	Inputs	Fees	Accounts	Events	Static data	Note amount O/S (b/f)	Credit events	Terms
Collection Account (24437302)								
Opening Balance	95,768							
Fees								
Taxes, Registration owing by the Issuer	9,015							
Trustee and Administrator Charges	46,640							
Other Admin Expenses								
Credit Events								
Aggregate of all Cash Settlement Amounts	14,843,125.00							
Aggregate of all Re-instatement Amounts	—							
Cash Settlement Amounts	7,671,250.00							
Re-instatement Amounts	—							
Terms								
Repurchased Securities: Originator to Provide Figures								
Initial Purchase Price	114,750,000.00							
Payment of Principal on the notes to be made								
Agg. Collateral Account Replenishment Payment (to date)	653,476.05							
Aggregate Repurchase Price paid (to date)	22,514,375.00							
Repo Rate Payents Accrued and Unpaid	—							
Repo Rate Payments Paid	762,341.92							
Calculation Amount (for Unsettled Credit Events)	—							
Max Portfolio Notional Amount (p51)	841,500,000.00							
Credit Swap Payment	792,303.19							
Interest rec'd wrt to Securities sold by Issuer	—							
Discount Payments (After Repo term.)	—							

© Suleman Baig 2003.

Figure 13.6   Model input showing cash receipts to vehicle

REMAINING PURCHASE PRICE	100,560,351
Cash Settlement Amount	**7,671,250**
Payment of Principal on the notes to be made	—
Initial Purchase Price	114,750,000
Collateral Account Replenishment Payments	—
Repo Rate Payments accrued and unpaid	—
Repo Rate Payments Paid	762,342
Aggregate of Collateral Account Replenishment Amts paid	653,476
Aggregate of Repurchase Prices Paid	22,514,375
TERMS	
Issuance of Notes Proceeds	114,750,000
Excess Repo Securities	—
Calculation Amount (for Unsettled Credit Events)	—
Max Portfolio Notional Amount	841,500,000
Credit Swap Payment	792,303
Collateral Account Investment Income	762,342
Interest rec'd wrt to Securities sold by Issuer	—
Repo Rate Payment	762,342
Discount Payments (After Repo term.)	—
PAR COVERAGE TEST	
Ratio (at period start)	1.040774241
Value	1.11
Test	PASS
10/1/03	1.11
10/1/04	0
Thereafter	0
PURCHASED SECURITIES	**"A"**
Reviewed Weekly	
Applicable Percentage	1.03
Required Amount	88,288,743
De Minimis Amount	214,293
Condition	**MARGIN SURPLUS**
	TRUE
CREDIT EVENTS	**"B"**
Aggregate of all Cash Settlement Amounts	14,843,125
Aggregate of all Re-instatement Amounts	—
Cash Settlement Amounts	7,671,250
Re-instatement Amounts	—

SUFFICIENT FUNDS TO PAY CASH SETTLEMENT AMOUNT

Figure 13.7   Waterfall payment calculations.

INTEREST WATERFALL	1,650,413.23		
	Due	*Paid*	*Balance*
Taxes, Registration owing by the Issuer	—	—	1,650,413.23
Trustee and Administrator Charges	9,015	9,015	1,641,398.44
Other Admin Expenses	46,640	46,640	1,594,758.00
Expense Account Top Up	—	—	1,594,758.00
Interest payments on Class A-1	337,923	337,923	1,256,834.55
Interest payments on Class A-2	198,479	198,479	1,058,355.30
Interest payments on Class A-3	349,313	349,313	709,042.70
Par Coverage	709,043	709,043	—
Class B-1 Interest Distribution Amount	—	—	—

PRINCIPAL WATERFALL	—		
	Amounts Due	*Paid*	*Balance*
REVISED BALANCE ON PRINCIPAL PAYMENT DATE (Int. on subordinate Notes)			
Unpaid Taxes, Registration owing by the Issuer	—	—	—
Unpaid Trustee and Administrator Charges	—	—	—
Unpaid Other Admin Charges	—	—	—
Unpaid Expense Account Top Up	—	—	—
Unpaid Interest payments on Class A-1	—	—	—
Principal payments on Class A-1	38,250,000	—	—
Unpaid Interest payments on Class A-2	—	—	—
Principal payments on Class A-2	21,250,000	—	—
Interest payments on Class A-3	—	—	—
Principal payments on Class A-3	29,750,000	—	—
Class A-3 Deferred interest	—	—	—
B-1Note Rate Interest	—	—	—
Principal payments on Class B-1	10,656,875	—	—
Principal payments on Class B-2	5,279,156	—	—

© Suleman Baig 2003

Figure 13.8 Bank account movements.

COLLATERAL ACCOUNT		PAYMENT ACCOUNT (BALANCE AT PAY DATE)	
Opening Balance (bf)	31,716.84	Opening Balance	—
Net Proceeds of the Notes	99,906,875.00	Transfer from Collection Account	1,650,413
Repo Securities (Market Value)	105,027,176	Waterfall Payments	1,650,413
Replenishment Payment	709,043	Revenue	1,650,413
Principal Amortisation Payment (c/f)	—	Principal	—
B-2 Note Principal Balance Adjustment	—	Excess Repo Securites	—
Reinstatement Amounts	—	Closing Balance	—
Cash Settlement Amount	7,671,250	Closing Balance	198,003,561

EXPENSE ACCOUNT		COLLECTION ACCOUNT	
Opening Balance	60,640	Opening Balance	95,768.12
Movements	—	Credit Swap Receipts	792,303.19
Condition as per O.C.	—	Collateral Investment Income	762,341.92
Unpaid Issuer Expenses	—	Interest rec'd wrt to Securities sold by Issuer	—
Other Net Movements	0	Repo Receipts	762,341.92
Closing Balance*	60,640	Discount Payments (After Repo term.)	—
		Transfer Balance to Payment Account	1,650,413.23

* On Final Principal Pay Date, balance transferred to Payment Account
© Suleman Baig 2003.

References and Bibliography

Moody's Investors Service, *The Binomial Expansion Technique*, Moody's special report, 2001.

Picone, D., *Collateralised Debt Obligations*, City University Business School, Working Paper 2001.

It ain't bragging if you can back it up.

— Muhammad Ali

Synthetic Mortgage-Backed Securities

The securitisation technique has been applied widely in capital markets worldwide since its introduction in the US mortgage market in the 1970s. It is now common to see esoteric assets such as funeral home receivables as well as musicians' royalties securitised to provide backing for ABS bonds. In addition to the obvious benefits of funding, capital management and diversification, the great benefit of securitisation has been the way it has been instrumental in the development and progress of the debt capital markets. It has been an impressive tool for intermediation, bringing the suppliers and users of capital together in never more efficient ways.

It is no surprise that the synthetic securitisation technique has lent itself to other asset classes. Up to now, all of Part II of this book has been devoted to the synthetic CDO. In this final chapter, we look at synthetic mortgage-backed securitisation, which was introduced in the European market. We can see that it is based on exactly the same principles as the CSO market, and that deals are originated for similar reasons to balance sheet static synthetic CDOs.[1]

Transaction Description

As has been observed in the CSO market, the European CMBS and RMBS markets have witnessed a range of different synthetic deal structures. The first deal was issued in 1998. As with CSOs, synthetic MBS deal structures

---

[1] Residential MBS and Commercial MBS (RMBS and CMBS) follow the same principles that we discussed in Chapter 9. For more detail on MBS structures, see Hayre (2001), referenced in Chapter 9, or the author's own *Bond Market Securities* (FT Prentice Hall 2001), Chapter 8.

involve the removal of the credit risk associated with a pool of mortgages by means of credit derivatives, rather than by recourse to a true sale to an SPV. The originator, typically a mortgage bank, is the credit protection buyer and retains ownership, as well as the economic benefit, of the assets. The credit risk is transferred to the investors, who are the protection sellers. As with synthetic CDOs, there exist funded and unfunded synthetic MBS deals, as well as partially funded deals. The type of structure adopted by the originator depends on the legal jurisdiction, the regulatory environment, capital requirements and also the preferences of investors.

The main market for synthetic MBS to date has been Germany, although deals have also involved UK, Swedish and Dutch originators.

Deal structures

Unfunded synthetic MBS

An unfunded synthetic MBS deal uses CDS to transfer the credit risk of a pool of mortgages from the originator to a swap counterparty. There is no note issue and frequently no SPV involved. The investor receives the CDS premium during the life of the transaction, in return for which they agree to pay out on any losses incurred by the originator on the pool of assets. The CDS references the pool of mortgages, which remain on the originator's balance sheet.

The CDS protection seller pays out on the occurrence of a credit event. The precise definition and range of credit events differs by transaction and jurisdiction, but generally there are fewer credit events associated with a synthetic MBS compared to a synthetic CDO deal. This reflects the nature of the reference assets. The common credit events described in a synthetic MBS are:

* failure to pay, and;
* bankruptcy.

Credit events are defined in the deal documentation and their occurrence triggers a payment from the protection seller.

As with vanilla CDS, in an unfunded synthetic MBS, the investor is exposed to counterparty risk if the originator is unable to continue paying its premium. To overcome this, some shorter maturity deals are arranged with a one-off premium aid at the start of the deal, that covers the credit protection for the life of the deal. Conversely, the risk for the protection buyer is if the protection seller becomes bankrupt, upon which the former will no longer be receiving any credit protection.

As there is no SPV involved, unfunded deals can be brought to market relatively quickly, and this is a key advantage over funded deals. Because the CDS counterparty must be rated equivalently to an OECD bank, the investor base is narrower than for funded deals.

Funded synthetic MBS

In a funded synthetic MBS structure, an SPV is set up that issues a tranched series of CLNs. These CLNs are referenced to the credit performance and risk exposure of a portfolio of reference assets, which may be residential mortgages, real-estate loans or commercial mortgages. The proceeds of the CLNs are either:

- invested in eligible collateral, such as a GIC account or AAA-rated government securities; or,
- passed to the originator or a third party.

If the note issue proceeds are invested in collateral, this is known as a collateralised funded synthetic MBS, otherwise the deal is uncollateralised.

Although fully-funded synthetic MBS deals have been observed, it is more common to see partially funded transactions, in which a portion of the reference pool credit risk is transferred via a CDS. This achieves a credit risk transfer from the SPV to investors without any funding issues.

Figure 14.1 shows a typical funded synthetic MBS structure. Figure 14.2 shows a simplified structure for a synthetic CMBS where the originator is transferring credit risk on assets spread across more than one legal jurisdiction.

Generally, the structure is initially brought to market by the originator entering into a credit protection agreement with the SPV, which requires it to pay the protection premium (or interest on par value) to the SPV, and secondly by the SPV ("issuer") transferring this risk exposure to investors by means of the note issue. These investors ultimately pay out on occurrence of a triggering event. The credit risk of the CLNs is, in effect, linked to the aggregated credit performance for the relevant tranche of risk of the reference pool. It is also linked to the risk profile of the collateral assets, but this is not significant because only high-quality investments are eligible for the collateral pool.

If the CLN note(s) is (are) to be collateralised, the cash raised from the issue is used to purchase eligible securities or placed in a reserve cash account. The note collateral is used to back the coupon payments on the CLNs; it is also a reserve fund that can be used to cover losses in the

Figure 14.1 Funded Synthetic MBS generic structure.

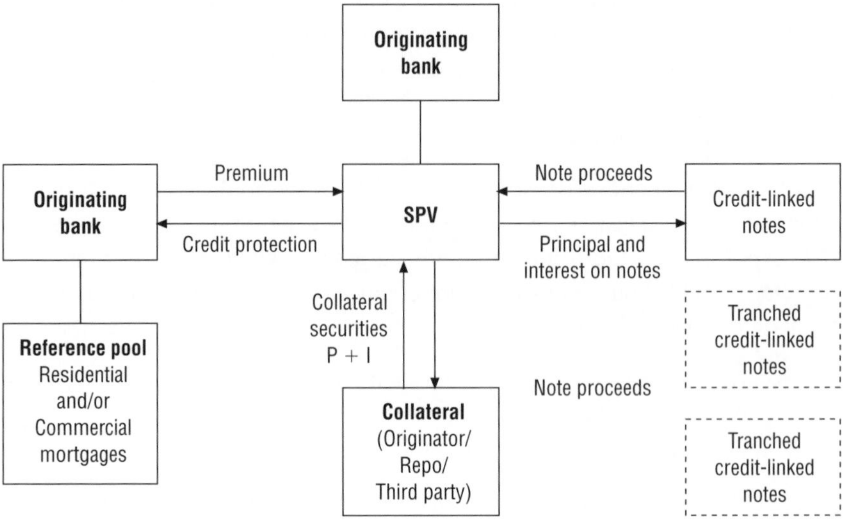

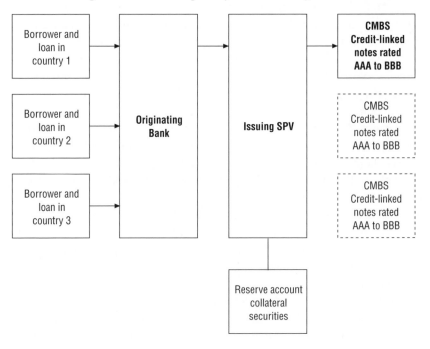

Figure 14.2 Pan-European Synthetic CMBS generic structure.

reference asset pool and to pay expenses associated with the vehicle. If the losses suffered by the reference assets are greater than the reserve account balance, or the nominal value of the junior note, the note collateral is available to cover the originator for the loss. This is the loss borne by the investors who purchased the CLNs. This arrangement, because it is funded, eliminates the counterparty risk (for the protection buyer) associated with unfunded structures, because investors have covered the credit risk exposure with an up-front payment. If the CLN notes are not to be collateralized, the note proceeds are passed to the originator directly or to a third-party agent. The originator or third party is obliged to repay principal on the CLNs on maturity, but only if no triggering events have occurred.

On occurrence of losses in the reference pool, the effect follows established synthetic deal procedures. Each loss is applied only to the most junior CLN (or CDS in an unfunded or partially funded deal) outstanding. More senior noteholders should not see their cash flows effected until the note below them is fully absorbed by continuing losses.

Partially funded synthetic MBS

In a partially-funded deal, the issue of CLNs is combined with a CDS which transfers part of the credit risk on an unfunded basis. Frequently this is a basket or portfolio CDS that is ranked above the CLNS, so becomes a super-senior CDS.

A selection of synthetic RMBS deals in Europe is listed in Figure 14.3.

Investor Considerations

Traditional cash MBS and synthetic MBS deals have several features in common, and both aim to achieve several common objectives. The main one of these is the transfer of the credit risk associated with a pool of mortgage assets away from the originating bank, usually via an SPV. Key to the attraction of a synthetic deal is the fact that it can be customised to investors' requirements more closely. In a synthetic deal, the credit risk exposure that is transferred is (in theory) defined precisely, compared to a cash deal where any and all risks associated with the assets are transferred. Thus a synthetic deal can be structured and documented to transfer precisely the risk exposures that the investors are looking for.

In this section we highlight those areas of difference between the two products.

Figure 14.3   Selected European synthetic MBS deals, 2000–2002.

Close date	Name	Origin of assets	Size of reference pool m	Funded portion m	Unfunded portion m	Loss definition
Jun-00	Eurohypo 2000–1	Germany	500	500	—	Principal plus accrued interest
Nov-00	Haus 200–2	Germany	2,885	159	2,726	Principal only
Dec-00	Neuschwanstein 2000–1	Germany	279	—	273	Principal only
Sep-01	Residence 2001–1	Germany	1,541	—	1,404	Principal only
Oct-01	HVB Real Estate 2001–1	Germany	1,311	44	1,232	Principal only
Oct-01	Provide-A-2001–1	Germany	1,000	145	855	Principal plus external enforcement costs plus accrued interest of 4% p.a.
Nov-01	FARMS Securitisation Limited	Sweden	1,535	203	1,332	Principal
Mar-02	Provide-Gems-2002–1	Germany	1,052	159	873	Principal plus external enforcement costs plus accrued interest of 4% p.a.
Jun-02	Bouwfonds 2002	Netherlands	1,000	—	1,000	Principal losses plus 3-month interest accrual plus enforcement costs
Jul-02	Provide Resident 2002–1	Germany	1,508	210	1,267	Principal losses plus enforcement costs

Source: Moody's. Used with permission.

Originator issues

As a synthetic MBS does not involve a true sale of assets, investors' fortunes are still connected with those of the originator. Therefore, if the originator becomes insolvent, the deal can be expected to terminate. Should this happen, an estimated loss is calculated, which is then applied to the most junior note in the structure.[2] The collateral assets are then realized and the proceeds are used to pay off the outstanding CLNs.

Cash flow liquidity risk

In a traditional cash MBS, a shortfall in cash in the vehicle may lead to disruption of cash receipts by investors. Typically, cash MBS deals are structured with a *liquidity provider* or *liquidity facility* to cover such temporary shortfalls, which may be the arranging bank for the deal. With such an arrangement, the credit rating of the deal is linked to some extent to that of the liquidity provider. With a synthetic MBS this does not apply. Losses in the reference pool are applied to the note structure in priority order, not when a credit event has been verified, but when the loss has been realized. In these circumstances, investors should continue to receive cash flows during the time interval up to the loss realisation, and so a liquidity provider is not required.

Loss severity

In a customised structure aimed at transferring credit risk, the probability of default is an important factor, but not the sole factor. The severity of loss is also significant, and the impact of this differs according to whether it is a cash or synthetic deal. Under a cash structure, if an event occurs which results in potential loss to investors, any outstanding principal, together with accrued interest and recovery costs, needs to be recovered from the securities. So the performance of a cash deal is dependant on the recovery time and costs incurred during the process (such as legal costs of administration).

---

[2]   Under this approach, an expected loss is calculated on non-performing loans, but which may not have become a credit event.

With a synthetic deal, the originator may customize the type and level of risk protection that it pays for. So it may, if it wishes, purchase protection for one or a combination of the following:

- Principal outstanding;
- Interest costs, capped or uncapped;
- Recovery costs.

Figure 14.3 shows the type of protection adopted by the various deals. We can see that for two of the deals, where accrued interest was covered, the cost was capped at 4%.

Well times have changed,
And time sure has changed you ...
Can't you see you've really changed?

— The Thrills, "Till the Tide Creeps In",
from *So Much For The City* (Virgin 2003)

15

Synthetic Conduit and Repackaged Transactions

In this final chapter we show how the concept of synthetic securitisation has been applied to other established structured finance vehicles. Conduits are vehicles that are set up to issue commercial paper on behalf of their sponsor, while "repacks" are repackaging vehicles, set up to transform an existing asset or basket of asset into another form of liability.[1] We also show how synthetic structures have presented new opportunities for funding.

To set the discussion in the proper context, it is necessary to discuss the cash securitisation vehicles first, before considering how the synthetic version of these structures is put together.

Commercial Paper conduits

Commercial paper (CP) is a short-term money market funding instrument issued by corporates. Companies short-term capital and working capital requirement is usually sourced directly from banks, in the form of bank loans. An alternative short-term funding instrument is commercial paper (CP), which is available to corporates that have a sufficiently strong credit rating. Commercial paper is an unsecured promissory note. The issuer of the note promises to pay its holder a specified amount on a specified maturity date. CP normally has a zero coupon and trades at a discount to its face value. CP is typically issued in bearer form, although some issues are in registered form.

---

[1] Actually, "conduit" is another term for an SPV, and this author is at a loss to explain logically why a vehicle that issues asset-backed short-term paper is a conduit while one that issues asset-backed long-term paper is a CDO! A repack is also effected through an SPV.

Originally the CP market was restricted to borrowers with high credit rating, and although lower-rated borrowers do now issue CP, sometimes by obtaining credit enhancements or setting up collateral arrangements, issuance in the market is still dominated by highly-rated companies. The majority of issues are very short-term, from 30 to 90 days in maturity; it is extremely rare to observe paper with a maturity of more than 270 days or nine months. This is because of regulatory requirements in the US,[2] which states that debt instruments with a maturity of less than 270 days need not be registered. Companies therefore issue CP with a maturity lower than nine months and so avoid the administration costs associated with registering issues with the SEC.

Table 15.1 Comparison of US CP and Eurocommercial CP.

	US CP	Eurocommercial CP
Currency	US dollar	Any Euro currency
Maturity	1–270 days	2–365 days
Common maturity	30–50 days	30–90 days
Interest	Zero coupon, issued at discount	Usually zero-coupon, issued at discount
Quotation	On a discount rate basis	On a discount rate basis or yield basis
Settlement	T + 0	T + 2
Registration	Bearer form	Bearer form
Negotiable	Yes	Yes

There are two major markets, the US dollar market with outstanding amount in 2003 just over $1 trillion, and the Eurocommercial paper market with outstanding value of $390 billion at the end of 2003.[3] Commercial paper markets are wholesale markets, and transactions are typically very large size. In the US over a third of all CP is purchased by money market unit trusts, known as mutual funds; other investors include pension fund managers, retail or commercial banks, local authorities and corporate treasurers.

Although there is a secondary market in CP, very little trading activity takes place since investors generally hold CP until maturity. This is to be expected because investors purchase CP that match their specific maturity

---

[2] This is the Securities Act of 1933. Registration is with the Securities and Exchange Commission.
[3] Source: BIS.

requirement. When an investor does wish to sell paper, it can be sold back to the dealer or, where the issuer has placed the paper directly in the market (and not via an investment bank), it can be sold back to the issuer.

Commercial paper programmes

The issuers of CP are often divided into two categories of company, banking and financial institutions and non-financial companies. The majority of CP issues are by financial companies. Financial companies include not only banks but the financing arms of corporates such as General Motors, Ford Motor Credit and Daimler-Chrysler Financial. Most of the issuers have strong credit ratings, but lower-rated borrowers have tapped the market, often after arranging credit support from a higher-rated company, such as a letter of credit from a bank, or by arranging collateral for the issue in the form of high-quality assets such as Treasury bonds. CP issued with credit support is known as credit-supported commercial paper, while paper backed with assets is known naturally enough, as asset-backed commercial paper (ABCP or AB-CP). We consider ABCP in the next section. Paper that is backed by a bank letter of credit is termed LOC paper. Although banks charge a fee for issuing letters of credit, borrowers are often happy to arrange for this, since by so doing they are able to tap the CP market. The yield paid on an issue of CP will be lower than a commercial bank loan.

Although CP is a short-dated security, typically of three- to six-month maturity, it is issued within a longer term programme, usually for three to five years for euro paper; US CP programmes are often open-ended. For example a company might arrange a five-year CP programme with a limit of $100 million. Once the programme is established the company can issue CP up to this amount, say for maturities of 30 or 60 days. The programme is continuous and new CP can be issue at any time, daily if required. The total amount in issue cannot exceed the limit set for the programme. A CP programme can be used by a company to manage its short-term liquidity, that is its working capital requirements. New paper can be issued whenever a need for cash arises, and for an appropriate maturity.

Issuers often roll over their funding and use funds from a new issue of CP to redeem a maturing issue. There is a risk that an issuer might be unable to roll over the paper where there is a lack of investor interest in the new issue. To provide protection against this risk issuers often arrange a stand-by line of credit from a bank, normally for all of the CP programme, to draw against in the event that it cannot place a new issue.

There are two methods by which CP is issued, known as direct-issued or direct paper and dealer-issued or dealer paper. Direct paper is sold by the issuing firm directly to investors, and no agent bank or securities house is involved. It is common for financial companies to issue CP directly to their customers, often because they have continuous programmes and constantly roll-over their paper. It is therefore cost-effective for them to have their own sales arm and sell their CP direct. The treasury arms of certain non-financial companies also issue direct paper; this includes for example British Airways plc corporate treasury, which runs a continuous direct CP programme, used to provide short-term working capital for the company. Dealer paper is paper that is sold using a banking or securities house intermediary. In the US, dealer CP is effectively dominated by investment banks, as retail (commercial) banks were until recently forbidden from underwriting commercial paper. This restriction has since been removed and now both investment banks and commercial paper underwrite dealer paper.

Asset-backed Commercial Paper

During the 1980s and 1990s the rise in popularity in the use of securitisation as a means of diversifying bank liquidity led to the introduction of short-term money market paper backed by the cash flows from other assets, known as asset-backed commercial paper (ABCP). Vehicles through which ABCP is issued are usually called conduits. These issues paper backed by the cash flows from a specified assets, such as residential mortgages, car loans or commercial bank loans, as backing for an issue of bonds. The assets themselves are transferred from the original owner (the originator) to a specially created legal entity, the SPV.

Generally securitisation is used as a funding instrument by companies for three main reasons: it offers lower-cost funding compared with traditional bank loan or bond financing; it is a mechanism by which assets such as corporate loans or mortgages can be removed from the balance sheet, thus improving the lenders return on assets or return on equity ratios; and it increases a borrower's funding options. When entering into securitisation, an entity may issue term securities against assets into the public or private market, or it may issue commercial paper via a special vehicle known as a conduit. These conduits are usually sponsored by commercial banks.

Entities usually access the commercial paper market in order to secure permanent financing, rolling over individual issues as part of a longer-term programme and using interest-rate swaps to arrange a fixed rate if required.

Conventional CP issues are typically supported by a line of credit from a commercial bank, and so this form of financing is in effect a form of bank funding. Issuing ABCP enables an originator to benefit from money market financing that it might otherwise not have access to because its credit rating is not sufficiently strong. A bank may also issue ABCP for balance sheet or funding reasons. ABCP trades however, exactly as conventional CP. The administration and legal treatment is more onerous however, because of the need to establish the CP trust structure and issuing SPV. The servicing of an ABCP programme follows that of conventional CP and is carried out by the same entities, such as the "Trust" arms of banks such JPMorgan Chase, Deutsche Bank and Bank of New York.

Example 15.1 details an hypothetical ABCP issue and typical structure.

Example 15.1   Illustration of ABCP structure

In Figure 15.1 we illustrate an hypothetical example of a securitisation of bank loans in an ABCP structure. The loans have been made by ABC Bank plc and are secured on borrowers' specified assets. They are denominated in sterling. These might be a lien on property, cash flows of the borrowers' business or other assets. The bank makes a "true sale" of the loans to a special purpose vehicle, named Claremont Finance. This has the effect of removing the loans from its balance sheet and also protecting them in the event of bankruptcy or liquidation of ABC Bank. The SPV raises finance by issuing commercial paper, via its appointed CP dealer(s), which is the Treasury desk of MC investment bank. The paper is rated A-1/P-1 by the rating agencies and is issued in US dollars. The liability of the CP is met by the cash flow from the original ABC Bank loans.

ABC Manager is the SPV manager for Claremont Finance, a subsidiary of ABC Bank. Liquidity for Claremont Finance is provided by ABC Bank, who also act as the hedge provider. The hedge is effected by means of a swap agreement between Claremont and ABC Bank; in fact ABC will fix a currency swap with a swap bank counterparty, who is most likely to be the swap desk of MC investment bank. The trustee for the transaction is Trust Bank Limited, who act as security trustee and represent the investors in the event of default.

Figure 15.1   "Claremont Finance ABCP structure.

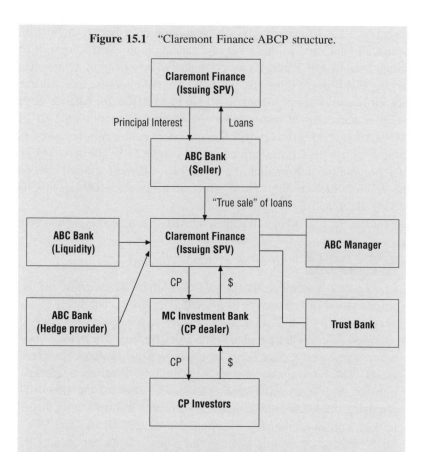

The other terms of the structure are as follows:

Programme facility limit: US$500 million

Facility term: The facility is available on an uncommitted basis renewable annually by the agreement of the SPV manager and the security trustee. It has a final termination date five years from first issue.

Tenor of paper: Seven days to 270 days

Prepayment guarantee: In the event of pre-payment of a loan, the seller will provide Claremont Finance with a guaranteed rate of interest for the relevant interest period.

Hedge agreement:	Claremont Finance will enter into currency and interest-rate swaps with the hedge provider to hedge any interest-rate or currency risk that arises.
Events of default:	Under event of default the issuance programme will cease and in certain events will lead to Claremont Finance to pay loan collections into a segregated specific collection account. Events of default can include non-payment by Claremont Finance under the transaction documentation, insolvency or raking of charge (where the charge ceases to be a first ranking charge over the assets of Claremont Finance.
Loans guarantee:	Loans purchased by Claremont Finance will meet a range of eligibility criteria, specified in the transaction offering circular. These criteria will include requirements on currency of the loans, their term to maturity, confirmation that they can be assigned, that they are not in arrears, and so on.

Evolution of ABCP programmes

Once the basic premise that assets may be securitised to provide cash flow backing for an issue of liabilities (debt financing), there is in principle no significant difference between this process being used to originate short-term paper in the form of CP or long-term paper in the form of bonds such as ABS. A key difference between CP and ABS is of course the shorter time required for refinancing with the former: a CP issuer must roll-over paper every a maximum of every 270 days (or 364 days with euro-CP). As with conventional CP programmes, as paper matures it is redeemed with the proceeds of a roll-over issue. If for any reason a roll-over issue cannot be placed in the market (for example there is a market correction and investor confidence disappears, or the Issuer suffers a credit rating downgrade), the Issuer will need to call on a bank lone of credit to repay investors. This line of credit is known as a liquidity facility. The liquidity facility acts as a form of credit enhancement to investors, providing comfort that in the last resort, there will be sufficient funds available to repay them. Another form of credit enhancement is over-collateralisation, which is when (say) 115% worth of assets are used as securitisation backing for issue of 100% nominal of paper.

ABCP conduits have followed the evolutionary path thus:

First generation:	A fully-supported programme backed by 100% Letters-of-Credit (LOC) from sponsor banks
Second generation:	Partially-supported programmes with multi-asset backing, with 100% bank LOC and 10–15% credit enhancement
Third generation:	Security arbitrage vehicles that are unsupported by bank LOCs and have minimal credit enhancement. These conduits issue both CP and medium-term notes (MTNs), so are also known as Structured Investment Vehicles (SIVs)
Fourth generation:	Multi-asset conduits also viewed as finance companies in their own right, with credit ratings based on quality of underlying assets. There is no bank LOC and the companies invest in high-quality assets and project finance programmes. Credit enhancement in SIV-type structures may take the form of subordinated notes and capital notes or "equity".

Figure 15.2 shows a single-seller ABCP structure.

Figure 15.2 Single-seller ABCP Conduit structure.

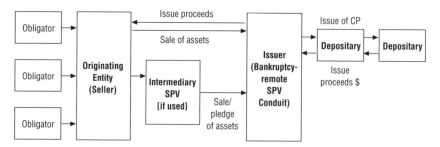

A single-seller conduit is established for the sale of assets originated by one entity. Typically it is 100% supported by a bank liquidity facility and by 10% credit enhancement. The liquidity provided is usually required by the credit ratings agencies to have a short-term rating of A-1/P-1/F.

A multi-seller conduit would have more than one seller into the conduit SPV.

Liquidity and credit enhancement

ABCP conduits require liquidity support to cover 100% of their outstanding CP for 364 days. A liquidity facility will guarantee timely repayment of CP as it matures, and is vital because most conduits do not match the term structure of their assets and liabilities. Facilities are typically required to purchase assets, in accordance with a pre-specified formula. Generally the facility will be called upon in the event of bankruptcy occurring with respect to the conduit, if it otherwise unable to honour its liabilities as they fall due, or if the underlying assets become rated at Caa1 or lower by Moodys and CCC+ or lower by Standard & Poor's and Fitch.

Liquidity support can be in the form of either a Liquidity Asset Purchase agreement (LAPA) or a Liquidity Loan agreement (LLA), which differ as follows:

- LAPA: the liquidity provider(s) purchase non-defaulted assets when called upon;
- LLA: the liquidity provider(s) lend money to the conduit in return for security pledge over the underlying asset cash flows.

A liquidity facility also covers other risks such as dilution, hedging and legal issues.

Other forms of credit enhancement are also set in place. If it is transaction-specific, credit enhancement provides the first layer of protection against shortfalls from the underlying collateral on specific asset pools, typically in the form of over-collateralisation, excess spread, a bank LOC or surety bond. The main features are that they are maintained as protection against delinquencies, losses or dilution, and that reserves are generally based on a multiple of the seller's historical delinquency, net losses and dilutions of the pool of assets.

If it is programme-wide, credit enhancement provides the second-layer of protection coverage for repurchase of cash receivables or guarantee of losses on the receivables. It supplements the seller's reserves, and will be used only after the seller's reserves are depleted. Its main features are:

- it is calculated as a percentage of the entire ABCP conduit;
- it is mainly in the form of a LOC, surety bond, subordinated notes, cash collateral bank account, or a total return swap;
- traditional receivables and loan programmes are sized at a minimum 5% of the total size and fluctuates in accordance with the credit quality of the asset pool.

Note that the enhancement for security arbitrage conduits and SIVs is usually at 0%, provided that the underlying assets are rated at AA-/Aa3/AA- or better.

Structural development

During 2001 and 2002 new structures were observed in the market that built on the first- and second-generation conduits first introduced. These focused on arrangements that reduced the need for bank liquidity support, and set up alternative sources of liquidity and credit enhancement. This was a response to the increasing difficulty in arranging traditional liquidity: for instance, the number of banks rated A-1/P-1 was in decline, banks were conserving their liquidity lines, investors were demanding higher return to reflect the true level of risk involved in these vehicles, and the growing popularity of conduits themselves made liquidity more expensive.

The newer generation of conduits featured alternative sources of liquidity including:

- capturing liquidity from the underlying assets, through matching asset/liability profiles, and capturing the excess spread between assets and liabilities;
- using non-bank liquidity providers, such as highly-rated entities;
- using investors as proxy liquidity providers, through issue of extendible notes and structured liquidity notes, and through issue of long-dated MTNs;
- use of derivative structures, such as total return swaps, credit default swaps and credit-linked notes;
- using monoline insurance firms to provide support backing to the conduit.

Vehicles such as arbitrage conduits and SIVs have much lower levels of credit enhancement, typically ranging from 0%–4% rather than to 10%–15%.

Another development in the US and euro-CP market is floating-rate CP. Unlike traditional CP which is discount paper, this is issued as interest-bearing CP at par. The paper is rolled typically at one-month or three-month Libor reset dates. Interest is paid to investors at each Libor reset date. Floating-rate paper is preferred by issuers to discount CP if they are expecting short-term interest rates to fall.

The newer vehicles securitise a wider range of assets, including equities and synthetic structures. We consider the synthetic ABCP conduit next.

The synthetic ABCP conduit

The latest development in conduits is the synthetic structure. Exactly as with synthetic structured credit products, this uses credit derivatives to make an economic transfer of risk and exposure between the originator and the issuer, so that there is not necessarily a sale of assets from the originator to the Issuer. We describe synthetic conduits by means of an hypothetical transaction, "Golden Claw Funding", which is a Total Return Swap-backed ABCP structure.

Example 15.2 **Hypothetical case study: Golden Claw Funding**

Figure 15.3 is a structure diagram for a synthetic ABCP vehicle that uses total return swaps (TRS) in its structure. It illustrates an hypothetical conduit, Golden Claw Funding Ltd, which issues paper into both the US CP market and the Euro CP market. It has been set up as a funding vehicle, with the originator accessing the CP market to fund assets that it holds on its balance sheet. The originator can be a bank, non-bank financial institution such as a hedge fund, or a corporate. In our case study the originator is a Hedge Fund called ABC Fund Limited.

The structure shown at Figure 15.3 has the following features:

- the CP issuance vehicle and SPV 2 are based off-shore at a location such as Jersey, Ireland or Cayman Islands;
- the conduit issues CP in the USD market via a co-issuer based in Delaware. It also issues euro-CP via an off-shore SPV;

Figure 15.3 Synthetic ABCP conduit, hypothetical deal "Golden Claw Funding".

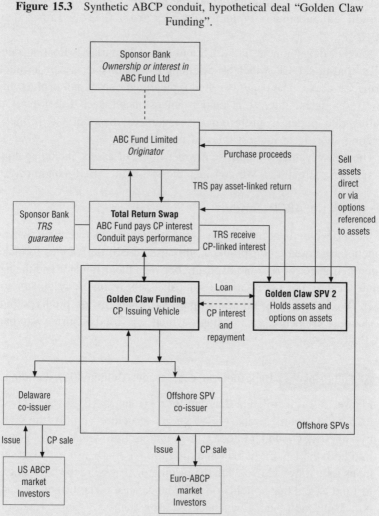

- proceeds of the CP issue are loaned to SPV 2, which uses these funds to purchase assets from the Originator. As well as purchasing assets directly, the vehicle may also acquire an "interest" in assets that are held by ABC Fund Limited via a contract for difference option called a zero-strike call (ZSC). (We describe ZSCs in box 15.3). If assets are purchased directly onto the balance sheet of SPV 2, this is akin to what happens in a conventional ABCP structure. If interests in the assets are acquired via a ZSC then they are not actually sold to SPV 2, and remain on the balance sheet of ABC Fund Limited. Assets can be bonds, structured finance bonds, equities, mutual funds, hedge fund shares, convertible bonds, synthetic products and private equity;

- simultaneously as it purchases assets or ZSCs on assets, SPV 2 enters into a TRS contract with ABC Fund Limited, under which it pays the performance on the assets and receives interest on the CP proceeds it has used to purchase assets and ZSCs. The TRS is the means by which ABC Fund retains the economic interest in the assets it is funding, and the means by which SPV 2 receives the interest it needs to pay back to Golden Claw as CP matures.
- the issue vehicle itself may also purchase assets and ZSCs, so we show at Figure 15.3 that it also has a TRS between itself and ABC Fund Limited

We reproduce the term sheet for the TRS contract below. This states that the notional value and maturity of the TRS matches those of the CP issue.

The Golden Claw structure is a means by which funds can be raised without a true sale structure. The TRS is guaranteed by the sponsor bank, so will ensure that the conduit is rated at least at the short-term rating of the sponsor bank. As CP matures, it will be repaid with a roll-over issue of CP, with interest received via the TRS contract. If CP cannot rolled over, then the PC or the Issuer will need to sell assets or exercise ZSCs in assets to repay principal, or otherwise the TRS guarantor will need to cover the repayment.

Example 15.3   Zero–strike call

A zero-strike call (ZSC) is a call option with strike price set at zero. It is written on an underlying asset such as a bond or shares in a hedge fund, and is sold at par. It is essentially a means by which an interest in illiquid assets can be transferred to a customer. Consider the two following examples showing how ZSCs might be used:

- Buying a ZSC: a hedge fund of funds wishes to acquire an interest in assets that are not on its balance sheet. It buys a ZSC from a hedge fund that holds the assets, who writes the ZSC. If the asset appreciates in value, the gain is realised by the hedge fund of funds.
- Selling a ZSC: a hedge fund of funds holds assets on its books, which a client (investor) wishes to acquire an interest in. The fund of funds writes a ZSC to the investor, enabling the investor to acquire an interest in the assets.

These examples are illustrated below at Figure 15.4.

Frequently the ZSC is transacted as part of a leveraged investment play, so that in the example above described as "selling a ZSC", the fund of funds will invest its own funds in a leveraged proportion to those of the client. For example, for every $25 invested by the client, the fund of funds will invest $75, as part of a notional $100 investment in a ZSC option.

Figure 15.4   Zero-strike call options.

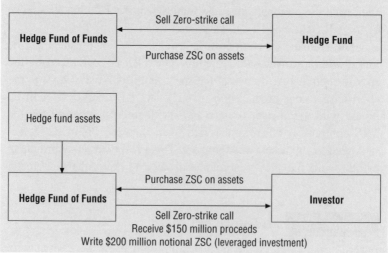

Synthetic ABCP conduit: example TRS term sheet

To illustrate the terms of the TRS used in the Golden Claw Funding Limited hypothetical case study, we produce below an example of what the term sheet for the TRS contract might look like. This describes the terms of the TRS used in the structure and has been produced for the Sponsoring Bank that is the guarantor to the TRS.

ABC Fund Limited

Golden Claw FUNDING LIMITED

TOTAL RETURN SWAP TERM SHEET

Programme summary

Golden Claw is set up to raise money in the US CP and Euro CP market. It will lend this money to Golden Claw Purchase Company (PC). PC will buy assets such as bonds or equities from ABC Fund Limited. Golden Claw PC simultaneously enters into a Total Return Swap (TRS) contract with ABC Fund Limited. The TRS contract is the means by which ABC Fund Limited retains the price risk of the assets. Via the TRS, Golden Claw PC will transfer the return on the assets to ABC Fund Limited, and receive sufficient interest from ABC Fund Limited to pay Golden Claw the interest on maturing CP. The mark-to-market on the TRS will be set in line with CP repayment dates. The TRS payments are guaranteed by the Sponsor Bank.

General Terms	A Total Return Swap (TRS) is entered into between Golden Claw PC and ABC Fund Limited. One leg of the TRS pays the performance of the underlying assets, while the other leg will pay the maturing CP interest. These payments are made two days after the TRS reset dates, which coincide with the CP issue maturity date. A TRS is entered into simultaneously each time CP is issued. The notional value of each TRS will be equivalent to the outstanding nominal value of each CP issue. The maturity of the TRS will match the maturity of the CP issue.

Assets
Each of the Issuer and each PC will own a portfolio of assets of a particular type. Initially, the types of assets will include debt securities; equity securities; and hedge fund investments (including zero strike calls relating to such investments).

Total Return Swaps
The Issuer and the PC will enter into a TRS ("Swap") with the Swap Counterparty (as defined below). The aggregate amount paid to the Issuer or PC under the Swap shall be sufficient to pay: (a) the interest payable on the CP issued to fund the related Assets through maturity and (b) expenses of the Issuer or the PC, including the fees of the Issuer's or PC's agents, taxes, rating agency and legal fees. All payments received in relation to the Assets held by the Issuer or the PC, will be paid to the related Swap Counterparty. Each Swap Agreement may also provide for periodic transfer (a) by the Issuer or the PC to the Swap Counterparty of market value increases of the related Assets and (b) by the Swap Counterparty to the Issuer or the PC, of market value decreases of the related Assets.

Swap counterparty
[tbc]

TRS Bookings
The Issuer or PC will enter into a TRS with ABC Fund Limited under which the Issuer or PC will (a) pay the performance on the TRS reference asset to KBC Bank and (b) receive proceeds equivalent to maturing CP interest and costs.

ABC Fund Limited will enter into a TRS with Issuer or PC under which it will (b) pay proceeds equivalent to maturing CP interest and other costs and (a) receive the performance on the TRS reference assets.

The notional value of the Swap will be equal to the nominal value of outstanding CP. A Swap will be written each time there is an issue of CP. Net payments will be exchanged on Swap payment dates (value two days after Swap reset date), which will coincide with CP maturity payment date and Swap maturity.

Issue mechanics   Golden Claw will issue CP on Trade date for settlement on T+2. Simultaneously, on T+0 PC will (a) enter into a loan with Golden Claw for the CP settlement proceeds, value date T+2, loan to expire on CP maturity date (b) will transact to purchase assets to the value of the loan from ABC Fund Limited, or ZSCs written on assets held by ABC Fund Limited, for asset delivery to PC on T+2 (c) will enter into a TRS agreement with ABC Fund Limited, for value date T+2, for the nominal value of the CP issue. The TRS reset date will be two days prior to CP maturity. ABC Fund Limited will pay CP interest and receive asset performance on this Swap.

On T+0 ABC Fund Limited will enter into a TRS with PC for nominal value of CP issue, for value T+2. PC will pay asset performance and receive CP maturing interest on this Swap.

The term sheet describes the mechanics of the swap arrangement for the synthetic asset-backed CP structure.

Essentially, the TRS is the means by which the conduit can be used to secure Libor-flat based funding for the originator, as long as payments under it are guaranteed by a sponsor or guarantor bank. Alternatively, the originator can arrange for a banking institution to provide a stand-by liquidity back-up for the TRS in the event that it cannot roll over maturing CP. This service would be provided for a fee.

Example 15.4   **"Golden Claw" synthetic AB–CP conduit cashflow mechanics**

Assume the first issue of CP by the Golden Claw structure. The vehicle issues $100 nominal of one-month CP at an all-in price of $99.50. These funds are lent by the vehicle to its SPV 2, which uses these funds to buy $99.50 – worth of assets synthetically from ABC Fund, in the form of par-priced options referenced to these assets. Simultaneously it enters into a TRS with ABC Fund, for a nominal amount of $100.

On CP maturity, assume that the reference assets are valued at $103. This represents an increase in value of $3. ABC Fund will pay this increase in value to SPV2, which would then pay this, under the terms of the TRS, back to ABC Fund (in practice, this cashflow nets to zero so no money actually moves). Also under the terms of the TRS, ABC Fund pays the maturing CP interest of $0.50, plus any expenses and costs of Golden Claw itself, to the purchase company, which in turn pays this to Golden Claw, enabling it to repay CP interest to investors. The actual nominal amount of the CP issue is repaid by rolling it over (re-issuing it).

If for any reason CP cannot be rolled over on maturity, the full nominal value of the CP must be paid under the terms of the TRS by ABC Fund to the purchase company.

Synthetic Repackaging structures

Repackaging structures or "repacks" were introduced in the cash securitisation market first, before also becoming a feature of the synthetic markets. In its simplest form, a repack is an underlying security or group of securities that have been packaged-up and transformed into a new note or class of notes that are more attractive to investors than the original securities. This may have been done because the original security has become illiquid or otherwise not tradeable.[4] Repacks were originally classed as "single-asset" or "multi-asset" repacks according to how many underlying securities they represented. Multi-asset repacks may be considered prototype CDOs.

In the synthetic market, investment banks have also structured repacks using credit derivatives. Often this will be to transform a particular feature of an existing bond (or bonds) in ways other than to make it more attractive to new investors, for example to transfer an existing credit exposure or to reduce balance sheet capital requirement. In other words, synthetic market repacks make use of the credit derivatives market to hedge out risk exposure on other bonds, which are frequently also structured products.

---

[4] For instance, one of the first repacks was of Japanese convertible bonds. With the bear market in Japanese equities during the 1990s, these became illiquid as they no longer were attractive to investors. Individual convertibles or groups of convertibles were packaged up, often with an enhanced coupon or additional new feature of attraction, and sold on to new investors.

Repackaging structures or "repacks" were introduced in the cash securitisation market first, before also becoming a feature of the synthetic markets. In its simplest form, a repack is an underlying security or group of securities that have been packaged-up and transformed into a new note or class of notes that are more attractive to investors than the original securities. This may have been done because the original security has become illiquid or otherwise not tradeable.[5] Repacks were originally classed as "single-asset" or "multi-asset" repacks according to how many underlying securities they represented. Multi-asset repacks may be considered prototype CDOs.

In the synthetic market, investment banks have also structured repacks using credit derivatives. Often this will be to transform a particular feature of an existing bond (or bonds) in ways other than to make it more attractive to new investors, for example to transfer an existing credit exposure or to reduce balance sheet capital requirement. In other words, synthetic market repacks make use of the credit derivatives market to hedge out risk exposure on other bonds, which are frequently also structured products.

Synthetic repack motivations

A synthetic repack uses funded or unfunded credit derivatives in its structure. It may be originated for the following reasons:

- by an investment bank that is tasked with making an asset "tradeable" again;
- by a broker-dealer to transform a current interest-rate or credit risk exposure;
- by a portfolio manager looking to extract value from assets currently held on the balance sheet or assets in the market that are trading below fair value.

The assets in question are often existing structured finance securities, such as CDO notes or CLNs. Hence if the repack vehicle SPV issues securities this will be a repacj of securities issued by another SPV. Hence a repack structure is usually similar in certain respects to a synthetic CDO and often targeted at the same class of investors.

---

[5] For instance, one of the first repacks was of Japanese convertible bonds. With the bear market in Japanese equities during the 1990s, these became illiquid as they no longer were attractive to investors. Individual convertibles or groups of convertibles were packaged up, often with an enhanced coupon or additional new feature of attraction, and sold on to new investors.

Example deal structure

To illustrate the mechanics of a synthetic repack, we present an hypothetical transaction that is a repack of a synthetic CDO. The repack has been structured by an investment bank, ABC Securities Limited, to hedge a position it holds in the junior tranche of a CDO. Through this transaction the bank hedges the credit risk exposure in its existing holding while also meeting the needs of client investors who seek an exposure to the risk-reward profile the repack represents.

It is necessary to describe first the original synthetic CDO deal. We then consider the motivation behind and structure of the repack.

All names and situations quoted are of course hypothetical.

Synthetic CDO: Black Island Finance Ltd

The underlying CDO is a fully unfunded synthetic CDO ("Black Island Finance Ltd"). This is a CDO originated on a pool of 100% risk-weighted bank assets, with the credit risk and regulatory capital requirements of the assets transferred via a tranched series of credit default swaps to investors. Figure 15.5 shows the structure of Black Island Finance Ltd.

The liabilities of the CDO are split into a series of credit default swaps, which pay a premium based on their seniority. If there are any credit events amongst reference assets then the nominal amounts of the CDS contracts is reduced (thereby reducing the interest receivable by protection sellers) in order of priority. On issue ABC Securities invests in the junior tranche of Black Island CDO. This represents the 2.5% to 10% tranche of risk in the reference pool. Assume it is at BBB level and so would represent this level of risk-return for the investor.

Later on in the deal life, ABC Securities Ltd decides to hedge its unhedged position in the 2.5%–10% risk piece of Black Island CDO. It also identifies a client requirement for a funded investment at a BBB-rated risk-return level. It therefore structures a repackage vehicle, let us call it Red Sea Finance Limited to meet this client requirement while simultaneously hedging its exposure in Black Island CDO.[6]

---

[6] The author has no qualms that he is a keen fan of the works of Georges Remi, in particular the adventures of Tintin...

Figure 15.5   Black Island Finance Ltd, hypothetical unfunded synthetic CDO.

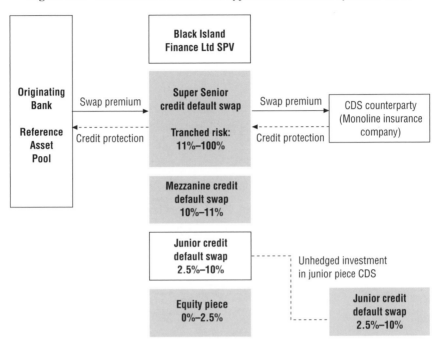

Synthetic repackage vehicle: Red Sea Finance Ltd

The purpose of Red Sea Finance Ltd is to hedge out the ABC Securities Ltd exposure in Black Island Finance CDO, which is a position in the junior CDS of that deal. The client order however, is for a funded position. Red Sea Finance Ltd is set up to repackage the exposure, thus transforming it from a credit default swap into a credit-linked note. An SPV is set up to issue the CLN to the investor. The liabilities of Red Sea CDO are the single CLN, that is, there is no tranching. This is placed with the client investor. The proceeds of the note issue are invested in eligible investments, which are risk-free securities. These are repo'd out with a bank and act as a reserve against losses suffered due to credit events in Black Island CDO.

The structure diagram for Red Sea Finance Ltd CDO is shown at Figure 15.6.

Figure 15.6   Red Sea Finance Ltd, hypothetical synthetic repack vehicle.

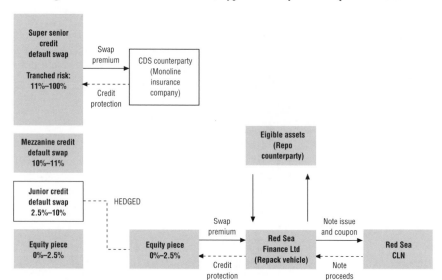

By structuring its holding via a synthetic repack, ABC Securities has transferred its credit risk exposure in its initial investment, whilst also meeting the needs of its client.

Synthetic Funding Structures

Investment banks are increasingly turning to off-shore synthetic structured solutions for their funding, regulatory capital and accounting treatment requirements. We saw in chapter 4 how total return swaps could be used to obtain off-balance sheet funding of assets at close to Libor, and earlier in this chapter we saw how synthetic conduit structures can be used to access the asset-backed commercial market at Libor or close to Libor.[1] In this section

---

[1]   For more information on asset-backed commercial paper, see Choudhry (2004b)

we discuss synthetic structures that issue in both the CP and medium-term note (MTN) market, and are set up to provide funding for investment bank portfolios or reference portfolios of their clients. There are a number of ways to structure these deals, some using multiple SPVs, and new variations are being introduced all the time.

We illustrate the approach taken when setting up these structures by describing two different hypothetical funding vehicles

Offshore synthetic funding behicle

A commercial bank or investment bank can set up an offshore SPV that issues both CP and MTNs to fund underlying assets that are acquired synthetically. We describe this here, as "Long-term Funding Ltd".

Assume an investment bank wishes to access the CP and MTN markets and borrow funds at close to Libor. It sets up an offshore SPV, Long-term Funding Limited, which has the freedom to issue the following liabilities as required:

- commercial paper;
- medium-term notes;
- guaranteed investment contracts (GICs); these are deposit contracts that pay either a fixed coupon to lenders or a fixed spread over Libor;
- repo agreements.

These liabilities are used to fund the purchase of assets that are held by the investment bank. These assets are purchased synthetically via TRS contracts or sometimes in cash form as a reverse repo trade. The vehicle is illustrated at Figure 15.7.

The vehicle is structured in such a way that the liabilities it issues are rated at A-1/F-1 and Aaa/AAA. It enables the originating bank to access the money and capital markets at rates that are lower than it would otherwise obtain in the interbank (unsecured) market. The originator invests its own capital in the structure in the form of an equity piece. At the same time, a liquidity facility is also put in place, to be used in the event that the vehicle is not able to pay maturing CP and MTNs. The liquidity facility is an additional factor that provides comfort to the rating agencies.

The types of assets and liabilities that can be held are described below.

Figure 15.7 "Long-term Funding Ltd.", offshore synthetic funding vehicle.

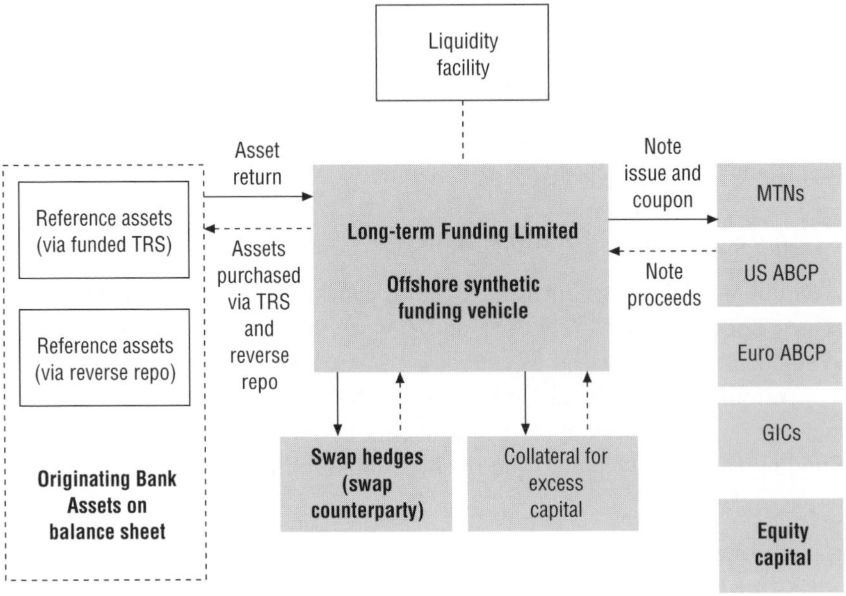

Vehicle capital stucture
MTNs Maximum $5,000 million (Aaa/AAA)
USCP Maximum $4,000 million (A-1/F-1)
ECP Maximum $1,000 million (A-1/F-1)

Underlying reference assets

The vehicle's asset structure is composed of mainly synthetic securities, accessed using funded TRS contracts. However to retain flexibility the vehicle is also able to bring in assets in cash form in the form of reverse repo transactions.

Possible types of assets that can be "acquired" by Long-term Funding Ltd" include:

- short-term money market instruments rated AAA;
- bullet corporate bonds rated from AAA to BB;
- structured finance securities including ABS, RMBS and CMBS securities rated from AAA to BB;
- government agency securities such as those issued by Ginnie Mae, Fannie Mae and Freddie Mac, as well as Pfandbriefe securities;
- secondary market bank loans and syndicated loans rated at AAA to BBB.

Reference assets can be denominated in any currency, and currency swaps are entered into to hedge currency mismatch as the vehicle only issues liabilities in US dollars and euros.

As well as the quality of the underlying reference assets, the credit rating of the TRS and repo counterparties is also taken into consideration when the liabilities are rated.

Liability transactions

Long-term Funding Ltd finances the purchase of TRS and reverse repos by issuing CP, MTNs and GICs. The interest-rate risk that arises from issuing GICs is hedged using interest-rate swaps.

The ability of Long-term Funding Ltd to issue different types of liabilities means that the originating bank can access funding at any maturity from one-month to very long-term, and across a variety of sources. For instance, CP may be bought by banks, corporates, money market funds and super-national institutions such as the World Bank; GIC contracts are frequently purchased by insurance companies.

Multi–SPV synthetic conduit funding structure

One of the main drivers behind the growth of synthetic funding structures has been the need for banks to reduce regulatory capital charges. While this has been achieved by setting up an offshore SPV that issues liabilities and references assets synthetically, recent proposals on changing accounting treatment for SPVs means that this approach may not be sufficient for some institutions.[2] The structure we describe here can reference an entire existing SPV synthetically, in effect a synthetic transfer of assets that have already been synthetically transferred. The vehicle would be used by banks or fund managers to obtain funding and capital relief for an entire existing portfolio without having to move any of the assets themselves.

---

[2] We refer to proposed new US accounting rules on consolidating SPVs that are not deemed truly arms-length. This was in response to the Enron episode, which uncovered the use of SPVs for less-than-savoury purposes. While we discuss a new synthetic structure that would enable banks to maintain separate accounting treatment for offshore companies, the subject of accounting treatment is outside the scope of this book.

The key to the synthetic multi-SPV conduit is the CP and MTN issuance vehicle, which is a stand-alone vehicle established by a commercial or investment bank. This provides funding to an existing SPV or SPVs, and acquires the assets of the assets synthetically. The assets are deemed as being held within the structure and as such attract a 0% risk-weighting under Basel I.

The structure is illustrated at Figure 15.8.

Figure 15.8 Multi-SPV offshore synthetic conduit funding structure.

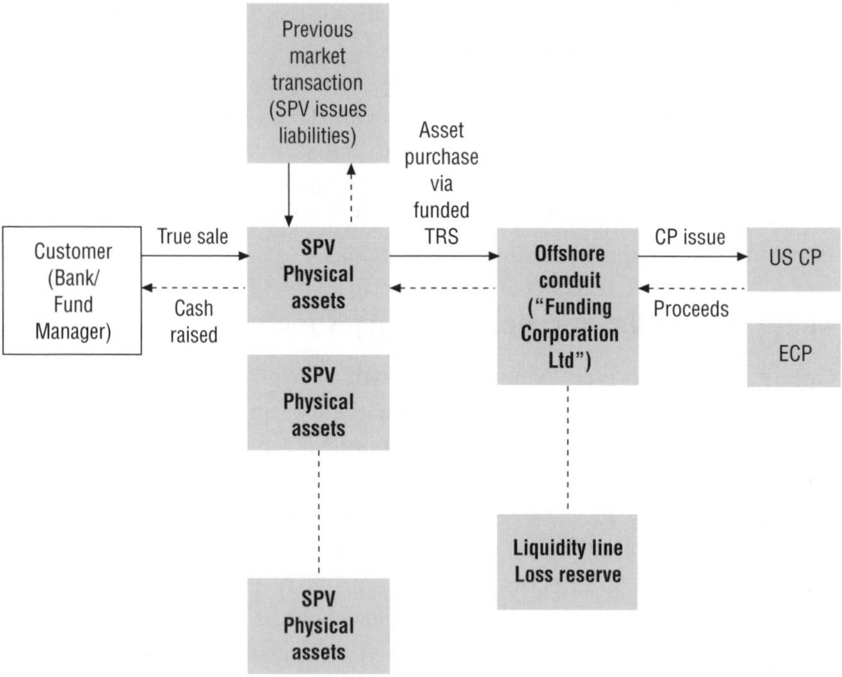

This structure has the following features:

- an offshore SPV that issues CP into the US and Euro markets;
- a synthetic purchase of the entire balance sheet of an existing SPV; the funds issued in the CP market are used to provide a funded TRS contract to the SPV whose assets are being funded;
- the customer realises funds and also retains the return on the assets; however it benefits from reduced capital charge and no more necessity to mark-to-market the assets;

- the investment bank originator, and CP investors (in that order) offer to wear any losses on the reference portfolio due to credit events or default, and earn a fee income for setting up this facility;
- assets and additional SPVs can be added at any time;
- a liquidity facility is in place in the event that CP cannot be issued.

This structure is yet another example of the flexibility and popularity of credit derivatives, and structured credit products created from credit derivatives, in the debt capital markets today.

Bibliography and References

Choudhry, M., *Fixed Income Markets: Instruments, Applications, Mathematics*, John Wiley & Sons 2004(a).

Choudhry, M., *The Money Markets: A Practitioner's Guide*, John Wiley & Sons 2004(b).

Now when we go to buy clothes, we don't go to clothes shops, do we? Strictly sports shops, innit?!

— Phil Broadhurst, *The Mighty Utterance* 1987

Glossary

A

ABS: Asset-backed security.

A note: A tranche of a CDO that is senior to other note tranches.

Amortising: A financial instrument whose nominal principal amount decreases in size during its life.

Arbitrage: The process of buying securities in one country, currency or market, and selling identical securities in another to take advantage of price differences. When this is carried out simultaneously, it is in theory a risk-free transaction. There are many forms of arbitrage transactions. For instance in the cash market a bank might issue a money market instrument in one money centre and invest the same amount in another centre at a higher rate, such as an issue of three-month US dollar CDs in the United States at 5.5% and a purchase of three-month Eurodollar CDs at 5.6%. In the futures market arbitrage might involve buying three-month contracts and selling forward six-month contracts.

Arbitrage CDO: A Collateralised Debt Obligation (CDO) that has been issued by an asset manager and in which the collateral is purchased solely for the purpose of securitising it to exploit the difference in yields ("arbitrage") between the underlying market and securitisation market.

Asset-backed securities: Securities that have been issued by a special purpose legal entity (SPV) and which are backed by principal and interest payments on existing assets, which have been sold to the SPV by the deal originator. These assets can include commercial bank loans, credit card loans, auto loans, equipment lease receivables, and so on.

Asset & Liability Management (ALM): The practice of matching the term structure and cashflows of an organisation's asset and liability portfolios to maximise returns and minimise risk.

Asset swap: An interest rate swap or currency swap used in conjunction with an underlying asset such as a bond investment.

Asset swap spread: The spread over Libor that is received by the person selling the asset swap. This spread reflects the credit quality of the asset.

Average life: The weighted-average life of a bond, the estimated time to return principal based on an assumed prepayment speed. It is the average number of years that each unit of unpaid principal remains outstanding.

B

Balance sheet CDO: A CDO backed by a static pool of assets that were previously on the balance sheet of the originator.

Basel rules: The set of rules that require banks to set aside a minimum level of capital to back assets. Now known as Basel 1 because they are being replaced by new rules (Basel 2) from the end of 2007.

Basis: The underlying cash market price minus the futures price. In the case of a bond futures contract, the futures price must be multiplied by the conversion factor for the cash bond in question.

Basis points: In interest rate quotations, 0.01 percent.

Basis swap: An interest rate swap where both legs are based on floating rate payments.

Binary default swap: See **digital credit default swap**.

Bullet: A loan/deposit has a bullet maturity if the principal is all repaid is maturity. See amortising.

C

CDO: Collateralised debt obligation, a structured financial product.

CMBS: Commercial mortgage-backed securities

Cash flow CDO: A CDO that is structured by securitising bonds or loans, undertaken by selling these assets to an issuing company ("SPV") that funds this purchase through the issue of note liabilities. The buyers of the notes take on the credit risk of the securitised assets.

Cashflow waterfall: The rules by which the cashflow that the issuer can pay to investors, after all expenses have been paid, is allocated to sevice issue liabilities and pay investors in order of seniority.

Credit event: A term used to refer to a number of occurrences that trigger payment under a credit derivative contract. These occurrences include default on payment of interest or principal, bankruptcy, administration and loan restructuring.

Credit (or default) risk: The risk that a loss will be incurred if a counterparty to a derivatives transaction does not fulfil its financial obligations in a timely manner.

Credit default swaps: Agreement between two counterparties to exchange disparate cashflows, at least one of which must be tied to the performance of a credit-sensitive asset or to a portfolio or index of such assets. The other cashflow is usually tied to a floating-rate index (such as Libor) or a fixed rate or is linked to another credit-sensitive asset.

Credit derivatives: Financial contracts that involve a potential exchange of payments in which at least one of the cashflows is linked to the performance of a specified underlying credit-sensitive asset or liability.

Credit enhancement: A level of investor protection built into a structured finance deal to absorb losses among the underlying assets. This may take the form of cash, "equity" subordinated note tranches, subordinated tranches, cash reserves, excess spread reserve, insurance protection ("wrap"), and so on.

Credit risk (or default risk) exposure: The value of the contract exposed to default. If all transactions are marked to market each day, such positive market value is the amount of previously recorded profit that might have to be reversed and recorded as a loss in the event of counterparty default.

Credit spread: The interest rate spread between two debt issues of similar duration and maturity, reflecting the relative creditworthiness of the issuers.

Credit spread option: A credit derivative contract that confers the option buyer with the right but not the obligation to enter into a credit spread position at a pre-specified spread level. The underlying spread position can be an asset swap, a floating-rate note bond or another credit derivative such as a credit default swap.

D

Default: A failure by one party to a contractual agreement to live up to its obligations under the agreement; a breach of contract such as non-payment of debt service interest or principal.

Default correlation: The degree of covariance between the probabilities of default of a given set of counterparties. For example, in a set of counterparties with positive default correlation, a default by one counterparty suggests an increased probability of a default by another counterparty.

Digital credit default swap: A credit default swap contract in which the payment made by the protection seller on occurrence of a credit event is a fixed pre-determined amount. Also known as a **binary default swap**.

Diversity score: A Moody's CDO calculation that assigns a numeric value to an asset portfolio that represents the number of uncorrelated assets theoretically in the portfolio. A low diversity score indicates industry and/or geographical concentration and will be penalised in the ratings procees.

E

Equity: Generally, the ownership share of a joint-stock company. Also known as a *share*. In the context of structured credit products, the most junior tranche note of a structured credit vehicle, so known as the **Equity Note**. It is also known as the *first-loss piece*, because losses in the vehicle are taken out of its value first. Its return is comprised of excess return in the vehicle, afet all other note liabilities have been paid.

Equity-linked swap: Swap where one of the cashflows is based on an equity instrument or index, when it is known as an equity index swap.

Equivalent life: The weighted average life of the principal of a bond where there are partial redemptions, using the **present values** of the partial redemptions as the weights.

Excess spread: Total cash left over in a securitisation, after paying all costs.

Expected (credit) loss: Estimate of the amount a derivatives counterparty is likely to lose as a result of default from a derivatives contract, with a given level of probability. The expected loss of any derivative position can be derived by combining the distributions of credit exposures, rate of recovery and probabilities of default.

Expected default rate: Estimate of the most likely rate of default of a counterparty expressed as a level of probability.

Expected rate of recovery: See **rate of recovery**.

F

Face value: The principal amount of a security generally repaid ('redeemed') all at maturity, but sometimes repaid in stages, on which the **coupon** amounts are calculated.

First-to-default basket: A credit default swap contract written on a pool or "basket" of reference assets, on which the protection seller sells protection on all the assets, and pays out on occurrence of the first credit event in the basket. There are also 2nd-, 3rd, and Nth-to-default contracts.

Floating rate: An interest rate set with reference to an external index. Also an instrument paying a floating rate is one where the rate of interest is refixed in line with market conditions at regular intervals such as every three or six months. In the current market, an exchange rate determined by market forces with no government intervention.

Floating rate note: Capital market instrument on which the rate of interest payable is refixed in line with market conditions at regular intervals (usually six months).

G

GIC: Guaranteed investment contract. A bank account that pays either a fixed rate for its life, or a fixed spread under Libor for its life.

H

Hedging: Protecting against the risks arising from potential market movements in exchange rates, interest rates or other variables. See cover, **arbitrage, speculation**.

Historic volatility: The actual **volatility** recorded in market prices over a particular period.

Hybrid: A term used to refer to a structure comprising elements of cash and synthetic securitisation.

I

Implied volatility: The volatility used by a dealer to calculate an option price; conversely, the volatility implied by the price actually quoted.

Index swap: A total return swap contract in which the total return payer pays the counterparty the return on a specified index, such as a bond index or credit reference index.

Interbank: The market in unsecured lending and trading between banks of roughly similar credit quality.

Interest rate swap: An agreement to exchange a series of cashflows determined in one currency, based on fixed or **floating** interest payments on an agreed **notional** principal, for a series of cashflows based in the same currency but on a different interest rate. May be combined with a **currency swap**.

Internal rate of return: The yield necessary to discount a series of cashflows to a net present value of zero.

Investment grade: Debt rated at or above BBB− by Standard & Poors or Baa3 by Moodys.

L

Liability swap: An interest rate swap or currency swap used in conjunction with an underlying liability such as a borrowing. See **asset swap**.

LIBID: The London Interbank Bid Rate, the rate at which banks will pay for funds in the interbank market.

LIBOR: The London Interbank Offered Rate, the lending rate for all major currencies up to one-year set at 11am each day by the British Bankers Association.

Liquidity: A word describing the ease with which one can undertake transactions in a particular market or instrument. A market where there are always ready buyers and sellers willing to transact at competitive prices is regarded as liquid. In banking, the term is also used to describe the requirement that a portion of a banks assets be held in short-term risk free instruments, such as government bonds, T-Bills and high quality Certificates of Deposit.

Long: A long position is a surplus of purchases over sales of a given currency or asset, or a situation which naturally gives rise to an organisation benefiting from a strengthening of that currency or asset. To a money market dealer, however, a long position is a surplus of borrowings taken in over money lent out, (which gives rise to a benefit if that currency weakens rather than strengthens). See **short**.

Long-term assets: Assets which are expected to provide benefits and services over a period longer than one year.

Long-term liabilities: Obligations to be repaid by the firm more than one year later.

M

Market-maker: Market participant who is committed, explicitly or otherwise, to quoting two-way bid and offer prices at all times in a particular market.

Market risk: Risks related to changes in prices of tradable macroeconomics variables, such as exchange rate risks.

Mark-to-market: The act of revaluing securities to current market values. Such revaluations should include both coupon accrued on the securities outstanding and interest accrued on the cash.

Maturity date: Date on which stock is redeemed.

Mezzanine: The intermediate tranche note of a structured credit product such as a CDO or MBS issue, senior to the Equity note.

N

Net present value: The net present value of a series of cashflows is the sum of the present values of each cashflow (some or all of which may be negative).

Nominal amount: Same as **face value** of a security.

Non-performing: A loan or other asset that is no longer being serviced, or has experienced default.

Normal: A normal **probability distribution** is a particular distribution assumed to prevail in a wide variety of circumstances, including the financial markets. Mathematically, it corresponds to the probability density function:

$$\frac{1}{\sqrt{2\pi}}e^{-\frac{1}{2}\phi^2}$$

Notional: In a bond futures contract, the bond bought or sold is a standardised non-existent notional bond, as opposed to the actual bonds which are **deliverable** at maturity. **Contracts for differences** also require a notional principal amount on which settlement can be calculated. Otherwise, the balance that is used as the basis for calculating interest or credit protection due with respect to an obligation.

NPV: See net present value.

O

OTC: Over the counter. Strictly speaking any transaction not conducted on a registered stock exchange. Trades conducted via the telephone between banks, and contracts such as FRAs and (non-exchange traded) options are said to be "over-the-counter" instruments. OTC also refers to non-standard instruments or contracts traded between two parties; for example a client with a requirement for a specific risk to be hedged with a tailor-made instrument may enter into an OTC structured option trade with a bank that makes markets in such products.

Over the counter: An OTC transaction is one dealt privately between any two parties, with all details agreed between them, as opposed to one dealt on an exchange — for example, a forward deal as opposed to a futures contract.

Overcollateralisation: A capital structure in which assets exceed liabilities.

P

Paper: Another term for a bond or debt issue.

Par: In foreign exchange, when the **outright** and **spot** exchange rates are equal, the **forward swap** is zero or par. When the price of a security is equal to the face value, usually expressed as 100, it is said to be trading at par. A par swap rate is the current market rate for a fixed **interest rate swap** against **Libor**.

Par yield curve: A curve plotting maturity against yield for bonds priced at par.

Plain vanilla: See **vanilla**.

Present value: The amount of money which needs to be invested now to achieve a given amount in the future when interest is added. See **time value of money**, **future value**.

Primary market: The market for new debt, into which new bonds are issued. The primary market is made up of borrowers, investors and the investment banks which place new debt into the market, usually with their clients. Bonds that trade after they have been issued are said to be part of the secondary market.

Principal protected note: A financial instrument that guarantees repayment of its principal amount (par amount) to investors on maturity or on termination. This feature is often added to higher-risk notes such as credit-linked notes referenced to a risky security. The addition of a principal protected feature lowers the coupon that would otherwise be paid to investors in the note.

Protection seller: In a credit default swap transaction, the party that accepts the credit risk associated with specified assets. If losses are incurred on the assets, the protection seller makes credit protection payments to the protection buyer. A fee is payable for this protection.

Q

Quanto swap: A **swap** where the payments one or both legs are based on a measurement (such as the interest rate) in one currency but payable in another currency.

R

RMBS: Residential mortgage-backed security.

Rate of recovery: Estimate of the percentage of the amount exposed to default — i.e., the credit risk exposure — that is likely to be recovered an institution if a counterparty defaults.

Record date: A coupon or other payment due on a security is paid by the issuer to whoever is registered on the record date as being the owner. See **ex-dividend, cum-dividend**.

Redeem: A security is said to be redeemed when the principal is repaid.

Redemption yield: The rate of interest at which all future payments (coupons and redemption) on a bond are discounted so that their total equals the current price of the bond (inversely related to price).

Return on equity: The net earning of a company divided by its equity.

S

Secondary market: The market in instruments after they have been issued. Bonds are bought and sold after their initial issue by the borrower, and the marketplace for this buying and selling is referred to as the secondary market. The new issues market is the primary market.

Securitisation: An issue of securities backed by specific assets.

Security: A financial asset sold initially for cash by a borrowing organisation (the 'issuer'). The security is often negotiable and usually has a maturity date when it is redeemed.

Short: A short position is a surplus of sales over purchases of a given currency or asset, or a situation which naturally gives rise to an organisation benefiting from a weakening of that currency or asset. To a money market dealer, however, a short position is a surplus of money lent out over borrowings taken in (which give rise to a benefit if that currency strengthens rather than weakens). See **long**.

Special: A security which for any reason is sought after in the repo market, thereby enabling any holder of the security to earn incremental income (in excess of the General Collateral rate) through lending them via a repo transaction. The repo rate for a special will be below the GC rate, as this is the rate the borrower of the cash is paying in returning for supplying the special bond as collateral. An individual security can be in high demand for a variety of reasons, for instance if there is sudden heavy investor demand for it, or (if it is a benchmark issue) it is required as a hedge against a new issue of similar maturity paper.

SPV: Special Purpose Vehicle, a legal entity set up to effect securitisation.

Synthetic: A package of transactions which is economically equivalent to a different transaction. In the structured finance market, a transaction that replicates some of the economic effects of a cash securitisation without recourse to an actual sale of assets, and which involves the use of credit derivatives.

Synthetic CDO: A CDO in which true sale of assets to an SPV does not take place. Rather, the economic effect of transferring the credit risk of the assets is created through the use of credit derivatives that reference the assets.

T

Time value for money: The concept that a future cashflow can be valued as the amount of money which it is necessary to invest now in order to achieve that cashflow in the future. See **present value**, **future value**.

Total return swap (TRS): A credit derivative contract in which the total return payer pays the return on a reference asset to the counterparty, who in return pays Libor or Libor plus a spread. If a funded TRS, the market value of the reference asset is exchanged up-front.

Trustee: A third-party specialist appointed to act on behalf of investors.

U

Underlying: The underlying of a futures or option contract is the commodity of financial instrument on which the contract depends. Thus underlying for a bond option is the bond; the underlying for a short-term interest rate futures contract is typically a three-month deposit.

Underwriting: An arrangement by which a company is guaranteed that an issue of debt (bonds) will raise a given amount of cash. Underwriting is carried out by investment banks, who undertake to purchase any part of the debt issue not taken up by the public. A commission is charged for this service.

Unexpected default rate: The distribution of future default rates is often characterised in terms of an expected default rate (e.g., 0.05%) and a worst-case default rate (e.g., 1.05%). The difference between the worst-case default rate and the expected default rate is often termed the 'unexpected default' (i.e., $1\% = 1.05 = 0.05\%$).

Unexpected loss: The distribution of credit losses associated with a derivative instrument is often characterised in terms of an expected loss or a worst-case loss. The unexpected loss associated with an instrument is the difference between these two measures.

V

Value-at-risk (VAR): Formally, the probabilistic bound of market losses over a given period of time (known as the holding period) expressed in terms of a specified degree of certainty (known as the confidence interval). Put more simply, the VAR is the worst-case loss that would be expected over the holding period within the probability set out by the confidence interval. Larger losses are possible but with a low probability. For instance, a portfolio whose VAR is $20 million over a one-day holding period, with a 95% confidence interval, would have only a 5% chance of suffering an overnight loss greater than $20 million.

Value date: The date on which a deal is to be consummated. In some bond markets, the value date for coupon accruals can sometimes differ from the settlement date.

Vanilla: A vanilla transaction is a straightforward one.

VAR: See value-at-risk

Variance (σ^2): A measure of how much the values of something fluctuate around its mean value. Defined as the average of (value $-$ mean)^2. See **standard deviation**.

Variance-covariance methodology: Methodology for calculating the **value-at-risk** of a portfolio as a function of the **volatility** of each asset or liability position in the portfolio and the correlation between the positions.

Volatility: The standard deviation of the continuously compounded return on the underlying. Volatility is generally annualised. See historic volatility, implied volatility.

Y

Yield: The interest rate which can be earned on an investment, currently quoted by the market or implied by the current market price for the investment — as opposed to the coupon paid by an issuer on a security, which is based on the coupon rate and the face value. For a bond, generally the same as yield to maturity unless otherwise specified.

Yield curve: Graphical representation of the maturity structure of interest rates, plotting yields of bonds that are all of the same class or credit quality against the maturity of the bonds.

Index

D

G

H

I

J

L

M

S

Y

Z